The Complete Cheesecake Cookbook:

766 Insanely Delicious Recipes to Bake at Home, with Love!

Anna Goldman

TABLE OF CONTENTS WITH RECIPE NAMES IS ON THE NEXT PAGE

Main Table .... *A*
Baking Basics *1*
   Ingredients 1
   Equipment 4
   Know Your Measurements 5
Cheesecakes *7*
Bonus: Cookie Recipes *119*
Bonus: Cake Recipes *237*
Bonus: Muffins and Cupcakes *416*
Bonus: French Desserts *641*
About the Author *675*

MAIN TABLE

Baking Basics 1

    Ingredients 1

    Equipment 4

    Know Your Measurements 5

Cheesecakes 7

        Almond Coconut Cheesecake 7
        Almond Praline Cheesecake 8
        Almond Vanilla Cheesecake 9
        Amaretti Cheesecake 10
        Amaretto Cheesecake 10
        Apple Cinnamon Cheesecake 11
        Apple Pie Cheesecake 12
        Apricot Compote Ricotta Cheesecake 13
        Baklava Cheesecake 14
        Banana Caramel Cheesecake 15
        Banoffee Pie Cheesecake 16
        Basque Burnt Cheesecake 17
        Berry Mascarpone Cheesecake 18
        Blackberry Ginger Cheesecake 19
        Blueberry Lime Cheesecake 19
        Brown Sugar Amaretto Cheesecake 20
        Brownie Cheesecake 21
        Brownie Mango Cheesecake 22
        Burnt Orange Cheesecake 24
        Cappuccino Cheesecake 25
        Caramel Drizzled Cheesecake 26
        Caramel Pecan Cheesecake 26
        Caramel Swirl Cheesecake 28
        Chai Cheesecake 28
        Chai Latte Cheesecake 29
        Cherry Chocolate Cheesecake 30
        Cherry Vanilla Cheesecake 31
        Chocolate Banana Cheesecake 32
        Chocolate Chip Banana Cheesecake 33
        Chocolate Chip Cheesecake 34

Chocolate Chip Mint Cheesecake	35
Chocolate Fudge Cheesecake	36
Chocolate Peanut Butter Cheesecake	37
Chocolate Pumpkin Cheesecake	38
Chocolate Sauce Cheesecake	39
Chocolate Strawberry Cheesecake	40
Chunky Banana Cheesecake	41
Citrus Cheesecake	42
Classic Vanilla Cheesecake	43
Coffee Glazed Cheesecake	44
Colorful Blueberry Cheesecake	45
Condensed Milk Cheesecake	46
Cranberry Eggnog Cheesecake	46
Cranberry Sauce Cheesecake	47
Creamy Lemon Cheesecakes	48
Crème Brulee Cheesecake	49
Crème Fraiche Cheesecake	50
Crustless Orange Cheesecake	51
Crustless Vanilla Cheesecake	52
Dark Cherry Cheesecake	52
Decadent Chocolate Cheesecake	53
Dried Fruit Cheesecake	55
Dulce De Leche Cheesecake	56
Dulce De Leche Cheesecake	56
Duo Cheesecake	57
Frangelico Cheesecake	58
Funfetti Chocolate Cheesecake	59
Ginger Eggnog Cheesecake	61
Gingersnap Cheesecake	61
Hazelnut Chocolate Cheesecake	62
Honey Fig Ricotta Cheesecake	63
Honey Ricotta Cheesecake	64
Individual Mocha Cheesecakes	65
Individual Pumpkin Cheesecakes	66
Irish Cream Cheesecake	67
Japanese Cheesecake	67
Kahlua Chocolate Cheesecake	68
Lavender Lemon Cheesecake	69
Lemon Coconut Cheesecake	70

Lemon Curd Cheesecake 71
Lemony Strawberry Cheesecake 72
Lime Pineapple Cheesecake 73
Mango Ripple Cheesecake.. 74
Maple Cinnamon Cheesecake 75
Marsala Infused Cheesecake 76
Meringue Cheesecake 77
Mini Ginger Cheesecakes.. 78
Mini Raspberry Cheesecakes 78
Minty Cheesecake... 79
Mixed Berry Cheesecake 80
Mocha Chocolate Cheesecake.. 81
New York Cheesecakes... 82
No Bake Mascarpone Cheesecake.. 83
No Bake Passionfruit Cheesecake... 84
No Crust Citrus Cheesecake.. 85
Nutella Cheesecake 86
Nutella Mocha Cheesecake 87
Nutmeg Ricotta Cheesecake... 88
Nutmeg Sweet Potato Cheesecake... 88
Oatmeal Crust Cheesecake... 89
Passionfruit Blueberry Cheesecake 90
Passionfruit Cheesecake 91
Peppermint Chocolate Cheesecake 92
Pistachio Paste Cheesecake.. 93
Pure Coconut Vanilla Cheesecake 94
Raisin Marsala Cheesecake... 95
Raspberry Chocolate Cheesecake... 96
Red Velvet Cheesecake... 97
Refreshing Kiwi Cheesecake 98
Rhubarb Strawberry Cheesecake 98
Ricotta Cheesecake With Balsamic Strawberries 100
S'mores Cheesecake 101
Salted Chocolate Cheesecake 102
Shortcrust Pastry Cheesecake 103
Snickers Cheesecake... 104
Sour Cream Mango Cheesecake 105
Spiced Honey Cheesecake 106
Spiced Pumpkin Cheesecake 107

Strawberry Jam Cheesecake 108
Strawberry Lemon Cheesecake 109
The Ultimate No Crust Cheesecake 109
Tiramisu Cheesecake 110
Tiramisu Inspired Cheesecake 111
Twix Cheesecake 112
Vanilla Crumble Cheesecake 113
Very Vanilla Cheesecake 114
Walnut Cheesecake 115
Walnut Crumble Cheesecake 116
White Chocolate Caramel Cheesecake 117
White Chocolate Cheesecake 118

Bonus: Cookie Recipes *119*

Brown Sugar Chocolate Chip Cookies 119
Brown Butter Chocolate Oatmeal Cookies 120
Brown Butter Chocolate Chip Cookies 120
Brown Butter American Cookies 121
Banana Oatmeal Cookies 122
Banana Chocolate Cookies 123
Banana Chocolate Chip Cookies 123
Apricot Coconut Cookies 124
Anzac Cookies 125
American Chocolate Chunk Cookies 126
Amaretti Cookies 127
Amaretti Cookies 127
Almond Cookies 128
Almond Blueberry Cookies 129
Chocolate Nutella Cookies 130
Chocolate Hazelnut Cookies 130
Chocolate Drizzled Lavender Cookies 131
Chocolate Dipped Sugar Cookies 132
Chocolate Crinkles 133
Chocolate Chunk Cookies 134
Chocolate Chip Pecan Cookies 135
Chocolate Buttercream Cookies 135
Chili Chocolate Cookies 136
Chewy Sugar Cookies 137
Chewy Coconut Cookies 138
Cashew Cranberry Cookies 139

Cardamom Chocolate Chip Cookies 140
Candy Cane Chocolate Cookies 140
Candied Ginger Oatmeal Cookies 141
Cakey Chocolate Chip Cookies 142
Butter Vanilla Cookies.. 143
Lemony Lavender Cookies 143
Lemon Ricotta Cookies 144
Lemon Poppy Seed Cookies 145
Layered Chocolate Chip Cookies 146
Icing Decorated Cookies 147
Honey Lemon Cookies 147
Honey Cornflake Cookies 148
Healthy Banana Cookies 149
Hazelnut Chocolate Chip Cookies 150
Gooey Chocolate Cherry Cookies 151
Gingersnap Cookies 151
Gingerbread Cookies 152
Gingerbread Cookies 153
Ginger Quinoa Cookies 154
Ginger Chocolate Oatmeal Cookies 154
Ginger Butter Cookies.. 155
Ginger Almond Biscotti 156
German Chocolate Cookies 157
Fudgy Chocolate Cookies 158
Fruity Cookies 159
Fresh Blueberry Cookies 159
Four Ingredient Peanut Butter Cookies 160
Flourless Peanut Butter Cookies 161
Fig and Almond Cookies 162
Everything 162
Eggless Cookies.. 163
Earl Grey Cookies 164
Dried Prune Oatmeal Cookies.. 165
Dried Fruit Wholesome Cookies 165
Dried Cranberry Oatmeal Cookies 166
Double Ginger Cookies 167
Double Chocolate Espresso Cookies 168
Double Chocolate Cookies 169
Date Pecan Ginger Cookies.. 169

Custard Powder Cookies 170
Cranberry Biscotti 171
Cracked Sugar Cookies 172
Cornflake Chocolate Chip Cookies 173
Confetti Cookies 173
Colorful Chocolate Cookies 174
Coffee Shortbread Cookies 175
Coffee Gingersnap Cookies 176
Coconut Shortbread Cookies 176
Coconut Macaroons 177
Coconut Lime Butter Cookies 178
Coconut Florentine Cookies 179
Coconut Butter Cookies 179
Clove Sugar Cookies 180
Cinnamon Sugar Cookies 181
Cinnamon Snap Cookies 182
Cinnamon Oatmeal Cookies 183
Chunky Peanut Butter Cookies 183
Chocolate Star Anise Cookies 184
Chocolate Sandwich Cookies With Passionfruit Ganache 185
Chocolate Pecan Cookies 186
Chocolate Orange Shortbread Cookies 187
White Chocolate Pistachio Cookies 188
White Chocolate Cranberry Cookies 189
White Chocolate Chunk Cookies 189
Walnut Crescent Cookies 190
Walnut Banana Cookies 191
Vanilla Sugared Cookies 192
Vanilla Malted Cookies 193
Triple Chocolate Cookies 193
Toffee Chocolate Chip Cookies 194
Toffee Apple Cookies 195
Thin Coconut Cookies 196
Sugar Covered Cookies 197
Spiced Chocolate Cookies 197
Spiced Apple Cookies 198
Soft Ginger Cookies 199
Soft Chocolate Chip Cookies 200
Soft Baked Chocolate Cookies 200

Salted Chocolate Cookies 201
Russian Tea Cookies 202
Rocky Road Cookies 203
Rice Flour Cookies 204
Raspberry Jam Cookies 204
Rainbow Cookies 205
Quick Brown Butter Cookies 206
Puffed Rice Cookies 207
Praline Cookies 207
Polenta Cookies 208
Pink Dotted Sugar Cookies 209
Pine Nut Cookies 210
Pecan Studded Cookies 210
Pecan Marshmallow Cookies 211
Pecan Cream Cheese Cookies 212
Pecan Butter Cookies 213
Peanut Butter Shortbread Cookies 213
Peanut Butter Pretzel Cookies 214
Peanut Butter Oatmeal Cookies 215
Peanut Butter Nutella Cookies 216
Peanut Butter Cups Cookies 217
Peanut Butter Cinnamon Cookies 217
Peanut Butter Chocolate Cookies 218
Outrageous Chocolate Cookies 219
Orange Pumpkin Cookies 220
Orange Poppy Seed Cookies 221
Orange Pistachio Cookies 221
Orange Passionfruit Cookies 222
Olive Oil Chocolate Chip Cookies 223
Oatmeal Raisins Cookies 224
Oatmeal Cookies 224
Nutty Cookies 225
Muesli Cookies 226
Monster Cookie Recipes 227
Molten Chocolate Cookies 228
Molasses Cookies 228
Minty Chocolate Cookies 229
Minty Chocolate Cookies 230
Milky Cookies 231

Marshmallow Chocolate Chip Cookies 232
Maple Sesame Cookies 232
Maple Flavored Cookies 233
Mango Crunch Cookies 234
Macadamia Cookies 235
M&M Cookies 235
Lentil Cookies 236

Bonus: Cake Recipes **237**

Yogurt Strawberry Cake 237
Yogurt Bundt Cake 239
Yeasted Plum Cake 239
Whole Pear Sponge Cake 240
White Chocolate Blackberry Cake 241
Walnut Honey Pound Cake 242
Walnut Coffee Cake 243
Walnut Carrot Cake 244
Walnut Banana Cake 245
Victoria Sponge Cake With Strawberries 246
Vanilla White Chocolate Chip Cake 247
Vanilla Strawberry Cake 248
Vanilla Genoise Cake 249
Vanilla Funfetti Cake 249
Vanilla Cardamom Cake 250
Tropical Carrot Cake 251
Tiramisu Cake 253
The Ultimate Chocolate Cake 253
Tahini Cake 254
Sweet Potato Bundt Cake 255
Summer Fruit Cake 256
Sultana Cake 257
Strawberry Yogurt Cake 258
Strawberry Polenta Cake 258
Strawberry Lemon Olive Oil Cake 259
Strawberry Crumble Cake 260
Strawberry Cake 261
Spicy Chocolate Cake 262
Spiced Walnut Cake 263
Spiced Pumpkin Sheet Cake 263
Sour Cherry Chocolate Cake 264

Snickerdoodle Bundt Cake 265
Rum Pineapple Upside Down Cake 266
Rich Vanilla Cake 267
Rhubarb Upside Down Cake 268
Raspberry Ricotta Cake 269
Raspberry Matcha Cake 269
Raspberry Lemon Olive Oil Cake 270
Raspberry Ganache Cake 271
Raspberry Chocolate Mud Cake 272
Raspberry Chocolate Cake 273
Rainbow Cake 274
Poppy Seed Lemon Bundt Cake 274
Pomegranate Cake 275
Plum Polenta Cake 276
Pistachio Cake 277
Pistachio Bundt Cake 278
Peppermint Chocolate Cake 279
Pecan Rum Cake 280
Pecan Carrot Bundt Cake 281
Pecan Butter Cake 282
Pear Cinnamon Bundt Cake 283
Pear Brownie Cake 283
Peanut Butter Jelly Cake 284
Peanut Butter Chocolate Bundt Cake 285
Peach Upside Down Cake 286
Peach Meringue Cake 287
Peach Brandy Cake 288
Parsnip Carrot Cake 289
Orange Ricotta Cake 290
Orange Pumpkin Bundt Cake 291
Orange Pound Cake 292
Orange Chocolate Mud Cake 292
Orange Chocolate Cake 293
Olive Oil Pistachio Cake 294
Natural Red Velvet Cake 295
Morello Cherry Cake 296
Molasses Pear Bundt Cake 296
Moist Pumpkin Cake 297
Moist Chocolate Cake 298

Moist Apple Cake 299
Mississippi Mud Cake 300
Milk Chocolate Chunk Cake 301
Meringue Black Forest Cake.. 301
Matcha Pound Cake 302
Matcha Chocolate Cake 303
Marble Cake 304
Maple Syrup Apple Cake 305
Mango Ice Box Cake 306
Madeira Cake 306
Lime Pound Cake... 307
Lemon Sprinkle Cake... 308
Lemon Ricotta Cake 309
Lemon Raspberry Pound Cake 310
Lemon Ginger Cake 311
Lemon Blueberry Bundt Cake 312
Jam Studded Cake 313
Hot Chocolate Bundt Cake 313
Honey Fig Cake.. 314
Holiday Pound Cake 315
Healthier Carrot Cake.. 316
Hazelnut Chocolate Cake 317
Granny Smith Cake.. 318
Grand Marnier Infused Loaf Cake 318
Grand Marnier Infused Loaf Cake 319
Graham Cracker Pumpkin Cake 320
Graham Cracker Cake.. 321
Gingersnap Pumpkin Bundt Cake.. 322
Gingerbread Chocolate Cake 323
Ginger Whole Orange Cake... 324
Ginger Sweet Potato Cake 325
German Fruit Bundt Cake.. 326
Ganache Chocolate Cake 326
Funfetti Cake... 327
Fudgy Chocolate Cake 328
Fudgy Chocolate Cake 329
Fruity Bundt Cake.. 330
Fruit and Brandy Cake... 331
French Apple Cake 332

Fluffy Pear Bundt Cake 332
Duo Bundt Cake 333
Devils Bundt Cake 334
Decadent Chocolate Cake 335
Dark Rum Pecan Cake 336
Dark Chocolate Coffee Cake 337
Cream Cheese Pumpkin Cake 338
Cream Cheese Pumpkin Cake 339
Cream Cheese Apple Cake 340
Cream Bundt Cake 341
Cranberry Upside Down Cake 342
Coconut Raspberry Cake 342
Coconut Carrot Bundt Cake 343
Classic Fruit Cake 344
Citrus Poppy Seed Bundt Cake 345
Cinnamon Streusel Raspberry Cake 346
Cinnamon Maple Pumpkin Cake 347
Cinnamon Frosted Banana Cake 348
Cinnamon Chocolate Cake 349
Chocolate Pumpkin Cake 350
Chocolate Peppermint Cake 351
Chocolate Peanut Butter Bundt Cake 352
Chocolate Olive Oil Cake 353
Chocolate Nutella Cake 353
Chocolate Mousse Cake 354
Chocolate Hazelnut Cake 355
Chocolate Hazelnut Cake 356
Chocolate Fudge Cake 357
Chocolate Dulce De Leche Cake 358
Chocolate Coffee Cake 359
Chocolate Coconut Cake 360
Chocolate Chip Pumpkin Bundt Cake 361
Chocolate Chip Bundt Cake 362
Chocolate Chip Blackberry Cake 363
Chocolate Bundt Cake 363
Chocolate Biscuit Cake 364
Chia Seed Chocolate Cake 365
Chestnut Puree Chocolate Cake 366
Cherry Liqueur Soaked Cake 367

Cherry Chocolate Cake 368
Cherry Brownie Cake 368
Chai Spiced Streusel Cake 369
Chai Spiced Cake 370
Cardamom Carrot Cake 371
Caramel Spice Cake 372
Caramel Pumpkin Cake 374
Caramel Pineapple Upside Down Cake 375
Caramel Banana Cake 376
Caramel Apple Cake 377
Candied Ginger Applesauce Cake 378
Buttery Zucchini Cake 379
Buttery Orange Cake 379
Butterscotch Sweet Potato Cake 380
Butterscotch Pecan Cake 381
Buttermilk Chocolate Cake 382
Buttermilk Chocolate Cake 383
Butter Cake 384
Brown Sugar Pineapple Bundt Cake 384
Brown Sugar Cake 385
Brown Butter Walnut Cake 386
Boozy Raisin Bundt Cake 387
Boozy Chocolate Cake 388
Blueberry Streusel Cake 389
Blueberry Cake 390
Blood Orange Olive Oil Cake 391
Blood Orange Cornmeal Cake 392
Blackberry Bundt Cake 392
Black Pepper Chocolate Cake 393
Berry Meringue Cake 394
Berry Lemon Cake 395
Beetroot Chocolate Fudge Cake 396
Beetroot Carrot Cake 396
Banana Peanut Butter Cake 397
Banana Mars Bar Cake 398
Banana Chocolate Chip Cake 399
Banana Cake 400
Banana Bundt Cake With Peanut Butter Frosting 401
Apricot Yogurt Loaf Cake 402

Apricot Cake 402
Applesauce Carrot Cake 403
Apple Vanilla Loaf Cake 404
Apple Pound Cake 405
Apple and Pear Molasses Cake 406
Amaretto Almond Cake 407
Almond White Chocolate Cake 408
Almond Strawberry Cake 408
Almond Strawberry Cake 409
Almond Honey Cake 410
Almond Fig Cake 411
Almond Date Cake 412
Almond Butter Banana Cake 412
Almond Apple Cake 413
All Butter Cake 414

Bonus: Muffins and Cupcakes 416

Zucchini Chocolate Muffins 416
Zucchini Carrot Muffins 417
Zesty Pistachio Muffins 417
Yogurt Vanilla Berry Muffins 418
Yogurt Blackberry Muffins 419
Wholesome Blueberry Muffins 420
Wholemeal Muffins 420
Whole Wheat Strawberry Muffins 421
Whole Wheat Banana Muffins 422
White Chocolate Pumpkin Cupcakes 423
White Chocolate Pumpkin Cupcakes 424
White Chocolate Lime Cupcakes 425
Walnut Banana Muffins 427
Vodka Cupcakes 427
Vegan Chocolate Muffins 429
Vegan Blueberries Muffins 429
Vanilla Cupcakes With Maple Frosting 430
Vanilla Cupcakes With Chocolate Buttercream 431
Turkish Delight Muffins 432
The Ultimate Vanilla Cupcakes 433
The Ultimate Blueberry Muffins 434
Sweet Raspberry Corn Muffins 435
Sweet Potato Zucchini Muffins 436

Sweet Potato Maple Muffins 437
Sweet Potato Cupcakes... 438
Sweet Potato Cinnamon Cupcakes 439
Sultana Bran Muffins... 440
Sugary Pumpkin Muffins 441
Sugary Blueberry Muffins 442
Sugarless Muffins... 442
Streusel Cranberry Muffins 443
Streusel Banana Muffins 444
Strawberry Muffins 445
Strawberry Matcha Muffins 446
Strawberry Chia Seed Muffins 447
Strawberry and Cream Cupcakes 447
Sprinkles Chocolate Cupcakes 448
Spicy Pineapple Muffins.. 449
Spiced Zucchini Muffins 450
Spiced Strawberry Cupcakes 451
Spiced Cupcakes With Cream Cheese Cupcakes 452
Spelt Zucchini Muffins... 453
Sour Cream Muffins 454
Snickers Cupcakes 454
Snickerdoodle Muffins 455
Simple Lavender Cupcakes 456
S'mores Chocolate Cupcakes 457
Ricotta Lemon Muffins.. 459
Rich Chocolate Muffins 459
Rhubarb Streusel Muffins 460
Rhubarb Strawberry Muffins 461
Red Wine Fig Cupcakes 462
Red Velvet Cupcakes... 463
Red Berries Cream Cheese Muffins.. 464
Raspberry White Chocolate Muffins 465
Raspberry Vanilla Cupcakes 466
Raspberry Ricotta Muffins 467
Raspberry Muffins... 468
Raspberry Jam Muffins 469
Raisin Bran Muffins 469
Quinoa Peach Muffins... 470
Quinoa Cranberry Muffins 471

Quick Coffee Muffins	472
Pure Vanilla Muffins	472
Pumpkin Pecan Crunch Muffins	473
Pumpkin Nutella Muffins	474
Pumpkin Chocolate Chip Muffins	475
Pumpkin Apple Streusel Muffins	476
Pumpkin Apple Muffins	477
Plum Whole Wheat Muffins	478
Pink Velvet Cupcakes	479
Pink Lemonade Cupcakes	480
Pink Coconut Cupcakes	481
Persimmon Muffins	482
Pecan Pie Muffins	483
Pear and Ginger Muffins	484
Peanut Butter Banana Cupcakes	484
Peachy Muffins	485
Peach and Cream Muffins	486
Passionfruit Cupcakes	487
Oreo Cream Cupcakes	488
Orange Yogurt Muffins	489
Orange Soda Cupcakes	490
Orange Poppy Seed Muffins	491
Orange Pecan Muffins	491
Orange Olive Oil Muffins	492
Orange Iced Cupcakes	493
Orange Glazed Cupcakes	494
Orange Almond Muffins	495
Oatmeal Cranberry Muffins	496
Oatmeal Carrot Muffins	497
Nutty Double Chocolate Muffins	498
Nutty Chocolate Chip Muffins	499
Nutella Stuffed Strawberry Muffins	499
Nutella Peanut Butter Cupcakes	500
Multigrain Muffins	501
Muesli Apple Muffins	502
Morning Muffins	503
Morning Glory Muffins	504
Moist Chocolate Coffee Cupcakes	504
Moist Banana Muffins	506

Moist Banana Muffins	506
Mocha Madness Cupcakes	507
Mocha Cupcakes	508
Mocha Chocolate Chip Banana Muffins	509
Mixed Berry Buttermilk Muffins	510
Minty Chocolate Cupcakes	511
Millet Flour Plum Muffins	512
Milky Banana Muffins	513
Milk Chocolate Cupcakes	514
Mexican Chocolate Muffins	515
Matcha Strawberry Cupcakes	516
Maple Syrup Pecan Cupcakes	517
Maple Spice Muffins	518
Mango Buttermilk Muffins	518
Loaded Muffins	519
Lemon Ricotta Muffins	520
Lemon Poppy Seed Muffins	521
Lemon Glazed Apple Cider Muffins	522
Lemon Fig Muffins	522
Lemon Curd Cupcakes	523
Lemon Chia Seed Muffins	524
Lemon Blueberry Muffins	525
Intense Chocolate Cupcakes	526
Hummingbird Muffins	527
Honey Spiced Muffins	528
Honey Pumpkin Muffins	528
Honey Pear Muffins	529
Honey Nutmeg Peach Muffins	530
Honey Lemon Muffins	531
Honey Cardamom Cupcakes	532
Healthy Chocolate Muffins	533
Hazelnut Fig Muffins	533
Harvest Muffins	534
Grapefruit Cream Cheese Cupcakes	535
Grain Free Apple Cinnamon	536
Gluten Free Maple Muffins	537
Gluten Free Chocolate Muffins	538
Gluten Free Chocolate Cupcakes With Pumpkin Frosting	539
Gingerbread Muffins	540

Ginger Pineapple Muffins 541
German Chocolate Cupcakes 541
Funfetti Cream Cheese Cupcakes 543
Funfetti Banana Muffins 544
Fudgy Chocolate Muffins 545
Fudgy Chocolate Date Muffins 545
Fresh Ginger Muffins 546
Fragrant Date Banana Muffins 547
Flaxseed Pumpkin Muffins 548
Fig Walnut Muffins 549
Extra Chocolate Muffins 549
Espresso Sour Cream Cupcakes 550
Eggless Pumpkin Muffins 551
Duo Chocolate Chip Muffins 552
Double Chocolate Nutella Muffins 553
Double Chocolate Muffins 554
Double Chocolate Cupcakes 555
Double Berry Cupcakes 556
Deep Chocolate Pumpkin Muffins 556
Decadent Brownie Muffins 557
Cranberry Eggnog Muffins 558
Coconut Muffins 559
Coconut Mango Muffins 560
Coconut Lemon Chia Seed Muffins 561
Coconut Flakes Cupcakes 561
Coconut Cupcakes 562
Coconut Caramel Cupcakes 563
Citrus Iced Coconut Cupcakes 565
Citrus Coconut Muffins 565
Cinnamon Plum Muffins 566
Cinnamon Blueberry Muffins 567
Cinnamon Autumn Muffins 568
Cinnamon Apple Cupcakes 569
Chunky Banana Muffins 570
Chocolate Tahini Muffins 571
Chocolate Spice Cupcakes 571
Chocolate Raspberry Cupcakes 572
Chocolate Raspberry Crumble Muffins 574
Chocolate Pretzel Muffins 575

Chocolate Pear Muffins 576
Chocolate Peanut Butter Cupcakes 576
Chocolate Malt Cupcakes 577
Chocolate Graham Cupcakes 579
Chocolate Drizzle Cupcakes 580
Chocolate Cupcakes With Peanut Butter Frosting 581
Chocolate Chunk Cupcakes 582
Chocolate Chip Muffins 583
Chocolate Chip Cinnamon Muffins 584
Chocolate Candied Orange Muffins 585
Chocolate Avocado Cupcakes 585
Cherry Muffins 587
Cherry Coconut Muffins 587
Chai Vanilla Frosted Cupcakes 588
Carrot White Chocolate Muffins 589
Carrot Cake Pecan Muffins 590
Caribbean Muffins 591
Caramel Vanilla Cupcakes 592
Cakey Blueberry Muffins 593
Butternut Almond Muffins 594
Brown Sugar Bourbon Cupcakes 595
Brown Butter Streusel Pumpkin Muffins 596
Brown Butter Chocolate Chip Muffins 597
Brown Butter Banana Muffins 597
Brown Butter Banana Cupcakes 598
Brooklyn Blackout Cupcakes 599
Breakfast Muffins 601
Bran Flax Blueberry Muffins 602
Bourbon Glazed Pumpkin Muffins 603
Blueberry White Chocolate Muffins 603
Blueberry Poppy Seed Muffins 604
Blueberry Oatmeal Muffins 605
Blueberry Lemon Cupcakes 606
Blueberry Frosted Cupcakes 607
Blueberry Cheese Muffins 608
Blueberry Banana Muffins 609
Blackberry White Chocolate Muffins 610
Blackberry Oat Bran Muffins 610
Blackberry Muffins 611

Blackberry Bran Muffins 612
Black Sesame Cupcakes With Cream Cheese Frosting 613
Black Magic Cupcakes... 614
Black Forest Muffins 615
Black Forest Cupcakes 616
Black Bottom Muffins 617
Beetroot Raspberry Muffins 618
Basic Muffins 619
Basic Chocolate Muffins 619
Banana Yogurt Muffins 620
Banana Pear Muffins 621
Banana Peanut Butter Muffins 622
Banana Peanut Butter Cups Muffins 623
Banana Olive Oil Muffins 623
Banana Mascarpone Cupcakes 624
Banana Honey Muffins 625
Banana Crunch Muffins 626
Banana Chocolate Chip Muffins 627
Banana Chia Muffins 627
Banana Buttermilk Muffins.. 628
Apricot Rosemary Muffins 629
Apricot Orange Muffins 630
Apple Puree Muffins 631
Apple Pie Caramel Cupcakes 632
Apple Muffins 633
Apple Cranberry Muffins 634
Almond White Chocolate Cupcakes 635
Almond Vanilla Cupcakes 636
Almond Vanilla Cupcakes 637
Almond Rose Cupcakes... 638
Almond Poppy Seed Muffins 639

Bonus: French Desserts *641*

Chocolate Tart 641
Chocolate Éclairs.. 642
Chewy Almond Macaroons.. 643
Cherry Clafoutis 644
Buttery Madeleines 644
Butter Cookies 645
Boozy Chocolate Truffles 646

Fiadone 647
Almond Sables.. 647
French Beignets.. 648
French Apple Tart... 649
Fig Galette 650
Far Breton 651
Dried Cranberry Pear Clafoutis 652
Deep Chocolate Soufflé 653
Crepes Suzzette.. 653
Crème Caramel 654
Crème Brulee 655
Classic French Toast With Honey 655
Pure Chocolate Buche De Noel 656
Port Wine Poached Pears... 657
Pistachio Financiers.. 658
Pepin's Apple Tart 659
Orange Marmalade Soufflés 660
Orange Apple Terrine... 660
Mousse Au Chocolat 661
Mocha Pots De Crème 662
Red Wine Chocolate Cake:... 662
Meringues 663
Lemon Cheese Soufflé.. 664
Iles Flottantes... 665
Honey Fig and Goat Cheese Tart 665
Gateau Basque 666
Gascon Flan 667
French Lemon Tart 668
French Canneles 669
Tarte Tropezienne... 669
Tart Tatin 672
Rustic Pear Galette... 672
Rhubarb Tart 673

About the Author 675

BAKING BASICS

Baking required no introduction. It is one of the oldest and most popular cooking methods known to mankind. These days, pretty much every kitchen has the food ingredients and equipment required to bake some delicious goodies.

Baking is a fairly simple process that can be used to prepare food ranging from simple breads to spectacular confectionery.

Before we jump into the recipes, let us take a look at the ingredients and equipment you will need. If you're a veteran baker already, feel free to jump straight into the recipes. If you're a newbie, stick around for a while longer.

Ingredients

In this section we will discuss a few of the most commonly used ingredients in baking recipes.

BUTTER

Butter has an amazing flavour and texture by itself, and when used in baking recipes, it greatly enhances the flavour and texture of the final product. Unsalted butter is best as it gives you full control over the taste of your recipes.

MILK

Milk is one of the most important ingredients when it comes to baking. It makes the four tender, and also forms the base for quite a few recipes.

FLOUR

Always sift the flour before you use in a baking recipe. Pretty much every kind of flour out there can be used for baking, but the most popular kind used for making is "All Purpose Flour". It is easily available, doesn't cost much, and easy to work with.

"Cake Flour" is another kind of flour that is smoother than all purpose flour. It is great for making cake sponges and other tender & spongy baked recipes.

"Pastry Flour" is another flour which works pretty much like cake flour.

"Self-Rising Flour" is basically all-purpose flour mixed with baking powder. To make your own, mix one teaspoon of baking powder for each cup of flour.

"Rye Flour" is a healthy flour with great nutritional benefits. However, it doesn't form gluten strands, making it ill-suited for yeasted dough.

"Oat Flour" is loaded with fiber and protein. It is commonly used in healthy baking recipes.

Almond flour, coconut flour, tapioca flour are a few other flours that are used in baking recipes today.

BAKING POWDER

Baking powder is basically a mixture of baking soda and an acidic component. It is a leavening agent on its own, and doesn't require addition of an acidic ingredient to do its work.

Hundreds of branks make baking powder, and they are all pretty much the same. Just make sure the baking powder you buy is free of aluminium. Baking powder has a shelf life of about six months, so make sure you use it all before that.

BAKING SODA

Baking soda is a leavening agent that requires another acidic ingredient to do its job. It can be stored safely for years.

YEAST

Found commonly in bread, dinner rolls and similar pastries, yeast is a natural leavening agent which does its job by fermenting in the batter or dough, causing a rise in volume by absorbing air.

SUGAR

Excess of sugar leads to a spike in blood glycogen levels, and is rightly blamed for many health problems. Eat sugary delights in moderation, and as a side to a healthy balanced diet. Sugar adds texture, sweetness, and moisture to baked recipes, making it an important ingredient in some of the sweet baked goodies. It promotes the growth of yeast in a few of the recipes too.

There are many kinds of sugars available out there, and every recipe will specify the kind of sugar used. If not mentioned, use the regular granulated sugar. Brown sugar is unrefined white sugar, and has a strong taste of its own, making it unsuitable most of the recipes. However, in some recipes, the flavour of brown sugar compliments the flavour of the recipe.

CHOCOLATE

If a recipe in this book calls for dark chocolate, it is best to use a chocolate that has a cocoa content higher than 70%. Dark chocolate is the most commonly used chocolate in this book, as it has low sugar content, and has a strong flavour and great texture. If a recipe calls for chocolate chips, and you don't have those on hand, just chop up a chunk of dark chocolate into small bits and you're good to go!

White and milk chocolates are quite popular too these days, and taste great due to the high sugar content.

COCOA POWDER

Today, two kinds of cocoa powers are popular- natural cocoa powder, and Dutch processed cocoa powder.

Unless stated otherwise, all cocoa powder used in this book is Dutch processed cocoa powder due to its darker colour and intense taste.

EGGS

Free ranch fresh eggs are best. Unless stated otherwise, all eggs used in this book are medium-sized.

Eggs are one of the most commonly used ingredients in baking as they greatly enhance the texture of cakes and cookies, and allow air to be absorbed into the batter, making it fluffy. They are also help keep the recipes moist.

Eggs are delicious and nutritious on their own, and when used in baking recipes, impart their nutrition, taste, and colour to the recipes.

GELATIN

Gelatin or gelatine is a translucent, colorless, flavorless food ingredient, derived from collagen extracted from animal body parts. It is brittle when dry and gummy when moist. It is used to to stabilize creams or jellies and it needs to be bloomed before use. If you boil it, it loses its strength, so don't do that.

Unless stated otherwise, all gelatin used in this book is powdered or granulated. Leafed gelatin comes in handy sometimes too.

NUTS

Nuts are rich in healthy fats, and taste absolutely scrumptious on pretty much everything baked. Some of the most commonly used nuts in baked recipes are: almonds, coconut, hazelnuts, pecans, peanuts, walnuts, pistachio, macadamia nuts, cashew nuts, etc. Nuts are best used fresh.

SALT

Salt is a common ingredient in all kinds of cooking, and baking is no exception. Salt strengthens the gluten structure, enhances the flavour, and highly useful with yeast.

SPICES

Spices are delicious and nutritious, and add a variety of flavours to baked recipes. One of the most commonly used spices in baking is vanilla. A natural extract of vanilla is best. Cinnamon, ginger, nutmeg, cardamom, orange zest, lemon zest, cloves, lavender, etc are some other spices commonly used in baking.

Equipment

Some cheap basic equipment is all you really need to start baking. You probably already have most of the stuff I am about to list.

BAKING PANS

Small pans, large pans, they all get the job done. Just make sure you have some.

Cake pans are great for making cakes. If you don't intend to make multiple cakes simultaneously, just one pan is all you really need. A basic pan with a diameter of eight to nine inches usually gets the job done. They are easily available in stores, and on amazon.

Bundt cake pans are used to give spectacular shapes to your cakes. They come in pretty much all shapes, sizes, and patterns. Just remember that the more complex the design gets, the harder they are to clean.

Muffin tins are really useful for making muffins, and are easily available on amazon, and in stores around you. I personally prefer muffin tins with minimum 12 cups, as I have a family of 4, and 12 cups hits the spot. If you get a smaller one, just reduce the amount of ingredients you use proportionally.

Pie and tart pans are also handy little pans, and it is a good idea to have minimum one of each if you wish to make these recipes.

MIXER

You can do all the mixing you will need using your hand and a spoon or whisk, but having a mixer sure makes the job easier. Any old small mixer will do. But then again, it is really not necessary if you don't mind some manual stirring and whisking.

WHISK

Whisks are indispensable tools when it comes to baking. There are manual and electronic whisks easily available today, and they will both get the job done.

SPATULAS AND WOODEN SPOONS

Some mixtures need to be blended slowly to prevent gluten strands from forming, and that is why it is always a good idea to keep spatulas and wooden spoons handy.

FOOD PROCESSOR

Food processors are cheap, and can make certain grinding tasks a piece of cake!

MEASURING SPOONS AND CUPS

You will need some a few measuring instruments as all recipes call for specific quantities of ingredients. If you're a veteran cook, you're probably good at approximation by now, but measuring instruments are indispensable for the newbies.

American measuring sets are quite cheap, and one set contains all standard measurements used in this book, so go grab a set if you don't have one already.

MIXING BOWLS

Steel and glass mixing containers are my favourite.

BAKING PAPER OR PARCHMENT PAPER

Baking paper is indispensable for baking. Not only does it protect the ingredients from burning or baking too quickly, but also making the cleaning process after baking a piece of cake!

KNOW YOUR MEASUREMENTS

American cooks use standard containers, the 8-ounce cup and a tablespoon that takes exactly 16 level fillings to fill that cup level. Measuring by cup makes it very difficult to give weight equivalents, as the density plays an important role when it comes to weight. The easiest way therefore to deal with cup measurements in recipes is to take the amount by volume rather than by weight. Thus, the equation reads:

1 cup = 240ml = 8 fluid Ounces

½ cup = 120ml = 4 fluid ounces

It is possible to buy a set of American cup measures in major stores around the world.

In the States, butter is sometimes measured in sticks. One stick is the equivalent of 8 tablespoons. One tablespoon of butter is therefore the equivalent to ½ ounce/15 grams.

Liquid Measures

1 Teaspoon= 5 Millilitres

1 Tablespoon = 14 millilitres

2 Tablespoons= 1 Fluid Ounce

Solid Measures

1 Ounce= 28 Grams

16 Ounces= 1 Pound

CHEESECAKES

ALMOND COCONUT CHEESECAKE

Total Time Taken: 1 ½ hours
Yield: 12 Servings
Ingredients:

Crust:

- ¼ cup butter
- ¼ cup coconut cream
- 1 ½ cups graham crackers, crushed

Filling:

- ½ cup coconut milk
- ½ cup sliced almonds
- ½ cup sweetened condensed milk
- 1 cup shredded coconut
- 1 pinch salt
- 1 teaspoon vanilla extract
- 3 cups cream cheese
- 3 eggs

Directions:

1. To make the crust, combine the ingredients in a container. Move to a 9-inch round cake pan covered with parchment paper and press it thoroughly on the bottom of the pan.
2. To make the filling, combine the ingredients in a container until creamy.
3. Pour the mixture over the crust , preheat your oven and bake at 330F for about fifty minutes or until the cheesecake looks slightly in the center when you shake the pan lightly.
4. When finished, take it out of the oven and let cool down completely before you serve.

Nutritional Content of One Serving:

Calories: 419 ‖ Fat: 35.1g ‖ Protein: 8.9g ‖ Carbohydrates: 19.4g

ALMOND PRALINE CHEESECAKE

Total Time Taken: 1 ½ hours

Yield: 12 Servings

Ingredients:

Crust:

- 1 ½ cups graham crackers, crushed
- 1 tablespoon dark rum
- 1/3 cup butter, melted

Filling:

- ½ cup almond flour
- ½ cup sour cream
- ½ cup white sugar
- ½ teaspoon almond extract
- 1 pinch salt
- 1 teaspoon vanilla extract
- 2 eggs
- 3 cups cream cheese

Topping:

- ½ cup white sugar
- 1 cup blanched almonds

Directions:

1. To make the crust, combine the ingredients in a container. Move the mixture to a 9-inch round cake pan covered with parchment paper and press it thoroughly on the bottom of the pan.
2. To make the filling, combine all the ingredients in a container until creamy. Pour the filling over the crust , preheat your oven and bake at 330F for about forty minutes or until the center of the cake looks slightly set is you shake the pan.
3. Let the cheesecake cool in the pan when done.
4. For the topping, melt the sugar in a heavy saucepan until it sppears amber in colour.
5. Turn off the heat and mix in the almonds. Combine until coated then spoon on a baking tray coated with baking paper. Let cool down and set.
6. Once chilled, crack into smaller pieces. Top the cheesecake with the almond praline and serve the cheesecake fresh.

Nutritional Content of One Serving:

Calories: 442 ‖ Fat: 33.7g ‖ Protein: 8.3g ‖ Carbohydrates: 28.7g

ALMOND VANILLA CHEESECAKE

Total Time Taken: 1 ¼ hours
Yield: 10 Servings
Ingredients:

Crust:

- ¼ cup ground almonds
- ½ cup butter, melted
- 1 cup graham crackers, crushed
- 2 tablespoons cocoa powder
- 2 tablespoons light brown sugar

Filling:

- ¼ teaspoon salt
- ½ teaspoon almond extract
- 1 cup sour cream
- 1 teaspoon vanilla extract
- 2/3 cup white sugar
- 3 cups cream cheese
- 3 eggs

Directions:

1. To make the crust, combine the ingredients in a food processor and pulse until combined.
2. Move the mixture to a 9-inch round cake pan coated with baking paper and press it thoroughly on the bottom of the pan.
3. To make the filling, combine all the ingredients in a container. Pour the filling over the crust , preheat your oven and bake at 330F for about forty-five minutes.
4. Let cool down before you serve.

Nutritional Content of One Serving:

Calories: 503 ‖ Fat: 41.8g ‖ Protein: 9.0g ‖ Carbohydrates: 25.7g

AMARETTI CHEESECAKE

Total Time Taken: 1 ¼ hours
Yield: 10 Servings
Ingredients:

Crust:

- ¼ cup butter, melted
- 6 oz. Amaretti cookies, crushed

Filling:

- ½ cup white sugar
- 1 teaspoon vanilla extract
- 3 cups cream cheese
- 3 eggs
- 4 oz. Amaretti cookies, crushed

Directions:

1. To make the crust, combine the ingredients in a container. Move to a 8-inch round cake pan and press it thoroughly on the bottom of the pan.
2. To make the filling, combine the cream cheese, eggs, sugar and vanilla in a container. Fold in the cookies then pour the batter in the pan.
3. Pre-heat the oven and bake at 330F for about forty minutes or until a golden-brown colour is achieved on the edges.
4. Let cool down before you serve.

Nutritional Content of One Serving:

Calories: 476 ‖ Fat: 35.7g ‖ Protein: 8.0g ‖ Carbohydrates: 32.4g

AMARETTO CHEESECAKE

Total Time Taken: 1 ¼ hours
Yield: 12 Servings
Ingredients:

Crust:

- ½ cup butter, melted
- 1 ½ cups graham crackers, crushed

- 1 tablespoon Amaretto liqueur

Filling:

- ¼ cup Amaretto liqueur
- ½ cup light brown sugar
- 1 pinch salt
- 1 tablespoon cornstarch
- 1 teaspoon vanilla extract
- 2 tablespoons butter, melted
- 3 cups cream cheese
- 3 eggs
- 3 oz. dark chocolate, melted

Directions:

1. To make the crust, combine the ingredients in a food processor and pulse until thoroughly combined. Move to a 9-inch round cake pan and press it thoroughly on the bottom of the pan.
2. To make the filling, combine the cream cheese with melted chocolate until creamy. Put in the remaining ingredients and mix thoroughly.
3. Pour the mixture over the crust, preheat your oven and bake at 330F for about forty-five minutes.
4. Let the cheesecake cool down and serve, sliced.

Nutritional Content of One Serving:

Calories: 431 ‖ Fat: 34.1g ‖ Protein: 7.1g ‖ Carbohydrates: 20.5g

APPLE CINNAMON CHEESECAKE

Total Time Taken: 1 ¼ hours
Yield: 12 Servings
Ingredients:

Crust:

- ½ cup butter, melted
- 2 cups graham crackers, crushed

Filling:

- ½ cup sour cream

- 1 teaspoon cinnamon powder
- 1 teaspoon vanilla extract
- 2 Granny Smith apples, peeled, cored and diced
- 2 tablespoons cornstarch
- 2/3 cup white sugar
- 3 cups cream cheese
- 3 eggs

Directions:

1. To make the crust, combine the ingredients in a container then move to a 9-inch round cake pan and press it thoroughly on the bottom of the pan.
2. Top the crust with apple dices and drizzle with cinnamon powder.
3. To make the filling, combine the ingredients in a container. Pour the filling over the apples , preheat your oven and bake at 330F for about forty-five minutes until the center of the cheesecake looks set.
4. Let the cheesecake cool down and serve, sliced.

Nutritional Content of One Serving:

Calories: 429 ‖ Fat: 32.4g ‖ Protein: 7.2g ‖ Carbohydrates: 29.3g

APPLE PIE CHEESECAKE

Total Time Taken: 1 ½ hours
Yield: 14 Servings
Ingredients:

Crust:

- ¼ teaspoon cinnamon powder
- ¼ teaspoon ground ginger
- 1 ½ cups graham crackers, crushed
- 1/3 cup butter, melted
- 2 tablespoons dark brown sugar

Filling:

- ¼ cup light brown sugar
- ½ cup heavy cream
- ½ cup white sugar
- 1 cinnamon stick

- 1 tablespoon cornstarch
- 1 tablespoon lemon juice
- 1 teaspoon vanilla extract
- 2 eggs
- 2 Granny Smith apples, peeled and diced
- 3 cups cream cheese

Directions:

1. To make the crust, combine the ingredients in a container until well combined and fragrant. Move to a 9-inch round cake pan and press it thoroughly on the bottom of the pan.
2. To make the filling, start by mixing the apples, brown sugar, lemon juice and cinnamon stick in a saucepan. Add to a boil and cook until tender,
3. about 5-seven minutes on low heat.
4. Let cool and then place it over the crust.
5. To make the filling, combine the cream cheese, heavy cream, eggs, cornstarch, sugar and vanilla in a container.
6. Pour over the apples , preheat your oven and bake at 330F for about fifty minutes or until set in the center.
7. Let cool in the pan before you serve.

Nutritional Content of One Serving:

Calories: 333 ‖ Fat: 24.9g ‖ Protein: 5.4g ‖ Carbohydrates: 23.6g

APRICOT COMPOTE RICOTTA CHEESECAKE

Total Time Taken: 1 ½ hours
Yield: 10 Servings
Ingredients:

Crust:

- ½ cup butter, melted
- 1 ½ cups graham crackers, crushed

Filling:

- ½ cup sour cream

- 1 cup cream cheese
- 1 tablespoon cornstarch
- 1 tablespoon lemon zest
- 2 cups ricotta cheese
- 2/3 cup white sugar
- 4 eggs

Apricot compote:

- ½ cup fresh orange juice
- 1 pound apricots, pitted and sliced
- 1 teaspoon orange zest

Directions:

1. To make the crust, combine the ingredients in a container. Move the mixture to a 9-inch round cake pan and press it thoroughly on the bottom of the pan.
2. To make the filling, combine the ricotta cheese, cream cheese, sour cream, eggs, lemon zest, cornstarch and sugar. Spoon the mixture over the crust and preheat your oven and bake at 350F for about forty minutes.
3. Let the cheesecake cool in the pan.
4. To make the compote, combine the ingredients in a saucepan and cook for five minutes using moderate heat.
5. Serve the cheesecake with warm or chilled apricot compote.

Nutritional Content of One Serving:

Calories: 415 ‖ Fat: 27.0g ‖ Protein: 11.6g ‖ Carbohydrates: 34.0g

BAKLAVA CHEESECAKE

Total Time Taken: 1 ½ hours
Yield: 12 Servings
Ingredients:

Crust:

- ¼ cup butter, melted
- 4 phyllo dough sheets, crumbled

Filling:

- 4 cups cream cheese

- 3 eggs
- 1 tablespoon vanilla extract
- 1 tablespoon cornstarch
- 1 pinch salt
- 2/3 cup white sugar

Topping:

- ¼ cup honey
- 1 cup walnuts, chopped

Directions:

1. To make the crust, combine the phyllo dough and butter in a 9-inch baking pan coated with baking paper.
2. Press slightly to position the dough in an even layer.
3. To make the filling, combine all the ingredients in a container until creamy. Pour the mixture over the phyllo dough , preheat your oven and bake at 330F for about forty-five minutes or until the center looks set.
4. Let the cheesecake cool down then top with walnuts and honey.

Best served chilled.

Nutritional Content of One Serving:

Calories: 472 ‖ Fat: 38.4g ‖ Protein: 10.2g ‖ Carbohydrates: 24.2g

BANANA CARAMEL CHEESECAKE

Total Time Taken: 1 ½ hours
Yield: 12 Servings
Ingredients:

Crust:

- ½ cup butter, melted
- 2 cups graham crackers, crushed

Filling:

- ½ cup caramel sauce
- ½ cup sour cream
- 1 pinch salt

- 1 tablespoon lemon juice
- 1 teaspoon vanilla extract
- 2 bananas, mashed
- 3 cups cream cheese
- 3 eggs

Directions:

1. To make the crust, combine the crackers and butter and mix thoroughly. Move the mixture to a 9-inch round cake pan and press it thoroughly on the bottom of the pan.
2. To make the filling, combine all the ingredients in a container and mix thoroughly. Pour the mixture over the crust.
3. Preheat your oven and bake the cheesecake at 330F for about fifty minutes.
4. Let the cheesecake cool to room temperature and serve, sliced.

Nutritional Content of One Serving:

Calories: 419 ‖ Fat: 32.5g ‖ Protein: 7.5g ‖ Carbohydrates: 26.4g

BANOFFEE PIE CHEESECAKE

Total Time Taken: 1 ½ hours
Yield: 12 Servings
Ingredients:

Crust:

- ½ cup butter, melted
- 2 cups graham crackers, crushed

Filling:

- ¼ cup heavy cream
- ¼ cup light brown sugar
- 1 cup dulce de leche
- 1 pinch salt
- 1 tablespoon cornstarch
- 1 teaspoon vanilla extract
- 2 bananas, sliced
- 2 eggs
- 3 cups cream cheese

Directions:

1. To make the crust, combine the crackers and butter in a container. Move the mixture to a 9-inch round cake pan and press it on the bottom and sides of the pan.
2. Top the crust with banana slices and dulce de leche.
3. Mix the cream cheese, eggs, cream, vanilla, sugar, salt and cornstarch in a container.
4. Spoon the filling over the dulce de leche and preheat your oven and bake the cheesecake at 330F for about forty minutes or until set in the center.

This cheesecake tastes best chilled.

Nutritional Content of One Serving:

Calories: 454 ‖ Fat: 32.0g ‖ Protein: 7.9g ‖ Carbohydrates: 35.9g

BASQUE BURNT CHEESECAKE

Total Time Taken: 1 hour
Yield: 10 Servings
Ingredients:

- 1 ½ cups white sugar
- 1 cup heavy cream
- 1 pinch salt
- 1 tablespoon all-purpose flour
- 3 cups cream cheese
- 4 eggs
- Butter to grease the pan

Directions:

1. Grease a 9-inch round cake pan with butter.
2. Mix the cream cheese until fluffy and pale. Put in the eggs, one at a time, then mix in the remaining ingredients and mix thoroughly.
3. Pour the batter in the readied pan, preheat your oven and bake at 400F for about forty minutes or until the cheesecake has a dark brown color.
4. Let cool in the pan and serve, sliced.

Nutritional Content of One Serving:

Calories: 425 ‖ Fat: 30.5g ‖ Protein: 7.8g ‖ Carbohydrates: 32.9g

BERRY MASCARPONE CHEESECAKE

Total Time Taken: 1 ¼ hours
Yield: 10 Servings
Ingredients:

Crust:
- ¼ cup butter, melted
- 1 ½ cups Oreo cookies

Filling:
- ¾ cup white sugar
- 1 ½ cups mascarpone cheese
- 1 pinch salt
- 1 tablespoon lemon zest
- 1 teaspoon vanilla extract
- 2 cups cream cheese
- 3 eggs

Topping:
- 2 cups mixed berries

Directions:

1. To make the crust, place the cookies in a food processor and pulse until ground. Put in the butter and mix thoroughly. Move the mixture to a 9-inch round cake pan and press it thoroughly on the bottom of the pan.
2. To make the filling, combine the cheese, eggs, vanilla, lemon zest, salt and sugar in a container. Pour the mixture over the crust , preheat your oven and bake at 330F for about forty-five minutes or until set.
3. Let cool in the pan then top with fresh berries before you serve.

Nutritional Content of One Serving:

Calories: 361 ‖ Fat: 27.1g ‖ Protein: 9.6g ‖ Carbohydrates: 21.2g

BLACKBERRY GINGER CHEESECAKE

Total Time Taken: 1 ½ hours
Yield: 16 Servings
Ingredients:

Crust:

- 20 gingersnap cookies, crushed
- 1/3 cup butter, melted

Filling:

- ½ cup sour cream
- 1 ½ cups fresh blackberries
- 1 pinch salt
- 1 tablespoon lemon zest
- 1 teaspoon orange zest
- 2 tablespoons all-purpose flour
- 2/3 cup white sugar
- 3 cups cream cheese
- 3 eggs

Directions:

1. To make the crust, combine the ingredients well then move to a 9-inch round cake pan coated with baking paper. Press the mixture thoroughly on the bottom of the pan.
2. Drizzle the blackberries with flour then place them over the crust.
3. To make the filling, combine the cream cheese, sour cream, sugar, lemon zest, orange zest, eggs and salt in a container.
4. Pour this mixture over the blackberries, preheat your oven and bake at 330F for about fifty minutes or until the center looks set.
5. Let the cheesecake cool down and serve, sliced.

Nutritional Content of One Serving:

Calories: 455 ‖ Fat: 29.6g ‖ Protein: 6.4g ‖ Carbohydrates: 42.6g

BLUEBERRY LIME CHEESECAKE

Total Time Taken: 1 ¼ hours
Yield: 12 Servings
Ingredients:

Crust:

- ½ cup butter, melted
- 1 1/2 cups graham crackers, crushed

Filling:

- ½ cup sour cream
- ½ cup white sugar
- 1 cup fresh blueberries
- 1 lime, zested and juiced
- 1 tablespoon cornstarch
- 1 teaspoon vanilla extract
- 2 eggs
- 3 cups cream cheese

Directions:

1. To make the crust, combine the ingredients in a container until well combined. Move to a 8-inch round cake pan and press it thoroughly on the bottom of the pan.
2. To make the filling, combine the cream cheese, sour cream, vanilla, lime zest and lime juice, eggs, cornstarch and sugar until creamy.
3. Pour the filling over the crust then top with blueberries.
4. Pre-heat the oven and bake at 330F for about fifty minutes or until the cheesecake looks set in the center.
5. Let cool in the pan before you serve.

Nutritional Content of One Serving:

Calories: 389 ‖ Fat: 31.7g ‖ Protein: 6.5g ‖ Carbohydrates: 21.4g

BROWN SUGAR AMARETTO CHEESECAKE

Total Time Taken: 1 ¼ hours
Yield: 10 Servings
Ingredients:

Crust:

- ¼ cup butter, melted
- ½ cup graham crackers, crushed
- 1 cup Amaretti biscuits, crushed

Filling:

- ¼ cup Amaretto liqueur
- ½ cup light brown sugar
- 1 ½ pounds cream cheese
- 1 pinch salt
- 1 teaspoon vanilla extract
- 2 egg yolks
- 2 eggs

Directions:

1. To make the crust, combine the biscuits, crackers and butter in a container until well combined. Move to a 9-inch round cake pan and press it thoroughly on the bottom of the pan.
2. To make the filling, combine all the ingredients in a container and mix thoroughly.
3. Pour the filling over the crust , preheat your oven and bake at 330F for about forty-five minutes or until set.
4. Let cool in the pan and serve, sliced.

Nutritional Content of One Serving:

Calories: 369 ‖ Fat: 30.6g ‖ Protein: 7.2g ‖ Carbohydrates: 12.8g

BROWNIE CHEESECAKE

Total Time Taken: 1 ½ hours
Yield: 12 Servings
Ingredients:

Brownie layer:

- ¼ cup butter, melted
- ¼ cup white sugar
- ½ cup all-purpose flour
- 1 pinch salt
- 2 eggs
- 3 oz. dark chocolate, melted

Filling:

- ½ cup sour cream
- ½ cup white sugar
- 1 pinch salt
- 1 tablespoon cornstarch
- 1 teaspoon orange zest
- 1 teaspoon vanilla extract
- 2 eggs
- 3 cups cream cheese

Directions:

1. To make the brownie layer, combine the chocolate and butter in a container. Put in the eggs and sugar and mix thoroughly.
2. Fold in the flour then pour the batter in a 9-inch round cake pan covered with parchment paper.
3. Pre-heat the oven and bake at 350F for about ten minutes.
4. To make the filling, combine all the ingredients in a container.
5. Pour the filling over the brownie layer and carry on baking at 330F for another forty minutes or until the cheesecake looks set when shaking the pan.
6. When finished, take it out of the oven and let cool down in the pan before you serve.

Nutritional Content of One Serving:

Calories: 385 ‖ Fat: 29.7g ‖ Protein: 7.6g ‖ Carbohydrates: 23.4g

BROWNIE MANGO CHEESECAKE

Total Time Taken: 1 ½ hours
Yield: 12 Servings
Ingredients:

Crust:

- ¼ cup all-purpose flour
- ¼ cup butter
- ¼ cup light brown sugar
- 1 cup dark chocolate chips
- 1 pinch salt
- 2 eggs

Filling:

- ½ cup white sugar
- 1 cup sour cream
- 1 mango, peeled and cubed
- 1 tablespoon cornstarch
- 1 teaspoon lemon juice
- 1 teaspoon lemon zest
- 1 teaspoon vanilla extract
- 2 cups ricotta cheese
- 2 eggs

Directions:

1. To make the crust, melt the butter and chocolate chips in a heatproof container. Put in the remaining ingredients and mix thoroughly.
2. Pour the mixture in a 9-inch round cake pan coated with baking paper.
3. Pre-heat the oven and bake at 330F for about ten minutes.
4. Place aside when baked.
5. To make the filling, combine all the ingredients in a blender and pulse until the desired smoothness is achieved.
6. Pour the mixture over the brownie crust , preheat your oven and bake at 330F for about fifty minutes or until set in the center.
7. Let cool down before you serve.

Nutritional Content of One Serving:

Calories: 268 ‖ Fat: 15.3g ‖ Protein: 8.2g ‖ Carbohydrates: 26.6g

BURNT ORANGE CHEESECAKE

Total Time Taken: 1 hour
Yield: 12 Servings
Ingredients:

Crust:

- ¼ cup butter, melted
- ½ cup ground hazelnuts
- 1 1/2 cups graham crackers, crushed

Filling:

- ½ cup heavy cream
- 1 cup white sugar
- 1 pinch salt
- 1 teaspoon vanilla extract
- 3 cups cream cheese
- 3 eggs

Topping:

- ½ cup light brown sugar
- 2 blood oranges, sliced

Directions:

1. To make the crust, combine the crackers, hazelnuts and butter in a container. Move the mixture to a 9-inch round cake pan covered with parchment paper and press it thoroughly on the bottom of the pan.
2. To make the filling, combine the cream cheese, sugar, eggs, salt, vanilla and cream in a container. Pour the filling over the crust , preheat your oven and bake at 330F for about fifty minutes.
3. When finished, take it out of the oven and let cool down.
4. Top the cheesecake with orange slices and drizzle with brown sugar.
5. Using a blowtorch, caramelize the sugar on top.

This cheesecake tastes best chilled.

Nutritional Content of One Serving:

Calories: 434 ‖ Fat: 30.0g ‖ Protein: 7.4g ‖ Carbohydrates: 36.6g

CAPPUCCINO CHEESECAKE

Total Time Taken: 1 ¼ hours
Yield: 10 Servings
Ingredients:

Crust:

- ½ cup butter, melted
- 1 ½ cups graham crackers
- 1 teaspoon vanilla extract

Filling:

- ¼ cup milk powder
- 1 pinch salt
- 1 tablespoon Amaretto liqueur
- 1 tablespoon cornstarch
- 1 teaspoon instant coffee
- 1 teaspoon vanilla extract
- 2 tablespoons cocoa powder
- 2/3 cup white sugar
- 3 cups cream cheese
- 3 eggs

Directions:

1. Make the crust by mixing the crackers and butter in a container. Move the mixture to a 9-inch round cake pan and press it thoroughly on the bottom of the pan.
2. To make the filling, combine all the ingredients in a container and give them a good mix.
3. Pour the filling over the crust and preheat your oven and bake the cheesecake at 330F for about fifty minutes or until the center of the cheesecake looks set if you shake it slightly.
4. Let the cheesecake cool down before you serve.

Nutritional Content of One Serving:

Calories: 471 ‖ Fat: 36.2g ‖ Protein: 9.3g ‖ Carbohydrates: 28.1g

CARAMEL DRIZZLED CHEESECAKE

Total Time Taken: 1 ¼ hours

Yield: 12 Servings

Ingredients:

Crust:

- ½ cup butter, melted
- 1 ½ cups graham crackers, crushed
- 1 pinch salt

Filling:

- ½ cup caramel sauce
- ½ cup sour cream
- 1 tablespoon cornstarch
- 1 teaspoon vanilla extract
- 2 eggs
- 3 cups cream cheese

Topping:

- 1 cup caramel sauce

Directions:

1. To make the crust, combine the crackers and butter in a container. Move the mixture to a 9-inch round cake pan coated with baking paper. Press well on the bottom of the pan.
2. To make the filling, mix the cream cheese and the remaining ingredients in a container. Stir thoroughly to mix then pour the mixture over the crust, preheat your oven and bake at 330F for about fifty minutes or until set.
3. Let the cheesecake cool to room temperature then sprinkle it with caramel sauce and serve it.

Nutritional Content of One Serving:

Calories: 453 ‖ Fat: 31.7g ‖ Protein: 7.0g ‖ Carbohydrates: 37.8g

CARAMEL PECAN CHEESECAKE

Total Time Taken: 1 ½ hours
Yield: 14 Servings
Ingredients:

Crust:

- ½ cup butter, melted
- 2 cups graham crackers, crushed

Filling:

- ¼ cup light brown sugar
- ½ cup heavy cream
- ½ cup white sugar
- 1 pinch salt
- 1 tablespoon cornstarch
- 1 teaspoon vanilla extract
- 2 tablespoons dark rum
- 3 eggs
- 4 cups cream cheese

Topping:

- ½ cup heavy cream
- 1 cup pecans
- 1 cup white sugar

Directions:

1. To make the crust, combine the ingredients in a container. Move the mixture to a 10-inch round cake pan and press it thoroughly on the bottom of the pan.
2. To make the filling, combine all the ingredients in a container until creamy. Pour the filling over the crust and preheat your oven and bake the cheesecake at 330F for about fifty minutes or until set in the center.
3. Let cool down completely once baked.
4. For the topping, melt the sugar in a heavy saucepan until it sppears amber in colour.
5. Put in the cream and stir thoroughly until melted.
6. Stir in the pecans and turn off the heat. Let cool down.
7. Top the cheesecake with the caramel and pecans just before you serve.

Nutritional Content of One Serving:

Calories: 481 ‖ Fat: 35.0g ‖ Protein: 7.3g ‖ Carbohydrates: 35.8g

CARAMEL SWIRL CHEESECAKE

Total Time Taken: 1 hour
Yield: 10 Servings
Ingredients:

Crust:

- 1 ½ cups graham crackers, crushed
- 1/3 butter, melted

Filling:

- ½ cup sour cream
- ½ cup white sugar
- 1 cup caramel sauce
- 1 pinch salt
- 1 tablespoon cornstarch
- 1 teaspoon vanilla extract
- 3 cups cream cheese
- 3 eggs

Directions:

1. To make the crust, combine the crackers and butter in a container. Move the mixture to a 9-inch round cake pan covered with parchment paper.
2. Press it thoroughly on the bottom of the pan.
3. To make the filling, combine the cream cheese, sour cream, eggs, sugar, vanilla, salt and cornstarch in a container.
4. Spoon the filling over the crust then sprinkle the filling with caramel sauce.
5. Use a fork to swirl the caramel sauce into the cheesecake.
6. Pre-heat the oven and bake at 330F for about forty-five minutes or until the center looks set.
7. Let cool down in the pan and serve, sliced.

Nutritional Content of One Serving:

Calories: 464 || Fat: 29.3g || Protein: 8.6g || Carbohydrates: 44.5g

CHAI CHEESECAKE

Total Time Taken: 1 ¼ hours
Yield: 10 Servings
Ingredients:

Crust:

- ¼ cup ground almonds
- ¼ teaspoon cinnamon powder
- ½ cup butter, melted
- ½ teaspoon ground ginger
- 1 ½ cups graham crackers, crushed

Filling:

- ½ cup sour cream
- ½ cup white sugar
- ½ teaspoon cinnamon powder
- ½ teaspoon ground cardamom
- ½ teaspoon ground ginger
- 1 pinch nutmeg
- 1 pinch salt
- 3 cups cream cheese
- 3 eggs

Directions:

1. To make the crust, combine all the ingredients in a container. Move the mixture to a 9- inch round cake pan covered with parchment paper and press it thoroughly on the bottom of the pan.
2. To make the filling, combine the cream cheese and the remaining ingredients in a container until creamy.
3. Pour the filling over the crust , preheat your oven and bake at 330F for 40-45 minutes or until the center of the cheesecake looks set.
4. Take out of the oven when done and let it cool down before you serve.

Nutritional Content of One Serving:

Calories: 473 ‖ Fat: 39.7g ‖ Protein: 8.8g ‖ Carbohydrates: 22.8g

CHAI LATTE CHEESECAKE

Total Time Taken: 1 ¼ hours

Yield: 10 Servings

Ingredients:

Crust:

- 1 ½ cups gingersnaps, crushed
- 1/3 cup butter, melted

Filling:

- ¼ cup milk powder
- ½ cup sour cream
- ½ cup white sugar
- ½ teaspoon cinnamon powder
- ½ teaspoon ground ginger
- 1 pinch salt
- 1 teaspoon vanilla extract
- 2 eggs
- 24 oz. cream cheese

Directions:

1. To make the crust, combine the gingersnaps and butter in a container until well combined. Move the mixture to a 9-inch round cake pan and press it thoroughly on the bottom of the pan with your fingertips.
2. To make the filling, combine the cream cheese and the remaining ingredients in a container until creamy.
3. Pour the filling over the crust , preheat your oven and bake at 330F for about fifty minutes or until set in the center if you shake the pan.
4. Let cool in the pan and serve, sliced.

Nutritional Content of One Serving:

Calories: 394 ‖ Fat: 33.7g ‖ Protein: 8.1g ‖ Carbohydrates: 16.4g

CHERRY CHOCOLATE CHEESECAKE

Total Time Taken: 1 ¼ hours

Yield: 12 Servings

Ingredients:

Crust:

- ½ cup butter, melted
- 1 ½ cups chocolate biscuits, crushed

Filling:

- ½ cup sour cream
- 1 tablespoon cornstarch
- 1 teaspoon vanilla extract
- 2 cups cherries, pitted
- 2 tablespoons all-purpose flour
- 2/3 cup white sugar
- 3 cups cream cheese
- 3 eggs
- 4 oz. dark chocolate, melted

Directions:

1. To make the crust, combine the chocolate biscuits and butter in a container. Move the mixture to a 9-inch round cake pan and press it thoroughly on the bottom of the pan.
2. To make the filling, combine the cream cheese with the melted chocolate. Put in the sugar, eggs, cornstarch and sour cream, as well as vanilla and mix thoroughly.
3. Pour the filling over the crust.
4. Mix the cherries with the flour. Top the cheesecake with the cherries.
5. Pre-heat the oven and bake at 330F for about fifty minutes.
6. Let the cheesecake cool down before you serve.

Nutritional Content of One Serving:

Calories: 432 ‖ Fat: 34.3g ‖ Protein: 7.2g ‖ Carbohydrates: 25.3g

CHERRY VANILLA CHEESECAKE

Total Time Taken: 1 ¼ hours
Yield: 10 Servings
Ingredients:

Crust:

- 1 cup pecans, ground
- ¼ cup butter, melted

- 1/2 cup graham crackers, crushed

Filling:
- ½ cup white sugar
- 1 cup cherries, pitted
- 1 pinch salt
- 1 tablespoon cornstarch
- 1 tablespoon vanilla extract
- 24 oz. cream cheese
- 3 eggs

Directions:
1. To make the crust, combine the ingredients in a food processor and pulse until thoroughly combined. Move to a 9-inch round cake pan and press it thoroughly on the bottom of the pan.
2. Top the crust with cherries.
3. To make the filling, combine the cream cheese, sugar, vanilla, salt, eggs and cornstarch in a container. Pour the filling over the cherries and preheat your oven and bake the cheesecake at 330F for about fifty minutes or until the center looks set.
4. Let cool down in the pan and serve, sliced.

Nutritional Content of One Serving:

Calories: 377 ‖ Fat: 31.1g ‖ Protein: 7.3g ‖ Carbohydrates: 18.3g

CHOCOLATE BANANA CHEESECAKE

Total Time Taken: 1 ½ hours
Yield: 12 Servings
Ingredients:

Crust:
- ½ cup butter, melted
- 2 cups chocolate biscuits, crushed
- 2 tablespoons dark rum

Filling:
- 1 cup mascarpone cheese

- 1 pinch salt
- 1 tablespoon cornstarch
- 2 bananas, sliced
- 2 tablespoons dark rum
- 2/3 cup white sugar
- 3 cups cream cheese
- 4 eggs
- 4 oz. dark chocolate, melted and chilled

Directions:

1. Mix the ingredients in a container. Move the mixture to a 9-inch round cake pan and press it thoroughly on the bottom of the pan.
2. Position the banana slices over the crust.
3. To make the filling, combine the mascarpone cheese and chocolate. Stir in the cream cheese, rum, salt, eggs, cornstarch and sugar and mix thoroughly.
4. Spoon the mixture over the banana slices , preheat your oven and bake at 330F for about fifty minutes or until set.
5. Let the cheesecake cool down and serve, sliced.

Nutritional Content of One Serving:

Calories: 461 ‖ Fat: 35.3g ‖ Protein: 9.8g ‖ Carbohydrates: 25.7g

CHOCOLATE CHIP BANANA CHEESECAKE

Total Time Taken: 1 ½ hours
Yield: 12 Servings
Ingredients:

Crust:

- ½ cup butter, melted
- 2 cups graham crackers, crushed

Filling:

- ½ cup dark chocolate chips
- ½ cup heavy cream
- ½ cup white sugar

- 1 pinch salt
- 1 tablespoon cornstarch
- 1 teaspoon lemon juice
- 1 teaspoon vanilla extract
- 2 bananas, mashed
- 3 cups cream cheese
- 3 eggs

Directions:

1. To make the crust, combine the crackers and butter in a container until well combined. Move the mixture to a round cake pan coated with baking paper and press it thoroughly on the bottom of the pan.
2. To make the filling, combine the bananas with lemon juice in a container.
3. Put in the remaining ingredients and mix thoroughly.
4. Fold in the chocolate chips then pour the mixture over the crust.
5. Pre-heat the oven and bake at 330F for about forty-five minutes or until the center looks set.
6. Let cool down and serve, sliced.

Nutritional Content of One Serving:

Calories: 438 ‖ Fat: 33.6g ‖ Protein: 7.4g ‖ Carbohydrates: 29.3g

CHOCOLATE CHIP CHEESECAKE

Total Time Taken: 1 ½ hours
Yield: 12 Servings
Ingredients:

Crust:

- 1 ½ cups graham crackers, crushed
- 2 tablespoons cocoa powder
- 1/2 cup butter, melted

Filling:

- ½ cup white sugar
- 1 cup dark chocolate chips
- 1 pinch salt
- 1 tablespoon cornstarch

- 1 teaspoon vanilla extract
- 2 tablespoons milk
- 4 cups cream cheese
- 4 eggs

Directions:

1. To make the crust, combine the ingredients in a container until well combined. Move to a 9-inch round cake pan and press the mixture well on the bottom of the pan.
2. To make the filling, combine the cream cheese, eggs, sugar, salt, vanilla, milk and cornstarch in a container.
3. Fold in the chocolate chips then spoon the filling over the crust.
4. Preheat your oven and bake the cheesecake at 330F for about fifty minutes or until set in the center.
5. Let the cheesecake cool down and serve, sliced.

Nutritional Content of One Serving:

Calories: 488 ‖ Fat: 40.0g ‖ Protein: 9.4g ‖ Carbohydrates: 26.5g

CHOCOLATE CHIP MINT CHEESECAKE

Total Time Taken: 1 ¼ hours
Yield: 12 Servings
Ingredients:

Crust:

- ½ cup butter, melted
- 2 cups Oreo cookies, crushed

Filling:

- ¼ cup butter, melted
- ½ cup dark chocolate chips
- ½ cup white sugar
- 1 pinch salt
- 1 tablespoon cornstarch
- 1 teaspoon peppermint extract
- 24 oz. cream cheese
- 3 eggs

Topping:

- 1 ½ cups heavy cream, whipped

Directions:

1. To make the crust, combine the cookies and butter in a container until well combined. Move to a 9-inch round cake pan and press it thoroughly on the bottom of the pan.
2. To make the filling, combine all the ingredients in a container. Pour the mixture over the crust, preheat your oven and bake at 330F for about fifty minutes or until set in the center.
3. Let cool in the pan then top with whipped cream.

This cheesecake tastes best chilled.

Nutritional Content of One Serving:

Calories: 433 ‖ Fat: 39.6g ‖ Protein: 6.5g ‖ Carbohydrates: 15.5g

CHOCOLATE FUDGE CHEESECAKE

Total Time Taken: 1 ½ hours
Yield: 14 Servings
Ingredients:

Crust:

- ½ cup butter, melted
- 8 oz. chocolate biscuits, crushed

Filling:

- ½ cup heavy cream
- ¾ cup sweetened condensed milk
- 1 pinch salt
- 1 teaspoon vanilla extract
- 3 cups cream cheese
- 6 oz. dark chocolate, melted

Directions:

1. To make the crust, combine all the ingredients in a container. Move the mixture to a 9- inch round cake pan covered with parchment paper and press it thoroughly on the bottom of the pan.
2. To make the filling, combine the ingredients in a container. Pour the filling over the crust , preheat your oven and bake at 330F for about forty-five minutes or until the center looks set.
3. Let the cheesecake cool down and serve, sliced.

Nutritional Content of One Serving:

Calories: 441 ‖ Fat: 33.4g ‖ Protein: 7.5g ‖ Carbohydrates: 28.4g

CHOCOLATE PEANUT BUTTER CHEESECAKE

Total Time Taken: 1 ¼ hours
Yield: 10 Servings
Ingredients:

Crust:

- ¼ cup butter
- ¼ cup smooth peanut butter
- 1 ½ cups graham crackers, crushed
- 1 tablespoon dark brown sugar

Filling:

- ¼ cup light brown sugar
- ½ cup smooth peanut butter
- ½ cup white sugar
- 1 cup sour cream
- 1 pinch salt
- 1 teaspoon vanilla extract
- 2 cups cream cheese
- 3 eggs

Directions:

1. To make the crust, combine the ingredients well then transfer the mixture in a 9-inch round cake pan coated with baking paper.

2. Press the mixture thoroughly on the bottom of the pan and set aside for later.
3. To make the filling, combine all the ingredients in a container until smooth and creamy.
4. Pour the filling over the crust then preheat your oven and bake the cheesecake at 330F for about fifty minutes or until the center of the cheesecake looks set.
5. Let the cheesecake cool down and serve, sliced.

Nutritional Content of One Serving:

Calories: 494 ‖ Fat: 37.9g ‖ Protein: 11.7g ‖ Carbohydrates: 30.3g

CHOCOLATE PUMPKIN CHEESECAKE

Total Time Taken: 1 ¼ hours
Yield: 12 Servings
Ingredients:

Crust:

- 1 ½ cups Oreo cookies, crushed
- 1/3 cup butter, melted

Filling:

- ½ cup dark chocolate chips
- ½ cup light brown sugar
- 1 cup pumpkin puree
- 1 pinch salt
- 1 tablespoon cornstarch
- 1 teaspoon vanilla extract
- 3 cups cream cheese
- 3 eggs

Topping:

- 1 ½ cups heavy cream, whipped Cocoa powder

Directions:

1. To make the crust, combine the cookies and butter in a container. Move the mixture to a 9-inch round cake pan and press it thoroughly on the bottom of the pan.
2. To make the filling, combine the ingredients in a container.
3. Pour the mixture over the crust , preheat your oven and bake at 330F for about fifty minutes or until set in the center.
4. Let cool in the pan.
5. Top the cheesecake with whipped cream and garnish with a dusting of
6. cocoa powder.

This cheesecake tastes best fresh.

Nutritional Content of One Serving:

Calories: 376 ‖ Fat: 33.5g ‖ Protein: 6.7g ‖ Carbohydrates: 14.2g

CHOCOLATE SAUCE CHEESECAKE

Total Time Taken: 1 ¼ hours
Yield: 10 Servings
Ingredients:

Crust:

- 1 ½ cups Oreo cookies, crushed
- 1/3 cup butter, melted

Filling:

- 1 pinch salt
- 1 tablespoon cornstarch
- 1 teaspoon vanilla extract
- 2/3 cup white sugar
- 3 cups cream cheese
- 3 eggs

Chocolate sauce:

- 1 cup dark chocolate chips
- 1 cup heavy cream

Directions:

1. To make the crust, combine the cookies and butter in a container until well combined. Move the mixture to a 8-inch round cake pan and press it thoroughly on the bottom of the pan.
2. To make the filling, combine the cream cheeses, eggs, sugar, vanilla, salt and cornstarch in a container. Pour the filling over the crust.
3. Preheat your oven and bake the cheesecake at 330F for about forty-five minutes or until the center looks set.
4. Let cool in the pan.
5. For the sauce, bring the cream to a boil in a saucepan. Turn off the heat and mix in the chocolate. Stir until melted and smooth.
6. Serve the cheesecake with chocolate sauce.

Nutritional Content of One Serving:

Calories: 472 ‖ Fat: 39.6g ‖ Protein: 8.1g ‖ Carbohydrates: 25.1g

CHOCOLATE STRAWBERRY CHEESECAKE

Total Time Taken: 1 ½ hours
Yield: 10 Servings
Ingredients:

Crust:

- 1 ½ cups Oreo cookies, crushed
- 1/3 cup butter, melted

Filling:

- ½ cup dark chocolate chips
- 1 pinch salt
- 1 tablespoon cornstarch
- 1 teaspoon vanilla extract
- 2/3 cup white sugar
- 3 cups cream cheese
- 3 eggs

Topping:

- 2 cups strawberries, sliced

Directions:

1. To make the crust, mxi the cookies and butter in a container. Move to a 9-inch round cake pan covered with parchment paper and press it thoroughly on the bottom of the pan.
2. To make the filling, mix the cream cheese and the remaining ingredients in a container and stir until creamy.
3. Fold in the chocolate chips then pour the mixture over the crust.
4. Preheat your oven and bake the cheesecake at 330F for about fifty minutes or until the center looks set.
5. Let cool down completely in the pan.
6. When chilled, top the cheesecake with strawberry slices.

This cheesecake tastes best chilled.

Nutritional Content of One Serving:

Calories: 409 ‖ Fat: 33.5g ‖ Protein: 7.6g ‖ Carbohydrates: 22.4g

CHUNKY BANANA CHEESECAKE

Total Time Taken: 1 ½ hours
Yield: 12 Servings
Ingredients:

Crust:

- ½ cup butter, melted
- 1 tablespoon dark brown sugar
- 2 cups graham crackers

Filling:

- ½ cup plain yogurt
- ½ cup white sugar
- 1 pinch salt
- 1 tablespoon cornstarch
- 1 teaspoon vanilla extract
- 2 bananas, sliced
- 2 eggs
- 3 cups cream cheese

Directions:

1. To make the crust, combine all the ingredients in a container. Move the mixture to a deep dish baking pan coated with baking paper and press it thoroughly on the bottom and sides of the pan.
2. Position the banana slices over the crust.
3. To make the filling, combine all the ingredients in a container until creamy pour the filling into the crust , preheat your oven and bake at 330F for about forty minutes or until the center of the cheesecake looks slightly set.
4. Let the cheesecake cool down in the pan then serve, sliced. Place it in your refrigerator for not more than four days.

Nutritional Content of One Serving:

Calories: 402 ‖ Fat: 30.2g ‖ Protein: 7.1g ‖ Carbohydrates: 27.3g

CITRUS CHEESECAKE

Total Time Taken: 1 ¼ hours
Yield: 14 Servings
Ingredients:

Crust:

- 1 ½ cups graham crackers, crushed
- 1/3 cup butter, melted

Filling:

- ½ cup white sugar
- 1 lemon, zested
- 1 lime, zested
- 1 orange, zested
- 1 pinch salt
- 1 teaspoon vanilla extract
- 3 eggs
- 4 cups cream cheese
- Fresh raspberries to garnish

Directions:

1. To make the crust, combine the crackers and butter in a container. Move the mixture to a 9-inch round cake coated with baking paper. Press it thoroughly on the bottom of the pan.
2. To make the filling, combine all the ingredients in a container until creamy. Pour the mixture over the crust , preheat your oven and bake at 330F for about fifty minutes or until set in the center.
3. Let cool in the pan and serve, sliced.

Nutritional Content of One Serving:

Calories: 358 ‖ Fat: 29.4g ‖ Protein: 7.1g ‖ Carbohydrates: 18.3g

CLASSIC VANILLA CHEESECAKE

Total Time Taken: 1 ¼ hours
Yield: 10 Servings
Ingredients:

Crust:

- ½ cup butter, melted
- 1 ½ cups graham crackers
- 1 pinch salt
- 2 tablespoons light brown sugar

Filling:

- 1 tablespoon cornstarch
- 1 tablespoon vanilla extract
- 2/3 cup white sugar
- 26 oz. cream cheese
- 3 eggs

Directions:

1. To make the crust, combine all the ingredients in a food processor and pulse until thoroughly combined.
2. Press well on the bottom of the pan.
3. To make the filling, combine all the ingredients in a container. Spoon the filling over the crust , preheat your oven and bake at 330F for about forty minutes.
4. Let cool down before you serve.

Nutritional Content of One Serving:

Calories: 474 ‖ Fat: 37.5g ‖ Protein: 8.2g ‖ Carbohydrates: 27.7g

---

COFFEE GLAZED CHEESECAKE

Total Time Taken: 1 ½ hours
Yield: 12 Servings
Ingredients:

Crust:

- ½ cup butter, melted
- 1 ½ cups chocolate biscuits, crushed
- 1 teaspoon vanilla extract

Filling:

- ½ cup sour cream
- 1 pinch salt
- 1 tablespoon cornstarch
- 2 teaspoons instant coffee
- 2/3 cup white sugar
- 3 cups cream cheese
- 3 eggs

Topping:

- ½ cup dark chocolate chips
- ¾ cup heavy cream
- 1 cup white chocolate chips
- 2 teaspoons instant coffee

Directions:

1. To make the crust, combine the ingredients in a container. Move the mixture to a 9-inch round cake pan and press it thoroughly on the bottom of the pan.
2. To make the filling, combine all the ingredients in a container until creamy. Pour the mixture over the crust , preheat your oven and bake at 330F for about fifty minutes.
3. When finished, let cool in the pan completely.
4. For the topping, heat the cream in a saucepan just to a boil.

5. Turn off the heat and mix in the chocolate chips and coffee. Stir thoroughly to mix then let cool down.
6. Pour the glaze over the baked cheesecake and serve the dessert fresh.

Nutritional Content of One Serving:

Calories: 483 ‖ Fat: 39.9g ‖ Protein: 7.5g ‖ Carbohydrates: 26.5g

COLORFUL BLUEBERRY CHEESECAKE

Total Time Taken: 1 ¼ hours
Yield: 10 Servings
Ingredients:

Crust:

- ½ cup butter, melted
- 1 ½ cups graham crackers, crushed

Filling:

- 1 cup fresh blueberries
- 1 pinch salt
- 1 tablespoon lemon juice
- 1 teaspoon lemon zest
- 2 eggs
- 2 tablespoons cornstarch
- 2/3 cup white sugar
- 3 cups cream cheese

Directions:

1. To make the crust, combine the crackers and butter in a container. Move the mixture to a 9-inch round cake pan and press it thoroughly on the bottom of the pan.
2. To make the filling, combine all the ingredients in a blender and pulse until the desired smoothness is achieved.
3. Pour the mixture over the filling.
4. Preheat your oven and bake the cheesecake at 350F for about fifty minutes or until the cheesecake looks set in the center if you shake the pan lightly.
5. When finished, take it out of the oven and let cool down before you serve.

Nutritional Content of One Serving:

Calories: 455 ‖ Fat: 35.7g ‖ Protein: 7.5g ‖ Carbohydrates: 28.6g

CONDENSED MILK CHEESECAKE

Total Time Taken: 1 ¼ hours

Yield: 10 Servings

Ingredients:

Crust:

- 1 ½ cups Oreo cookies, crushed
- 1/3 cup butter, melted

Filling:

- ½ cup dark chocolate chips
- 1 pinch salt
- 1 teaspoon vanilla extract
- 16 oz. cream cheese
- 2 eggs
- 2/3 cup sweetened condensed milk

Directions:

1. To make the crust, combine the cookies and butter in a container until well combined. Move the mixture to a 9-inch round cake pan and press it thoroughly on the bottom of the pan.
2. To make the filling, combine the milk, cream cheese, vanilla, eggs and salt in a container. Fold in the chocolate chips.
3. Pour the filling over the crust , preheat your oven and bake at 330F for about fifty minutes or until the center looks set.
4. Let cool down and serve, sliced.

Nutritional Content of One Serving:

Calories: 325 ‖ Fat: 26.4g ‖ Protein: 6.6g ‖ Carbohydrates: 17.2g

CRANBERRY EGGNOG CHEESECAKE

Total Time Taken: 1 ¼ hours
Yield: 12 Servings
Ingredients:

Crust:

- 1 ½ cups graham crackers, crushed
- 1/3 cup butter, melted

Filling:

- ¼ cup eggnog
- ½ cup sour cream
- ½ cup white sugar
- 1 cup cranberries
- 1 pinch salt
- 1 tablespoon cornstarch
- 1 teaspoon vanilla extract
- 2 eggs
- 3 cups cream cheese

Directions:

1. To make the crust, combine the ingredients in a container then transfer the mixture in a 9- inch round cake pan and press it thoroughly on the bottom of the pan.
2. Top the crust with cranberries.
3. To make the filling, combine all the ingredients in a container and mix thoroughly.
4. Pour the mixture over the cranberries , preheat your oven and bake at 330F for about fifty minutes or until well set in the center.
5. Let cool in the pan before you serve.

Nutritional Content of One Serving:

Calories: 370 ‖ Fat: 29.5g ‖ Protein: 6.6g ‖ Carbohydrates: 20.6g

CRANBERRY SAUCE CHEESECAKE

Total Time Taken: 1 ½ hours
Yield: 10 Servings
Ingredients:

Crust:

- 1 ½ cups graham crackers, crushed
- 1 teaspoon vanilla extract
- 1/3 cup butter, melted

Filling:

- ½ cup white sugar
- 1 tablespoon cornstarch
- 1 teaspoon vanilla extract
- 24 oz. cream cheese
- 3 eggs

Cranberry sauce:

- ¼ cup white sugar
- 1 cup cranberries
- 1 tablespoon lemon juice

Directions:

1. To make the crust, combine the crackers, butter and vanilla in a container until well combined. Move the mixture to a 9-inch round cake pan and press it thoroughly on the bottom of the pan.
2. To make the filling, combine all the ingredients in a container until creamy and smooth.
3. Pour the filling over the crust , preheat your oven and bake at 330F for about forty-five minutes or until set.
4. Let cool in the pan.
5. For the sauce, combine the ingredients in a saucepan and place over low heat. Cook until the cranberries become tender.
6. Slice the cheesecake and top it with the sauce just before you serve.

Nutritional Content of One Serving:

Calories: 432 ‖ Fat: 32.5g ‖ Protein: 7.7g ‖ Carbohydrates: 28.5g

CREAMY LEMON CHEESECAKES

Total Time Taken: 1 ½ hours
Yield: 10 Servings
Ingredients:

Crust:

- ½ cup butter, melted
- 1 ½ cups vanilla biscuits
- 1 teaspoon lemon zest

Filling:

- ¾ cup white sugar
- 1 lemon, zested and juiced
- 1 tablespoon cornstarch
- 1 teaspoon vanilla extract
- 3 cups cream cheese
- 3 eggs

Directions:

1. To make the crust, combine all the ingredients in a container. Move the mixture to a 9- inch round cake pan coated with baking paper and press it thoroughly on the bottom of the pan.
2. To make the filling, combine the cream cheese and the remaining ingredients in a container and stir for a few seconds to mix.
3. Pour the filling over the crust , preheat your oven and bake at 330F for about forty-five minutes or until mildly golden-brown on the edges and set in the center.

This cheesecake tastes best chilled.

Nutritional Content of One Serving:

Calories: 448 ‖ Fat: 35.8g ‖ Protein: 7.8g ‖ Carbohydrates: 25.9g

CRÈME BRULEE CHEESECAKE

Total Time Taken: 1 ¼ hours
Yield: 12 Servings
Ingredients:

Crust:

- ½ cup butter, melted
- 1 ½ cups Oreo cookies, crushed

Filling:

- 1 pinch salt
- 1 teaspoon orange zest
- 1 teaspoon vanilla extract
- 2/3 cup white sugar
- 3 eggs
- 4 cups cream cheese

Topping:

- 1/2 cup white sugar

Directions:

1. To make the crust, combine the cookies and butter in a container. Move the mixture to a 9-inch round cake pan and press it thoroughly on the bottom of the pan.
2. To make the filling, combine the ingredients in a container until creamy. Spoon the filling over the crust , preheat your oven and bake at 330F for about forty-five minutes or until set.
3. When finished, take it out of the oven and let cool down slightly.
4. Top with sugar and place under the broiler for at least two minutes until caramelized.
5. Let cool down before you serve.

Nutritional Content of One Serving:

Calories: 429 ‖ Fat: 35.8g ‖ Protein: 7.3g ‖ Carbohydrates: 21.8g

CRÈME FRAICHE CHEESECAKE

Total Time Taken: 1 ¼ hours
Yield: 10 Servings
Ingredients:

Crust:

- 1 ½ cups vanilla cookies, crushed
- 1 teaspoon vanilla extract
- 1/3 cup butter, melted

Filling:

- 1 cup cream cheese
- 1 pinch salt
- 1 tablespoon cornstarch
- 1 teaspoon vanilla extract
- 2 cups crème fraiche
- 3 eggs

Directions:

1. To make the crust, combine the ingredients in a container until well combined. Move to a 9-inch round cake pan and press it thoroughly on the bottom of the pan.
2. To make the filling, combine all the ingredients in a container until creamy.
3. Pour the filling over the crust and preheat your oven and bake the cheesecake at 330F for about fifty minutes or until the center of the cheesecake looks slightly set if you shake the pan.

This cheesecake tastes best chilled.

Nutritional Content of One Serving:

Calories: 285 ‖ Fat: 27.0g ‖ Protein: 5.7g ‖ Carbohydrates: 7.0g

CRUSTLESS ORANGE CHEESECAKE

Total Time Taken: 1 ½ hours
Yield: 10 Servings

Ingredients:

- ½ cup sour cream
- 1 tablespoon orange zest
- 1 teaspoon vanilla extract
- 2 tablespoons cornstarch
- 2/3 cup white sugar
- 3 cups cream cheese
- 3 eggs

Directions:

1. Combine all the ingredients in a container.

2. Grease a 8-inch baking pan with butter then pour the cheesecake mix in the pan.
3. Pre-heat the oven and bake at 330F for about fifty minutes or until set.
4. Let the cheesecake cool down and serve, sliced.

Nutritional Content of One Serving:

Calories: 344 ‖ Fat: 28.0g ‖ Protein: 7.3g ‖ Carbohydrates: 17.4g

CRUSTLESS VANILLA CHEESECAKE

Total Time Taken: 1 hour
Yield: 10 Servings
Ingredients:

- ¾ cup white sugar
- 1 cup sour cream
- 1 pinch salt
- 1 tablespoon vanilla extract
- 2 tablespoons all-purpose flour
- 24 oz. cream cheese
- 4 eggs
- Butter to grease the pan

Directions:

1. Mix all the ingredients in a container.
2. Grease a 9-inch round cake pan with butter. Pour the filling in the pan, preheat your oven and bake at 330F for about forty minutes or until set.
3. Let the cake cool in the oven before you serve.

Nutritional Content of One Serving:

Calories: 378 ‖ Fat: 30.3g ‖ Protein: 8.2g ‖ Carbohydrates: 19.3g

DARK CHERRY CHEESECAKE

Total Time Taken: 1 ¼ hours
Yield: 12 Servings
Ingredients:

Crust:

- ½ cup butter, melted
- 1 ½ cups Oreo cookies

Filling:

- ¼ cup heavy cream
- ¾ cup white sugar
- 1 pinch salt
- 1 tablespoon cornstarch
- 1 tablespoon dark rum
- 2 cups dark cherries, pitted
- 2 tablespoons cocoa powder
- 3 eggs
- 4 cups cream cheese
- 4 oz. dark chocolate, melted

Directions:

1. To make the crust, place the cookies in a food processor and pulse until ground.
2. Put in the melted butter and mix thoroughly then move to a 9-inch round cake pan and press it thoroughly on the bottom of the pan.
3. Top with the pitted cherries.
4. To make the filling, combine the cream cheese and chocolate in a container.
5. Put in the remaining ingredients and mix thoroughly.
6. Spoon the filling over the cherries and preheat your oven and bake the cheesecake at 330F for about fifty minutes or until set in the center.
7. Let the cheesecake cool in the pan and serve, sliced.

Nutritional Content of One Serving:

Calories: 480 ‖ Fat: 39.6g ‖ Protein: 8.5g ‖ Carbohydrates: 24.7g

DECADENT CHOCOLATE CHEESECAKE

Total Time Taken: 1 ½ hours
Yield: 14 Servings
Ingredients:

Crust:

- ½ cup butter, melted
- 1 ½ cups chocolate cookies, crushed

Filling:

- ¾ cup white sugar
- 1 cup dark chocolate chips, melted
- 1 cup heavy cream
- 1 tablespoon cornstarch
- 1 teaspoon vanilla extract
- 3 cups cream cheese
- 3 eggs

Topping:

- 1 ¼ cups dark chocolate chips
- 1 cup heavy cream

Directions:

1. To make the crust, combine the ingredients in a container. Move the mixture to a 9-inch round cake pan coated with baking paper and press it thoroughly on the bottom of the pan.
2. To make the filling, combine the ingredients in a container until creamy. Pour the mixture over the crust , preheat your oven and bake at 330F for about fifty minutes.
3. Let cool down in the pan.
4. For the topping, bring the cream to a boil.
5. Turn off the heat and put in the chocolate. Stir until melted then let cool.
6. Top the cheesecake with the chilled topping chocolate cream.

This cheesecake tastes best chilled.

Nutritional Content of One Serving:

Calories: 489 ‖ Fat: 38.0g ‖ Protein: 7.4g ‖ Carbohydrates: 34.7g

DRIED FRUIT CHEESECAKE

Total Time Taken: 1 ½ hours
Yield: 12 Servings
Ingredients:

Crust:

- ½ cup butter, melted
- 2 cups graham crackers, crushed
- 2 tablespoons brandy

Filling:

- ¼ cup brandy
- ½ cup white sugar
- 1 cup mixed dried fruits, chopped
- 1 cup ricotta cheese
- 1 pinch salt
- 1 tablespoon vanilla extract
- 2 tablespoons cornstarch
- 3 cups cream cheese
- 4 eggs

Directions:

1. To make the crust, combine the ingredients well in a container then transfer the mixture in a 9-inch round cake pan covered with parchment paper.
2. Press well on the bottom of the pan and set aside for later.
3. To make the filling, first of all combine the fruits with brandy in a container and allow to soak up for about half an hour.
4. Mix the cream cheese, ricotta, sugar, vanilla, eggs, salt and cornstarch in a container.
5. Fold in the dried fruits then pour the filling over the crust.
6. Pre-heat the oven and bake at 330F for about forty-five minutes or until the center of the cake is set if you shake the pan.
7. Let the cheesecake cool to room temperature and serve, sliced.

Nutritional Content of One Serving:

Calories: 492 ‖ Fat: 32.5g ‖ Protein: 10.2g ‖ Carbohydrates: 38.8g

DULCE DE LECHE CHEESECAKE

Total Time Taken: 1 ¼ hours
Yield: 10 Servings
Ingredients:

Crust:

- ½ cup butter, melted
- 1 ½ cups graham crackers, crushed

Filling:

- ¾ cup white sugar
- 1 tablespoon cornstarch
- 1 tablespoon vanilla extract
- 4 cream cheese
- 4 eggs

Topping:

- 1 cup dulce de leche

Directions:

1. To make the crust, combine the crackers with the butter in a container. Move the mixture to a 9-inch round cake pan coated with baking paper. Press the mixture thoroughly on the bottom of the pan.
2. To make the filling, combine the cream cheese, eggs, sugar, vanilla and cornstarch in a container until creamy.
3. Spoon the filling over the crust , preheat your oven and bake at 330F for about forty minutes.
4. When finished, allow the cheesecake to cool down in the pan.
5. Top the chilled cheesecake with dulce de leche and serve it immediately.

Nutritional Content of One Serving:

Calories: 325 ‖ Fat: 14.8g ‖ Protein: 5.1g ‖ Carbohydrates: 44.2g

DULCE DE LECHE CHEESECAKE

Total Time Taken: 1 ¼ hours
Yield: 12 Servings
Ingredients:

Crust:

- 1 ½ cups graham crackers, crushed
- 1/3 cup butter, melted

Filling:

- 1 cup dulce de leche
- 1 pinch salt
- 1 tablespoon cornstarch
- 1 teaspoon vanilla extract
- 3 cups cream cheese
- 3 eggs

Directions:

1. To make the crust, combine the two ingredients in a container. Move the mixture to a 9- inch round cake pan and press it thoroughly on the bottom of the pan.
2. To make the filling, combine all the ingredients in a container until creamy.
3. Pour the filling over the crust and preheat your oven and bake the cheesecake at 330F for about forty minutes or until the center looks set.
4. Let cool in the pan and serve, sliced.

Nutritional Content of One Serving:

Calories: 385 ‖ Fat: 28.5g ‖ Protein: 7.9g ‖ Carbohydrates: 25.7g

DUO CHEESECAKE

Total Time Taken: 1 ½ hours
Yield: 12 Servings
Ingredients:

Crust:

- ½ cup butter, melted
- 1 teaspoon vanilla extract
- 2 cups graham crackers, crushed

White layer:

- ¼ cup sour cream
- ¼ cup white sugar
- 1 ½ cups cream cheese
- 1 tablespoon cornstarch
- 1 teaspoon vanilla extract
- 2 eggs

Dark layer:

- ¼ cup light brown sugar
- 1 teaspoon vanilla extract
- 2 cups cream cheese
- 2 eggs
- 2 oz. dark chocolate, melted and chilled

Directions:

1. To make the crust, combine the ingredients in a container. Move the mixture to a 9-inch round cake pan and press it thoroughly.
2. For the white layer, combine all the ingredients in a container until creamy.
3. Pour the mixture over the crust.
4. For the dark layer, combine the cream cheese with the melted chocolate. Put in the remaining ingredients then pour the mixture over the white one.
5. Swirl it around using a fork , preheat your oven and bake at 330F for about fifty minutes or until the center looks set.

This cheesecake tastes best chilled.

Nutritional Content of One Serving:

Calories: 452 ‖ Fat: 36.5g ‖ Protein: 8.5g ‖ Carbohydrates: 23.5g

FRANGELICO CHEESECAKE

Total Time Taken: 1 ¼ hours
Yield: 10 Servings
Ingredients:

Crust:

- ½ cup butter, melted

- 1 ½ cups graham crackers, crushed

Filling:

- ¼ cup Frangelico liqueur
- ½ cup white sugar
- 1 pinch salt
- 1 tablespoon cornstarch
- 1 teaspoon vanilla extract
- 3 cups cream cheese
- 3 eggs

Topping:

- 2 cups strawberries, sliced

Directions:

1. To make the crust, combine the ingredients in a container. Move the mixture to a 9-inch round cake pan and press it thoroughly on the bottom of the pan.
2. To make the filling, combine the ingredients in a container until creamy and airy.
3. Spoon the filling over the crust, preheat your oven and bake at 330F for about forty-five minutes or until the center of the cheesecake looks set if you shake the pan.
4. When finished, take it out of the oven and let cool down.
5. Top the cheesecake with fresh strawberries.

This cheesecake tastes best chilled.

Nutritional Content of One Serving:

Calories: 465 ‖ Fat: 36.2g ‖ Protein: 8.1g ‖ Carbohydrates: 24.6g

FUNFETTI CHOCOLATE CHEESECAKE

Total Time Taken: 1 ½ hours
Yield: 10 Servings
Ingredients:

Crust:

- 1 ½ cups Oreo cookies, crushed

- 1/3 cup butter, melted

Filling:
- ½ cup colourful sprinkles
- ½ cup sour cream
- ½ cup white sugar
- 1 pinch salt
- 1 tablespoon cornstarch
- 1 teaspoon vanilla extract
- 2 eggs
- 20 oz. cream cheese
- 6 oz. dark chocolate, melted

Directions:

1. To make the crust, combine the cookies and butter in a container until well combined. Move the mixture to a 9-icnh round cake pan and press it thoroughly on the bottom of the pan.
2. To make the filling, combine the cream cheese, sour cream, chocolate and vanilla in a container. Put in the remaining ingredients and mix thoroughly.
3. Fold in the sprinkles then pour the filling over the crust.
4. Pre-heat the oven and bake at 330F for about fifty minutes or until set in the center.
5. Let cool in the pan and serve, sliced.

Nutritional Content of One Serving:

Calories: 441 ‖ Fat: 34.9g ‖ Protein: 7.4g ‖ Carbohydrates: 26.0g

GINGER EGGNOG CHEESECAKE

Total Time Taken: 1 ¼ hours
Yield: 12 Servings
Ingredients:

Crust:

- 1 ½ cups gingersnaps, crushed
- 1/3 cup butter, melted

Filling:

- ¼ cup light brown sugar
- ½ cup eggnog
- 1 pinch nutmeg
- 1 tablespoon cornstarch
- 1 teaspoon vanilla extract
- 3 cups cream cheese
- 3 eggs

Topping:

- 2 cups heavy cream, whipped

Directions:

1. To make the crust, combine the gingersnaps and butter in a container. Move the mixture to a 9-inch round cake batter and press it thoroughly on the bottom of the pan.
2. To make the filling, combine all the ingredients in a container until creamy.
3. Pour the mixture over the crust, preheat your oven and bake at 330F for about fifty minutes or until set in the center.
4. Let cool in the pan before you serve.

Nutritional Content of One Serving:

Calories: 373 ‖ Fat: 35.0g ‖ Protein: 6.8g ‖ Carbohydrates: 9.1g

GINGERSNAP CHEESECAKE

Total Time Taken: 1 ¼ hours
Yield: 14 Servings
Ingredients:

Crust:

- ½ cup butter, melted
- 16 gingersnaps

Filling:

- ½ cup sour cream
- 1 cup light brown sugar
- 1 teaspoon ground ginger
- 1 teaspoon vanilla extract
- 2 eggs
- 28 oz. cream cheese

Directions:

1. To make the crust, mix the gingersnaps and butter in a food processor and pulse until thoroughly combined.
2. Move the mixture to a 9-inch pan and press it thoroughly on the bottom of the pan.
3. To make the filling, combine all the ingredients in a container. Pour the mixture over the crust and preheat your oven and bake the cheesecake at 330F for around forty minutes.
4. When finished, allow the cheesecake to cool in the pan then serve, sliced.

Nutritional Content of One Serving:

Calories: 483 ‖ Fat: 34.4g ‖ Protein: 7.7g ‖ Carbohydrates: 37.4g

HAZELNUT CHOCOLATE CHEESECAKE

Total Time Taken: 1 ¼ hours
Yield: 12 Servings
Ingredients:

Crust:

- ¼ cup butter, melted
- 1 cup graham crackers

- 1 cup ground hazelnuts

Filling:

- ¾ cup white sugar
- 1 tablespoon cornstarch
- 1 teaspoon vanilla extract
- 2 tablespoons hazelnut liqueur
- 3 cups cream cheese
- 3 eggs
- 3 oz. dark chocolate, melted

Directions:

1. To make the crust, combine the hazelnuts, crackers and butter in a container. Move the mixture to a 9-inch round cake pan and press it thoroughly on the bottom of the pan.
2. To make the filling, combine the cream cheese and the melted chocolate in a container. Stir in the remaining ingredients. Pour the mixture over the crust then preheat your oven and bake the cheesecake at 330F for about fifty minutes or until set in the center.
3. Let the cheesecake cool down before you serve.

Nutritional Content of One Serving:

Calories: 418 ‖ Fat: 32.2g ‖ Protein: 7.8g ‖ Carbohydrates: 25.9g

HONEY FIG RICOTTA CHEESECAKE

Total Time Taken: 1 ¼ hours
Yield: 10 Servings
Ingredients:

Crust:

- ½ cup butter, melted
- 1 ½ cups graham crackers, crushed

Filling:

- ¼ cup honey
- ¼ cup white sugar
- 1 ½ pounds ricotta cheese

- 1 tablespoon cornstarch
- 1 teaspoon vanilla extract
- 4 eggs

Topping:

- ¼ cup honey
- 1 pound fresh figs, quartered

Directions:

1. To make the crust, combine the crackers with melted butter in a container then transfer the mixture in a 9-inch round cake pan coated with baking paper. Press it thoroughly on the bottom of the pan.
2. To make the filling, combine the cheese, eggs, vanilla, honey, sugar and cornstarch in a container.
3. Pour the mixture over the crust and preheat your oven and bake at 350F for about forty-five minutes or until set in the center.
4. When finished, let cool then top with fresh figs.
5. Sprinkle with honey just before you serve.

Nutritional Content of One Serving:

Calories: 441 ‖ Fat: 18.0g ‖ Protein: 12.5g ‖ Carbohydrates: 62.1g

HONEY RICOTTA CHEESECAKE

Total Time Taken: 1 hour
Yield: 8 Servings
Ingredients:

- ¼ cup honey
- ¼ cup light brown sugar
- ½ cup golden raisins Butter to grease the pan
- 1 ½ pounds ricotta cheese
- 1 teaspoon cornstarch
- 1 teaspoon vanilla extract
- 3 eggs

Directions:

1. Combine all the ingredients in a container.

2. Grease a 8-inch round cake pan with butter then pour the cheesecake mixture in the pan.
3. Pre-heat the oven and bake at 330F for about forty minutes or until the edges turn mildly golden brown.
4. Let the cheesecake cool down before you serve.

Nutritional Content of One Serving:

Calories: 220 ‖ Fat: 8.4g ‖ Protein: 12.1g ‖ Carbohydrates: 25.2g

INDIVIDUAL MOCHA CHEESECAKES

Total Time Taken: 1 ¼ hours
Yield: 12 Servings
Ingredients:

Crust:

- ½ cup butter, melted
- 2 cups Oreo cookies, crushed

Filling:

- ¼ cup cocoa powder
- ½ cup white sugar
- 1 cup sour cream
- 1 pinch salt
- 3 cups cream cheese
- 3 eggs
- 3 teaspoons instant coffee

Directions:

1. To make the crust, combine the cookies and butter in a container. Move to a muffin tin covered with muffin papers and press it thoroughly on the bottom of the muffin cups.
2. To make the filling, combine all the ingredients in a container until creamy. Pour the mixture over the crust, preheat your oven and bake at 330F for about twenty minutes or until the center looks set if you shake the pan slightly.
3. Let cool in the pan before you serve.

Nutritional Content of One Serving:

Calories: 370 ‖ Fat: 33.6g ‖ Protein: 6.9g ‖ Carbohydrates: 13.0g

INDIVIDUAL PUMPKIN CHEESECAKES

Total Time Taken: 1 ¼ hours
Yield: 12 Servings
Ingredients:

Crust:
- ½ cup butter, melted
- 2 cups gingersnaps, crushed

Filling:
- ¼ teaspoon cinnamon powder
- ¼ teaspoon salt
- ½ cup light brown sugar
- ½ teaspoon ground ginger
- ½ teaspoon vanilla extract
- 1 cup pumpkin puree
- 2 eggs
- 3 cups cream cheese

Directions:

1. To make the crust, combine the ingredients in a container. Spoon the mixture in a muffin tin covered with muffin papers and press it thoroughly on the bottom of the pan.
2. To make the filling, combine all the ingredients in a container and stir until creamy.
3. Pour the filling over the crust, preheat your oven and bake at 330F for about twenty minutes or until the center looks set.
4. Let cool in the pan before you serve.

Nutritional Content of One Serving:

Calories: 335 ‖ Fat: 29.5g ‖ Protein: 5.9g ‖ Carbohydrates: 12.9g

IRISH CREAM CHEESECAKE

Total Time Taken: 1 ¼ hours
Yield: 12 Servings
Ingredients:

Crust:

- 1 ½ cups Oreo cookies, crushed
- 1/3 cup butter, melted

Filling:

- 24 oz. cream cheese
- 2 tablespoons cocoa powder
- ¼ cup Irish cream liqueur
- 1 pinch salt
- 3 eggs
- ½ cup sour cream
- 2/3 cup white sugar

Directions:

1. To make the crust, combine the ingredients in a container until well combined. Move to a 9-inch round cake pan and press it thoroughly on the bottom of the pan.
2. To make the filling, combine all the ingredients in a container. Pour the filling over the crust and preheat your oven and bake the cheesecake at 350F for about fifty minutes or until the center looks set if you shake the pan lightly.
3. Let the cheesecake cool in the pan and serve, sliced.

Nutritional Content of One Serving:

Calories: 381 ‖ Fat: 30.4g ‖ Protein: 6.7g ‖ Carbohydrates: 18.4g

JAPANESE CHEESECAKE

Total Time Taken: 1 ¼ hours
Yield: 10 Servings

Ingredients:

- ¼ cup white sugar

- 1 pinch salt
- 1 teaspoon vanilla extract
- 6 eggs, separated
- 6 oz. cream cheese
- 6 oz. white chocolate chips, melted

Directions:

1. Mix the white chocolate, cream cheese and vanilla in a container.
2. Put in the egg yolks and mix thoroughly.
3. Whip the egg whites with a pinch of salt until fluffy. Put in the sugar and carry on mixing until shiny and firm.
4. Fold the whipped whites into the cream cheese mixture.
5. Pour the mixture in a small round cake pan coated with baking paper.
6. Pre-heat the oven and bake at 330F for about half an hour.
7. Let cool in the pan then serve, sliced.

Nutritional Content of One Serving:

Calories: 209 ‖ Fat: 14.0g ‖ Protein: 5.6g ‖ Carbohydrates: 15.8g

KAHLUA CHOCOLATE CHEESECAKE

Total Time Taken: 1 ¼ hours
Yield: 10 Servings
Ingredients:

Crust:

- ¼ cup butter, melted
- 1 ½ cups Oreo cookies, crushed
- 1 tablespoon Kahlua

Filling:

- ½ cup light brown sugar
- 1 cup dark chocolate chips, melted
- 1 pinch salt
- 1 tablespoon cornstarch
- 1 teaspoon vanilla extract
- 2 tablespoons Kahlua
- 3 cups cream cheese

- 3 eggs

Directions:

1. To make the crust, combine the cookies, butter and Kahlua in a container until well combined. Move to a 9-inch round cake pan and press it thoroughly on the bottom of the pan.
2. To make the filling, combine all the ingredients in a container. Pour the mixture over the crust, preheat your oven and bake at 330F for about fifty minutes or until the center looks set if you shake the pan.
3. Let cool down and serve, sliced.

Nutritional Content of One Serving:

Calories: 411 ‖ Fat: 33.6g ‖ Protein: 7.8g ‖ Carbohydrates: 20.2g

LAVENDER LEMON CHEESECAKE

Total Time Taken: 1 ¼ hours
Yield: 12 Servings
Ingredients:

Crust:

- ½ cup gingersnaps, crushed
- 1 cup graham crackers, crushed
- 1/3 cup butter, melted

Filling:

- ¼ cup butter, melted
- ½ cup white sugar
- 1 pinch salt
- 1 tablespoon cornstarch
- 1 tablespoon lemon zest
- 1 teaspoon lavender buds
- 1 teaspoon vanilla extract
- 2 tablespoons lemon juice
- 24 oz. cream cheese
- 3 eggs

Topping:

- 2 cups heavy cream, whipped

Directions:

1. To make the crust, combine all the ingredients in a container until well combined.
2. Move to a 9-inch round cake pan and press it thoroughly on the bottom of the pan.
3. To make the filling, combine all the ingredients in a container until creamy and smooth. Pour the mixture over the crust then bake in the preheated oven at 330F for
4. about fifty minutes or until set in the center.
5. Let cool in the pan then top with whipped cream.
6. Serve the cheesecake fresh and chilled.

Nutritional Content of One Serving:

Calories: 443 ‖ Fat: 38.4g ‖ Protein: 6.9g ‖ Carbohydrates: 19.4g

LEMON COCONUT CHEESECAKE

Total Time Taken: 1 ½ hours
Yield: 10 Servings
Ingredients:

Crust:

- ¼ cup coconut oil, melted
- ½ cup shredded coconut
- 1 cup vanilla biscuits, crushed

Filling:

- ½ cup white sugar
- 1 ½ pounds cream cheese
- 1 tablespoon cornstarch
- 1 tablespoon lemon zest
- 1 teaspoon vanilla extract
- 2 egg yolks
- 2 eggs
- 2 tablespoons lemon juice

Directions:

1. To make the crust, combine all the ingredients in a food processor and pulse until combined. Move the mixture to a 9-inch round cake pan coated with baking paper and press it thoroughly on the bottom of the pan.
2. To make the filling, combine all the ingredients in a container then pour the filling over the crust.
3. Preheat your oven and bake the cheesecake at 330F for about fifty minutes or until the center looks set.
4. Let the cheesecake cool down and serve, sliced.

Nutritional Content of One Serving:

Calories: 408 ‖ Fat: 33.3g ‖ Protein: 7.7g ‖ Carbohydrates: 21.2g

LEMON CURD CHEESECAKE

Total Time Taken: 1 ¼ hours
Yield: 14 Servings
Ingredients:

Cheesecake:

- ¼ cup butter, melted
- ½ cup white sugar
- 1 tablespoon lemon zest
- 1 teaspoon vanilla extract
- 2 tablespoons cornstarch
- 3 cups cream cheese
- 3 eggs
- Butter to grease the pan

Lemon curd:

- ½ cup butter
- 1 cup white sugar
- 1 pinch salt
- 1/3 cup lemon juice
- 2 tablespoons lemon zest
- 4 egg yolks

Directions:

1. For the cheesecake, combine all the ingredients in a container and mix thoroughly.
2. Coat an 8-inch round cake pan with baking paper then pour the filling in the pan.
3. Pre-heat the oven and bake at 330F for about fifty minutes or until the center looks set.
4. Let cool in the pan then move to a platter.
5. For the lemon curd, combine all the ingredients in a heatproof container. Put the container over a hot water bath and cook for about twenty minutes, stirring all the time using a spatula or whisk, until it becomes thick and creamy.
6. Let cool down then spread it over the cheesecake.

Best served chilled.

Nutritional Content of One Serving:

Calories: 377 ‖ Fat: 29.5g ‖ Protein: 5.9g ‖ Carbohydrates: 24.5g

LEMONY STRAWBERRY CHEESECAKE

Total Time Taken: 1 ¼ hours
Yield: 10 Servings
Ingredients:

Crust:

- ½ cup butter, melted
- 1 ½ cups vanilla biscuits, crushed

Filling:

- 1 lemon, zested and juiced
- 1 pinch salt
- 1 tablespoon cornstarch
- 2 cups fresh strawberries
- 2/3 cup white sugar
- 3 cups cream cheese
- 3 eggs

Directions:

1. To make the crust, combine the biscuits and butter in a container. Move to a 9-inch round cake pan coated with baking paper and press it thoroughly on the bottom of the pan.
2. To make the filling, combine the cream cheese, lemon zest, lemon juice, sugar, salt, eggs and cornstarch in a container.
3. Pour the mixture over the crust and preheat your oven and bake at 350F for about fifty minutes.
4. When finished, let cool down then top with fresh strawberries.

This cheesecake tastes best chilled.

Nutritional Content of One Serving:

Calories: 450 ‖ Fat: 35.9g ‖ Protein: 8.0g ‖ Carbohydrates: 26.4g

LIME PINEAPPLE CHEESECAKE

Total Time Taken: 1 ¼ hours
Yield: 10 Servings
Ingredients:

Crust:

- ½ cup butter, melted
- 1 ½ cups graham crackers, crushed

Filling:

- ½ cup white sugar
- 1 cup crushed pineapple, drained
- 1 cup sour cream
- 1 lime, zested and juiced
- 1 pinch salt
- 1 tablespoon cornstarch
- 3 cups cream cheese
- 3 eggs

Directions:

1. To make the crust, combine the two ingredients in a container. Move to a 9-inch round cake pan and press it thoroughly on the bottom of the pan.
2. Top the crust with pineapple.

3. To make the filling, combine the cream cheese, sour cream, eggs, cornstarch, sugar, lime zest, lime juice and salt in a container. Pour the mixture over the pineapple.
4. Pre-heat the oven and bake at 350F for about forty-five minutes or until the center looks set.
5. Let the cheesecake cool in the pan and serve, sliced.

Nutritional Content of One Serving:

Calories: 496 ‖ Fat: 40.9g ‖ Protein: 8.8g ‖ Carbohydrates: 26.2g

MANGO RIPPLE CHEESECAKE

Total Time Taken: 1 ½ hours
Yield: 12 Servings
Ingredients:

Crust:
- ½ cup butter, melted
- 1 ½ cups graham crackers

Filling:
- ¼ cup light brown sugar
- ¼ cup plain yogurt
- ¾ cup white sugar
- 1 lime, zested and juiced
- 1 mango, peeled and cubed
- 1 teaspoon vanilla extract
- 4 cups cream cheese
- 4 eggs

Directions:

1. To make the crust, combine the crackers and butter in a container. Move the mixture to a deep dish baking pan coated with baking paper.
2. Press the mixture thoroughly on the bottom of the pan.
3. To make the filling, mixing the cream cheese, eggs, sugar, vanilla and yogurt and mix thoroughly. Pour the mixture over the crust.
4. For the mango ripple, combine the mango flesh, lime zest and juice and sugar in a blender and pulse until the desired smoothness is achieved.

5. Sprinkle the mixture over the cheesecake and swirl it around using a fork.

This cheesecake tastes best chilled.

Nutritional Content of One Serving:

Calories: 480 ‖ Fat: 37.3g ‖ Protein: 8.9g ‖ Carbohydrates: 29.6g

MAPLE CINNAMON CHEESECAKE

Total Time Taken: 1 ¼ hours
Yield: 12 Servings
Ingredients:

Crust:

- ½ cup ground walnuts
- 1 ½ cups gingersnaps, crushed
- 1/3 cup butter, melted

Filling:

- ¼ teaspoon cinnamon powder
- ½ cup maple syrup
- 1 cup ricotta cheese
- 1 teaspoon vanilla extract
- 2 tablespoons butter, melted
- 3 cups cream cheese
- 3 eggs

Directions:

1. To make the crust, combine the ingredients in a container. Move the mixture to a 9-inch round cake pan coated with baking paper.
2. Press it thoroughly on the bottom of the pan.
3. To make the filling, combine all the ingredients in a container until creamy. Pour the mixture over the crust.
4. Pre-heat the oven and bake at 330F for about fifty minutes or until set in the center if you shake the pan.
5. Let cool in the pan before you serve.

Nutritional Content of One Serving:

Calories: 388 || Fat: 33.5g || Protein: 9.6g || Carbohydrates: 13.9g

MARSALA INFUSED CHEESECAKE

Total Time Taken: 1 ½ hours
Yield: 10 Servings
Ingredients:

Crust:

- ¼ cup butter, melted
- 1 ½ cups vanilla cookies, crushed
- 2 tablespoons Marsala wine

Filling:

- ½ cup Marsala wine
- ½ cup sour cream
- 1 cup sultanas
- 1 tablespoon cornstarch
- 1 teaspoon vanilla extract
- 2/3 cup white sugar
- 3 cups cream cheese
- 3 eggs

Directions:

1. To make the crust, combine the cookies, butter and wine in a container. Move the mixture to a 9-inch round cake pan and press it thoroughly on the bottom of the pan.
2. To make the filling, combine the sultanas and wine in a container and allow to soak up for about half an hour.
3. Mix the cream cheese, sour cream, eggs, cornstarch and vanilla in a container.
4. Put in the sultanas and wine and mix thoroughly. Pour the mixture over the crust and preheat your oven and bake at 350F for about fifty minutes or until the center looks set.
5. Let the cheesecake cool down before you serve.

Nutritional Content of One Serving:

Calories: 409 || Fat: 32.8g || Protein: 7.5g || Carbohydrates: 20.4g

MERINGUE CHEESECAKE

Total Time Taken: 1 ½ hours
Yield: 12 Servings
Ingredients:

Crust:

- 1 ½ cups graham crackers, crushed
- 1/3 cup butter, melted

Filling:

- 1 lemon, zested and juiced
- 1 tablespoon cornstarch
- 1 teaspoon vanilla extract
- 2 eggs
- 2/3 cup white sugar
- 24 oz. cream cheese

Topping:

- ½ cup sugar
- 2 egg whites

Directions:

1. To make the crust, combine the ingredients in a container. Move the mixture to a 8-inch round cake pan and press it thoroughly on the bottom of the pan.
2. To make the filling, combine all the ingredients in a container until creamy. Pour the filling over the crust and preheat your oven and bake the cheesecake at 330F for about forty-five minutes or until the center looks set.
3. Let the cheesecake cool in the pan.
4. For the topping, mix the egg whites and sugar in a container and place over a hot water bath. Cook, stirring all the time, just until the sugar has dissolved.
5. Turn off the heat and whip using an electric mixer for about five to seven minutes until firm and shiny.
6. Top the cheesecake with the whipped whites and place under the broiler for a couple of minutes just to brown mildly.

This cheesecake tastes best chilled.

Nutritional Content of One Serving:

Calories: 379 ‖ Fat: 26.7g ‖ Protein: 6.6g ‖ Carbohydrates: 30.2g

MINI GINGER CHEESECAKES

Total Time Taken: 1 ¼ hours

Yield: 12 Servings

Ingredients:

Crust:

- ½ cup butter, melted
- ½ teaspoon ground ginger
- 2 cups graham crackers, crushed

Filling:

- ¼ teaspoon cinnamon powder
- ½ cup light brown sugar
- 1 pinch salt
- 1 tablespoon cornstarch
- 1 teaspoon grated ginger
- 3 cups cream cheese
- 3 eggs

Directions:

1. To make the crust, combine the ingredients in a container. Spoon the mixture in a muffin tin covered with muffin papers. Press it thoroughly on the bottom of the tin.
2. To make the filling, combine all the ingredients in a container. Pour the filling over the crust and preheat your oven and bake at 350F for about twenty minutes or until set in the center.
3. Let cool down before you serve.

Nutritional Content of One Serving:

Calories: 372 ‖ Fat: 30.4g ‖ Protein: 6.8g ‖ Carbohydrates: 19.1g

MINI RASPBERRY CHEESECAKES

Total Time Taken: 1 ½ hours

Yield: 14 Servings

Ingredients:

Crust:

- ½ cup butter, melted
- 1 teaspoon vanilla extract
- 2 cups graham crackers, crushed

Filling:

- 1 cup raspberry puree
- 1 tablespoon cornstarch
- 1 teaspoon vanilla extract
- 2/3 cup white sugar
- 4 cups cream cheese
- 4 eggs

Directions:

1. To make the crust, combine the crackers, butter and vanilla in a container. Move the mixture toto 12 muffin cups covered with muffin papers and press it thoroughly on the bottom of each cup.
2. To make the filling, combine the cream cheese, eggs, sugar, vanilla and cornstarch in a container.
3. Evenly pour the mixture into the muffin cups.
4. Top the cheesecakes with a spoonful of raspberry puree. Swirl the puree into the cheesecake using a fork.
5. Pre-heat the oven and bake at 330F for about twenty-five minutes or until set.

Best served chilled.

Nutritional Content of One Serving:

Calories: 455 ‖ Fat: 32.2g ‖ Protein: 7.6g ‖ Carbohydrates: 36.1g

MINTY CHEESECAKE

Total Time Taken: 1 ¼ hours
Yield: 14 Servings
Ingredients:

Crust:

- 1 ½ cups graham crackers, crushed

- 1/3 cup butter, melted

Filling:
- ½ cup white sugar
- 1 cup white chocolate chips
- 1 pinch salt
- 1 teaspoon peppermint extract
- 1 teaspoon vanilla extract
- 3 cups cream cheese
- 3 eggs
- 4 oz. dark chocolate, melted

Directions:
1. To make the crust, combine the crackers and butter in a container. Move to a 9-inch round cake pan and press it thoroughly on the bottom of the pan.
2. To make the filling, mix the cream cheese, chocolate, eggs, vanilla, peppermint extract, salt and sugar in a container and stir until creamy.
3. Fold in the chocolate chips.
4. Pour the mixture over the crust , preheat your oven and bake at 330 for about fifty minutes or until the center looks set.
5. Let cool down and serve, sliced.

Nutritional Content of One Serving:

Calories: 401 ‖ Fat: 29.9g ‖ Protein: 6.9g ‖ Carbohydrates: 27.5g

MIXED BERRY CHEESECAKE

Total Time Taken: 1 ¼ hours
Yield: 12 Servings
Ingredients:

Crust:
- ½ cup butter, melted
- 1 ½ cups graham crackers, crushed
- 1 teaspoon vanilla extract

Filling:
- ¾ cup white sugar

- 1 tablespoon cornstarch
- 1 tablespoon vanilla extract
- 4 cups cream cheese
- 4 eggs

Topping:

- 2 cups mixed berries

Directions:

1. To make the crust, combine the crackers, butter and vanilla in a container. Move the mixture to a 9-inch round cake pan and press it thoroughly on the bottom of the pan.
2. To make the filling, combine the cream cheese, sugar, vanilla, eggs and cornstarch in a container pour the mixture over the crust , preheat your oven and bake at 330F for about fifty minutes or until set in the center.
3. Let the cheesecake cool down in the pan then top with mixed berries.

Nutritional Content of One Serving:

Calories: 470 ‖ Fat: 37.2g ‖ Protein: 8.7g ‖ Carbohydrates: 26.4g

MOCHA CHOCOLATE CHEESECAKE

Total Time Taken: 1 ¼ hours
Yield: 12 Servings
Ingredients:

Crust:

- ½ cup butter, melted
- 1 ½ cups Oreo cookies, crushed

Filling:

- 1 pinch salt
- 1 tablespoon dark rum
- 2 teaspoons instant coffee
- 2/3 cup white sugar
- 3 eggs
- 4 cups cream cheese
- 4 oz. dark chocolate, melted

Directions:

1. To make the crust, combine the cookies and butter in a container. Move the mixture to a 9-inch round cake pan covered with parchment paper and press it thoroughly on the bottom of the pan.
2. To make the filling, combine all the ingredients in a container until creamy.
3. Pour the mixture over the crust , preheat your oven and bake at 330F for about forty minutes or until the center looks slightly set.
4. When finished, allow the cheesecake to cool down and serve, sliced.
5. Top it with whipped cream if you want.

Nutritional Content of One Serving:

Calories: 449 ‖ Fat: 38.6g ‖ Protein: 8.0g ‖ Carbohydrates: 19.0g

NEW YORK CHEESECAKES

Total Time Taken: 1 ¼ hours
Yield: 12 Servings
Ingredients:

Crust:

- ¼ cup butter, melted
- 1 ½ cups Oreo cookies, crushed

Filling:

- 24 oz. cream cheese
- 3 eggs
- 1 teaspoon vanilla extract
- 2/3 cup white sugar

Topping:

- ½ cup white sugar
- 1 teaspoon vanilla extract
- 2 cups sour cream

Directions:

1. To make the crust, combine all the ingredients in a container. Move to a 9-inch round cake pan and press it thoroughly on the bottom of the pan.

2. To make the filling, combine all the ingredients in a container. Pour the filling over the crust.
3. Coat the pan using aluminium foil and place it in a deep baking pan.
4. Pour hot water in the bigger pan, surrounding the cheesecake.
5. Pre-heat the oven and bake at 330F for about forty-five minutes or until the center looks set.
6. Take out of the oven.
7. Mix the ingredients for the topping in a container.
8. Top the cheesecake with the sour cream mixture and place back in the oven for 10 additional minutes.
9. Let cool down before you serve.

Nutritional Content of One Serving:

Calories: 408 ‖ Fat: 32.9g ‖ Protein: 6.9g ‖ Carbohydrates: 23.3g

NO BAKE MASCARPONE CHEESECAKE

Total Time Taken: 2 hours
Yield: 10 Servings
Ingredients:

Crust:

- 1 ½ cups graham crackers, crushed
- 1/3 cup butter, melted

Filling:

- ¾ cup powdered sugar
- 1 ½ cups mascarpone cheese
- 1 cup cream cheese
- 1 cup heavy cream, whipped
- 1 pinch salt
- 1 tablespoon vanilla extract
- 1 teaspoon gelatin
- 2 cups cherries, pitted
- 2 tablespoons cold water

Directions:

1. To make the crust, combine the ingredients in a container. Move the mixture to a 9-inch round cake pan covered with parchment paper and press it thoroughly on the bottom of the pan.
2. To make the filling, combine the mascarpone cheese, sugar and cream cheese in a container for five minutes until airy and light.
3. Bloom the gelatin in cold water for about ten minutes.
4. Mix the cheese mixture with vanilla. Melt the gelatin and mix in the melted gelatin.
5. Fold in the whipped cream then put in the cherries.
6. Spoon the mixture over the crust and store in the refrigerator to set for minimum an hour.

Nutritional Content of One Serving:

Calories: 353 ‖ Fat: 24.8g ‖ Protein: 7.8g ‖ Carbohydrates: 25.0g

NO BAKE PASSIONFRUIT CHEESECAKE

Total Time Taken: 2 hours
Yield: 10 Servings
Ingredients:

Crust:

- ¼ cup butter, melted
- 1 ½ cups vanilla biscuits, crushed
- 1 teaspoon vanilla extract

Filling:

- ¼ cup passionfruit juice
- 1 cup heavy cream, whipped
- 1 cup powdered sugar
- 1 teaspoon gelatin
- 1 teaspoon vanilla extract
- 2 cups cream cheese
- 2 tablespoons cold water

Directions:

1. To make the crust, combine the biscuits, butter and vanilla in a container. Move the mixture to a 9-inch round cake pan covered with parchment paper and press it thoroughly on the bottom of the pan.
2. Bloom the gelatin in cold water for about ten minutes.
3. To make the filling, combine the cream cheese, sugar and vanilla in a container until fluffy.
4. Melt the gelatin and stir it in the cream cheese mixture.
5. Put in the passionfruit juice then fold in the whipped cream. Spoon the mixture over the crust and store in the refrigerator to set for minimum an hour.

This cheesecake tastes best chilled.

Nutritional Content of One Serving:

Calories: 341 ‖ Fat: 26.2g ‖ Protein: 5.1g ‖ Carbohydrates: 21.9g

NO CRUST CITRUS CHEESECAKE

Total Time Taken: 1 hour
Yield: 10 Servings
Ingredients:

- ¼ cup butter, melted
- ¾ cup white sugar
- 1 ½ pounds cream cheese
- 1 pinch salt
- 1 pinch salt
- 1 tablespoon cornstarch
- 1 teaspoon lemon zest
- 1 teaspoon lime zest
- 1 teaspoon orange zest
- 1 teaspoon vanilla extract
- 3 eggs
- Butter to grease the pan

Directions:

1. Mix all the ingredients in a container and stir for a few seconds to mix.

2. Grease a 8-inch round cake pan with butter then pour the cheesecake mixture in the pan.
3. Pre-heat the oven and bake at 330F for about forty minutes or until the center looks set.
4. Let the cheesecake cool down and serve, sliced.

Nutritional Content of One Serving:

Calories: 358 ‖ Fat: 29.6g ‖ Protein: 6.8g ‖ Carbohydrates: 17.8g

NUTELLA CHEESECAKE

Total Time Taken: 1 ¼ hours
Yield: 10 Servings
Ingredients:

Crust:

- 1 ½ cups graham crackers, crushed
- 1/3 cup butter, melted

Filling:

- ¼ cup milk
- 1 cup Nutella
- 1 pinch salt
- 1 tablespoon cornstarch
- 1 teaspoon vanilla extract
- 2 tablespoons cocoa powder
- 3 cups cream cheese
- 3 eggs

Directions:

1. To make the crust, combine the ingredients in a container until well combined. Move the mixture to a baking tray covered with parchment paper and press it thoroughly on the bottom of the pan.
2. To make the filling, combine all the ingredients in a container until creamy.
3. Pour the filling over the crust, preheat your oven and bake at 330F for about fifty minutes or until the center of the cake looks set in the center.
4. Let the cheesecake cool down in the pan and serve, sliced.

Nutritional Content of One Serving:

Calories: 399 ‖ Fat: 34.4g ‖ Protein: 8.4g ‖ Carbohydrates: 15.6g

NUTELLA MOCHA CHEESECAKE

Total Time Taken: 1 ¼ hours
Yield: 12 Servings
Ingredients:

Crust:
- 1 ½ cups chocolate cookies, crushed
- 1/3 cup butter, melted

Filling:
- ½ cup Nutella
- ½ cup white sugar
- 1 pinch salt
- 1 teaspoon vanilla extract
- 2 teaspoons instant coffee
- 24 oz. cream cheese
- 3 eggs

Topping:
- 1 ½ cups heavy cream, whipped
- 1 teaspoon instant coffee

Directions:

1. To make the crust, combine the ingredients in a container until well combined. Move the mixture to a 9-inch round cake pan and press it thoroughly on the bottom of the pan.
2. To make the filling, combine all the ingredients in a separate container until creamy. Pour the mixture over the crust , preheat your oven and bake at 330F for about fifty minutes or until the center of the cheesecake looks set if you shake the cheesecake.
3. Let cool in the pan and serve, sliced.

Nutritional Content of One Serving:

Calories: 420 ‖ Fat: 34.5g ‖ Protein: 7.1g ‖ Carbohydrates: 22.3g

NUTMEG RICOTTA CHEESECAKE

Total Time Taken: 1 ¼ hours
Yield: 10 Servings
Ingredients:

Crust:

- ½ cup butter, melted
- 1 ½ cups graham crackers, crushed

Filling:

- ¼ cup butter, melted
- ¼ teaspoon ground nutmeg
- ½ cup heavy cream
- 1 pinch salt
- 1 tablespoon cornstarch
- 1 teaspoon vanilla extract
- 2 eggs
- 2/3 cup white sugar
- 24 oz. ricotta cheese

Directions:

1. To make the crust, combine the ingredients in a container. Move the mixture to a 9-inch round cake pan and press it thoroughly on the bottom of the pan.
2. To make the filling, combine all the ingredients in a container until creamy.
3. Pour the mixture over the crust, preheat your oven and bake at 330F for about forty minutes or until set in the center.

This cheesecake tastes best chilled.

Nutritional Content of One Serving:

Calories: 357 ‖ Fat: 23.6g ‖ Protein: 10.0g ‖ Carbohydrates: 27.6g

NUTMEG SWEET POTATO CHEESECAKE

Total Time Taken: 1 ¼ hours
Yield: 12 Servings
Ingredients:

Crust:

- ½ cup butter, melted
- 2 cups gingersnaps, crushed

Filling:

- ¼ cup heavy cream
- ¼ teaspoon nutmeg
- ½ cup light brown sugar
- 1 cup sweet potato puree
- 1 pinch salt
- 1 tablespoon cornstarch
- 3 cups cream cheese
- 3 eggs

Directions:

1. To make the crust, combine the gingersnaps and butter in a container until well combined. Move the mixture to a 9-inch round cake pan and press it thoroughly on the bottom of the pan.
2. To make the filling, combine the ingredients in a container until creamy and smooth.
3. Spoon the filling over the crust, preheat your oven and bake at 330F for about fifty minutes or until the cheesecake looks set in the center.
4. Let cool in the pan and serve, sliced.

Nutritional Content of One Serving:

Calories: 365 ‖ Fat: 30.8g ‖ Protein: 6.6g ‖ Carbohydrates: 16.8g

OATMEAL CRUST CHEESECAKE

Total Time Taken: 1 ¼ hours
Yield: 12 Servings
Ingredients:

Crust:

- ½ cup graham crackers, crushed
- ½ cup smooth peanut butter
- 1 cup rolled oats

Filling:

- ¼ cup smooth peanut butter
- ½ cup light brown sugar
- ½ cup plain yogurt
- 1 pinch salt
- 1 teaspoon vanilla extract
- 24 oz. cream cheese
- 3 eggs

Directions:

1. To make the crust, combine the ingredients in a container until well combined. Move the mixture to a 9-inch round cake pan covered with parchment paper.
2. To make the filling, combine the cream cheese, peanut butter, sugar, vanilla, salt, eggs and yogurt in a container. Pour the mixture over the crust.
3. Pre-heat the oven and bake at 330F for about fifty minutes or until the center looks set.
4. Let cool down before you serve.

Nutritional Content of One Serving:

Calories: 380 ‖ Fat: 29.9g ‖ Protein: 11.4g ‖ Carbohydrates: 18.7g

PASSIONFRUIT BLUEBERRY CHEESECAKE

Total Time Taken: 1 ¼ hours
Yield: 10 Servings
Ingredients:

Crust:

- ½ cup butter, melted
- 1 ½ cups vanilla biscuits, crushed

Filling:

- 4 cups cream cheese
- 1 tablespoon vanilla extract

- 3 eggs
- 1 tablespoon cornstarch
- ¼ cup passionfruit juice
- 1 cup fresh blueberries
- 2/3 cup white sugar

Directions:

1. To make the crust, combine the ingredients in a container. Move the mixture to a 9-inch round cake pan and press it thoroughly on the bottom of the pan.
2. To make the filling, combine the cream cheese, sugar, vanilla, eggs, cornstarch and passionfruit juice in a container. Pour the filling over the crust.
3. Top with blueberries then bake in the preheated oven at 330F for about forty-five minutes or until the set looks set.
4. Let the cheesecake cool down in the pan and serve, sliced.

Nutritional Content of One Serving:

Calories: 447 ‖ Fat: 36.6g ‖ Protein: 8.0g ‖ Carbohydrates: 22.8g

PASSIONFRUIT CHEESECAKE

Total Time Taken: 1 ¼ hours
Yield: 10 Servings
Ingredients:

Crust:

- ½ cup butter, melted
- 1 ½ cups vanilla biscuits, crushed
- 1 teaspoon orange zest

Filling:

- ¼ cup passionfruit juice
- ½ cup sour cream
- ¾ cup white sugar
- 1 tablespoon cornstarch
- 1 teaspoon orange zest
- 1 teaspoon vanilla extract
- 24 oz. cream cheese

- 3 eggs

Directions:

1. To make the crust, combine the biscuits with melted butter and orange zest. Move to a 9-inch baking pan and press it thoroughly on the bottom of the pan.
2. To make the filling, combine all the ingredients in a container until creamy.
3. Pour the filling over the crust then preheat your oven and bake the cheesecake at 330F for about fifty minutes.
4. Let the cheesecake cool down and serve, sliced.

Nutritional Content of One Serving:

Calories: 439 ‖ Fat: 37.2g ‖ Protein: 7.5g ‖ Carbohydrates: 20.6g

PEPPERMINT CHOCOLATE CHEESECAKE

Total Time Taken: 1 ¼ hours
Yield: 12 Servings
Ingredients:

Crust:

- ½ cup butter, melted
- 1 ½ cups chocolate biscuits, crushed

Filling:

- 1 pinch salt
- 1 teaspoon vanilla extract
- 2/3 cup white sugar
- 3 cups cream cheese
- 3 eggs
- 4 oz. dark chocolate, melted

Topping:

- 1 cup dark chocolate chips
- 1 cup heavy cream
- 1 teaspoon peppermint extract
- Crushed candy canes to garnish

Directions:

1. To make the crust, combine the ingredients in a container then move to a 9-inch round cake pan covered with parchment paper.
2. Press the mixture thoroughly on the bottom of the pan.
3. To make the filling, combine the cream cheese and chocolate in a container until creamy.
4. Put in the remaining ingredients and stir thoroughly until blended.
5. Let the cheesecake cool down.
6. For the topping, bring the cream to a boil in a saucepan. Turn off the heat and put in the chocolate. Stir thoroughly to mix then mix in the peppermint extract.
7. Top the cheesecake with the chocolate glaze.

This cheesecake tastes best chilled.

Nutritional Content of One Serving:

Calories: 476 ‖ Fat: 39.0g ‖ Protein: 7.6g ‖ Carbohydrates: 27.2g

PISTACHIO PASTE CHEESECAKE

Total Time Taken: 1 ¼ hours
Yield: 10 Servings
Ingredients:

Crust:

- 1 ½ cups Oreo cookies, crushed
- 1/3 cup butter, melted

Filling:

- ½ cup pistachio paste
- ½ cup white sugar
- 1 pinch salt
- 1 tablespoon cornstarch
- 1 teaspoon vanilla extract
- 3 cups cream cheese
- 3 eggs

Directions:

1. To make the crust, combine the ingredients in a container. Move the mixture to a 9-inch round cake pan covered with parchment paper. Press the mixture thoroughly on the bottom of the pan.
2. To make the filling, combine the cream cheese, pistachio paste, eggs, vanilla, salt, sugar and cornstarch in a container until creamy.
3. Pour the mixture over the crust and preheat your oven and bake the cheesecake at 330F for about fifty minutes or until set in the center.
4. Let the cheesecake cool down and serve, sliced.
5. Store the cheesecake in your refrigerator.

Nutritional Content of One Serving:

Calories: 427 ‖ Fat: 37.0g ‖ Protein: 8.6g ‖ Carbohydrates: 17.7g

PURE COCONUT VANILLA CHEESECAKE

Total Time Taken: 1 ¼ hours
Yield: 12 Servings
Ingredients:

Crust:

- ¼ cup coconut oil, melted
- 1 cup graham crackers, crushed
- 1 cup shredded coconut

Filling:

- ½ cup coconut sugar
- ½ cup shredded coconut
- 1 cup coconut cream
- 1 pinch salt
- 1 tablespoon coconut flour
- 1 tablespoon vanilla extract
- 3 cups cream cheese
- 3 eggs

Directions:

1. To make the crust, combine the ingredients in a container until thoroughly combined. Move to a 9- inch round cake pan and press it thoroughly on the bottom of the pan.

2. To make the filling, combine all the ingredients in a container and mix thoroughly. Pour the filling over the crust.
3. Pre-heat the oven and bake at 330F for about fifty minutes or until the center of the cheesecake looks set if you shake the pan.
4. Let the cheesecake cool in the pan and serve, sliced.

Nutritional Content of One Serving:

Calories: 404 ‖ Fat: 34.8g ‖ Protein: 7.1g ‖ Carbohydrates: 18.1g

RAISIN MARSALA CHEESECAKE

Total Time Taken: 1 ¼ hours
Yield: 10 Servings
Ingredients:

Crust:

- ½ cup butter, melted
- 1 ½ cups graham crackers
- 1 tablespoon dark brown sugar
- 1 tablespoon Marsala

Filling:

- ¼ cup Marsala
- ½ cup white sugar
- 1 cup golden raisins
- 1 pinch salt
- 1 tablespoon cornstarch
- 1 teaspoon vanilla extract
- 3 cups cream cheese
- 3 eggs

Directions:

1. To make the crust, combine the crackers in a food processor until ground. Put in the sugar and butter and mix thoroughly then transfer the mixture in a round cake pan coated with baking paper. Press it thoroughly on the bottom of the pan.
2. To make the filling, combine all the ingredients in a container until creamy.

3. Pour the mixture over the crust and preheat your oven and bake the cheesecake at 330F for about fifty minutes.
4. Let the cheesecake cool down in the pan and serve, sliced.

Nutritional Content of One Serving:

Calories: 491 ‖ Fat: 36.1g ‖ Protein: 8.3g ‖ Carbohydrates: 35.0g

RASPBERRY CHOCOLATE CHEESECAKE

Total Time Taken: 1 ½ hours
Yield: 10 Servings
Ingredients:

Crust:

- 1 ½ cups Oreo cookies, crushed
- 1/3 cup butter, melted

Filling:

- ½ cup white sugar
- 1 pinch salt
- 1 teaspoon vanilla extract
- 3 cups cream cheese
- 3 eggs
- 6 oz. dark chocolate, melted and chilled

Topping:

- 2 cups fresh raspberries

Directions:

1. To make the crust, combine the cookies and butter in a container. Move the mixture to a baking tray covered with parchment paper and press it thoroughly on the bottom of the pan.
2. To make the filling, combine the cream cheese, chocolate, eggs, salt, sugar and vanilla in a container. Pour the filling over the crust, preheat your oven and bake at 330F for about fifty minutes or until the center looks set.
3. Let the cheesecake cool down in the pan then move to a platter. Top with fresh raspberries just before you serve.

Nutritional Content of One Serving:

Calories: 460 ‖ Fat: 37.0g ‖ Protein: 8.6g ‖ Carbohydrates: 25.2g

RED VELVET CHEESECAKE

Total Time Taken: 1 ¼ hours
Yield: 10 Servings
Ingredients:

Crust:

- 1 ½ cups Oreo cookies, crushed
- 1/3 cup butter, melted

Filling:

- ½ cup white sugar
- 1 cup sour cream
- 1 pinch salt
- 1 tablespoon cornstarch
- 1 teaspoon lemon juice
- 1 teaspoon red food colouring
- 1 teaspoon vanilla extract
- 3 cups cream cheese

Directions:

1. To make the crust, combine the cookies and butter in a container until combined. Move the mixture to a 9-inch round cake pan and press it thoroughly on the bottom of the pan.
2. To make the filling, combine all the ingredients in a container and stir until creamy.
3. Pour the filling over the crust then bake in the preheated oven at 330F for about forty-five minutes or until set in the center.
4. Let cool down and serve, sliced.

Nutritional Content of One Serving:

Calories: 389 ‖ Fat: 35.3g ‖ Protein: 6.1g ‖ Carbohydrates: 13.8g

REFRESHING KIWI CHEESECAKE

Total Time Taken: 1 ½ hours

Yield: 10 Servings

Ingredients:

Crust:

- 1 ½ cups vanilla biscuits, crushed
- 1/3 cup butter, melted

Filling:

- ¼ cup heavy cream
- 1 pinch salt
- 1 tablespoon cornstarch
- 1 teaspoon vanilla extract
- 2 tablespoons butter, melted
- 2/3 cup white sugar
- 3 cups cream cheese
- 3 eggs

Topping:

- 1 pound kiwi fruits

Directions:

1. To make the crust, combine the biscuits and butter in a container. Move the mixture to a 9-inch round cake pan and press it thoroughly on the bottom of the pan.
2. To make the filling, combine all the ingredients in a container. Pour the mixture over the crust, preheat your oven and bake at 330F for about fifty minutes or until the center of the cheesecake looks set.
3. When finished, take it out of the oven and let cool down.
4. Top the freshly baked cheesecake with kiwi fruit slices and serve it fresh.

Nutritional Content of One Serving:

Calories: 472 ‖ Fat: 36.4g ‖ Protein: 8.3g ‖ Carbohydrates: 30.4g

RHUBARB STRAWBERRY CHEESECAKE

Total Time Taken: 1 ½ hours
Yield: 12 Servings
Ingredients:

Crust:

- ½ cup butter, melted
- 1 ½ cups graham crackers, crushed

Filling:

- 1 cup heavy cream
- 1 tablespoon cornstarch
- 1 teaspoon vanilla extract
- 2/3 cup white sugar
- 24 oz. cream cheese
- 3 eggs

Topping:

- ¼ cup light brown sugar
- ½ pound strawberries, halved
- 2 rhubarb stalks, sliced

Directions:

1. To make the crust, combine the crackers and butter well then move to a 9-inch cake pan coated with baking paper. Press the mixture thoroughly on the bottom of the pan.
2. To make the filling, combine the cream cheese, cream, eggs, cornstarch, sugar and vanilla in a container. Pour the filling over the crust, preheat your oven and bake at 330F for about forty-five minutes or until the center looks set.
3. Let the cheesecake cool down in the pan.
4. For the topping, combine the ingredients in a deep dish baking pan and cook in the preheated oven at 350F for about fifteen minutes until softened. Let cool down.
5. Top the cheesecake with the rhubarb strawberry mixture and serve it fresh.

Nutritional Content of One Serving:

Calories: 425 ‖ Fat: 33.4g ‖ Protein: 6.9g ‖ Carbohydrates: 26.5g

RICOTTA CHEESECAKE WITH BALSAMIC STRAWBERRIES

Total Time Taken: 1 ½ hours
Yield: 10 Servings
Ingredients:

Crust:

- ½ cup olive oil
- 1 1/2cups graham crackers, ground
- 2 tablespoons dark brown sugar

Filling:

- 1 tablespoon cornstarch
- 1 teaspoon lemon zest
- 1 teaspoon vanilla extract
- 2/3 cup white sugar
- 3 cups ricotta cheese
- 4 eggs

Topping:

- 1 tablespoon balsamic vinegar
- 1 tablespoon olive oil
- 2 cups strawberries, halved

Directions:

1. To make the crust, combine the ingredients in a container. Move the mixture to a 9-inch round cake pan coated with baking paper and press it thoroughly on the bottom of the pan.
2. To make the filling, combine the ricotta cheese, eggs, vanilla, lemon zest, sugar and cornstarch in a container.
3. Pour the mixture over the crust and preheat your oven and bake the cheesecake at 350F for about forty-five minutes or until it looks set in the center.
4. Let the cheesecake cool down and serve, sliced.

Nutritional Content of One Serving:

Calories: 327 ‖ Fat: 20.0g ‖ Protein: 11.5g ‖ Carbohydrates: 27.1g

S'MORES CHEESECAKE

Total Time Taken: 1 ½ hours
Yield: 14 Servings
Ingredients:

Crust:

- ½ cup butter, melted
- 2 cups graham crackers, crushed

Filling:

- ¼ cup cocoa powder
- ¼ teaspoon salt
- 1 cup white sugar
- 1 tablespoon cornstarch
- 1 teaspoon vanilla extract
- 2 tablespoons chocolate liqueur
- 26 oz. cream cheese
- 3 eggs
- 4 oz. dark chocolate, melted

Topping:

- ½ cup white sugar
- 1 teaspoon vanilla extract
- 2 egg whites

Directions:

1. To make the crust, combine the ingredients in a container until well combined.
2. Move the mixture to a 9-inch round cake pan coated with baking paper and press it thoroughly on the bottom of the pan.
3. To make the filling, combine the cream cheese and melted chocolate in a container.
4. Put in the remaining ingredients and mix thoroughly.
5. Pour the filling over the crust.
6. Pre-heat the oven and bake at 330F for about fifty minutes or until the center of the cheesecake looks set.
7. For the topping, whip the egg whites in a container until fluffy. Put in the sugar, progressively and stir until fluffy and shiny.
8. Stir in the vanilla then spread the meringue over the cheesecake.

9. Place under the broiler for at least two minutes just until mildly browned on top.
10. Let cool down before you serve.

Nutritional Content of One Serving:

Calories: 462 ‖ Fat: 30.8g ‖ Protein: 7.6g ‖ Carbohydrates: 41.1g

SALTED CHOCOLATE CHEESECAKE

Total Time Taken: 1 ¼ hours
Yield: 10 Servings
Ingredients:

Crust:

- 1 ½ cups graham crackers, crushed
- 1/3 cup butter, melted
- 2 tablespoons cocoa powder

Filling:

- ½ cup white sugar
- 1 tablespoon cornstarch
- 1 teaspoon salt
- 1 teaspoon vanilla extract
- 2 tablespoons cocoa powder
- 24 oz. cream cheese
- 3 eggs
- 8 oz. dark chocolate chips, melted

Directions:

1. To make the crust, combine the crackers, cocoa powder and butter in a container. Move the mixture to a 9-inch round cake pan and press it thoroughly on the bottom of the pan.
2. To make the filling, combine the cream cheese and chocolate in a container until creamy.
3. Put in the remaining ingredients and mix thoroughly.
4. Pour the filling over the crust, preheat your oven and bake at 330F for about fifty minutes or until set in the center.
5. Let cool in the pan and serve, sliced.

Nutritional Content of One Serving:

Calories: 430 ‖ Fat: 32.3g ‖ Protein: 8.0g ‖ Carbohydrates: 32.2g

SHORTCRUST PASTRY CHEESECAKE

Total Time Taken: 1 ½ hours
Yield: 12 Servings
Ingredients:

Crust:

- ¼ cup powdered sugar
- ½ cup butter, softened
- 1 ¾ cups all-purpose flour
- 1 egg yolk
- 1 pinch salt

Filling:

- ½ cup white sugar
- 1 cup sour cream
- 1 pinch salt
- 1 tablespoon cornstarch
- 1 teaspoon vanilla extract
- 2 tablespoons butter, melted
- 3 cups cream cheese
- 3 eggs

Directions:

1. To make the crust, combine the butter and sugar in a container until creamy. Put in the egg yolk and mix thoroughly then mix in the remaining ingredients.
2. Transfer the dough to a floured working surface and roll the dough into a slim sheet.
3. Move the dough to a 9-inch round cake pan and press it thoroughly on the bottom and sides of the pan.
4. Preheat your oven and bake the crust at 350F for about twelve minutes then let cool down.

5. To make the filling, combine all the ingredients in a container. Pour the mixture into the crust, preheat your oven and bake at 300F for about forty-five minutes or until set in the center.

This cheesecake tastes best chilled.

Nutritional Content of One Serving:

Calories: 459 ‖ Fat: 35.5g ‖ Protein: 8.6g ‖ Carbohydrates: 27.9g

SNICKERS CHEESECAKE

Total Time Taken: 1 ¼ hours
Yield: 10 Servings
Ingredients:

Crust:

- ¼ cup butter
- 1 cup graham crackers
- 1 tablespoon Dark rum
- 2 tablespoons cocoa powder

Filling:

- 24 oz. cream cheese, softened
- 3 eggs
- 1 teaspoon vanilla extract
- 1 tablespoon cornstarch
- 4 Snickers bars, chopped
- 2/3 cup white sugar

Directions:

1. To make the crust, combine the ingredients in a food processor and pulse until thoroughly combined. Move the mixture to a 8-inch round cake pan and press it thoroughly on the bottom of the pan.
2. To make the filling, combine the cream cheese, sugar, eggs, vanilla and cornstarch in a container. Fold in the chopped Snickers then pour the mixture in the readied pan, over the crust.
3. Pre-heat the oven and bake at 330F for about fifty minutes or until the center looks set.

4. Let the cheesecake cool down and serve, sliced.

Nutritional Content of One Serving:

Calories: 456 ‖ Fat: 33.8g ‖ Protein: 8.8g ‖ Carbohydrates: 31.5g

SOUR CREAM MANGO CHEESECAKE

Total Time Taken: 1 ¼ hours
Yield: 10 Servings
Ingredients:

Crust:

- ½ cup butter, melted
- 1 ½ cups graham cracker, crushed

Filling:

- ¾ cup white sugar
- 1 tablespoon cornstarch
- 1 teaspoon vanilla extract
- 2 cups cream cheese
- 2 cups sour cream
- 3 eggs

Topping:

- ¼ cup fresh orange juice
- ¼ cup light brown sugar
- 1 mango, peeled and cubed

Directions:

1. To make the crust, combine the ingredients in a container. Move the mixture to a 9-inch round cake pan coated with baking paper.
2. To make the filling, combine all the ingredients in a container. Pour the mixture over the crust, preheat your oven and bake at 330F for about forty-five minutes or until set in the center.
3. Let cool down in the pan.
4. For the topping, combine all the ingredients in a saucepan and cook until softened.
5. Let cool and then top the cheesecake with the mango compote.

This cheesecake tastes best fresh.

Nutritional Content of One Serving:

Calories: 491 ‖ Fat: 37.6g ‖ Protein: 7.6g ‖ Carbohydrates: 33.0g

SPICED HONEY CHEESECAKE

Total Time Taken: 1 ¼ hours
Yield: 14 Servings
Ingredients:

Crust:
- ¼ teaspoon cinnamon powder
- ½ cup butter, melted
- 10 gingersnaps
- 10 graham crackers

Filling:
- ¼ teaspoon ground nutmeg
- ½ cup light brown sugar
- ½ teaspoon cinnamon powder
- ½ teaspoon ground cardamom
- ½ teaspoon ground ginger
- 1 cup sour cream
- 1 pinch salt
- 1 tablespoon cornstarch
- 1 teaspoon vanilla extract
- 1/4 cup honey
- 3 cups cream cheese
- 3 eggs

Directions:

1. To make the crust, combine all the ingredients in a food processor and pulse until thoroughly combined. Move the mixture to a 9-inch round cake pan and press it thoroughly on the bottom of the pan.

2. To make the filling, combine all the ingredients in a container. Pour the container over the crust and preheat your oven and bake the cheesecake at 330F for around forty minutes or until a golden-brown colour is achieved.
3. Let the cheesecake cool down in the pan and serve, sliced.

Nutritional Content of One Serving:

Calories: 464 ‖ Fat: 32.9g ‖ Protein: 7.7g ‖ Carbohydrates: 36.2g

SPICED PUMPKIN CHEESECAKE

Total Time Taken: 1 ½ hours
Yield: 10 Servings
Ingredients:

Crust:

- ½ cup butter, melted
- 4 oz. gingersnaps, crushed

Filling:

- ½ teaspoon cinnamon powder
- ½ teaspoon ground ginger
- ½ teaspoon ground star anise
- 1 cup pumpkin puree
- 1 pinch salt
- 1 tablespoon cornstarch
- 1 teaspoon vanilla extract
- 2 eggs
- 3 cups cream cheese
- ½ teaspoon ground whole cloves

Directions:

1. To make the crust, combine the gingersnap and butter in a container. Move the mixture to a 9-inch round cake pan coated with baking paper.
2. To make the filling, combine the ingredients in a container until creamy. Pour the filling over the crust.
3. Preheat your oven and bake the cheesecake at 330F for about fifty minutes or until aromatic.
4. Let the cheesecake cool down and serve, sliced.

Nutritional Content of One Serving:

Calories: 404 ‖ Fat: 36.3g ‖ Protein: 7.5g ‖ Carbohydrates: 13.2g

STRAWBERRY JAM CHEESECAKE

Total Time Taken: 1 ¼ hours
Yield: 14 Servings
Ingredients:

Crust:

- 1 ½ cups graham crackers, crushed
- 1/3 cup butter, melted

Filling:

- ½ cup white sugar
- 1 cup strawberry jam
- 1 tablespoon cornstarch
- 1 teaspoon vanilla extract
- 3 eggs
- 4 cups cream cheese

Directions:

1. To make the crust, combine all the ingredients in a container until well combined. Move to a 9-inch round cake pan and press it thoroughly on the bottom of the pan.
2. To make the filling, combine the cream cheese, eggs, sugar, vanilla and cornstarch in a container. Pour the mixture over the crust.
3. Top the cheesecake with dollops of strawberry jam.
4. Pre-heat the oven and bake at 330F for about fifty minutes or until the center of the cake looks set.
5. Let cool in the pan then serve, sliced.

Nutritional Content of One Serving:

Calories: 438 ‖ Fat: 29.4g ‖ Protein: 6.9g ‖ Carbohydrates: 37.7g

STRAWBERRY LEMON CHEESECAKE

Total Time Taken: 1 ¼ hours
Yield: 10 Servings
Ingredients:

Crust:

- 1 ¼ cups graham crackers, crushed
- ½ cup butter, melted
- 1 teaspoon lemon zest

Filling:

- ½ cup plain yogurt
- ¾ cup white sugar
- 1 lemon, zested and juiced
- 1 tablespoon cornstarch
- 1 teaspoon vanilla extract
- 2 eggs
- 3 cups cream cheese

Topping:

- 2 cups fresh strawberries

Directions:

1. To make the crust, combine all the ingredients in a container then move to a 9-inch round cake pan. Press it thoroughly on the bottom of the pan.
2. To make the filling, combine all the ingredients in a container. Pour the filling over the crust and preheat your oven and bake at 350F for about forty minutes until set in the center.
3. When finished, take it out of the oven and let it cool.
4. Put the strawberries on top and serve chilled.

Nutritional Content of One Serving:

Calories: 462 ‖ Fat: 35.7g ‖ Protein: 8.1g ‖ Carbohydrates: 29.4g

THE ULTIMATE NO CRUST CHEESECAKE

Total Time Taken: 1 hour

Yield: 12 Servings

Ingredients:

- ½ cup sour cream
- 1 cup cream cheese
- 1 cup sweetened condensed milk
- 1 pinch salt
- 1 tablespoon cornstarch
- 1 teaspoon vanilla extract
- 2 cups ricotta cheese
- 2 tablespoons butter, melted
- 3 eggs
- Butter to grease the pan

Directions:

1. Grease 1 9-inch round cake pan with butter.
2. Mix the ricotta cheese and the remaining ingredients in a container until creamy.
3. Pour the mixture in the greased pan and preheat your oven and bake at 350F for forty minutes or until mildly golden-brown on the edges and set in the center.
4. Let the cheesecake cool down in the pan and serve, sliced.

Nutritional Content of One Serving:

Calories: 263 ‖ Fat: 17.2g ‖ Protein: 9.9g ‖ Carbohydrates: 17.6g

TIRAMISU CHEESECAKE

Total Time Taken: 1 ½ hours

Yield: 10 Servings

Ingredients:

Crust:

- ½ cup butter, melted
- 1 ½ cups chocolate biscuits
- 1 teaspoon instant coffee

Filling:

- ¼ cup espresso
- ¾ cup white sugar
- 1 tablespoon cornstarch
- 1 teaspoon vanilla extract
- 3 cups cream cheese
- 3 eggs

Topping:

- ¼ cup cocoa powder

Directions:

1. To make the crust, place the biscuits in a food processor and pulse until ground. Put in the butter and mix thoroughly then transfer the mixture in a 9-inch round cake pan and press it thoroughly on the bottom of the pan.
2. To make the filling, combine all the ingredients in a container. Pour the mixture over the crust and preheat your oven and bake the cheesecake at 330F for about fifty minutes.
3. Let the cheesecake cool in the pan then top it with a dusting of cocoa powder.
4. Serve the cheesecake fresh and chilled.

Nutritional Content of One Serving:

Calories: 446 ‖ Fat: 37.3g ‖ Protein: 7.9g ‖ Carbohydrates: 22.9g

TIRAMISU INSPIRED CHEESECAKE

Total Time Taken: 1 ¼ hours
Yield: 10 Servings
Ingredients:

Crust:

- 1 ½ cups Oreo cookies, crushed
- 1 tablespoon cocoa powder
- 1/3 cup butter, melted

Filling:

- ½ cup white sugar
- 1 cup mascarpone cheese

- 1 pinch salt
- 1 tablespoon instant coffee
- 1 teaspoon vanilla extract
- 3 cups cream cheese
- 3 eggs
- Cocoa powder for dusting

Directions:

1. To make the crust, combine all the ingredients in a container. Move the mixture to a 9- inch round cake pan and press it thoroughly on the bottom of the pan.
2. To make the filling, combine all the ingredients in a container until creamy and thick. Pour the filling over the crust , preheat your oven and bake at 330F for about forty-five minutes or until set in the center.
3. Let cool down then dust with cocoa powder.

This cheesecake tastes best chilled.

Nutritional Content of One Serving:

Calories: 404 ‖ Fat: 35.2g ‖ Protein: 9.9g ‖ Carbohydrates: 13.8g

TWIX CHEESECAKE

Total Time Taken: 1 ¼ hours
Yield: 14 Servings
Ingredients:

Crust:

- ½ cup butter, melted
- 2 cups Oreo cookies, crushed

Filling:

- ½ cup white sugar
- 1 cup sour cream
- 1 pinch salt
- 1 teaspoon vanilla extract
- 2 tablespoons cornstarch
- 3 cups cream cheese

- 4 eggs
- 4 Twix bars, chopped

Directions:

1. To make the crust, combine the ingredients in a container until combined. Move to a 9- inch round cake pan and press it thoroughly on the bottom of the pan.
2. To make the filling, combine the cream cheese, sour cream, eggs, cornstarch, vanilla, sugar and salt in a container. Fold in the bars and pour the mixture over the crust.
3. Pre-heat the oven and bake at 330F for about fifty minutes or until the center of the cheesecake looks set, but still slightly jiggly.
4. Let cool in the pan and serve, sliced.

Nutritional Content of One Serving:

Calories: 406 ‖ Fat: 32.9g ‖ Protein: 6.7g ‖ Carbohydrates: 22.0g

VANILLA CRUMBLE CHEESECAKE

Total Time Taken: 1 ¼ hours
Yield: 12 Servings
Ingredients:

Crust:

- ¼ cup butter, melted
- 1 ½ cups vanilla biscuits

Filling:

- ½ cup heavy cream
- 1 pinch salt
- 1 tablespoon cornstarch
- 1 tablespoon vanilla extract
- 2/3 cup white sugar
- 3 cups cream cheese
- 3 eggs

Topping:

- ½ cup butter, chilled

- ¾ cup all-purpose flour
- 1 pinch salt

Directions:

1. To make the crust, combine the two ingredients in a container then transfer the mixture in a 9-inch round cake pan coated with baking paper.
2. To make the filling, combine all the ingredients in a container. Pour the mixture over the crust.
3. For the topping, combine the butter, flour and salt in a container until crumbly, grainy.
4. Spread the crumble over the filling then preheat your oven and bake the cheesecake at 330F.
5. Bake for about fifty minutes or until a golden-brown colour is achieved and crusty.
6. Let cool down before you serve.

Nutritional Content of One Serving:

Calories: 449 ‖ Fat: 35.6g ‖ Protein: 7.4g ‖ Carbohydrates: 25.9g

VERY VANILLA CHEESECAKE

Total Time Taken: 1 ¼ hours
Yield: 10 Servings
Ingredients:

Crust:

- ½ cup butter, melted
- 1 ½ cups graham crackers, crushed
- 1 teaspoon vanilla extract

Filling:

- 1 cup sour cream
- 1 pinch salt
- 1 tablespoon cornstarch
- 1 vanilla bean, split along the length, seeds removed
- 3 cups cream cheese
- 3 eggs

Directions:

1. To make the crust, combine the ingredients in a container. Move the mixture to a 9-inch round cake pan and press it thoroughly on the bottom of the pan.
2. To make the filling, combine the cream cheese, sour cream, vanilla bean seeds, eggs, salt and cornstarch in a container.
3. Pour the mixture over the crust and preheat your oven and bake the cheesecake at 330F for about forty minutes. Place a pan filled with water under the cheesecake to guarantee a humid atmosphere in the oven so that the cheesecake has less chances to crack on top.
4. Let the cheesecake cool to room temperature and serve, sliced.

Nutritional Content of One Serving:

Calories: 460 ‖ Fat: 41.2g ‖ Protein: 8.9g ‖ Carbohydrates: 14.9g

WALNUT CHEESECAKE

Total Time Taken: 1 ¼ hours
Yield: 10 Servings
Ingredients:

Crust:

- ¼ cup butter, melted
- 1 cup walnuts
- 10 graham crackers

Filling:

- 1 cup sour cream
- 1 tablespoon cornstarch
- 1 teaspoon vanilla extract
- 2 cups cream cheese
- 2 oz. dark chocolate, melted
- 2 tablespoons dark rum
- 2/3 cup white sugar
- 3 eggs

Directions:

1. To make the crust, combine the ingredients in a food processor and pulse until thoroughly combined. Move to a 9-inch round cake pan and press it thoroughly on the bottom of the pan.

2. To make the filling, mix the ingredients in a blender and pulse until thoroughly combined. Pour the mixture into the crust, preheat your oven and bake at 330F for about forty minutes until set.
3. Let the cheesecake cool down and serve, sliced.

Nutritional Content of One Serving:

Calories: 498 ‖ Fat: 37.4g ‖ Protein: 10.3g ‖ Carbohydrates: 31.8g

WALNUT CRUMBLE CHEESECAKE

Total Time Taken: 1 ½ hours
Yield: 12 Servings
Ingredients:

Crust:

- 1 cup graham crackers, crushed
- 1 cup ground walnuts
- 2 tablespoons butter, melted

Filling:

- 1 pinch salt
- 1 tablespoon cornstarch
- 1 teaspoon vanilla extract
- 2 eggs
- 2 tablespoons dark rum
- 2/3 cup white sugar
- 24 oz. cream cheese

Topping:

- ¼ cup all-purpose flour
- 1 cup walnuts, chopped
- 1 pinch salt
- 2 tablespoons butter, chilled

Directions:

1. To make the crust, combine the ingredients in a food processor and pulse until ground and thoroughly combined.

2. Move to a 9-inch round cake pan coated with baking paper and press it thoroughly on the bottom of the pan.
3. To make the filling, combine all the ingredients in a container. Pour the mixture over the
4. crust.
5. For the topping, combine all the ingredients in a container until grainy.
6. Top the cheesecake with this mixture and preheat your oven and bake at 350F for about forty-five minutes or until set in the center.
7. Let cool down and serve, sliced.

Nutritional Content of One Serving:

Calories: 461 ‖ Fat: 37.4g ‖ Protein: 11.0g ‖ Carbohydrates: 22.8g

WHITE CHOCOLATE CARAMEL CHEESECAKE

Total Time Taken: 1 ¼ hours
Yield: 12 Servings
Ingredients:

Crust:

- 1 ½ cups graham crackers, crushed
- 1/3 cup butter, melted

Filling:

- ¼ cup caramel sauce
- 1 pinch salt
- 1 tablespoon cornstarch
- 1 tablespoon vanilla extract
- 24 oz. cream cheese
- 3 eggs
- 6 oz. white chocolate chips, melted

Directions:

1. To make the crust, combine the ingredients in a container. Move to a 9-inch round cake pan and press it thoroughly on the bottom of the pan.
2. To make the filling, combine the cream cheese and chocolate in a container.

3. Put in the remaining ingredients and mix thoroughly.
4. Pour the mixture over the crust , preheat your oven and bake at 330F for about fifty minutes or until the center looks set.
5. Let cool down in the pan and serve, sliced.

Nutritional Content of One Serving:

Calories: 403 ‖ Fat: 31.6g ‖ Protein: 7.4g ‖ Carbohydrates: 23.3g

WHITE CHOCOLATE CHEESECAKE

Total Time Taken: 1 ¼ hours
Yield: 10 Servings
Ingredients:

Crust:

- ½ cup butter, melted
- 1 ½ cups graham crackers, crushed

Filling:

- 1 pinch salt
- 1 teaspoon cornstarch
- 1 teaspoon vanilla extract
- 1/3 cups white sugar
- 3 cups cream cheese
- 3 eggs
- 4 oz. white chocolate, melted

Directions:

1. To make the filling, combine the ingredients in a container. Move to a 9-inch round cake pan and press it thoroughly on the bottom of the pan.
2. To make the filling, combine the cream cheese, white chocolate, eggs, vanilla, sugar, salt and cornstarch.
3. Pour the mixture over the crust , preheat your oven and bake at 330F for about fifty minutes or until the center looks set if you shake the pan slightly.
4. Let the cheesecake cool in the pan and serve, sliced.

Nutritional Content of One Serving:

Calories: 485 ‖ Fat: 39.7g ‖ Protein: 8.5g ‖ Carbohydrates: 25.3g

BONUS: COOKIE RECIPES

BROWN SUGAR CHOCOLATE CHIP COOKIES

Total Time Taken: 1 ½ hours
Yield: 40 Servings

Ingredients:

- ½ cup white sugar
- ½ teaspoon salt
- 1 ½ cups butter, softened
- 1 ½ cups dark chocolate chips
- 1 cup dark brown sugar
- 1 cup light brown sugar
- 1 teaspoon baking soda
- 1 teaspoon vanilla extract
- 2 eggs
- 3 cups all-purpose flour

Directions:

1. Mix the butter and sugars in a container until creamy and fluffy.
2. Put in the eggs and vanilla and mix thoroughly then fold in the remaining ingredients.
3. Drop spoonfuls of batter on a baking tray coated with baking paper.
4. Preheat your oven and bake the cookies at 350F for about fifteen minutes or until a golden-brown colour is achieved on the edges and crisp.
5. These cookies taste best chilled.

Nutritional Content of One Serving:

Calories: 157 || Fat: 8.4g || Protein: 1.6g || Carbohydrates: 19.8g

BROWN BUTTER CHOCOLATE OATMEAL COOKIES

Total Time Taken: 1 ¼ hours
Yield: 30 Servings

Ingredients:

- ¼ teaspoon salt
- ½ cup dark chocolate chips
- 1 1/2 cups rolled oats
- 1 cup all-purpose flour
- 1 cup butter
- 1 cup light brown sugar
- 1 egg
- 1 teaspoon baking soda
- 1 teaspoon vanilla extract

Directions:

1. Melt the butter in a saucepan until it becomes mildly golden.
2. Put in the sugar and mix thoroughly then mix in the egg and vanilla.
3. Put in the oats, flour, baking soda and salt then fold in the chocolate chips.
4. Drop spoonfuls of batter on a baking tray coated with baking paper.
5. Preheat your oven and bake the cookies at 350F for about fifteen minutes or until a golden-brown colour is achieved on the edges.
6. These cookies taste best chilled.

Nutritional Content of One Serving:

Calories: 115 ‖ Fat: 7.1g ‖ Protein: 1.4g ‖ Carbohydrates: 12.0g

BROWN BUTTER CHOCOLATE CHIP COOKIES

Total Time Taken: 2 hours
Yield: 20 Servings
Ingredients:

- ¼ teaspoon salt
- ½ cup butter
- ½ teaspoon baking soda
- 1 ½ cups all-purpose flour
- 1 cup dark chocolate chips
- 1 cup light brown sugar
- 1 egg
- 1 egg yolk
- 1 teaspoon baking powder
- 1 teaspoon vanilla extract

Directions:

1. Mix the flour, baking powder, baking soda and salt in a container.
2. Melt the butter in a saucepan until it starts to appear somewhat golden-brown and caramelized. Let cool and then move to a container.
3. Stir in the sugar, egg, egg yolk, vanilla and flour. Stir slowly until mixed using a spatula.
4. Fold in the chocolate chips then drop spoonfuls of dough on a baking sheet coated with baking paper.
5. Freeze the cookies for about half an hour then preheat your oven and bake at 350F for fifteen minutes until a golden-brown colour is achieved.

Best served chilled.

Nutritional Content of One Serving:

Calories: 137 ‖ Fat: 6.8g ‖ Protein: 1.8g ‖ Carbohydrates: 18.5g

BROWN BUTTER AMERICAN COOKIES

Total Time Taken: 1 ¼ hours
Yield: 20 Servings

Ingredients:

- ¼ teaspoon salt
- ½ cup pecans, chopped
- ½ teaspoon baking soda
- 1 ½ cups all-purpose flour
- 1 cup butter

- 1 cup light brown sugar
- 1 egg
- 1 teaspoon vanilla extract

Directions:

1. Put the butter in a saucepan and melt it then cook it until golden and caramelized. Let cool and then move to a container.
2. Mix the butter and sugar in a fluffy and pale.
3. Put in the egg and vanilla and mix thoroughly then mix in the flour, baking soda, salt and pecans.
4. Drop spoonfuls of batter on a baking tray coated with baking paper.
5. Pre-heat the oven and bake at 350F for about fifteen minutes or until a golden-brown colour is achieved on the edges.
6. These cookies taste best chilled.

Nutritional Content of One Serving:

Calories: 152 ‖ Fat: 10.0g ‖ Protein: 1.4g ‖ Carbohydrates: 14.4g

BANANA OATMEAL COOKIES

Total Time Taken: 1 hour
Yield: 10 Servings
Ingredients:

- ¼ teaspoon baking soda
- 1 cup rolled oats
- 1 pinch salt
- 2 tablespoons maple syrup
- 3 ripe bananas, mashed

Directions:

1. Combine all the ingredients in a container.
2. Drop spoonfuls of batter on a baking sheet coated with baking paper.
3. Preheat your oven and bake the cookies at 350F for about ten minutes or until a golden-brown colour is achieved on the edges.
4. These cookies taste best chilled.

Nutritional Content of One Serving:

Calories: 73 ‖ Fat: 0.7g ‖ Protein: 1.5g ‖ Carbohydrates: 16.3g

BANANA CHOCOLATE COOKIES

Total Time Taken: 1 ¼ hours
Yield: 20 Servings

Ingredients:

- ¼ cup butter, softened
- ¼ cup cocoa powder
- ¼ cup coconut oil, melted
- ¼ teaspoon baking soda
- ¼ teaspoon salt
- ½ cup walnuts, chopped
- ½ teaspoon baking powder
- 1 ¾ cups all-purpose flour
- 2 bananas, mashed
- 2/3 cup white sugar

Directions:

1. Mix the butter, oil and sugar in a container until creamy and fluffy.

2. Stir in the bananas then fold in the flour, baking soda, baking powder, salt and cocoa powder.

3. Put in the walnuts then drop spoonfuls of batter on a baking sheet coated with baking paper.

4. Preheat your oven and bake the cookies at 350F for fifteen minutes or until aromatic.

5. These cookies taste best chilled.

Nutritional Content of One Serving:

Calories: 141 ‖ Fat: 7.2g ‖ Protein: 2.2g ‖ Carbohydrates: 18.7g

BANANA CHOCOLATE CHIP COOKIES

Total Time Taken: 1 ¼ hours
Yield: 20 Servings

Ingredients:

- ¼ teaspoon salt
- ½ cup butter, melted
- ½ cup dark chocolate chips
- ½ cup white sugar
- 1 ½ cups all-purpose flour
- 1 egg
- 1 teaspoon baking powder
- 1 teaspoon vanilla extract
- 2 bananas, mashed

Directions:

1. Combine all the dry ingredients in a container.
2. Put in the rest of the ingredients and mix thoroughly using a spatula.
3. Drop spoonfuls of batter on a baking tray covered with parchment paper.
4. Preheat your oven and bake the cookies at 350F for about fifteen minutes or until a golden-brown colour is achieved on the edges.
5. These cookies taste best chilled.

Nutritional Content of One Serving:

Calories: 122 ‖ Fat: 5.8g ‖ Protein: 1.6g ‖ Carbohydrates: 17.0g

APRICOT COCONUT COOKIES

Total Time Taken: 1 ½ hours

Yield: 25 Servings

Ingredients:

- ¼ cup light brown sugar
- ¼ teaspoon salt
- ½ cup butter, softened
- ½ cup dark chocolate chips
- ½ cup dried apricots, chopped
- ½ cup rolled oats
- ½ cup white sugar
- ½ teaspoon baking soda
- 1 cup all-purpose flour
- 1 cup shredded coconut

- 1 teaspoon vanilla extract
- 2 eggs

Directions:

1. Mix the flour, coconut, oats, apricots, salt and baking soda in a container.
2. In a separate container, mix the butter and the sugars and vanilla and mix thoroughly.
3. Fold in the flour mixture and the chocolate chips.
4. Drop spoonful of batter on a baking sheet coated with baking paper.
5. Pre-heat the oven and bake at 350F for about fifteen minutes or until a golden-brown colour is achieved on the edges.
6. Let the cookies cool before you serve.

Nutritional Content of One Serving:

Calories: 107 ‖ Fat: 5.9g ‖ Protein: 1.5g ‖ Carbohydrates: 12.8g

ANZAC COOKIES

Total Time Taken: 1 ¼ hours
Yield: 20 Servings

Ingredients:

- ¼ teaspoon salt
- ½ cup shredded coconut
- ½ teaspoon baking soda
- ¾ cup all-purpose flour
- ¾ cup butter, melted
- 1 cup rolled oats
- 1 teaspoon lemon juice
- 4 tablespoons golden syrup

Directions:

1. Mix the oats, coconut, flour, baking soda and salt in a container.
2. Put in the rest of the ingredients and mix thoroughly.
3. Make small balls of dough and place them in a baking tray coated with baking paper.

4. Flatten the cookies slightly then preheat your oven and bake at 350F for about fifteen minutes or until a golden-brown colour is achieved on the edges.
5. These cookies taste best chilled.

Nutritional Content of One Serving:

Calories: 112 ‖ Fat: 7.9g ‖ Protein: 1.2g ‖ Carbohydrates: 9.8g

AMERICAN CHOCOLATE CHUNK COOKIES

Total Time Taken: 1 ¼ hours
Yield: 20 Servings

Ingredients:

- ½ cup smooth peanut butter
- ½ cup light brown sugar
- 1 egg
- 1 teaspoon vanilla extract
- 1 cup all-purpose flour
- ¼ teaspoon salt
- ½ teaspoon baking powder
- ½ cup peanuts, chopped
- 3 oz. dark chocolate, chopped
- 1/3 cup butter, softened

Directions:

1. Mix the peanut butter, butter and sugar in a container until fluffy and creamy.
2. Put in the egg and vanilla and mix thoroughly.
3. Fold in the flour, salt, baking powder, peanuts and dark chocolate.
4. Drop spoonfuls of batter on a baking tray coated with baking paper.
5. Preheat your oven and bake the cookies at 350F for about fifteen minutes or until a golden-brown colour is achieved on the edges.
6. These cookies taste best chilled.

Nutritional Content of One Serving:

Calories: 149 ‖ Fat: 9.7g ‖ Protein: 3.9g ‖ Carbohydrates: 12.8g

AMARETTI COOKIES

Total Time Taken: 1 ¼ hours

Yield: 10 Servings

Ingredients:

- ¼ cup all-purpose flour
- ¼ teaspoon salt 2 egg whites
- ½ cup light brown sugar
- ½ teaspoon baking powder
- 1 teaspoon vanilla extract
- 2 cups almond flour

Directions:

1. Whip the egg whites with salt and vanilla in a container until fluffy.
2. Put in the sugar and continue mixing until shiny and firm.
3. Drop spoonfuls of batter on a baking tray coated with baking paper.
4. Pre-heat the oven and bake at 350F for about twenty minutes or until a golden-brown colour is achieved and crisp.
5. These cookies taste best chilled.

Nutritional Content of One Serving:

Calories: 76 ‖ Fat: 2.8g ‖ Protein: 2.2g ‖ Carbohydrates: 10.9g

AMARETTI COOKIES

Total Time Taken: 1 hour

Yield: 10 Servings

Ingredients:

- 2 cups almond flour
- 1 teaspoon vanilla extract
- ½ teaspoon almond extract
- 2 egg whites

- 2/3 cup light brown sugar

Directions:

1. Mix the egg whites until fluffy.
2. Put in the vanilla and sugar and continue whipping until shiny and firm.
3. Fold in the almond flour then drop spoonfuls of batter on a baking tray coated with baking paper.
4. Preheat your oven and bake the cookies at 350F for about fifteen minutes or until a golden-brown colour is achieved on the edges.
5. These cookies taste best chilled.

Nutritional Content of One Serving:

Calories: 74 ‖ Fat: 2.8g ‖ Protein: 1.9g ‖ Carbohydrates: 10.8g

ALMOND COOKIES

Total Time Taken: 1 ¼ hours
Yield: 20 Servings

Ingredients:

- ½ cup butter, softened
- 1 teaspoon almond extract
- 2 egg yolks
- 1 ½ cups all-purpose flour
- ½ cup almond flour
- ¼ teaspoon salt
- 1 teaspoon baking powder
- ½ cup sliced almonds
- 2/3 cup white sugar

Directions:

1. Mix the butter, sugar and almond extract in a container until fluffy and pale.
2. Put in the egg yolks and stir thoroughly until blended.
3. Fold in the flours, salt and baking powder.
4. Drop spoonfuls of batter on a baking sheet coated with baking paper.
5. Top each cookie with sliced almonds and preheat your oven and bake at 350F for about fifteen minutes until a golden-brown colour is achieved on the edges.

6. These cookies taste best chilled.

Nutritional Content of One Serving:

Calories: 124 || Fat: 6.7g || Protein: 1.9g || Carbohydrates: 14.7g

ALMOND BLUEBERRY COOKIES

Total Time Taken: 1 ¼ hours
Yield: 20 Servings

Ingredients:

- ½ cup butter, softened
- 1 teaspoon lemon zest
- 1 egg
- ¼ cup whole milk
- 1 teaspoon almond extract
- 1 ¼ cups all-purpose flour
- 1 cup ground almonds
- ¼ teaspoon salt
- ½ teaspoon baking soda
- ½ cup dried blueberries
- ¼ cup sliced almonds
- 2/3 cup white sugar

Directions:

1. Mix the butter, sugar and lemon zest in a container until fluffy and pale.
2. Put in the egg and milk and mix thoroughly then fold in the flour, ground almonds, baking soda, salt and blueberries.
3. Drop spoonfuls of batter on a baking tray covered with parchment paper and top each cookie with almond slices.
4. Preheat your oven and bake the cookies at 350F for about fifteen minutes or until a golden-brown colour is achieved and fragrant.
5. Serve Chilled or store them in an airtight container for maximum 1 week.

Nutritional Content of One Serving:

Calories: 136 || Fat: 8.0g || Protein: 2.5g || Carbohydrates: 14.6g

CHOCOLATE NUTELLA COOKIES

Total Time Taken: 1 ¼ hours
Yield: 30 Servings

Ingredients:

- ¼ cup cocoa powder
- ¼ cup white sugar
- ½ teaspoon baking soda
- ½ teaspoon salt
- ¾ cup light brown sugar
- 1 cup butter, softened
- 1 cup dark chocolate chips
- 1 cup Nutella
- 1 teaspoon vanilla extract
- 2 cups all-purpose flour
- 2 eggs

Directions:

1. Mix the butter and sugars in a container until creamy and fluffy.
2. Put in the Nutella, vanilla and eggs and mix thoroughly.
3. Fold in the remaining ingredients then drop spoonfuls of batter on a baking tray covered with parchment paper.
4. Preheat your oven and bake the cookies at 350F for about fifteen minutes or until a golden-brown colour is achieved.
5. Serve the cookie chilled.

Nutritional Content of One Serving:

Calories: 136 || Fat: 8.0g || Protein: 1.8g || Carbohydrates: 15.5g

CHOCOLATE HAZELNUT COOKIES

Total Time Taken: 1 ½ hours
Yield: 30 Servings

Ingredients:

- ¼ cup cocoa powder

- ¼ teaspoon salt
- ½ cup cream cheese, softened
- ½ cup ground hazelnuts
- 1 ½ cups all-purpose flour
- 1 cup butter, softened
- 1 egg yolk

Directions:

1. Mix the butter, cream cheese and egg yolk in a container until creamy.
2. Put in the salt, flour, cocoa powder and hazelnuts and mix using a spatula.
3. Wrap the plastic wrap and store in the refrigerator for about half an hour.
4. Transfer the dough to a floured working surface and roll it into a slim sheet.
5. Cut into small cookies with a cookie cutter of your choices.
6. Put the cookies in a baking sheet coated with baking paper and preheat your oven and bake at 350F for about ten minutes or until a golden-brown colour is achieved on the edges.
7. These cookies taste best chilled.

Nutritional Content of One Serving:

Calories: 102 ‖ Fat: 8.6g ‖ Protein: 1.4g ‖ Carbohydrates: 5.5g

CHOCOLATE DRIZZLED LAVENDER COOKIES

Total Time Taken: 1 ½ hours
Yield: 20 Servings

Ingredients:

- ¼ cup cornstarch
- ¼ teaspoon baking soda
- ¼ teaspoon salt
- ½ cup butter, softened
- ½ cup powdered sugar
- ½ cup white chocolate chips, melted
- 1 ½ cups all-purpose flour
- 1 egg

- 1 egg yolk
- 1 teaspoon lavender buds
- 2 tablespoons whole milk

Directions:

1. Mix the butter with sugar in a container until fluffy and pale.
2. Stir in the egg and egg yolk and mix thoroughly.
3. Put in the milk and mix then fold in the remaining ingredients. Mix the dough then move it to a floured working surface and roll it into a slim sheet.
4. Cut into small cookies using a cookie cutter of your choices.
5. Position the cookies on a baking sheet coated with baking paper.
6. Pre-heat the oven and bake at 350F for about fifteen minutes or until a golden-brown colour is achieved on the edges.
7. When finished, let cool in the pan then sprinkle the cookies with melted chocolate.
8. Best served chilled.

Nutritional Content of One Serving:

Calories: 122 ‖ Fat: 6.6g ‖ Protein: 1.7g ‖ Carbohydrates: 14.2g

CHOCOLATE DIPPED SUGAR COOKIES

Total Time Taken: 1 ¼ hours
Yield: 30 Servings

Ingredients:

- ¼ teaspoon salt
- 1 cup butter, softened
- 1 cup dark chocolate, melted
- 1 cup powdered sugar
- 1 teaspoon baking powder
- 1 teaspoon vanilla extract
- 2 egg yolks
- 3 cups all-purpose flour

Directions:

1. Mix the butter and sugar in a container until pale and fluffy.
2. Stir in the egg yolks and vanilla and mix thoroughly.

3. Fold in the flour, baking powder and salt then wrap the dough in plastic wrap and store in the refrigerator for about half an hour.
4. Transfer the dough to a floured working surface and roll into a slim sheet.
5. Cut cookies using a cookie cutter of your choices and arrange them on a baking sheet coated with baking paper.
6. Pre-heat the oven and bake at 350F for about thirteen minutes or until mildly golden-brown on the edges.
7. When finished, allow the cookies to cool then immerse them in melted chocolate.
8. These cookies taste best chilled.

Nutritional Content of One Serving:

Calories: 149 ‖ Fat: 8.2g ‖ Protein: 2.0g ‖ Carbohydrates: 17.0g

CHOCOLATE CRINKLES

Total Time Taken: 2 hours
Yield: 40 Servings
Ingredients:

- ½ cup cocoa powder
- ½ cup coconut oil, melted
- ½ teaspoon salt
- 1 ½ teaspoons baking powder
- 1 teaspoon vanilla extract
- 2 cups all-purpose flour
- 2 cups powdered sugar
- 2 cups white sugar
- 4 eggs
- 4 oz. dark chocolate, melted

Directions:

1. Mix the coconut oil and melted chocolate in a container.
2. Put in the sugar and eggs and mix thoroughly then mix in the vanilla.
3. Fold in the flour, baking powder, cocoa and salt then cover the dough using plastic wrap.
4. Place in your refrigerator for an hour then form small balls of dough and roll them through powdered sugar.

5. Put the cookies on a baking tray coated with baking paper and preheat your oven and bake at 350F for about ten minutes.
6. These cookies taste best chilled.

Nutritional Content of One Serving:

Calories: 131 ‖ Fat: 4.2g ‖ Protein: 1.6g ‖ Carbohydrates: 23.1g

CHOCOLATE CHUNK COOKIES

Total Time Taken: 1 ¼ hours
Yield: 20 Servings

Ingredients:

- ¼ teaspoon salt
- ½ cup butter, softened
- 1 ½ cups all-purpose flour
- 1 egg
- 1 teaspoon baking powder
- 2 tablespoons honey
- 2/3 cup light brown sugar
- 4 oz. dark chocolate, chopped

Directions:

1. Mix the butter, honey and sugar in a container until fluffy and pale.
2. Put in the egg and mix thoroughly then mix in the flour, baking powder and salt.
3. Fold in the chocolate then drop spoonfuls of dough on a baking sheet coated with baking paper.
4. Preheat your oven and bake the cookies at 350F for fifteen minutes or until a golden-brown colour is achieved on the edges.
5. These cookies taste best chilled.

Nutritional Content of One Serving:

Calories: 133 ‖ Fat: 6.6g ‖ Protein: 1.8g ‖ Carbohydrates: 17.1g

CHOCOLATE CHIP PECAN COOKIES

Total Time Taken: 1 ¼ hours
Yield: 20 Servings

Ingredients:

- ¼ teaspoon salt
- ½ cup butter, softened
- ½ cup chocolate chips
- ½ cup powdered sugar
- ½ teaspoon baking soda
- 1 cup all-purpose flour
- 1 cup ground pecans
- 1 egg
- 2 tablespoon honey

Directions:

1. Mix the butter, sugar and honey in a container until creamy and pale.
2. Put in the egg and mix thoroughly then put in the flour, pecans, baking soda and salt.
3. Fold in the chocolate chips then drop spoonfuls of batter on a baking sheet coated with baking paper.
4. Pre-heat the oven and bake at 350F for about fifteen minutes or until a golden-brown colour is achieved and fragrant.
5. These cookies taste best chilled.

Nutritional Content of One Serving:

Calories: 112 ‖ Fat: 6.6g ‖ Protein: 1.4g ‖ Carbohydrates: 12.1g

CHOCOLATE BUTTERCREAM COOKIES

Total Time Taken: 1 ½ hours
Yield: 20 Servings
Ingredients:

Cookies:

- ½ cup butter, softened

- ½ cup cocoa powder
- ½ cup coconut oil
- ½ cup powdered sugar
- ½ teaspoon baking powder
- ½ teaspoon salt
- 1 egg
- 2 cups all-purpose flour
- 2 tablespoons whole milk

Filling:

- ½ cup butter, softened
- 1 cup powdered sugar

Directions:

1. For the cookies, combine the flour, cocoa powder, salt and baking powder in a container.
2. In a separate container, combine the coconut oil, butter and sugar in a container until creamy and fluffy.
3. Put in the egg and mix thoroughly, then mix in the flour and the milk.
4. Cover the dough with plastic wrap and store in the refrigerator for about half an hour.
5. Transfer the dough to a floured working surface and roll into a slim sheet.
6. Cut small round cookies and place them on a baking sheet.
7. Pre-heat the oven and bake at 350F for about fifteen minutes.
8. Let the cookies cool to room temperature.
9. For the filling, combine the butter with sugar until fluffy and creamy.
10. Fill the cookies, two by two with the buttercream.
11. Serve fresh or store in an airtight container.

Nutritional Content of One Serving:

Calories: 218 ‖ Fat: 15.4g ‖ Protein: 2.1g ‖ Carbohydrates: 19.8g

CHILI CHOCOLATE COOKIES

Total Time Taken: 1 ¼ hours

Yield: 30 Servings

Ingredients:

- ¼ cup dark brown sugar
- ½ cup cocoa powder
- ½ cup white sugar
- ½ teaspoon salt
- 1 cup butter, softened
- 1 cup dark chocolate chips
- 1 teaspoon baking powder
- 1 teaspoon chili powder
- 1 teaspoon vanilla extract
- 2 cups all-purpose flour
- 2 eggs

Directions:

1. Mix the butter and sugars in a container until creamy and fluffy.
2. Put in the vanilla and eggs and mix thoroughly.
3. Fold in the flour, cocoa powder, salt, chili powder and baking powder then put in the chocolate chips.
4. Drop spoonfuls of batter on a baking sheet coated with baking paper.
5. Preheat your oven and bake the cookies at 350F for about fifteen minutes or until risen and fragrant.
6. These cookies taste best chilled.

Nutritional Content of One Serving:

Calories: 129 ‖ Fat: 7.8g ‖ Protein: 1.8g ‖ Carbohydrates: 14.5g

CHEWY SUGAR COOKIES

Total Time Taken: 1 ¼ hours
Yield: 40 Servings

Ingredients:

- ½ teaspoon salt
- 1 cup butter, softened
- 1 teaspoon baking soda
- 1 teaspoon vanilla extract
- 2 ½ cups all-purpose flour
- 2 cups white sugar

- 2 eggs

Directions:

1. Mix the butter with sugar until creamy and pale. Put in the eggs, one at a time, then mix in the vanilla.
2. Fold in the flour, baking soda and salt then shape the dough into small balls.
3. Put the balls on a baking tray coated with baking paper and flatten them slightly.
4. Preheat your oven and bake the cookies at 350F for about fifteen minutes or until mildly golden brown.
5. These cookies taste best chilled.

Nutritional Content of One Serving:

Calories: 110 || Fat: 4.9g || Protein: 1.1g || Carbohydrates: 16.0g

CHEWY COCONUT COOKIES

Total Time Taken: 1 hour
Yield: 20 Servings
Ingredients:

- ¼ cup coconut oil, melted
- ¼ cup cornstarch
- ¼ teaspoon salt
- ½ teaspoon baking soda
- ½ teaspoon coconut extract
- 1 ¼ cups all-purpose flour
- 1 cup shredded coconut
- 1 cup white sugar
- 1 egg
- 1 teaspoon vanilla extract

Directions:

1. Mix the egg and sugar in a container until volume increases to twice what it was. Stir in the coconut oil then put in the coconut oil, vanilla and coconut extract.
2. Fold in the flour, cornstarch, baking soda, salt and coconut.
3. Drop spoonfuls of batter on a baking sheet pan coated with baking paper.

4. Preheat your oven and bake the cookies at 350F for about fifteen minutes or until a golden-brown colour is achieved on the edges.
5. These cookies taste best chilled.

Nutritional Content of One Serving:

Calories: 114 ‖ Fat: 4.4g ‖ Protein: 1.2g ‖ Carbohydrates: 18.1g

CASHEW CRANBERRY COOKIES

Total Time Taken: 1 ¼ house
Yield: 30 Servings

Ingredients:

- ¼ teaspoon salt
- ½ cup all-purpose flour
- ½ cup baking soda
- ½ cup coconut oil, melted
- ½ cup light brown sugar
- 1 ½ cups ground cashew nuts
- 1 cup dried cranberries
- 1 teaspoon vanilla extract
- 2 eggs
- 2 tablespoons golden syrup

Directions:

1. Mix the cashew nuts, flour, salt and baking soda in a container.
2. In a separate container, combine the coconut oil, eggs, vanilla, sugar and syrup until creamy.
3. Put in the flour mixture then fold in the cranberries.
4. Drop spoonfuls of batter on a baking sheet coated with baking paper.
5. Preheat your oven and bake the cookies at 350F for about fifteen minutes or until a golden-brown colour is achieved on the edges.
6. These cookies taste best chilled.

Nutritional Content of One Serving:

Calories: 106 ‖ Fat: 7.7g ‖ Protein: 2.0g ‖ Carbohydrates: 7.6g

CARDAMOM CHOCOLATE CHIP COOKIES

Total Time Taken: 1 hour
Yield: 20 Servings
Ingredients:

- ½ cup light brown sugar
- ½ cup white sugar
- ½ teaspoon salt
- 1 cup butter, softened
- 1 cup dark chocolate chips
- 1 teaspoon baking powder
- 1 teaspoon cardamom powder
- 2 ½ cups all-purpose flour
- 2 eggs

Directions:

1. Mix the butter and sugars in a container until creamy and fluffy.
2. Stir in the eggs, one at a time, then put in the flour, salt, baking powder and cardamom powder.
3. Fold in the chocolate chips then drop spoonfuls of batter on a baking sheet coated with baking paper.
4. Pre-heat the oven and bake at 350F for about fifteen minutes.
5. Let the cookies cool in the pan before you serve.

Nutritional Content of One Serving:

Calories: 206 ‖ Fat: 11.4g ‖ Protein: 2.7g ‖ Carbohydrates: 24.7g

CANDY CANE CHOCOLATE COOKIES

Total Time Taken: 1 ¼ hours
Yield: 20 Servings

Ingredients:

- ¼ cup cocoa powder
- ¼ cup shredded coconut

- ¼ teaspoon salt
- ½ cup butter, softened
- ½ cup crushed candy cane cookies
- ½ teaspoon baking soda
- 1 cup all-purpose flour
- 1 egg
- 1 teaspoon vanilla extract
- 2 tablespoons canola oil
- 2/3 cup light brown sugar

Directions:

1. Mix the butter, canola oil, sugar and vanilla in a container until fluffy and creamy.
2. Stir in the egg then put in the flour, cocoa powder, coconut, baking soda and salt.
3. Fold in the crushed candy then drop spoonfuls of batter on a baking sheet coated with baking paper.
4. Preheat your oven and bake the cookies at 350F for about fifteen minutes or until aromatic and risen.
5. These cookies taste best chilled.

Nutritional Content of One Serving:

Calories: 108 ‖ Fat: 7.0g ‖ Protein: 1.3g ‖ Carbohydrates: 10.8g

CANDIED GINGER OATMEAL COOKIES

Total Time Taken: 1 hour
Yield: 30 Servings
Ingredients:

- ¼ cup butter, softened
- ½ cup candied ginger, chopped
- ½ cup canola oil
- ½ teaspoon salt
- 1 cup light brown sugar
- 1 teaspoon baking soda
- 1 teaspoon vanilla extract
- 2 cups all-purpose flour

- 2 cups rolled oats
- 2 eggs

Directions:

1. Mix the butter and sugar in a container until creamy and pale.
2. Put in the eggs and mix thoroughly then mix in the vanilla.
3. Fold in the dry ingredients and ginger then drop spoonfuls of batter on a baking sheet coated with baking paper.
4. Preheat your oven and bake the cookies at 350F for about fifteen minutes or until it is aromatic and appears golden-brown on the edges.
5. These cookies taste best chilled.

Nutritional Content of One Serving:

Calories: 121 ‖ Fat: 5.9g ‖ Protein: 2.0g ‖ Carbohydrates: 15.0g

CAKEY CHOCOLATE CHIP COOKIES

Total Time Taken: 1 hour
Yield: 20 Servings
Ingredients:

- ¼ cup coconut oil, melted
- ¼ cup whole milk
- ¼ teaspoon salt
- ½ cup dark chocolate chips
- ½ cup white sugar
- ½ teaspoon baking powder
- 1 ½ cups all-purpose flour
- 1 egg

Directions:

1. Mix the egg and sugar in a container until volume increases to twice what it was.
2. Put in the coconut oil and milk and mix thoroughly.
3. Stir in the remaining ingredients then drop spoonfuls of batter on a baking tray coated with baking paper.
4. Preheat your oven and bake the cookies at 350F for about ten minutes or until it rises and appears golden.

5. Let cool in the pan before you serve.

Nutritional Content of One Serving:

Calories: 96 ‖ Fat: 3.9g ‖ Protein: 1.6g ‖ Carbohydrates: 14.4g

BUTTER VANILLA COOKIES

Total Time Taken: 1 hour
Yield: 30 Servings
Ingredients:

- ¼ cup cornstarch
- ¼ teaspoon salt
- ½ cup powdered sugar
- 1 cup butter, softened
- 1 egg
- 1 tablespoon vanilla extract
- 2 cups all-purpose flour

Directions:

1. Mix the butter and sugar in a container until fluffy and creamy.
2. Put in the egg and vanilla and mix thoroughly.
3. Fold in the flour, cornstarch and salt and mix thoroughly.
4. Drop spoonfuls of batter on a baking sheet coated with baking paper.
5. Pre-heat the oven and bake at 350F for about fifteen minutes or until a golden-brown colour is achieved on the edges.
6. These cookies taste best chilled.

Nutritional Content of One Serving:

Calories: 100 ‖ Fat: 6.4g ‖ Protein: 1.1g ‖ Carbohydrates: 9.4g

LEMONY LAVENDER COOKIES

Total Time Taken: 1 ¼ hours
Yield: 25 Servings
Ingredients:

- ½ cup butter, softened
- ½ cup white sugar
- ½ teaspoon baking soda
- ½ teaspoon salt
- 1 cup all-purpose flour
- 1 cup almond flour
- 1 egg
- 1 tablespoon lemon zest
- 1 teaspoon lavender buds
- 2 tablespoons honey

Directions:

1. Mix the butter, honey, egg, lemon zest, sugar and lavender in a container until pale and light.
2. Put in the rest of the ingredients and mix using a spatula.
3. Drop spoonfuls of batter on a baking tray coated with baking paper.
4. Preheat your oven and bake the cookies at 350F for about fifteen minutes or until a golden-brown colour is achieved on the edges.
5. These cookies taste best chilled.

Nutritional Content of One Serving:

Calories: 82 ‖ Fat: 4.5g ‖ Protein: 1.1g ‖ Carbohydrates: 9.9g

LEMON RICOTTA COOKIES

Total Time Taken: 2 hours
Yield: 40 Servings
Ingredients:

- ¼ cup butter, softened
- ½ teaspoon salt
- 1 cup ricotta cheese
- 1 cup white sugar
- 1 tablespoon lemon zest
- 1 teaspoon baking powder
- 2 eggs
- 2 tablespoons lemon juice 2 ½ cups all-purpose flour

Directions:

1. Mix the cheese, sugar, eggs and butter in a container until creamy.
2. Put in the lemon zest and lemon juice then fold in the flour, salt and baking powder.
3. Drop spoonfuls of baking batter on a baking tray covered with parchment paper.
4. Preheat your oven and bake the cookies at 350F for about fifteen minutes or until a golden-brown colour is achieved on the edges.
5. These cookies taste best chilled.

Nutritional Content of One Serving:

Calories: 69 ‖ Fat: 1.9g ‖ Protein: 1.8g ‖ Carbohydrates: 11.4g

LEMON POPPY SEED COOKIES

Total Time Taken: 1 hour
Yield: 20 Servings
Ingredients:

- ¼ cup butter, softened
- ¼ cup coconut oil
- ¼ cup cornstarch
- ¼ teaspoon salt
- ½ teaspoon baking soda
- 1 cup all-purpose flour
- 1 egg
- 1 tablespoon lemon zest
- 2 tablespoons lemon juice
- 2 tablespoons poppy seeds
- 2/3 cup white sugar

Directions:

1. Mix the butter, coconut oil and sugar in a container until fluffy and pale.
2. Put in the egg, lemon zest and lemon juice and mix thoroughly.
3. Fold in the remaining ingredients and mix using a spatula.
4. Drop spoonfuls of batter on baking trays coated with baking paper.

5. Preheat your oven and bake the cookies at 350F for about fifteen minutes or until a golden-brown colour is achieved or until a golden-brown colour is achieved on the edges.
6. These cookies taste best chilled.

Nutritional Content of One Serving:

Calories: 106 ‖ Fat: 5.7g ‖ Protein: 1.1g ‖ Carbohydrates: 13.2g

LAYERED CHOCOLATE CHIP COOKIES

Total Time Taken: 1 ¼ hours

Yield: 30 Servings

Ingredients:

- ¼ cup dark brown sugar
- ½ teaspoon salt
- ¾ cup light brown sugar
- 1 cup butter, softened
- 1 cup dark chocolate chips
- 1 teaspoon baking soda
- 1 teaspoon vanilla extract
- 2 ¼ cups all-purpose flour
- 2 eggs

Directions:

1. Mix the butter and sugars in a container until fluffy and pale.
2. Put in the eggs and mix thoroughly then fold in the remaining ingredients.
3. Drop spoonfuls of batter on baking trays covered with parchment paper.
4. Preheat your oven and bake the cookies at 350F for about thirteen minutes or until a golden-brown colour is achieved.
5. These cookies taste best chilled.

Nutritional Content of One Serving:

Calories: 130 ‖ Fat: 7.6g ‖ Protein: 1.7g ‖ Carbohydrates: 14.6g

ICING DECORATED COOKIES

Total Time Taken: 1 ¼ hours
Yield: 20 Servings
Ingredients:

Cookies:

- ¼ teaspoon salt
- ½ cup butter, softened
- ½ cup powdered sugar
- ½ teaspoon baking powder
- 1 ½ cups all-purpose flour
- 1 egg yolk

Icing:

- ¼ teaspoon vanilla extract
- 1 cup powdered sugar
- 1 egg white

Directions:

1. For the cookies, combine the butter and sugar in a container until fluffy and pale.
2. Put in the egg yolk and mix thoroughly then fold in the flour, salt and baking powder.
3. Transfer the dough to a floured working surface and roll the dough into slim sheet.
4. Cut into small cookies with a cookie cutter and arrange the cookies on a baking tray coated with baking paper.
5. Preheat your oven and bake the cookies at 350F for about ten minutes or until a golden-brown colour is achieved on the edges.
6. For the icing, combine the sugar, egg white and vanilla in a container.
7. Spoon the icing in a small piping bag and garnish the chilled cookies with it.

Nutritional Content of One Serving:

Calories: 114 ‖ Fat: 4.9g ‖ Protein: 1.3g ‖ Carbohydrates: 16.2g

HONEY LEMON COOKIES

Total Time Taken: 1 ¼ hours

Yield: 40 Servings

Ingredients:

- ¼ cup honey
- ½ teaspoon salt
- ¾ cup white sugar
- 1 cup butter, softened
- 1 egg
- 1 lemon, zested and juiced
- 1 teaspoon baking soda
- 3 cups all-purpose flour

Directions:

1. Sift the flour, baking soda and salt in a container.
2. In a separate container, combine the butter, sugar and honey and mix thoroughly.
3. Stir in the lemon zest and juice, as well as the egg.
4. Fold in the flour mixture then roll the dough into a slim sheet over a floured working surface.
5. Cut the cookies using a cookie cutter of your choices.
6. Put the cookies in the preheated oven at 350F for about fifteen minutes or until a golden-brown colour is achieved on the edges.
7. These cookies taste best chilled.

Nutritional Content of One Serving:

Calories: 97 ‖ Fat: 4.8g ‖ Protein: 1.2g ‖ Carbohydrates: 12.8g

HONEY CORNFLAKE COOKIES

Total Time Taken: 1 ¼ hours

Yield: 20 Servings

Ingredients:

- ¼ teaspoon salt
- ½ cup honey
- ½ cup light brown sugar
- 1 ¾ cups all-purpose flour

- 1 cup cornflakes
- 1 egg
- 1 teaspoon baking powder
- 1 teaspoon vanilla extract
- 2 tablespoons pine nuts
- 2/3 cup butter, softened

Directions:

1. Mix the butter, honey and sugar in a container.
2. Stir in the egg and vanilla and mix thoroughly then fold in the remaining ingredients.
3. Drop spoonfuls of batter on a baking sheet coated with baking paper.
4. Pre-heat the oven and bake at 350F for about fifteen minutes or until a golden-brown colour is achieved on the edges.
5. These cookies taste best chilled.

Nutritional Content of One Serving:

Calories: 148 ‖ Fat: 7.1g ‖ Protein: 1.7g ‖ Carbohydrates: 20.4g

HEALTHY BANANA COOKIES

Total Time Taken: 1 hour
Yield: 25 Servings
Ingredients:

- ¼ cup coconut flakes
- ¼ cup coconut oil, melted
- ¼ cup dried cranberries
- ¼ cup dried mango, chopped
- 1 cup dates, pitted and chopped
- 2 cups rolled oats
- 4 ripe bananas, mashed

Directions:

1. Mix the bananas and oil then mix in the rest of the ingredients.
2. Drop spoonfuls of batter on baking trays coated with baking paper.
3. Pre-heat the oven and bake at 350F for about fifteen minutes or until a golden-brown colour is achieved.

4. These cookies taste best chilled.

Nutritional Content of One Serving:

Calories: 114 ‖ Fat: 3.0g ‖ Protein: 1.3g ‖ Carbohydrates: 21.8g

HAZELNUT CHOCOLATE CHIP COOKIES

Total Time Taken: 1 ¼ hours
Yield: 30 Servings

Ingredients:

- ¼ cup sour cream
- ½ cup mini chocolate chip cookies
- ½ cup rolled oats, ground
- ½ teaspoon salt
- 1 cup butter, softened
- 1 cup ground hazelnuts
- 1 cup light brown sugar
- 1 egg
- 1 teaspoon baking powder
- 1 teaspoon vanilla extract
- 2 cups all-purpose flour

Directions:

1. Mix the butter and sugar in a container until creamy and fluffy.
2. Put in the egg and vanilla and sour cream and mix thoroughly the mix in the dry ingredients and chocolate chips.
3. Transfer the dough to a floured working surface and roll it into a slim sheet.
4. Cut into small cookies with your cookie cutters and place the cookies on baking trays coated with baking paper.
5. Preheat your oven and bake the cookies at 350F for about fifteen minutes or until a golden-brown colour is achieved on the edges.
6. These cookies taste best chilled.

Nutritional Content of One Serving:

Calories: 135 ‖ Fat: 8.6g ‖ Protein: 1.8g ‖ Carbohydrates: 13.1g

GOOEY CHOCOLATE CHERRY COOKIES

Total Time Taken: 1 hour
Yield: 20 Servings
Ingredients:

- ¼ cup white sugar
- ½ cup butter, melted
- ½ cup dark chocolate chips
- ½ cup glace cherries, halved
- ½ cup muscovado sugar
- 1 ½ cups all-purpose flour
- 1 egg
- 2 tablespoons cocoa powder

Directions:

1. Combine all the ingredients in a container using a spatula.
2. Drop spoonfuls of batter on a baking tray coated with baking paper.
3. Pre-heat the oven and bake at 350F for about ten minutes.
4. These cookies taste best chilled.

Nutritional Content of One Serving:

Calories: 128 ‖ Fat: 5.8g ‖ Protein: 1.7g ‖ Carbohydrates: 18.2g

GINGERSNAP COOKIES

Total Time Taken: 1 hour
Yield: 20 Servings
Ingredients:

- ¼ cup molasses
- ¼ teaspoon salt
- ½ teaspoon baking powder
- ½ teaspoon cinnamon powder
- ¾ cup canola oil
- ¾ cup light brown sugar
- 1 egg
- 1 teaspoon baking soda

- 1 teaspoon ground ginger
- 2 cups all-purpose flour

Directions:

1. Mix the oil, molasses and sugar in a container.
2. Put in the egg and stir until creamy and pale.
3. Fold in the remaining ingredients then form small balls and place them on baking trays coated with baking paper.
4. Preheat your oven and bake the cookies at 350F for about fifteen minutes or until crisp and fragrant.
5. These cookies taste best chilled.

Nutritional Content of One Serving:

Calories: 154 ‖ Fat: 8.5g ‖ Protein: 1.6g ‖ Carbohydrates: 18.1g

GINGERBREAD COOKIES

Total Time Taken: 1 ¼ hours

Yield: 30 Servings

Ingredients:

- ¼ teaspoon salt
- ½ cup golden syrup
- ½ cup white sugar
- ½ teaspoon ground cardamom
- 1 cup butter, softened
- 1 egg
- 1 teaspoon baking soda
- 1 teaspoon cinnamon powder
- 1 teaspoon ground ginger
- 2 cups all-purpose flour
- 2 tablespoons dark molasses

Directions:

1. Mix the butter, golden syrup, sugar and molasses in a container until fluffy and pale.
2. Put in the egg and mix thoroughly then fold in the flour, spices, baking soda and salt.

3. Make small balls of dough and arrange them on a baking sheet coated with baking paper.
4. Pre-heat the oven and bake at 350F for fifteen minutes or until it is aromatic and appears golden.
5. These cookies taste best chilled.

Nutritional Content of One Serving:

Calories: 119 ‖ Fat: 6.4g ‖ Protein: 1.1g ‖ Carbohydrates: 15.0g

GINGERBREAD COOKIES

Total Time Taken: 1 ¼ hours
Yield: 20 Servings

Ingredients:

- ¼ cup molasses
- ¼ teaspoon salt
- ½ cup butter, softened
- ½ cup ground almonds
- ½ cup light brown sugar
- ½ teaspoon baking soda
- ½ teaspoon cinnamon powder
- ½ teaspoon ground cloves
- ½ teaspoon ground ginger
- 1 egg
- 2 cups all-purpose flour

Directions:

1. Mix the butter, molasses and sugar in a container until pale and creamy.
2. Put in the egg and mix thoroughly then mix in the rest of the ingredients.
3. Make small balls of dough and place them on a baking tray coated with baking paper.
4. Preheat your oven and bake the cookies at 350F for about thirteen minutes or until aromatic, risen and golden.
5. These cookies taste best chilled.

Nutritional Content of One Serving:

Calories: 129 ‖ Fat: 6.2g ‖ Protein: 2.1g ‖ Carbohydrates: 16.8g

GINGER QUINOA COOKIES

Total Time Taken: 1 ¼ hours

Yield: 30 Servings

Ingredients:

- ¼ cup quinoa flakes
- ¼ cup quinoa flour
- ¼ teaspoon salt
- ½ cup almond flour
- ½ cup coconut oil, melted
- ½ cup light brown sugar
- ½ teaspoon baking soda
- ½ teaspoon cinnamon powder
- ½ teaspoon ground ginger
- 1 cup all-purpose flour
- 1 egg
- 2 tablespoons butter, softened
- 2 tablespoons molasses

Directions:

1. Mix the coconut oil and butter, molasses and sugar in a container until creamy and fluffy.
2. Put in the egg and mix thoroughly.
3. Stir in the remaining ingredients then drop spoonfuls of batter on a baking sheet coated with baking paper.
4. Preheat your oven and bake the cookies at 350F for about fifteen minutes or until a golden-brown colour is achieved on the edges.
5. These cookies taste best chilled.

Nutritional Content of One Serving:

Calories: 79 ‖ Fat: 5.0g ‖ Protein: 1.2g ‖ Carbohydrates: 7.6g

GINGER CHOCOLATE OATMEAL COOKIES

Total Time Taken: 1 ¼ hours
Yield: 30 Servings

Ingredients:

- ¼ teaspoon salt
- ½ teaspoon baking soda
- ½ teaspoon cinnamon powder
- 1 cup all-purpose flour
- 1 cup light brown sugar
- 1 cup rolled oats
- 1 egg
- 1 teaspoon grated ginger
- 2 tablespoons cocoa powder
- 2/3 cup butter, softened

Directions:

1. Mix the butter and sugar until fluffy and creamy. Stir in the egg and mix thoroughly.
2. Put in the rest of the ingredients and mix using a spatula.
3. Drop spoonfuls of batter on a baking sheet coated with baking paper.
4. Pre-heat the oven and bake at 350F for fifteen minutes.
5. These cookies taste best chilled.

Nutritional Content of One Serving:

Calories: 83 ‖ Fat: 4.5g ‖ Protein: 1.1g ‖ Carbohydrates: 10.0g

GINGER BUTTER COOKIES

Total Time Taken: 1 ¼ hours
Yield: 20 Servings

Ingredients:

- ¼ teaspoon salt
- ½ cup butter, softened
- ½ teaspoon baking soda
- ½ teaspoon ground cardamom
- ¾ cup light brown sugar
- 1 ½ cups all-purpose flour

- 1 egg
- 1 teaspoon ground ginger
- 1 teaspoon vanilla extract

Directions:

1. Mix the butter and sugar until fluffy and pale. Put in the egg and vanilla and mix thoroughly.
2. Stir in the flour, ginger, cardamom, salt and baking soda.
3. Drop spoonfuls of batter on baking trays coated with baking paper.
4. Preheat your oven and bake the cookies at 350F for about fifteen minutes or until a golden-brown colour is achieved and crisp on the edges.
5. These cookies taste best chilled.

Nutritional Content of One Serving:

Calories: 100 ‖ Fat: 4.9g ‖ Protein: 1.3g ‖ Carbohydrates: 12.6g

GINGER ALMOND BISCOTTI

Total Time Taken: 1 ¼ hours

Yield: 20 Servings

Ingredients:

- ¼ teaspoon baking soda
- ½ cup blanched almonds
- ½ cup butter, softened
- ½ teaspoon salt
- ¾ cup white sugar
- 1 teaspoon baking powder
- 1 teaspoon ground ginger
- 1 teaspoon vanilla extract
- 2 cups all-purpose flour
- 2 eggs
- 2 tablespoons dark brown sugar
- 2 tablespoons molasses

Directions:

1. Mix the sugars, molasses, eggs and butter in a container until creamy.
2. Put in the vanilla then fold in the remaining ingredients.

3. Transfer the dough to a baking tray covered with parchment paper and shape it into a log.
4. Preheat your oven and bake the log at 350F for fifteen minutes or until a golden-brown colour is achieved on the edges.
5. When finished, let cool down slightly then cut the log into thin slices and place them back on the baking tray with the cut facing up.
6. Preheat your oven and bake the cookies at 350F for another ten to fifteen minutes.
7. Serve the biscotti chilled.

Nutritional Content of One Serving:

Calories: 145 ‖ Fat: 6.4g ‖ Protein: 2.4g ‖ Carbohydrates: 20.2g

GERMAN CHOCOLATE COOKIES

Total Time Taken: 1 ¼ hours
Yield: 30 Servings

Ingredients:

- ¼ cup cocoa powder
- ½ cup coconut flakes
- ½ cup dark chocolate chips
- ½ cup white sugar
- ½ teaspoon salt
- 1 cup butter, softened
- 1 cup light brown sugar
- 1 cup pecans, chopped
- 1 teaspoon baking soda
- 2 ¼ cups all-purpose flour
- 2 eggs

Directions:

1. Mix the butter and sugars in a container until pale and creamy.
2. Put in the eggs and mix thoroughly then fold in the flour, cocoa powder, baking soda and salt.
3. Fold in the chocolate chips, coconut flakes and pecans.
4. Drop spoonfuls of batter on baking trays coated with baking paper.

5. Preheat your oven and bake the cookies at 350F for about fifteen minutes or until risen.
6. These cookies taste best chilled.

Nutritional Content of One Serving:

Calories: 142 || Fat: 7.9g || Protein: 1.8g || Carbohydrates: 17.2g

FUDGY CHOCOLATE COOKIES

Total Time Taken: 1 ¼ hours
Yield: 30 Servings

Ingredients:

- ¼ teaspoon salt
- ½ cup butter
- ½ cup light brown sugar
- 1 ½ cups dark chocolate chips
- 1 teaspoon baking powder
- 1 teaspoon vanilla extract
- 2 eggs
- 2 tablespoons white sugar
- 2/3 cup all-purpose flour

Directions:

1. Melt the butter and chocolate in a heatproof container over a hot water bath.
2. Mix the eggs and sugars in a container until fluffy and pale.
3. Stir in the chocolate and mix using a spatula.
4. Fold in the flour, baking powder and salt then drop spoonfuls of batter in a baking sheet coated with baking paper.
5. Preheat your oven and bake the cookies at 350F for about thirteen minutes.
6. These cookies taste best chilled.

Nutritional Content of One Serving:

Calories: 82 || Fat: 5.0g || Protein: 1.1g || Carbohydrates: 9.4g

FRUITY COOKIES

Total Time Taken: 1 ½ hours

Yield: 30 Servings

Ingredients:

- 2 tablespoons molasses
- 2 tablespoons golden syrup
- 1 egg
- ¼ cup milk
- 2 cups all-purpose flour
- ¼ teaspoon salt
- 1 teaspoon baking soda
- ½ cup sultanas
- ½ cup dried cranberries
- ½ cup raisins
- ½ cup dried apricots, chopped
- ¼ cup Grand Marnier
- 2/3 cup butter, softened
- 2/3 cup white sugar

Directions:

1. Mix the fruits with Grand Marnier in a container and allow to soak up for about half an hour.
2. Mix the butter, sugar, molasses and golden syrup in a container until pale.
3. Put in the egg and milk and mix thoroughly.
4. Put in the dry ingredients then fold in the fruits.
5. Drop spoonfuls of batter on a baking sheet coated with baking paper and preheat your oven and bake the cookies at 350F for fifteen minutes.
6. Let the cookies cool down before you serve.

Nutritional Content of One Serving:

Calories: 111 ‖ Fat: 4.4g ‖ Protein: 1.3g ‖ Carbohydrates: 15.7g

FRESH BLUEBERRY COOKIES

Total Time Taken: 1 ½ hours
Yield: 30 Servings

Ingredients:

- ¼ cup whole milk
- ½ teaspoon baking soda
- ½ teaspoon salt
- 1 cup butter, softened
- 1 cup fresh blueberries
- 1 cup powdered sugar
- 1 egg
- 1 tablespoon lemon zest
- 1 teaspoon vanilla extract
- 2 cups all-purpose flour

Directions:

1. Mix the butter, vanilla and sugar in a container until fluffy and light.
2. Put in the egg, milk and lemon zest and mix thoroughly.
3. Stir in the flour, salt and baking soda and mix using a spatula then fold in the blueberries.
4. Drop spoonfuls of batter on a baking tray covered with parchment paper.
5. Pre-heat the oven and bake at 350F for about thirteen minutes or until a golden-brown colour is achieved on the edges.
6. These cookies taste best chilled.

Nutritional Content of One Serving:

Calories: 107 ‖ Fat: 6.5g ‖ Protein: 1.2g ‖ Carbohydrates: 11.2g

FOUR INGREDIENT PEANUT BUTTER COOKIES

Total Time Taken: 1 hour
Yield: 20 Servings
Ingredients:

- 1 cup rolled oats
- 1 cup smooth peanut butter

- 1 egg
- 2/3 cup light brown sugar

Directions:

1. Mix the peanut butter, egg and sugar in a container until creamy then put in the oats.
2. Drop spoonfuls of batter on a baking tray coated with baking paper.
3. Preheat your oven and bake the cookies at 350F for about fifteen minutes or until a golden-brown colour is achieved on the edges.
4. These cookies taste best chilled.

Nutritional Content of One Serving:

Calories: 113 ‖ Fat: 7.0g ‖ Protein: 4.1g ‖ Carbohydrates: 10.1g

FLOURLESS PEANUT BUTTER COOKIES

Total Time Taken: 1 hour
Yield: 30 Servings
Ingredients:

- ½ teaspoon salt
- 1 cup light brown sugar
- 2 cups smooth peanut butter
- 2 eggs

Directions:

1. Combine all the ingredients in a container until the desired smoothness is achieved.
2. Drop spoonfuls of mixture on a baking sheet coated with baking paper.
3. Score the top of each cookie with a fork then preheat your oven and bake the cookies at 350F for about ten minutes.
4. These cookies taste best chilled.

Nutritional Content of One Serving:

Calories: 124 ‖ Fat: 9.0g ‖ Protein: 4.7g ‖ Carbohydrates: 8.1g

FIG AND ALMOND COOKIES

Total Time Taken: 1 ¼ hours

Yield: 20 Servings

Ingredients:

- ½ cup butter, softened
- ½ cup ground almonds
- ½ teaspoon baking soda
- ½ teaspoon salt
- 1 ½ cups dried figs, chopped
- 1 ¾ cups all-purpose flour
- 1 cup powdered sugar
- 1 egg
- 1 teaspoon vanilla extract

Directions:

1. Mix the butter, sugar and vanilla in a container until fluffy and pale.
2. Put in the egg and mix thoroughly then fold in the remaining ingredients.
3. Drop spoonfuls of batter on a baking tray coated with baking paper.
4. Pre-heat the oven and bake at 350F for about fifteen minutes or until a golden-brown colour is achieved on the edges and slightly crisp.
5. These cookies taste best chilled.

Nutritional Content of One Serving:

Calories: 159 ‖ Fat: 6.3g ‖ Protein: 2.5g ‖ Carbohydrates: 24.4g

EVERYTHING-BUT-THE-KITCHEN-SINK COOKIES

Total Time Taken: 1 ¼ hours

Yield: 20 Servings

Ingredients:

- ¼ cup applesauce
- ¼ cup coconut oil, melted
- ¼ cup dark chocolate chips
- ¼ cup dried apricots, chopped
- ¼ cup dried cranberries

- ¼ cup shredded coconut
- ¼ teaspoon cinnamon powder
- ½ cup walnuts, chopped
- ½ teaspoon ground ginger
- ½ teaspoon salt
- 1 cup rolled oats
- 1 cup whole wheat flour
- 1 egg
- 1 teaspoon vanilla extract
- 2 tablespoons butter, softened

Directions:

1. Mix the coconut oil, butter, vanilla, egg and applesauce in a container.
2. Put in the flour, oats, spices and salt then fold in the walnuts, apricots, cranberries, apricots, chocolate chips and coconut.
3. Drop spoonfuls of batter on baking trays coated with baking paper.
4. Preheat your oven and bake the cookies at 350F for about fifteen minutes or until a golden-brown colour is achieved and crisp on the edges.
5. These cookies taste best chilled.

Nutritional Content of One Serving:

Calories: 109 ‖ Fat: 7.0g ‖ Protein: 2.4g ‖ Carbohydrates: 9.8g

EGGLESS COOKIES

Total Time Taken: 1 hour
Yield: 20 Servings
Ingredients:

- ¼ cup whole milk
- ¼ teaspoon salt
- ½ cup butter, melted
- ½ cup dried cranberries
- ½ cup light brown sugar
- ½ teaspoon baking soda
- 1 ½ cups all-purpose flour

Directions:

1. Mix the flour, salt, baking soda and sugar in a container.
2. Stir in the butter and milk and mix using a spatula.
3. Fold in the cranberries then drop spoonfuls of batter on a baking sheet coated with baking paper.
4. Pre-heat the oven and bake at 350F for about fifteen minutes or until a golden-brown colour is achieved on the edges.
5. These cookies taste best chilled.

Nutritional Content of One Serving:

Calories: 92 ‖ Fat: 4.8g ‖ Protein: 1.1g ‖ Carbohydrates: 11.1g

EARL GREY COOKIES

Total Time Taken: 1 ¼ hours

Yield: 20 Servings

Ingredients:

- ½ cup powdered sugar
- ½ teaspoon salt
- 1 cup butter, softened
- 1 egg
- 1 tablespoon loose Earl grey leaves
- 1 teaspoon baking powder
- 1 teaspoon vanilla extract
- 2 cups all-purpose flour

Directions:

1. Mix the butter and sugar in a container until fluffy and pale.
2. Put in the egg and vanilla and mix thoroughly.
3. Stir in the remaining ingredients and mix using a spatula.
4. Transfer the dough to a floured working surface and roll it into a slim sheet.
5. Cut into small cookies with your cookie cutters and place them on a baking tray coated with baking paper.
6. Pre-heat the oven and bake at 350F for about ten minutes or until a golden-brown colour is achieved on the edges.
7. These cookies taste best chilled.

Nutritional Content of One Serving:

Calories: 143 ‖ Fat: 9.6g ‖ Protein: 1.7g ‖ Carbohydrates: 12.7g

DRIED PRUNE OATMEAL COOKIES

Total Time Taken: 1 ¼ hours

Yield: 25 Servings

Ingredients:

- ¼ teaspoon salt
- ½ cup coconut oil, melted
- ½ cup maple syrup
- ½ teaspoon baking soda
- ¾ cup all-purpose flour
- 1 cup dried prunes, chopped
- 1 teaspoon lemon juice
- 1 teaspoon vanilla extract
- 2 cups rolled oats

Directions:

1. Mix the prunes, oats, flour, baking soda and salt in a container.
2. Put in the rest of the ingredients and mix using a spatula.
3. Make small balls of dough and arrange them on a baking sheet coated with baking paper.
4. Preheat your oven and bake the cookies at 350F for about fifteen minutes or until a golden-brown colour is achieved.
5. These cookies taste best chilled.

Nutritional Content of One Serving:

Calories: 109 ‖ Fat: 4.9g ‖ Protein: 1.4g ‖ Carbohydrates: 15.9g

DRIED FRUIT WHOLESOME COOKIES

Total Time Taken: 1 ¼ hours

Yield: 20 Servings

Ingredients:

- ¼ cup applesauce
- ¼ cup coconut oil, melted
- ¼ cup dried apricots, chopped
- ¼ cup dried cranberries
- ¼ cup golden raisins
- ¼ cup rolled oats
- ¼ teaspoon salt
- ½ teaspoon baking soda
- ½ teaspoon cinnamon powder
- 1 ¼ cups whole wheat flour
- 1 egg
- 1 teaspoon vanilla extract

Directions:

1. Mix the coconut oil, applesauce, egg and vanilla and mix thoroughly.
2. Stir in the flour, salt, baking soda and cinnamon then put in the oats and dried fruits.
3. Drop spoonfuls of batter on a baking tray coated with baking paper.
4. Preheat your oven and bake the cookies at 350F for about ten minutes or until a golden-brown colour is achieved and crisp on the edges.
5. These cookies taste best chilled.

Nutritional Content of One Serving:

Calories: 68 ‖ Fat: 3.1g ‖ Protein: 1.3g ‖ Carbohydrates: 8.8g

DRIED CRANBERRY OATMEAL COOKIES

Total Time Taken: 1 ¼ hours

Yield: 20 Servings

Ingredients:

- ¼ teaspoon salt
- ½ cup butter, softened, melted
- ½ cup dried cranberries
- ½ cup light brown sugar
- ½ teaspoon cinnamon powder
- ½ teaspoon ground ginger

- 1 cup all-purpose flour
- 1 cup rolled oats
- 1 teaspoon baking soda
- 4 tablespoons golden syrup

Directions:

1. Mix the oats, flour, baking soda, spices, salt and cranberries in a container.
2. Stir in the butter, golden syrup and sugar and mix thoroughly.
3. Make small balls for dough and place the balls on a baking sheet coated with baking paper.
4. Flatten the cookies slightly and preheat your oven and bake at 350F for fifteen minutes or until a golden-brown colour is achieved and fragrant.
5. These cookies taste best chilled.

Nutritional Content of One Serving:

Calories: 106 ‖ Fat: 4.9g ‖ Protein: 1.2g ‖ Carbohydrates: 14.5g

DOUBLE GINGER COOKIES

Total Time Taken: 1 ¼ hours
Yield: 20 Servings

Ingredients:

- ¼ cup candied ginger, chopped
- ¼ teaspoon salt
- ½ teaspoon baking soda
- ½ teaspoon cinnamon powder
- 1 teaspoon ground ginger
- 1 teaspoon vanilla extract
- 1/3 cup butter, softened
- 2 cups all-purpose flour
- 2 tablespoons golden syrup
- 2/3 cup light brown sugar

Directions:

1. Sift the flour, ginger, cinnamon, salt and baking soda in a container.
2. Mix the butter, sugar, vanilla and syrup in a container until fluffy and pale.
3. Fold in the flour then put in the candied ginger.

4. Drop spoonfuls of batter on a baking sheet coated with baking paper.
5. Pre-heat the oven and bake at 350F for about fifteen minutes or until it rises and looks golden brown.
6. These cookies taste best chilled.

Nutritional Content of One Serving:

Calories: 98 || Fat: 3.2g || Protein: 1.4g || Carbohydrates: 16.1g

DOUBLE CHOCOLATE ESPRESSO COOKIES

Total Time Taken: 1 hour
Yield: 20 Servings
Ingredients:

- 2 eggs
- 1 teaspoon vanilla extract
- ¼ cup coconut oil, melted
- 1 teaspoon instant coffee
- 6 oz. dark chocolate
- ¼ cup butter
- 2 tablespoons all-purpose flour
- ¼ teaspoon salt
- 2/3 cup white sugar

Directions:

1. Mix the chocolate and butter in a heatproof container and place over a hot water bath. Melt them together until smooth and melted.
2. Mix the eggs and sugar in a container until fluffy and pale. Put in the vanilla and oil and stir lightly. Stir in the coffee.
3. Put in the melted chocolate and stir lightly then fold in the flour and salt.
4. Drop spoonfuls of batter on a baking tray coated with baking paper.
5. Pre-heat the oven and bake at 350F for about ten minutes or until set.
6. These cookies taste best chilled.

Nutritional Content of One Serving:

Calories: 124 || Fat: 8.0g || Protein: 1.3g || Carbohydrates: 12.4g

DOUBLE CHOCOLATE COOKIES

Total Time Taken: 1 ½ hours
Yield: 30 Servings

Ingredients:

- ¼ teaspoon salt
- ½ cup cocoa powder
- ½ cup mini chocolate chips
- ½ teaspoon baking powder
- 1 ½ cups all-purpose flour
- 1 cup white sugar
- 1 egg
- 1 teaspoon vanilla extract
- 2/3 cup butter, softened

Directions:

1. Mix the butter and sugar until fluffy and creamy.
2. Put in the egg and vanilla and mix thoroughly then fold in the remaining ingredients and mix thoroughly.
3. Cover the dough with plastic wrap and store in the refrigerator for about half an hour.
4. Transfer the dough to a floured working surface and roll it into a slim sheet.
5. Cut into small cookies using a cookie cutter of your choices and place them on a baking pan coated with baking paper.
6. Pre-heat the oven and bake at 350F for about fifteen minutes.
7. These cookies taste best chilled.

Nutritional Content of One Serving:

Calories: 93 ‖ Fat: 4.6g ‖ Protein: 1.2g ‖ Carbohydrates: 12.8g

DATE PECAN GINGER COOKIES

Total Time Taken: 1 ½ hours
Yield: 30 Servings

Ingredients:

- ¼ teaspoon salt

- ½ cup olive oil
- ½ cup whole wheat flour
- 1 cup all-purpose flour
- 1 cup dates, pitted and chopped
- 1 cup light brown sugar
- 1 cup pecans, chopped
- 1 egg
- 1 teaspoon baking powder
- 1 teaspoon grated ginger
- 1 teaspoon vanilla extract

Directions:

1. Mix the oil and sugar in a container until fluffy and pale.
2. Put in the vanilla and ginger and mix thoroughly then fold in the flours, baking powder and salt.
3. Stir in the dates and pecans then drop spoonfuls of batter on a baking sheet coated with baking paper.
4. Preheat your oven and bake the cookies at 350F for fifteen minutes or until a golden-brown colour is achieved on the edges.
5. These cookies taste best chilled.

Nutritional Content of One Serving:

Calories: 93 ‖ Fat: 3.9g ‖ Protein: 1.0g ‖ Carbohydrates: 14.2g

CUSTARD POWDER COOKIES

Total Time Taken: 1 ¼ hours
Yield: 20 Servings

Ingredients:

- ¼ cup whole milk
- ¼ teaspoon salt
- ½ cup butter, softened
- ½ cup vanilla custard powder
- ½ cup white sugar
- 1 ½ cups all-purpose flour
- 1 teaspoon baking powder

- 1 teaspoon vanilla extract

Directions:

1. Mix the butter and sugar in a container until creamy and fluffy.
2. Stir in the milk and vanilla then fold in the remaining ingredients.
3. Drop spoonfuls of batter on a baking sheet coated with baking paper.
4. Preheat your oven and bake the cookies at 350F for about fifteen minutes or until a golden-brown colour is achieved on the edges.
5. These cookies taste best chilled.

Nutritional Content of One Serving:

Calories: 115 ‖ Fat: 4.8g ‖ Protein: 1.1g ‖ Carbohydrates: 17.3g

CRANBERRY BISCOTTI

Total Time Taken: 1 ½ hours
Yield: 20 Servings

Ingredients:

- ¼ teaspoon salt
- ½ cup butter, softened
- ½ cup white sugar
- ½ teaspoon baking soda
- 1 cup dried cranberries
- 1 egg
- 1 tablespoon lemon zest
- 2 cups all-purpose flour

Directions:

1. Mix the butter and sugar in a container until creamy and fluffy.
2. Put in the egg and lemon zest and mix thoroughly.
3. Stir in the flour, baking soda and salt then put in the cranberries.
4. Put the dough on a baking tray coated with baking paper. Shape the dough into a log and bake it in the preheated oven at 350F for fifteen minutes.
5. Remove the tray from the oven and allow it to cool down for about ten minutes. Cut the log into 1cm wide slices and place them back on the tray with the cut facing up.

6. Carry on baking for fifteen minutes or until a golden-brown colour is achieved and crisp.
7. Let cool before you serve or storing.

Nutritional Content of One Serving:

Calories: 111 ‖ Fat: 5.0g ‖ Protein: 1.6g ‖ Carbohydrates: 15.1g

CRACKED SUGAR COOKIES

Total Time Taken: 1 ¼ hours
Yield: 30 Servings

Ingredients:

- ½ teaspoon salt
- 1 cup butter, softened
- 1 cup powdered sugar
- 1 cup white sugar
- 1 teaspoon baking soda
- 1 teaspoon vanilla extract
- 2 ½ cups all-purpose flour
- 3 egg yolks

Directions:

1. Mix the butter and sugar in a container until creamy and fluffy.
2. Put in the egg yolks and mix thoroughly then mix in the vanilla.
3. Fold in the flour, baking soda and salt then form small balls of dough and roll them through powdered sugar.
4. Put the balls on a baking tray coated with baking paper.
5. Pre-heat the oven and bake at 350F for about fifteen minutes or until mildly golden brown.
6. These cookies taste best chilled, handling them with care.

Nutritional Content of One Serving:

Calories: 139 ‖ Fat: 6.7g ‖ Protein: 1.4g ‖ Carbohydrates: 18.7g

CORNFLAKE CHOCOLATE CHIP COOKIES

Total Time Taken: 1 hour

Yield: 20 Servings

Ingredients:

- ½ cup butter, softened
- ½ cup dark chocolate chips
- ½ teaspoon baking soda
- ¾ cup white sugar
- 1 ¼ cup all-purpose flour
- 1 cup cornflakes
- 1 egg
- 1 teaspoon vanilla extract
- 2/4 teaspoon salt

Directions:

1. Mix the butter, sugar and vanilla in a container until creamy and pale.
2. Put in the egg then mix in the flour, baking soda and salt.
3. Fold in the cornflakes and chocolate chips.
4. Drop spoonfuls of batter on a baking sheet coated with baking paper.
5. Preheat your oven and bake the cookies at 350F for about fifteen minutes or until a golden-brown colour is achieved on the edges.
6. These cookies taste best chilled.

Nutritional Content of One Serving:

Calories: 120 ‖ Fat: 5.7g ‖ Protein: 1.4g ‖ Carbohydrates: 16.7g

CONFETTI COOKIES

Total Time Taken: 1 ¼ hours

Yield: 20 Servings

Ingredients:

- 1 teaspoon vanilla extract
- 1 egg
- 2 cups all-purpose flour
- 1 teaspoon baking powder

- ¼ teaspoon salt
- ½ cup colourful sprinkles
- 2/3 cup butter, softened
- 2/3 cup white sugar

Directions:

1. Mix the butter with sugar and vanilla in a container until creamy and fluffy.
2. Stir in the egg and mix thoroughly then fold in the remaining ingredients.
3. Drop in the sprinkles and mix using a spatula.
4. Drop spoonfuls of batter on a baking sheet coated with baking paper.
5. Pre-heat the oven and bake at 350F for about fifteen minutes or until a golden-brown colour is achieved on the edges.
6. These cookies taste best chilled.

Nutritional Content of One Serving:

Calories: 136 ‖ Fat: 6.7g ‖ Protein: 1.7g ‖ Carbohydrates: 17.5g

COLORFUL CHOCOLATE COOKIES

Total Time Taken: 1 ¼ hors
Yield: 30 Servings

Ingredients:

- ½ cup cocoa powder
- ½ cup crushed candy cane cookies
- ½ cup M&M candies
- ½ teaspoon salt
- 1 cup butter, softened
- 1 cup light brown sugar
- 1 egg
- 1 teaspoon baking powder
- 1 teaspoon vanilla extract
- 2 cups all-purpose flour

Directions:

1. Mix the butter, sugar and vanilla and stir thoroughly until fluffy and pale.
2. Stir in the egg and mix thoroughly then put in the remaining ingredients.
3. Drop spoonfuls of batter on a baking tray coated with baking paper.

4. Pre-heat the oven and bake at 350F for about fifteen minutes.
5. Let the cookies cool in the pan before you serve.

Nutritional Content of One Serving:

Calories: 129 ‖ Fat: 7.4g ‖ Protein: 1.5g ‖ Carbohydrates: 14.8g

COFFEE SHORTBREAD COOKIES

Total Time Taken: 1 hour
Yield: 20 Servings
Ingredients:

- ½ cup butter, softened
- ½ cup powdered sugar
- ½ teaspoon baking powder
- ½ teaspoon salt
- 1 egg
- 1 teaspoon vanilla extract
- 2 cups all-purpose flour
- 2 teaspoons instant coffee

Directions:

1. Mix the butter, sugar and vanilla and stir until smooth and fluffy.
2. Put in the egg and mix thoroughly then fold in the flour, salt, baking powder and coffee.
3. Put the dough on a floured working surface and roll it into a slim sheet.
4. Cut into small cookies using a cookie cutter of your choices and position the cookies on a baking sheet coated with baking paper.
5. Preheat your oven and bake the cookies at 350F for about fifteen minutes or until it is aromatic and appears golden-brown on the edges.
6. Serve Chilled or store them in an airtight container.

Nutritional Content of One Serving:

Calories: 102 ‖ Fat: 5.0g ‖ Protein: 1.6g ‖ Carbohydrates: 12.6g

COFFEE GINGERSNAP COOKIES

Total Time Taken: 1 ¼ hours

Yield: 20 Servings

Ingredients:

- ¼ cup coconut oil
- ¼ teaspoon salt
- ½ cup butter, softened
- ½ teaspoon ground cardamom
- 1 cup light brown sugar
- 1 egg
- 1 teaspoon baking soda
- 1 teaspoon cinnamon powder
- 1 teaspoon ground ginger
- 1 teaspoon vanilla extract
- 2 cups all-purpose flour
- 2 teaspoons instant coffee

Directions:

1. Mix the butter, coconut oil and brown sugar in a container until fluffy and creamy.
2. Put in the egg and vanilla and mix thoroughly.
3. Fold in the remaining ingredients then drop spoonfuls of batter on a baking sheet coated with baking paper.
4. Pre-heat the oven and bake at 350F for fifteen minutes or until aromatic and crunchy.
5. These cookies taste best chilled.

Nutritional Content of One Serving:

Calories: 142 ‖ Fat: 7.7g ‖ Protein: 1.7g ‖ Carbohydrates: 16.8g

COCONUT SHORTBREAD COOKIES

Total Time Taken: 2 hours

Yield: 20 Servings

Ingredients:

- ¼ teaspoon baking powder
- ¼ teaspoon salt
- ½ cup powdered sugar
- 1 cup butter, softened
- 1 cup shredded coconut
- 1 egg
- 1 teaspoon coconut extract
- 2 cups all-purpose flour

Directions:

1. Mix the butter, sugar and coconut extract in a container.
2. Stir in the egg and mix thoroughly then put in the flour, salt, coconut and baking powder.
3. Wrap the dough in a plastic wrap and store in the refrigerator for about half an hour.
4. Transfer the dough to a working surface and roll it into a slim sheet.
5. Cut the dough into small cookies with a cookie cutter of your choice.
6. Put the cookies in a baking tray coated with baking paper.
7. Pre-heat the oven and bake at 350F for about fifteen minutes or until a golden-brown colour is achieved on the edges.
8. Best served chilled.

Nutritional Content of One Serving:

Calories: 157 ‖ Fat: 10.9g ‖ Protein: 1.8g ‖ Carbohydrates: 13.2g

COCONUT MACAROONS

Total Time Taken: 1 ½ hours
Yield: 20 Servings

Ingredients:

- ¼ teaspoon salt
- ½ cup all-purpose flour
- 1 can sweetened condensed milk
- 1 teaspoon vanilla extract
- 4 cups shredded coconut

Directions:

1. Mix the coconut, salt and flour in a container.
2. Put in the milk and vanilla and mix thoroughly.
3. Drop spoonfuls of mixture on baking trays coated with baking paper.
4. Preheat your oven and bake the cookies at 350F for fifteen minutes or until crisp and golden brown.
5. These cookies taste best chilled.

Nutritional Content of One Serving:

Calories: 118 ‖ Fat: 6.7g ‖ Protein: 2.1g ‖ Carbohydrates: 13.2g

COCONUT LIME BUTTER COOKIES

Total Time Taken: 1 ¼ hours
Yield: 30 Servings

Ingredients:

- ½ teaspoon baking powder
- ½ teaspoon salt
- 1 cup butter, softened
- 1 cup shredded coconut
- 1 cup white sugar
- 1 lime, zested and juiced
- 1 teaspoon coconut extract
- 2 cups all-purpose flour
- 2 egg yolks

Directions:

1. Mix the butter and sugar in a container until creamy and pale.
2. Put in the egg yolks, lime zest and lime juice, as well as the coconut extract.
3. Stir in the flour, salt, coconut and baking powder then transfer the dough on a floured working surface.
4. Roll the dough into a slim sheet then cut small cookies using a cookie cutter of your choice.
5. Put the cookies on a baking tray covered with parchment paper.
6. Preheat your oven and bake the cookies at 350F for about fifteen minutes or until a golden-brown colour is achieved on the edges.
7. These cookies taste best chilled.

Nutritional Content of One Serving:

Calories: 124 ‖ Fat: 7.4g ‖ Protein: 1.2g ‖ Carbohydrates: 13.8g

COCONUT FLORENTINE COOKIES

Total Time Taken: 1 ¼ hours
Yield: 25 Servings

Ingredients:

- ¼ cup honey
- ¼ teaspoon salt
- ½ cup light brown sugar
- 1 ½ cups sliced almonds
- 1 cup butter, softened
- 1 cup shredded coconut
- 4 tablespoons all-purpose flour

Directions:

1. Mix the butter, sugar and honey in a heatproof container over a hot water bath until smooth and melted.
2. Turn off the heat and put in the coconut, almonds, salt and flour.
3. Drop spoonfuls of batter on a baking tray coated with baking paper.
4. Spread the mixture slightly then preheat your oven and bake the cookies at 350F for about fifteen minutes or until a golden-brown colour is achieved and crisp.
5. Let the cookies cool down before you serve.

Nutritional Content of One Serving:

Calories: 135 ‖ Fat: 11.3g ‖ Protein: 1.5g ‖ Carbohydrates: 8.3g

COCONUT BUTTER COOKIES

Total Time Taken: 1 ¼ hours
Yield: 20 Servings

Ingredients:

- ¼ teaspoon salt
- ½ cup coconut butter, softened
- 1 cup shredded coconut
- 1 egg
- 1 teaspoon baking powder
- 1 teaspoon coconut extract
- 2 cups all-purpose flour
- 2 tablespoons coconut oil
- 2/3 cup white sugar

Directions:

1. Mix the coconut butter, coconut oil and sugar in a container until pale and creamy.
2. Put in the egg and coconut extract and mix thoroughly.
3. Stir in the flour, coconut, baking powder and salt then form small balls of dough.
4. Put the balls on baking trays coated with baking paper and preheat your oven and bake at 350F for about fifteen minutes or until a golden-brown colour is achieved,
5. When finished, transfer the cookies in a container and dust them with powdered sugar.
6. These cookies taste best chilled.

Nutritional Content of One Serving:

Calories: 100 ‖ Fat: 3.0g ‖ Protein: 1.7g ‖ Carbohydrates: 17.0g

CLOVE SUGAR COOKIES

Total Time Taken: 1 ¼ hours

Yield: 30 Servings

Ingredients:

- ¼ teaspoon salt
- ½ cup powdered sugar
- ½ teaspoon baking powder
- 1 cup butter, softened
- 1 cup ground hazelnuts

- 1 egg yolk
- 1 teaspoon ground whole cloves
- 1 teaspoon vanilla extract
- 2 cups all-purpose flour

Directions:

1. Mix the butter and sugar in a container until pale and fluffy.
2. Put in the vanilla and egg yolk and mix thoroughly.
3. Fold in the flour, hazelnuts, cloves, salt and baking powder.
4. Transfer the dough to a floured working surface then roll the dough into a slim sheet.
5. Cut into small cookies with a cookie cutter and place them on a baking tray coated with baking paper.
6. Preheat your oven and bake the cookies at 350F for about fifteen minutes or until a golden-brown colour is achieved and fragrant.
7. These cookies taste best chilled.

Nutritional Content of One Serving:

Calories: 115 ‖ Fat: 7.9g ‖ Protein: 1.5g ‖ Carbohydrates: 9.7g

CINNAMON SUGAR COOKIES

Total Time Taken: 1 ½ hours
Yield: 25 Servings

Ingredients:

- ¼ teaspoon salt
- ½ cup coconut oil, melted
- ½ cup light brown sugar
- 1 cup white sugar
- 1 teaspoon baking powder
- 1 teaspoon cinnamon powder
- 1 teaspoon vanilla extract
- 2 cups all-purpose flour
- 2 eggs

Directions:

1. Mix the brown sugar and cinnamon in a container and set aside for later.

2. Combine the eggs and sugar in a separate container and stir until volume increases to twice what it was.
3. Put in the coconut oil and vanilla and mix thoroughly.
4. Put in the flour, salt and baking powder and mix using a spatula.
5. Make small balls of dough and roll them through cinnamon sugar.
6. Preheat your oven and bake the cookies at 350F for about fifteen minutes or until a golden-brown colour is achieved and fragrant.
7. These cookies taste best chilled.

Nutritional Content of One Serving:

Calories: 121 ‖ Fat: 4.8g ‖ Protein: 1.5g ‖ Carbohydrates: 18.6g

CINNAMON SNAP COOKIES

Total Time Taken: 1 ¼ hours

Yield: 30 Servings

Ingredients:

- ¼ cup cocoa powder
- ½ teaspoon ground cloves
- ½ teaspoon ground ginger
- ½ teaspoon salt
- 1 cup butter, softened
- 1 egg
- 1 teaspoon baking soda
- 1 teaspoon cinnamon powder
- 1 teaspoon vanilla extract
- 2 cups all-purpose flour
- 2 tablespoons golden syrup
- 2/3 cup white sugar

Directions:

1. Mix the butter, sugar, vanilla and golden syrup in a container until pale and creamy.
2. Put in the egg and mix thoroughly then put in the flour mixture.
3. Make small balls of dough and place the cookies on a baking sheet coated with baking paper.

4. Preheat your oven and bake the cookies at 350F for about fifteen minutes until it is aromatic and appears golden brown.
5. These cookies taste best chilled.

Nutritional Content of One Serving:

Calories: 109 ‖ Fat: 6.5g ‖ Protein: 1.2g ‖ Carbohydrates: 12.3g

CINNAMON OATMEAL COOKIES

Total Time Taken: 1 ¼ hours
Yield: 30 Servings

Ingredients:

- ¼ cup golden syrup
- 1 egg
- 2 cups rolled oats
- 1 teaspoon cinnamon powder
- ¼ teaspoon salt
- ½ teaspoon baking soda
- 2/3 cup butter
- 2/3 cup light brown sugar
- 2/3 cup all-purpose flour

Directions:

1. Mix the butter, sugar and syrup in a container until fluffy and creamy.
2. Put in the egg and mix thoroughly then fold in the remaining ingredients.
3. Drop spoonfuls of batter on a baking sheet coated with baking paper.
4. Preheat your oven and bake the cookies at 350F for about fifteen minutes or until a golden-brown colour is achieved on the edges.
5. Let the cookies cool down before you serve.

Nutritional Content of One Serving:

Calories: 89 ‖ Fat: 4.6g ‖ Protein: 1.2g ‖ Carbohydrates: 11.1g

CHUNKY PEANUT BUTTER COOKIES

Total Time Taken: 1 ¼ hours
Yield: 30 Servings

Ingredients:

- ¼ teaspoon salt
- ½ cup butter, softened
- 1 cup light brown sugar
- 1 cup peanut butter, softened
- 1 cup peanuts, chopped
- 1 egg
- 1 teaspoon baking powder
- 2 cups all-purpose flour

Directions:

1. Mix the butter and peanut butter in a container until creamy. Put in the sugar and mix for five minutes until fluffy.
2. Put in the egg and mix thoroughly then fold in the remaining ingredients.
3. Drop spoonfuls of batter on a baking tray coated with baking paper.
4. Preheat your oven and bake the cookies at 350F for about fifteen minutes or until a golden-brown colour is achieved on the edges.
5. Allow the cookies cool down before you serve.

Nutritional Content of One Serving:

Calories: 156 ‖ Fat: 10.0g ‖ Protein: 4.5g ‖ Carbohydrates: 13.7g

CHOCOLATE STAR ANISE COOKIES

Total Time Taken: 1 ¼ hours
Yield: 20 Servings

Ingredients:

- ½ cup butter, softened
- ½ cup cocoa powder
- ½ cup pecans, chopped
- ½ teaspoon baking soda
- ½ teaspoon salt
- ¾ cup white sugar
- 1 ½ cups all-purpose flour

- 1 egg
- 1 teaspoon ground star anise
- 2 tablespoons coconut oil

Directions:

1. Mix the butter and coconut oil in a container. Put in the sugar and stir until fluffy.
2. Stir in the egg and stir thoroughly until blended.
3. Fold in the remaining ingredients and mix using a spatula.
4. Drop spoonfuls of batter on baking trays covered with parchment paper.
5. Pre-heat the oven and bake at 350F for about fifteen minutes or until risen and fragrant.
6. These cookies taste best chilled.

Nutritional Content of One Serving:

Calories: 129 ‖ Fat: 7.1g ‖ Protein: 1.8g ‖ Carbohydrates: 16.1g

CHOCOLATE SANDWICH COOKIES WITH PASSIONFRUIT GANACHE

Total Time Taken: 2 hours
Yield: 30 Servings
Ingredients:

Cookies:

- ½ cup cocoa powder
- ½ teaspoon salt
- 1 cup white sugar
- 1 egg
- 1 teaspoon baking powder
- 1 teaspoon vanilla extract
- 2 cups all-purpose flour
- 2/3 cup butter, softened

Passionfruit Ganache:

- ¼ cup passionfruit juice
- ½ cup heavy cream

- 1 cup white chocolate chips
- 2 tablespoons butter

Directions:

1. For the cookies, combine the flour, cocoa powder, baking powder and salt in a container.
1. In a separate container, combine the butter and sugar until fluffy and pale.
2. Stir in the egg and vanilla and mix thoroughly then fold in the flour.
3. Transfer the dough to a floured working surface and roll it into a slim sheet.
4. Cut 40 small cookies using a round cookie cutter and arrange them on a baking sheet coated with baking paper.
5. For the ganache, bring the cream to a boil. Stir in the chocolate and stir until it melts completely. Put in the passionfruit juice and butter and mix thoroughly. Let cool in your refrigerator.
6. Fill the cookies with chilled ganache.

Nutritional Content of One Serving:

Calories: 143 ‖ Fat: 7.8g ‖ Protein: 1.7g ‖ Carbohydrates: 17.6g

CHOCOLATE PECAN COOKIES

Total Time Taken: 1 hour
Yield: 10 Servings
Ingredients:

- ¼ teaspoon salt
- ½ cup dark chocolate chips
- 1 cup ground pecans
- 1 teaspoon vanilla extract
- 2 egg whites
- 2/3 cup white sugar

Directions:

1. Whip the egg whites and salt in a container until fluffy and airy.
2. Put in the sugar, progressively, and stir until shiny.
3. Fold in the pecans and chocolate chips then drop spoonfuls of batter on a baking sheet coated with baking paper.

4. Preheat your oven and bake the cookies at 350F for about fifteen minutes or until a golden-brown colour is achieved.
5. These cookies taste best chilled.

Nutritional Content of One Serving:

Calories: 92 ‖ Fat: 2.6g ‖ Protein: 1.3g ‖ Carbohydrates: 17.6g

CHOCOLATE ORANGE SHORTBREAD COOKIES

Total Time Taken: 1 hour
Yield: 20 Servings
Ingredients:

- ¼ cup cocoa powder
- ¼ teaspoon salt
- ½ cup almond flour
- ½ cup butter, softened
- ½ cup white sugar
- ½ teaspoon baking soda
- 1 ½ cups all-purpose flour
- 1 egg
- 1 tablespoon orange zest
- 1 teaspoon vanilla extract

Directions:

1. Mix the butter, cocoa powder and sugar in a container until fluffy and pale.
2. Put in the egg, vanilla and orange zest and mix thoroughly.
3. Fold in the flour, almond flour, salt and baking soda then transfer the dough on a floured working surface.
4. Roll the dough into a slim sheet then cut small cookies using a cookie cutter of your choice.
5. Preheat your oven and bake the cookies at 350F for about fifteen minutes or until a golden-brown colour is achieved and fragrant.
6. These cookies taste best chilled.

Nutritional Content of One Serving:

Calories: 104 ‖ Fat: 5.4g ‖ Protein: 1.6g ‖ Carbohydrates: 13.0g

WHITE CHOCOLATE PISTACHIO COOKIES

Total Time Taken: 1 ¼ hours

Yield: 40 Servings

Ingredients:

- ¼ cup whole milk
- ½ cup light brown sugar
- ½ cup white chocolate chips
- ½ teaspoon baking powder
- ½ teaspoon salt
- 1 cup butter, softened
- 1 cup pistachio, chopped
- 1 cup white sugar
- 1 teaspoon baking soda
- 1 teaspoon vanilla extract
- 2 ½ cups all-purpose flour
- 2 eggs

Directions:

1. Mix the butter and sugars in a container until fluffy and pale.
2. Put in the eggs and mix thoroughly then mix in the vanilla.
3. Put in the rest of the ingredients and mix using a spatula.
4. Drop spoonfuls of batter on baking trays coated with baking paper.
5. Preheat your oven and bake the cookies at 350F for about fifteen minutes or until a golden-brown colour is achieved on the edges.
6. These cookies taste best chilled.

Nutritional Content of One Serving:

Calories: 119 ‖ Fat: 6.3g ‖ Protein: 1.6g ‖ Carbohydrates: 14.5g

WHITE CHOCOLATE CRANBERRY COOKIES

Total Time Taken: 1 ¼ hours
Yield: 30 Servings

Ingredients:

- ¼ cup coconut oil, melted
- ¼ teaspoon cinnamon powder
- ¼ teaspoon salt
- ½ cup butter, softened
- ½ cup dried cranberries
- ½ cup light brown sugar
- ½ cup white chocolate chips
- 1 ½ cups all-purpose flour
- 1 egg
- 1 tablespoon brandy
- 1 teaspoon baking powder

Directions:

1. Mix the butter, coconut oil and sugar in a container until fluffy and pale.
2. Put in the egg and brandy and mix thoroughly.
3. Fold in the remaining ingredients and mix using a spatula.
4. Drop spoonfuls of batter on a baking tray coated with baking paper.
5. Preheat your oven and bake the cookies at 350F for about fifteen minutes or until a golden-brown colour is achieved on the edges.
6. These cookies taste best chilled.

Nutritional Content of One Serving:

Calories: 95 ‖ Fat: 6.0g ‖ Protein: 1.0g ‖ Carbohydrates: 9.1g

WHITE CHOCOLATE CHUNK COOKIES

Total Time Taken: 1 ¼ hours
Yield: 30 Servings

Ingredients:

- ¼ cup white sugar
- ½ cup butter, softened
- ½ cup cocoa powder
- ½ teaspoon salt
- 1 cup light brown sugar
- 1 teaspoon baking soda
- 1 teaspoon vanilla extract
- 2 cups all-purpose flour
- 2 eggs
- 4 oz. white chocolate, chopped

Directions:

1. Mix the butter and sugars in a container until fluffy and pale.
2. Put in the vanilla and eggs and mix thoroughly.
3. Fold in the flour, cocoa powder, salt and baking soda.
4. Put in the white chocolate chips then drop spoonfuls of batter on baking trays coated with baking paper.
5. Preheat your oven and bake the cookies at 350F for about fifteen minutes or until risen.
6. These cookies taste best chilled.

Nutritional Content of One Serving:

Calories: 110 ‖ Fat: 4.8g ‖ Protein: 1.8g ‖ Carbohydrates: 15.8g

WALNUT CRESCENT COOKIES

Total Time Taken: 1 ¼ hours

Yield: 20 Servings

Ingredients:

- 1 teaspoon vanilla extract
- ½ teaspoon almond extract
- 1 egg
- 1 cup all-purpose flour
- 1 ½ cups ground walnuts
- ½ teaspoon salt
- ½ teaspoon baking powder

- 2/3 cup butter, softened
- 2/3 cup white sugar

Directions:

1. Mix the butter, sugar, vanilla and almond extract in a container until fluffy and creamy.
2. Put in the egg and mix thoroughly then fold in the flour, walnuts, salt and baking powder.
3. Take small pieces of dough and shape them into small logs.
4. Place them on a baking tray coated with baking paper and preheat your oven and bake at 350F for about fifteen minutes or until a golden-brown colour is achieved on the edges.
5. These cookies taste best chilled.

Nutritional Content of One Serving:

Calories: 164 ‖ Fat: 11.9g ‖ Protein: 3.2g ‖ Carbohydrates: 12.5g

WALNUT BANANA COOKIES

Total Time Taken: 1 hour
Yield: 20 Servings
Ingredients:

- ¼ cup dark brown sugar
- ½ cup all-purpose flour
- ½ cup butter, softened
- ½ cup dark chocolate chips
- ½ cup walnuts, chopped
- ½ cup white sugar
- ½ teaspoon baking powder
- ½ teaspoon salt
- 1 banana, mashed
- 1 cup whole wheat flour
- 1 egg
- 1 teaspoon vanilla extract

Directions:

1. Mix the butter and sugars in a container until fluffy and pale.

2. Put in the egg, vanilla and banana and mix thoroughly.
3. Stir in the flours, salt and baking powder then fold in the chocolate chips and walnuts.
4. Drop spoonfuls of batter on a baking tray covered with parchment paper and preheat your oven and bake at 350F for about thirteen minutes or until a golden-brown colour is achieved and crisp on the edges.
5. The cookies are best served chilled.

Nutritional Content of One Serving:

Calories: 143 ‖ Fat: 7.6g ‖ Protein: 2.3g ‖ Carbohydrates: 17.7g

VANILLA SUGARED COOKIES

Total Time Taken: 2 hours

Yield: 20 Servings

Ingredients:

- ¼ teaspoon baking powder
- ¼ teaspoon salt
- ½ cup butter, softened
- ½ cup powdered sugar
- 1 egg
- 1 tablespoon vanilla extract
- 2 cups all-purpose flour
- Powdered sugar for coating the cookies

Directions:

1. Mix the butter and sugar in a container until pale and light.
2. Put in the vanilla and egg and mix thoroughly.
3. Stir in the flour, salt and baking powder then transfer the dough on a plastic wrap and roll it into a log.
4. Wrap the dough and place it in the freezer for about half an hour.
5. When finished, cut the log of dough into thin slices.
6. Put the cookies in a baking tray covered with parchment paper and preheat your oven and bake at 350F for about ten minutes or until a golden-brown colour is achieved on the edges.
7. These cookies taste best chilled.

Nutritional Content of One Serving:

Calories: 103 ‖ Fat: 5.0g ‖ Protein: 1.6g ‖ Carbohydrates: 12.7g

VANILLA MALTED COOKIES

Total Time Taken: 1 ¼ hours

Yield: 30 Servings

Ingredients:

- ½ cup cream cheese
- ½ cup malted milk powder
- ½ cup white chocolate chips
- ½ teaspoon baking soda
- ½ teaspoon salt
- 1 cup butter, softened
- 1 cup white sugar
- 1 egg
- 1 teaspoon baking powder
- 1 teaspoon vanilla extract
- 2 ½ cups all-purpose flour

Directions:

1. Sift the flour, milk powder, baking powder, baking soda and salt.
2. Mix the butter, cream cheese and sugar in a container until creamy and fluffy.
3. Put in the vanilla and egg and mix thoroughly.
4. Fold in the flour mixture then put in the chocolate chips.
5. Drop spoonfuls of batter on a baking sheet coated with baking paper.
6. Preheat your oven and bake the cookies at 350F for about fifteen minutes or until a golden-brown colour is achieved on the edges.
7. These cookies taste best chilled.

Nutritional Content of One Serving:

Calories: 161 ‖ Fat: 8.8g ‖ Protein: 2.1g ‖ Carbohydrates: 19.0g

TRIPLE CHOCOLATE COOKIES

Total Time Taken: 1 ¼ hours
Yield: 30 Servings

Ingredients:

- ¼ cup cocoa powder
- ¼ teaspoon baking soda
- ¼ teaspoon salt
- ½ cup dark chocolate chips
- ½ cup dark chocolate chips, melted
- 1 ½ teaspoons baking powder
- 1 cup butter, softened
- 1 cup light brown sugar
- 1 teaspoon vanilla extract
- 2 cups all-purpose flour
- 2 eggs
- 2 tablespoons whole milk

Directions:

1. Mix the butter and sugar in a container until fluffy and pale.
2. Put in the melted chocolate, eggs and vanilla, as well as the milk.
3. Fold in the flour, cocoa powder, baking powder, baking soda and salt then put in the chocolate chips.
4. Drop spoonfuls of batter on a baking sheet coated with baking paper.
5. Preheat your oven and bake the cookies at 350F for about fifteen minutes or until the cookies are golden-brown on the edges.
6. These cookies taste best chilled.

Nutritional Content of One Serving:

Calories: 129 ‖ Fat: 7.7g ‖ Protein: 1.7g ‖ Carbohydrates: 14.4g

TOFFEE CHOCOLATE CHIP COOKIES

Total Time Taken: 1 ¼ hours
Yield: 30 Servings

Ingredients:

- ¼ cup white sugar
- ½ cup dark chocolate chips

- ½ cup light brown sugar
- ½ teaspoon salt
- 1 cup butter, softened
- 1 cup chopped toffee pieces
- 1 teaspoon baking powder
- 2 ½ cups all-purpose flour
- 2 eggs

Directions:

1. Mix the flour, salt and baking powder in a container.
2. In a separate container, mix the butter and sugars and mix thoroughly. Put in the eggs and stir thoroughly until blended.
3. Put in the flour then fold in the toffee pieces and chocolate chips.
4. Drop spoonfuls of batter on a baking sheet coated with baking paper.
5. Preheat your oven and bake the cookies at 350F for about fifteen minutes or until a golden-brown colour is achieved on the edges.
6. These cookies taste best chilled.

Nutritional Content of One Serving:

Calories: 129 ‖ Fat: 7.3g ‖ Protein: 1.7g ‖ Carbohydrates: 14.5g

TOFFEE APPLE COOKIES

Total Time Taken: 1 ¼ hours
Yield: 20 Servings

Ingredients:

- ¼ teaspoon salt
- ½ cup almond flour
- ½ cup butter, softened
- ½ cup toffee bits
- ½ teaspoon baking soda
- 1 ½ cups all-purpose flour
- 1 cup light brown sugar
- 2 apples, peeled and cored
- 2 egg yolks

Directions:

1. Mix the butter and sugar in a container until fluffy and pale.
2. Put in the egg yolks and mix thoroughly then mix in the almond flour, flour, baking soda and salt in the container.
3. Put in the eggs and toffee bits then drop spoonfuls of batter on a baking tray coated with baking paper.
4. Preheat your oven and bake the cookies at 350F for about fifteen minutes or until a golden-brown colour is achieved on the edges.
5. These cookies taste best chilled.

Nutritional Content of One Serving:

Calories: 129 || Fat: 5.8g || Protein: 2.1g || Carbohydrates: 17.8g

THIN COCONUT COOKIES

Total Time Taken: 1 hour
Yield: 20 Servings
Ingredients:

- ¼ cup all-purpose flour
- ¼ teaspoon salt
- ½ cup butter, softened
- ½ cup white sugar
- 1 ¾ cups shredded coconut
- 2 egg whites

Directions:

1. Combine all the ingredients in a container until creamy. Put the dough in your refrigerator until firm.
2. Make small balls of dough and place them on baking trays coated with baking paper.
3. Flatten the cookies and preheat you even and bake at 350F for about fifteen minutes or until a golden-brown colour is achieved and crisp on the edges.
4. These cookies taste best chilled.

Nutritional Content of One Serving:

Calories: 92 || Fat: 7.0g || Protein: 0.8g || Carbohydrates: 7.3g

SUGAR COVERED COOKIES

Total Time Taken: 1 ½ hours
Yield: 30 Servings

Ingredients:

- ¼ teaspoon salt
- ½ cup rice flour
- ½ cup white sugar
- ½ teaspoon baking powder
- 1 cup butter, softened
- 1 cup powdered sugar
- 1 egg
- 1 teaspoon vanilla extract
- 2 cups all-purpose flour
- 2 egg yolks

Directions:

1. Mix the butter and sugar in a container until fluffy and pale.
2. Put in the egg and egg yolks, as well as the vanilla and mix thoroughly.
3. Stir in the rice flour, flour, salt and baking powder in a container.
4. Make small balls and place them on baking trays coated with baking paper.
5. Flatten the cookies then preheat you even and bake at350F for about fifteen minutes or until a golden-brown colour is achieved on the edges.
6. Move the cookies to a container and dust them with powdered sugar.
7. These cookies taste best chilled.

Nutritional Content of One Serving:

Calories: 128 ‖ Fat: 6.7g ‖ Protein: 1.4g ‖ Carbohydrates: 15.9g

SPICED CHOCOLATE COOKIES

Total Time Taken: 1 ¼ hours
Yield: 20 Servings

Ingredients:

- ¼ cup cocoa powder

- ¼ teaspoon salt
- ½ cup butter, softened
- ½ cup dark brown sugar
- ½ teaspoon baking powder
- 1 ¼ cups all-purpose flour
- 1 egg
- 1 teaspoon all-spice powder
- 2 tablespoons honey

Directions:

1. Mix the butter, brown sugar and honey in a container until creamy and fluffy.
2. Put in the egg and mix thoroughly then fold in the flour, cocoa powder, salt, baking powder and all-spice powder.
3. Transfer the dough to a floured working surface and roll it into a slim sheet.
4. Cut the dough using a cookie cutter of your choices and move the cookies to a baking sheet coated with baking paper.
5. Pre-heat the oven and bake at 350F for about twelve minutes.
6. These cookies taste best chilled.

Nutritional Content of One Serving:

Calories: 95 ‖ Fat: 5.0g ‖ Protein: 1.4g ‖ Carbohydrates: 11.9g

SPICED APPLE COOKIES

Total Time Taken: 1 ¼ hours

Yield: 20 Servings

Ingredients:

- ¼ teaspoon salt
- ½ cup coconut oil, melted
- ½ cup light brown sugar
- ½ teaspoon cinnamon powder
- 1 ½ cups all-purpose flour
- 1 egg
- 1 teaspoon baking powder
- 2 red apples, cored and diced

- 2 tablespoons water

Directions:

1. Mix the oil, sugar and egg in a container until fluffy and light.
2. Put in the water and mix thoroughly then mix in the flour, salt, baking powder and cinnamon.
3. Put in the apples then drop spoonfuls of batter on a baking tray coated with baking paper.
4. Preheat your oven and bake the cookies at 350F for about fifteen minutes or until it is aromatic and appears golden brown.
5. These cookies taste best chilled.

Nutritional Content of One Serving:

Calories: 108 ‖ Fat: 5.8g ‖ Protein: 1.3g ‖ Carbohydrates: 13.4g

SOFT GINGER COOKIES

Total Time Taken: 1 ¼ hours
Yield: 30 Servings

Ingredients:

- ¼ teaspoon salt
- ¾ cup butter, softened
- 1 cup white sugar
- 1 egg
- 1 teaspoon baking soda
- 1 teaspoon ground ginger
- 1 teaspoon vanilla extract
- 1/2 teaspoon cinnamon powder
- 2 cups all-purpose flour
- 3 tablespoons molasses

Directions:

1. Mix the flour, salt, baking soda and spices in a container.
2. In a separate container, mix the butter and sugar and mix thoroughly. Put in the egg and molasses and stir thoroughly until blended. Stir in the vanilla.
3. Fold in the flour mixture then drop spoonfuls of batter on baking trays coated with baking paper.

4. Preheat your oven and bake the cookies at 350F for about fifteen minutes or until it is aromatic and appears golden brown.
5. These cookies taste best chilled.

Nutritional Content of One Serving:

Calories: 105 ‖ Fat: 4.8g ‖ Protein: 1.1g ‖ Carbohydrates: 14.6g

SOFT CHOCOLATE CHIP COOKIES

Total Time Taken: 1 ¼ hours
Yield: 20 Servings

Ingredients:

- ½ cup butter, softened
- ½ teaspoon salt
- 1 cup dark chocolate chips
- 1 cup light brown sugar
- 1 teaspoon baking powder
- 2 cups all-purpose flour
- 2 eggs

Directions:

1. Mix the butter and sugar in a container until fluffy and pale.
2. Put in the eggs, one at a time, stirring thoroughly after each addition.
3. Fold in the remaining ingredients then drop spoonfuls of batter on a baking sheet coated with baking paper.
4. Pre-heat the oven and bake at 350F for about fifteen minutes or until a golden-brown colour is achieved on the edges.
5. These cookies taste best chilled.

Nutritional Content of One Serving:

Calories: 148 ‖ Fat: 6.8g ‖ Protein: 2.3g ‖ Carbohydrates: 20.8g

SOFT BAKED CHOCOLATE COOKIES

Total Time Taken: 1 ½ hours

Yield: 30 Servings

Ingredients:

- ¼ cup light corn syrup
- ½ cup butter, softened
- ½ teaspoon baking soda
- ½ teaspoon salt
- 1 ¼ cups chocolate chips
- 1 cup dark brown sugar
- 1 teaspoon vanilla extract
- 2 ½ cups all-purpose flour
- 2 eggs

Directions:

1. Mix the butter and sugar in a container until pale and creamy.
2. Put in the corn syrup, eggs and vanilla and mix thoroughly.
3. Fold in the flour, salt and baking soda then put in the chocolate chips and mix thoroughly.
4. Drop spoonfuls of batter on baking trays coated with baking paper and preheat your oven and bake the cookies at 350F for about fifteen minutes or until a golden-brown colour is achieved and crisp on the edges.
5. These cookies taste best chilled.

Nutritional Content of One Serving:

Calories: 133 || Fat: 5.5g || Protein: 2.0g || Carbohydrates: 18.9g

SALTED CHOCOLATE COOKIES

Total Time Taken: 1 ½ hours

Yield: 30 Servings

Ingredients:

- ¼ cup cocoa powder
- ½ cup butter
- 1 ½ cups all-purpose flour
- 1 cup light brown sugar
- 1 teaspoon baking powder

- 1 teaspoon sea salt
- 2 cups dark chocolate chips
- 2 eggs
- 2 tablespoons coconut oil
- 2 tablespoons dark brown sugar

Directions:

1. Mix the chocolate and butter in a heatproof container over a hot water bath and melt them together until the desired smoothness is achieved.
2. Put in the coconut oil and mix thoroughly then mix in the sugars and eggs. Stir thoroughly to mix.
3. Fold in the remaining ingredients then drop spoonfuls of batter on a baking sheet coated with baking paper.
4. Preheat your oven and bake the cookies at 350F for fifteen minutes.
5. These cookies taste best chilled.

Nutritional Content of One Serving:

Calories: 122 ‖ Fat: 6.5g ‖ Protein: 1.7g ‖ Carbohydrates: 15.9g

RUSSIAN TEA COOKIES

Total Time Taken: 1 hour
Yield: 30 Servings
Ingredients:

- ¼ teaspoon salt
- ½ cup powdered sugar
- 1 cup butter, softened
- 1 cup ground walnuts
- 1 cup powdered sugar
- 1 egg
- 1 teaspoon baking powder
- 1 teaspoon vanilla extract
- 2 cups all-purpose flour

Directions:

1. Mix the butter and sugar in a container until creamy and pale.

2. Put in the egg and vanilla and mix thoroughly then mix in the flour, walnuts, salt and baking powder.
3. Make small balls of dough and place them on a baking tray coated with baking paper.
4. Transfer the baked cookies in a container and dust them with plenty of powdered sugar.
5. These cookies taste best chilled.

Nutritional Content of One Serving:

Calories: 136 ‖ Fat: 8.8g ‖ Protein: 2.1g ‖ Carbohydrates: 12.9g

ROCKY ROAD COOKIES

Total Time Taken: 1 ¼ hours
Yield: 20 Servings

Ingredients:

- ¼ cup light brown sugar
- ½ cup dried cranberries
- ½ cup glace cherries, halved
- ½ cup mini marshmallows
- ½ cup walnuts, chopped
- 1 cup all-purpose flour
- 1 cup macadamia nuts, chopped
- 1/3 cup butter, softened
- 2 eggs

Directions:

1. Mix the butter and sugar in a container until creamy.
2. Put in the eggs, one at a time, then mix in the flour, followed by the remaining ingredients.
3. Drop spoonfuls of batter on a baking tray coated with baking paper.
4. Preheat your oven and bake the cookies at 350F for about fifteen minutes or until a golden-brown colour is achieved on the edges.
5. These cookies taste best chilled.

Nutritional Content of One Serving:

Calories: 139 ‖ Fat: 10.5g ‖ Protein: 2.6g ‖ Carbohydrates: 9.7g

RICE FLOUR COOKIES

Total Time Taken: 1 hour

Yield: 20 Servings

Ingredients:

- ½ cup butter, softened
- 1 teaspoon vanilla extract
- 1 egg
- ½ cup all-purpose flour
- ½ cup rice flour
- 1 teaspoon baking powder
- ¼ teaspoon cardamom powder
- ¼ teaspoon salt
- 1/3 cup white sugar

Directions:

1. Mix the butter, sugar and vanilla and stir until fluffy.
2. Put in the egg and mix thoroughly then fold in the remaining ingredients.
3. Drop spoonfuls of batter on a baking sheet coated with baking paper.
4. Preheat your oven and bake the cookies at 350F for about fifteen minutes or until a golden-brown colour is achieved on the edges.
5. These cookies taste best chilled.

Nutritional Content of One Serving:

Calories: 83 ‖ Fat: 4.9g ‖ Protein: 0.9g ‖ Carbohydrates: 9.1g

RASPBERRY JAM COOKIES

Total Time Taken: 2 hours

Yield: 20 Servings

Ingredients:

- ¼ teaspoon salt
- ½ cup butter, softened
- ½ cup powdered sugar
- ½ cup seedless raspberry jam
- ½ teaspoon baking powder

- 1 ¼ cups all-purpose flour
- 1 cup almond flour
- 1 egg
- 2 tablespoons whole milk

Directions:

1. Mix the butter and sugar in a container until fluffy and creamy.
2. Stir in the egg and milk and mix thoroughly then fold in the flours, salt and baking powder.
3. Transfer the dough to a floured working surface and roll it into a slim sheet.
4. Cut 40 small cookies.
5. Preheat your oven and bake the cookies at 350F for about fifteen minutes.
6. When finished, chill the cookies and fill them two by two with raspberry jam.
7. Serve immediately.

Nutritional Content of One Serving:

Calories: 115 ‖ Fat: 5.7g ‖ Protein: 1.5g ‖ Carbohydrates: 14.9g

RAINBOW COOKIES

Total Time Taken: 1 ¼ hours
Yield: 25 Servings

Ingredients:

- ¼ cup coconut oil, melted
- ¼ teaspoon salt
- ½ cup colourful sprinkles
- ½ cup butter, softened
- 1 ½ cups all-purpose flour
- 1 cup white sugar
- 1 egg
- 1 teaspoon baking powder
- 1 teaspoon vanilla extract

Directions:

1. Mix the butter, coconut oil and sugar in a container until fluffy and pale.
2. Stir in the egg and vanilla and mix thoroughly.
3. Fold in the flour, salt and baking powder then put in the sprinkles.

4. Drop spoonfuls of batter on a baking sheet coated with baking paper.
5. Pre-heat the oven and bake at 350F for about fifteen minutes or until a golden-brown colour is achieved on the edges.
6. These cookies taste best chilled.

Nutritional Content of One Serving:

Calories: 118 ‖ Fat: 6.3g ‖ Protein: 1.1g ‖ Carbohydrates: 14.8g

QUICK BROWN BUTTER COOKIES

Total Time Taken: 1 hour
Yield: 20 Servings
Ingredients:

- ¼ teaspoon salt
- ½ cup sliced almonds
- ¾ cup butter
- ¾ cup white sugar
- 1 ½ cups all-purpose flour
- 1 egg
- 1 teaspoon baking powder
- 1 teaspoon vanilla extract

Directions:

1. Put the butter in a saucepan and cook it until melted and mildly golden.
2. Let cool and then move to a container and mix in the rest of the ingredients in the same order they are written in.
3. Drop spoonfuls of batter on a baking tray coated with baking paper.
4. Preheat your oven and bake the cookies at 350F for about fifteen minutes or until a golden-brown colour is achieved.
5. These cookies taste best chilled.

Nutritional Content of One Serving:

Calories: 141 ‖ Fat: 8.4g ‖ Protein: 1.8g ‖ Carbohydrates: 15.3g

PUFFED RICE COOKIES

Total Time Taken: 1 ¼ hours
Yield: 20 Servings

Ingredients:

- ½ cup butter, softened
- ½ cup light brown sugar
- ½ teaspoon salt
- 1 ½ cup all-purpose flour
- 1 egg
- 1 teaspoon baking powder
- 2 cups puffed rice cereals
- 2 tablespoons golden syrup

Directions:

1. Mix the butter, sugar and golden syrup in a container until fluffy and creamy.
2. Put in the egg and mix thoroughly then fold in the remaining ingredients.
3. Drop spoonfuls of batter on a baking sheet coated with baking paper.
4. Pre-heat the oven and bake at 350F for about fifteen minutes or until a golden-brown colour is achieved on the edges.
5. These cookies taste best chilled.

Nutritional Content of One Serving:

Calories: 103 ‖ Fat: 4.9g ‖ Protein: 1.4g ‖ Carbohydrates: 13.6g

PRALINE COOKIES

Total Time Taken: 1 ¼ hours
Yield: 30 Servings

Ingredients:

- ¼ teaspoon salt
- ½ cup butter, softened
- ½ cup light brown sugar
- ½ cup praline paste
- 1 tablespoon praline liqueur

- 1 teaspoon baking soda
- 1 teaspoon vanilla extract
- 2 cups all-purpose flour
- 2 eggs

Directions:

1. Mix the butter, praline paste and sugar in a container until pale and fluffy.
2. Put in the egg yolks, vanilla and praline liqueur and mix thoroughly.
3. Stir in the flour, salt and baking soda then mix using a spatula.
4. Transfer the dough to a floured working surface and roll it into a slim sheet.
5. Cut into small cookies with a cookie cutter and place them all on a baking tray coated with baking paper.
6. Preheat your oven and bake the cookies at 350F for about fifteen minutes or until a golden-brown colour is achieved on the edges.
7. These cookies taste best chilled.

Nutritional Content of One Serving:

Calories: 91 ‖ Fat: 4.6g ‖ Protein: 1.5g ‖ Carbohydrates: 10.9g

POLENTA COOKIES

Total Time Taken: 1 ¼ hours
Yield: 30 Servings

Ingredients:

- ¼ cup dark brown sugar
- ½ cup light brown sugar
- ½ teaspoon salt
- 1 ¾ cups all-purpose flour
- 1 cup butter, softened
- 1 cup polenta flour
- 1 egg
- 1 egg yolk
- 1 teaspoon baking powder
- 1 teaspoon vanilla extract

Directions:

1. Mix the flours, salt and baking powder in a container.

2. In a separate container, combine the butter and sugars in a container until fluffy and pale.
3. Put in the egg and egg yolk, as well as the vanilla and mix thoroughly.
4. Stir in the flour then drop spoonfuls of batter on a baking sheet coated with baking paper.
5. Pre-heat the oven and bake at 350F for about fifteen minutes or until a golden-brown colour is achieved on the edges.
6. Serve Chilled or store them in an airtight container.

Nutritional Content of One Serving:

Calories: 101 ‖ Fat: 6.5g ‖ Protein: 1.2g ‖ Carbohydrates: 9.7g

PINK DOTTED SUGAR COOKIES

Total Time Taken: 1 ½ hours
Yield: 20 Servings

Ingredients:

- ¼ teaspoon salt
- ½ cup butter, softened
- ½ cup pink sprinkles
- ½ cup powdered sugar
- 1 egg
- 1 teaspoon baking powder
- 2 cups all-purpose flour

Directions:

1. Mix the butter and sugar in a container until fluffy and creamy.
2. Stir in the egg then fold in the flour, salt and baking powder, as well as sprinkles.
3. Transfer the dough to a floured working surface and roll it into a slim sheet.
4. Cut the cookies using a cookie cutter of your choice then arrange them on a baking sheet coated with baking paper.
5. Preheat your oven and bake the cookies at 350F for about fifteen minutes or until a golden-brown colour is achieved on the edges.
6. These cookies taste best chilled.

Nutritional Content of One Serving:

Calories: 119 || Fat: 5.0g || Protein: 1.6g || Carbohydrates: 17.5g

PINE NUT COOKIES

Total Time Taken: 1 hour

Yield: 20 Servings

Ingredients:

- ¼ teaspoon salt
- ½ cup pine nuts
- ½ cup sugar
- 1 ½ cups almond paste
- 1 egg
- 2 egg whites

Directions:

1. Mix the almond paste, sugar and egg and stir thoroughly until creamy.
2. Whip the egg whites and salt until fluffy then fold the meringue into the almond paste.
3. Drop spoonfuls of mixture on baking trays coated with baking paper.
4. Top with pine nuts and preheat your oven and bake at 350F for about fifteen minutes or until a golden-brown colour is achieved and crisp.
5. These cookies taste best chilled.

Nutritional Content of One Serving:

Calories: 125 || Fat: 7.3g || Protein: 2.6g || Carbohydrates: 13.6g

PECAN STUDDED COOKIES

Total Time Taken: 1 hour

Yield: 20 Servings

Ingredients:

- ½ cup butter
- 1 teaspoon lemon juice
- 1 egg

- 1 ½ cups all-purpose flour
- ¼ cup cocoa powder
- ¼ teaspoon salt
- ½ teaspoon baking soda
- ½ cup dark chocolate chips
- 2/3 cup light brown sugar

Directions:

1. Melt the butter in a saucepan until it becomes mildly golden brown.
2. Turn off the heat and mix in the lemon juice and egg, as well as sugar.
3. Put in the rest of the ingredients and mix using a spatula.
4. Drop spoonfuls of batter on a baking tray coated with baking paper.
5. Preheat your oven and bake the cookies at 350F for about fifteen minutes or until mildly golden-brown and crisp on the edges.
6. These cookies taste best chilled.

Nutritional Content of One Serving:

Calories: 113 ‖ Fat: 5.9g ‖ Protein: 1.7g ‖ Carbohydrates: 14.5g

PECAN MARSHMALLOW COOKIES

Total Time Taken: 1 ½ hours
Yield: 30 Servings

Ingredients:

- ¼ teaspoon salt
- 1 cup mini marshmallows
- 1 cup pecans, chopped
- 1 cup white sugar
- 1 egg
- 1 teaspoon baking powder
- 1 teaspoon vanilla extract
- 2 ¼ cups all-purpose flour
- 2/3 cup butter

Directions:

1. Mix the butter and sugar in a container until fluffy and creamy.
2. Stir in the vanilla and egg then put in the flour, salt and baking powder.

3. Fold in the pecans and marshmallows then drop spoonfuls of batter on a baking sheet coated with baking paper.
4. Pre-heat the oven and bake at 350F for about fifteen minutes or until a golden-brown colour is achieved on the edges.
5. These cookies taste best chilled.

Nutritional Content of One Serving:

Calories: 104 ‖ Fat: 4.7g ‖ Protein: 1.2g ‖ Carbohydrates: 14.7g

PECAN CREAM CHEESE COOKIES

Total Time Taken: 2 hours
Yield: 40 Servings
Ingredients:

- 1 cup cream cheese
- 1 cup white sugar
- 1 teaspoon vanilla extract
- 1 egg
- 3 cups all-purpose flour
- 1 ½ cups ground pecans
- ¼ teaspoon salt
- 1 teaspoon baking powder
- 2/3 cup butter, softened

Directions:

1. Mix the cream cheese, butter, sugar and vanilla and mix thoroughly. Put in the egg and mix thoroughly.
2. Fold in the remaining ingredients then transfer the dough on plastic wrap and roll it into a log. Wrap tightly and place in the freezer for an hour.
3. Remove the dough from the freezer and cut into thin cookies.
4. Place them on a baking tray coated with baking paper and preheat your oven and bake at 350F for about fifteen minutes or until mildly golden-brown on the edges.
5. These cookies taste best chilled.

Nutritional Content of One Serving:

Calories: 105 ‖ Fat: 5.5g ‖ Protein: 1.6g ‖ Carbohydrates: 12.4g

PECAN BUTTER COOKIES

Total Time Taken: 1 ¼ hours

Yield: 20 Servings

Ingredients:

- ½ cup pecan butter, softened
- 1 egg
- 1 teaspoon vanilla extract
- 1 cup all-purpose flour
- 1 cup ground pecans
- ¼ teaspoon salt
- ½ teaspoon baking soda
- 1 cup pecans, chopped
- 1/3 cup dark brown sugar

Directions:

1. Mix the butter, sugar, egg and vanilla in a container.
2. Put in the flour, salt, baking soda and ground pecans. Fold in the chopped pecans then drop spoonfuls of batter on a baking tray coated with baking paper.
3. Pre-heat the oven and bake at 350F for about fifteen minutes or until it is aromatic and appears golden-brown on the edges.
4. Serve Chilled and store them in an airtight container.

Nutritional Content of One Serving:

Calories: 86 ‖ Fat: 5.9g ‖ Protein: 1.1g ‖ Carbohydrates: 7.4g

PEANUT BUTTER SHORTBREAD COOKIES

Total Time Taken: 2 hours

Yield: 25 Servings

Ingredients:

- ½ cup butter, softened
- ½ cup powdered sugar

- ½ cup smooth peanut butter
- ½ teaspoon baking powder
- ½ teaspoon salt
- 1 ¾ cups all-purpose flour
- 1 egg
- 1 tablespoon cocoa powder
- 1 teaspoon vanilla extract

Directions:

1. Mix the peanut butter, butter, sugar and vanilla in a container until creamy and fluffy.
2. Stir in the egg and mix thoroughly then put in the cocoa powder, flour, salt and baking powder.
3. Cover the dough with plastic wrap and store in the refrigerator for about half an hour.
4. Transfer the dough to a floured working surface and roll it into a slim sheet.
5. Cut into small cookies using a cookie cutter of your choice.
6. Put the cookies in a baking sheet coated with baking paper.
7. Pre-heat the oven and bake at 350F for about fifteen minutes until it is aromatic and appears golden.
8. These cookies taste best chilled.

Nutritional Content of One Serving:

Calories: 108 ‖ Fat: 6.6g ‖ Protein: 2.5g ‖ Carbohydrates: 10.3g

PEANUT BUTTER PRETZEL COOKIES

Total Time Taken: 1 ¼ hours
Yield: 30 Servings

Ingredients:

- ¼ teaspoon salt
- ½ cup smooth peanut butter
- ½ teaspoon baking soda
- ¾ cup butter, softened
- 1 cup crushed pretzels
- 1 cup light brown sugar

- 1 egg
- 1 teaspoon vanilla extract
- 2 cups all-purpose flour

Directions:

1. Mix the butter, peanut butter and sugar in a container until creamy and fluffy.
2. Put in the egg and vanilla and mix thoroughly.
3. Fold in the flour, salt and baking soda then put in the pretzels.
4. Drop spoonfuls of batter on a baking tray coated with baking paper.
5. Pre-heat the oven and bake at 350F for about twenty minutes or until a golden-brown colour is achieved on the edges.
6. These cookies taste best chilled.

Nutritional Content of One Serving:

Calories: 121 ‖ Fat: 7.0g ‖ Protein: 2.2g ‖ Carbohydrates: 12.7g

PEANUT BUTTER OATMEAL COOKIES

Total Time Taken: 1 ½ hours
Yield: 30 Servings

Ingredients:

- ¼ cup butter, softened
- ¼ cup heavy cream
- ¼ teaspoon salt
- ½ cup light brown sugar
- ½ cup smooth peanut butter
- ½ cup white sugar
- ½ teaspoon baking soda
- 1 cup all-purpose flour
- 1 egg
- 1 teaspoon vanilla extract
- 2 cups rolled oats

Directions:

1. Mix the peanut butter, butter and sugars in a container until pale and creamy.

2. Put in the egg and vanilla and mix thoroughly.
3. Put in the cream as well then fold in the flour, oats, baking soda and salt.
4. Drop spoonfuls of batter on a baking tray coated with baking paper.
5. Preheat your oven and bake the cookies at 350F for about fifteen minutes or until the cookies turn golden-brown on the edges.
6. These cookies taste best chilled.

Nutritional Content of One Serving:

Calories: 102 ‖ Fat: 4.6g ‖ Protein: 2.5g ‖ Carbohydrates: 13.5g

PEANUT BUTTER NUTELLA COOKIES

Total Time Taken: 1 ¼ hours

Yield: 20 Servings

Ingredients:

- ¼ cup butter, softened
- ¼ teaspoon salt
- ½ cup dark brown sugar
- ½ cup Nutella
- ½ cup peanut butter, softened
- ½ teaspoon baking powder
- ½ teaspoon baking soda
- 1 ½ cups all-purpose flour
- 1 egg
- 1 teaspoon vanilla extract

Directions:

1. Mix the butter, peanut butter and sugar in a container until creamy and fluffy.
2. Put in the egg and vanilla and stir thoroughly until blended.
3. Fold in the flour, baking soda, baking powder and salt.
4. Put in the Nutella and swirl it into the batter.
5. Drop spoonfuls of batter on a baking sheet coated with baking paper.
6. Preheat your oven and bake the cookies at 350F for fifteen minutes or until a golden-brown colour is achieved on the edges.
7. These cookies taste best chilled.

Nutritional Content of One Serving:

Calories: 120 ‖ Fat: 6.5g ‖ Protein: 3.0g ‖ Carbohydrates: 13.2g

PEANUT BUTTER CUPS COOKIES

Total Time Taken: 1 ¼ hours

Yield: 25 Servings

Ingredients:

- ¼ cup smooth peanut butter
- ¼ teaspoon salt
- ½ cup butter, softened
- ½ teaspoon baking soda
- ¾ cup light brown sugar
- 1 ½ cups all-purpose flour
- 1 cup peanut butter, chopped
- 1 egg
- 1 teaspoon vanilla extract
- 2 tablespoons golden syrup

Directions:

1. Mix the butter and smooth peanut butter in a container until smooth and creamy.
2. Put in the sugar and golden syrup then mix in the egg and vanilla extract.
3. Put in the flour, baking soda and salt then fold in the peanut butter cups.
4. Drop spoonfuls of batter on a baking tray covered with parchment paper.
5. Preheat your oven and bake the cookies at 350F for about fifteen minutes or until a golden-brown colour is achieved on the edges.
6. These cookies taste best chilled.

Nutritional Content of One Serving:

Calories: 160 ‖ Fat: 10.4g ‖ Protein: 4.3g ‖ Carbohydrates: 13.8g

PEANUT BUTTER CINNAMON COOKIES

Total Time Taken: 1 hour

Yield: 20 Servings

Ingredients:

- ¼ cup almond milk
- ½ cup white sugar
- ½ teaspoon baking soda
- ½ teaspoon salt
- 1 ½ cups smooth peanut butter
- 1 cup all-purpose flour
- 1 teaspoon cinnamon powder
- 2 eggs

Directions:

1. Mix the peanut butter, eggs and sugar in a container until creamy.
2. Put in the flour, salt, cinnamon and baking soda and stir for a few seconds to mix.
3. Drop spoonfuls of batter on baking trays covered with parchment paper and preheat your oven and bake the cookies at 350F for about fifteen minutes or until aromatic and crunchy on the edges.

These cookies taste best chilled

Nutritional Content of One Serving:

Calories: 168 ‖ Fat: 11.0g ‖ Protein: 6.1g ‖ Carbohydrates: 13.7g

PEANUT BUTTER CHOCOLATE COOKIES

Total Time Taken: 1 hour

Yield: 20 Servings

Ingredients:

- ¼ cup butter, softened
- ¼ cup smooth peanut butter
- ¼ teaspoon salt
- ½ cup chocolate chips
- ½ cup light brown sugar
- ½ teaspoon baking powder
- ½ teaspoon baking soda

- 1 cup all-purpose flour
- 1 egg

Directions:

1. Mix the butters and sugar in a container until creamy and fluffy.
2. Stir in the egg and mix thoroughly.
3. Fold in the flour, baking soda, baking powder and salt.
4. Put in the chocolate chips then drop spoonfuls of batter on a baking sheet coated with baking paper.
5. Preheat your oven and bake the cookies at 350F for about fifteen minutes or until a golden-brown colour is achieved.
6. Let the cookies cool in the pan before you serve.

Nutritional Content of One Serving:

Calories: 102 ‖ Fat: 5.5g ‖ Protein: 2.1g ‖ Carbohydrates: 11.5g

OUTRAGEOUS CHOCOLATE COOKIES

Total Time Taken: 1 ¼ hours
Yield: 20 Servings

Ingredients:

- ¼ cup butter, softened
- ¼ cup coconut oil
- ½ cup dark chocolate chips
- ½ teaspoon salt
- ¾ cup light brown sugar
- 1 cup all-purpose flour
- 1 teaspoon baking powder
- 1 teaspoon vanilla extract
- 2 eggs
- 4 oz. dark chocolate, melted

Directions:

1. Mix the butter, coconut oil and sugar in a container until pale and creamy.
2. Mix the eggs, one at a time, then mix in the chocolate and vanilla.
3. Fold in the flour, salt and baking powder, as well as the chocolate chips.
4. Drop spoonfuls of batter on a baking tray coated with baking paper.

5. Pre-heat the oven and bake at 350F for about fifteen minutes or until a golden-brown colour is achieved and it rises significantly.
6. These cookies taste best chilled.

Nutritional Content of One Serving:

Calories: 139 ‖ Fat: 8.0g ‖ Protein: 1.9g ‖ Carbohydrates: 15.7g

ORANGE PUMPKIN COOKIES

Total Time Taken: 1 hour
Yield: 20 Servings
Ingredients:

- ¼ teaspoon salt
- ½ cup almond flour
- ½ cup butter, softened
- ½ cup powdered sugar
- ½ cup pumpkin puree
- 1 ½ cups all-purpose flour
- 1 orange, zested and juiced
- 1 teaspoon baking powder

Directions:

1. Mix the butter and sugar in a container until pale and creamy.
2. Put in the orange zest and juice, as well as the pumpkin puree and mix thoroughly.
3. Fold in the flour, almond flour, salt and baking powder then drop spoonfuls of batter on a baking tray coated with baking paper.
4. Preheat your oven and bake the cookies at 350F for about fifteen minutes or until a golden-brown colour is achieved or until a golden-brown colour is achieved and fragrant.
5. These cookies taste best chilled.

Nutritional Content of One Serving:

Calories: 97 ‖ Fat: 5.1g ‖ Protein: 1.3g ‖ Carbohydrates: 12.0g

ORANGE POPPY SEED COOKIES

Total Time Taken: 1 ¼ hours
Yield: 20 Servings

Ingredients:

- ¼ teaspoon salt
- ½ cup butter, softened
- ½ cup white sugar
- ½ teaspoon baking powder
- 1 ½ cups all-purpose flour
- 1 egg
- 1 tablespoon orange zest
- 1 tablespoon poppy seeds

Directions:

1. Mix the butter and sugar in a container until fluffy and creamy.
2. Put in the egg and orange zest and mix thoroughly then fold in the flour, salt, baking powder and poppy seeds.
3. Drop spoonfuls of batter on a baking tray coated with baking paper.
4. Preheat your oven and bake the cookies at 350F for about fifteen minutes or until a golden-brown colour is achieved on the edges.
5. These cookies taste best chilled.

Nutritional Content of One Serving:

Calories: 100 ‖ Fat: 5.1g ‖ Protein: 1.4g ‖ Carbohydrates: 12.4g

ORANGE PISTACHIO COOKIES

Total Time Taken: 1 ¼ hours
Yield: 20 Servings

Ingredients:

- ¼ cup powdered sugar
- ¼ teaspoon salt
- ½ cup almond flour
- ½ cup butter, softened

- ½ cup ground pistachio
- ½ teaspoon baking soda
- 1 cup all-purpose flour
- 1 egg
- 1 teaspoon orange zest
- 2 tablespoons fresh orange juice

Directions:

1. Mix the almonds and pistachio in a container.
2. Mix the butter with sugar until fluffy and pale.
3. Stir in the egg, orange juice and orange zest.
4. Stir in the flour, salt, baking soda and pistachio mixture.
5. Drop spoonfuls of batter on a baking sheet coated with baking paper.
6. Preheat your oven and bake the cookies at 350F for about fifteen minutes or until a golden-brown colour is achieved on the edges.
7. These cookies taste best chilled.

Nutritional Content of One Serving:

Calories: 88 ‖ Fat: 5.7g ‖ Protein: 1.4g ‖ Carbohydrates: 8.0g

ORANGE PASSIONFRUIT COOKIES

Total Time Taken: 1 ¼ hours

Yield: 20 Servings

Ingredients:

- 1 teaspoon vanilla extract
- 1 egg
- 1 teaspoon orange zest
- Juice from 2 passionfruits
- 2 cups all-purpose flour
- ¼ teaspoon salt
- 1 teaspoon baking powder
- 2/3 cup butter, softened
- 2/3 cup white sugar

Directions:

1. Mix the butter, sugar and vanilla until creamy and fluffy.

2. Put in the egg, orange zest and passionfruit juice then mix in the dry ingredients.
3. Drop spoonfuls of batter on a baking tray coated with baking paper.
4. Preheat your oven and bake the cookies at 350F for about fifteen minutes or until the edges turn golden brown.
5. These cookies taste best chilled.

Nutritional Content of One Serving:

Calories: 129 ‖ Fat: 6.5g ‖ Protein: 1.6g ‖ Carbohydrates: 16.4g

OLIVE OIL CHOCOLATE CHIP COOKIES

Total Time Taken: 1 ¼ hours
Yield: 30 Servings

Ingredients:

- ¼ cup butter, softened
- ¼ cup white sugar
- ¼ teaspoon salt
- ½ cup dark chocolate chips
- ½ cup light brown sugar
- ½ cup olive oil
- ½ cup white chocolate chips
- 1 egg
- 1 teaspoon baking powder
- 1 teaspoon vanilla extract
- 2 cups all-purpose flour

Directions:

1. Mix the oil, butter and sugars in a container until creamy and fluffy.
2. Put in the vanilla and egg and mix thoroughly.
3. Fold in the flour, salt and baking powder, then put in the chocolate chips.
4. Drop spoonfuls of batter on a baking sheet coated with baking paper.
5. Pre-heat the oven and bake at 350F for about fifteen minutes or until a golden-brown colour is achieved on the edges.
6. These cookies taste best chilled.

Nutritional Content of One Serving:

Calories: 115 ‖ Fat: 6.6g ‖ Protein: 1.4g ‖ Carbohydrates: 13.5g

OATMEAL RAISINS COOKIES

Total Time Taken: 2 hours

Yield: 20 Servings

Ingredients:

- ¼ cup brandy
- ¼ teaspoon salt
- ½ cup golden raisins
- ½ cup light brown sugar
- 1 cup rolled oats
- 1 cup whole wheat flour
- 1 egg
- 1 teaspoon baking powder
- 1 teaspoon vanilla extract
- 2/3 cup butter, softened

Directions:

1. Mix the raisins and brandy in a container and let them soak up for an hour.
2. Mix the butter and sugar in a container until fluffy and pale.
3. Put in the egg and vanilla and mix thoroughly.
4. Put in the flour, salt, baking powder and oats then fold in the raisins.
5. Drop spoonfuls of batter on a baking sheet coated with baking paper.
6. Pre-heat the oven and bake at 350F for fifteen minutes or until the edges turn golden brown.
7. These cookies taste best chilled.

Nutritional Content of One Serving:

Calories: 124 ‖ Fat: 6.7g ‖ Protein: 1.6g ‖ Carbohydrates: 14.1g

OATMEAL COOKIES

Total Time Taken: 1 hour
Yield: 30 Servings
Ingredients:

- ½ cup dried cranberries
- ½ cup light brown sugar
- ½ teaspoon baking soda
- ½ teaspoon salt
- ¾ cup butter, softened
- 1 ½ cups all-purpose flour
- 1 cup pecans, chopped
- 1 cup rolled oats
- 1 egg
- 1 teaspoon vanilla extract
- 2 tablespoons dark brown sugar

Directions:

1. Mix the butter and sugars in a container until fluffy and creamy.
2. Stir in the egg and vanilla and mix thoroughly.
3. Fold in the remaining ingredients.
4. Drop spoonfuls of batter on a baking sheet coated with baking paper.
5. Preheat your oven and bake the cookies at 350F for fifteen minutes or until it rises significantly and seems golden.
6. Let the cookies cool in the pan before you serve.

Nutritional Content of One Serving:

Calories: 92 ‖ Fat: 5.3g ‖ Protein: 1.3g ‖ Carbohydrates: 9.8g

NUTTY COOKIES

Total Time Taken: 1 hour
Yield: 20 Servings
Ingredients:

- ¼ cup white sugar
- ¼ teaspoon salt
- ½ cup almond butter
- ½ cup ground cashew nuts

- ½ cup ground walnuts
- ½ cup light brown sugar
- ½ teaspoon baking soda
- 1 ¼ cups all-purpose flour
- 1 egg
- 1 teaspoon vanilla extract

Directions:

1. Mix the almond butter and sugars in a container until pale and light. Put in the egg and vanilla and mix thoroughly.
2. Stir in the remaining ingredients then drop spoonfuls of batter on a baking tray coated with baking paper.
3. Preheat your oven and bake the cookies at 350F for about fifteen minutes or until crisp and golden brown.
4. Serve Chilled or store them in an airtight container.

Nutritional Content of One Serving:

Calories: 138 ‖ Fat: 7.6g ‖ Protein: 3.9g ‖ Carbohydrates: 14.6g

MUESLI COOKIES

Total Time Taken: 1 ¼ hours

Yield: 20 Servings

Ingredients:

- ¼ teaspoon salt
- ½ cup butter, softened
- ½ cup white chocolate chips
- ½ cup white sugar
- 1 cup all-purpose flour
- 1 cup muesli
- 1 egg
- 1 teaspoon baking powder

Directions:

1. Mix the butter and sugar until fluffy and creamy. Put in the egg and mix thoroughly.

2. Stir in the flour, baking powder and salt then put in the muesli and chocolate chips.
3. Drop spoonfuls of batter on a baking sheet coated with baking paper.
4. Preheat your oven and bake the cookies at 350F for fifteen minutes or until a golden-brown colour is achieved on the edges.
5. These cookies taste best chilled.

Nutritional Content of One Serving:

Calories: 124 ‖ Fat: 6.5g ‖ Protein: 1.6g ‖ Carbohydrates: 15.6g

MONSTER COOKIE RECIPES

Total Time Taken: 1 ¼ hours
Yield: 30 Servings

Ingredients:

- ¼ cup white sugar
- ½ cup butter, softened
- ½ cup M&M candies
- ½ cup mini marshmallows
- ½ cup pecans, chopped
- ½ cup smooth peanut butter
- ½ cup walnuts, chopped
- ½ teaspoon salt
- ¾ cup light brown sugar
- 1 teaspoon baking soda
- 1 teaspoon vanilla extract
- 2 ¼ cups all-purpose flour
- 2 eggs

Directions:

1. Mix the butter, peanut butter and sugars in a container. Put in the vanilla and eggs and mix thoroughly.
2. Fold in the flour, salt and baking soda then put in the remaining ingredients.
3. Drop spoonfuls of batter on a baking tray covered with parchment paper.
4. Preheat your oven and bake the cookies at 350F for about fifteen minutes or until a golden-brown colour is achieved on the edges.
5. These cookies taste best chilled.

Nutritional Content of One Serving:

Calories: 149 ‖ Fat: 7.2g ‖ Protein: 3.2g ‖ Carbohydrates: 18.9g

MOLTEN CHOCOLATE COOKIES

Total Time Taken: 1 hour

Yield: 20 Servings

Ingredients:

- ¼ cup cocoa powder
- ¼ cup white sugar
- ¼ teaspoon salt
- ½ teaspoon baking soda
- 1 ¾ cups all-purpose flour
- 1 cup light brown sugar
- 1 egg
- 1 egg yolk
- 2/3 cup butter, melted

Directions:

1. Mix the butter, sugars, egg and egg yolk in container until creamy and fluffy.
2. Put in the rest of the ingredients then drop large spoonfuls of batter on a baking sheet coated with baking paper.
3. Pre-heat the oven and bake at 350F for about twelve minutes.
4. These cookies taste best chilled.

Nutritional Content of One Serving:

Calories: 139 ‖ Fat: 6.8g ‖ Protein: 1.8g ‖ Carbohydrates: 18.6g

MOLASSES COOKIES

Total Time Taken: 1 ½ hours

Yield: 20 Servings

Ingredients:

- ¼ teaspoon salt
- ½ cup butter, softened
- ½ cup light brown sugar
- 1 ½ cups all-purpose flour
- 1 egg
- 1 teaspoon baking powder
- 1 teaspoon vanilla extract
- 4 tablespoons dark molasses

Directions:

1. Mix the butter, molasses and sugar in a container until creamy and fluffy.
2. Put in the egg and vanilla and mix thoroughly.
3. Fold in the remaining ingredients then drop spoonfuls of batter on a baking tray coated with baking paper.
4. Preheat your oven and bake the cookies at 350F for about fifteen minutes or until aromatic and crunchy.
5. These cookies taste best chilled.

Nutritional Content of One Serving:

Calories: 104 ‖ Fat: 4.9g ‖ Protein: 1.3g ‖ Carbohydrates: 13.9g

MINTY CHOCOLATE COOKIES

Total Time Taken: 1 ¼ hours
Yield: 20 Servings

Ingredients:

- ¼ cup cocoa powder
- ¼ teaspoon salt
- ½ cup butter, softened
- ½ cup white sugar
- 1 ¼ cups all-purpose flour
- 1 egg
- 1 teaspoon baking powder
- 1 teaspoon peppermint extract
- 1 teaspoon vanilla extract
- 2 tablespoons honey

Directions:

1. Mix the butter, sugar, honey, peppermint and vanilla in a container until fluffy and pale.
2. Put in the egg and mix thoroughly then fold in the remaining ingredients.
3. Drop spoonfuls of batter on a baking sheet coated with baking paper.
4. Preheat your oven and bake the cookies at 350F for about fifteen minutes or until it rises completely and is aromatic.
5. These cookies taste best chilled.

Nutritional Content of One Serving:

Calories: 101 ‖ Fat: 5.0g ‖ Protein: 1.4g ‖ Carbohydrates: 13.5g

MINTY CHOCOLATE COOKIES

Total Time Taken: 1 ¼ hours
Yield: 20 Servings

Ingredients:

- ¼ cup cocoa powder
- ¼ teaspoon salt
- ½ cup dark chocolate chips
- ¾ cup butter, softened
- 1 1/4 cups all-purpose flour
- 1 cup light brown sugar
- 1 egg
- 1 teaspoon baking powder
- 1 teaspoon peppermint extract
- 1 teaspoon vanilla extract
- 2 tablespoons milk

Directions:

1. Mix the butter, sugar and vanilla in a container until creamy and pale.
2. Put in the milk, peppermint extract and egg and mix thoroughly then fold in the remaining ingredients.
3. Drop spoonfuls of batter on baking trays coated with baking paper.
4. Preheat your oven and bake the cookies at 350F for about thirteen minutes or until aromatic.

5. These cookies taste best chilled.

Nutritional Content of One Serving:

Calories: 139 ‖ Fat: 8.2g ‖ Protein: 1.6g ‖ Carbohydrates: 15.9g

MILKY COOKIES

Total Time Taken: 1 ¼ hours
Yield: 30 Servings

Ingredients:

- ¼ cup milk powder
- ¼ cup whole milk
- ¼ teaspoon salt
- 1 cup butter, softened
- 1 cup white sugar
- 1 teaspoon baking powder
- 1 teaspoon lemon zest
- 1 teaspoon vanilla extract
- 2 cups all-purpose flour
- 2 egg yolks

Directions:

1. Mix the butter, sugar, vanilla and lemon zest in a container until fluffy and pale.
2. Put in the egg yolks and milk and mix thoroughly then mix in the flour, milk powder, baking powder and salt.
3. Drop spoonfuls of batter on a baking tray coated with baking paper.
4. Pre-heat the oven and bake at 350F for about fifteen minutes or until a golden-brown colour is achieved on the edges.
5. Let the cookies cool before you serve.

Nutritional Content of One Serving:

Calories: 119 ‖ Fat: 6.6g ‖ Protein: 1.6g ‖ Carbohydrates: 13.8g

MARSHMALLOW CHOCOLATE CHIP COOKIES

Total Time Taken: 1 ¼ hours
Yield: 20 Servings

Ingredients:

- ¼ teaspoon salt
- ½ cup butter, softened
- ½ cup cornflakes
- ½ cup dark chocolate chips
- ½ teaspoon baking soda
- ¾ cup light brown sugar
- 1 ½ cups all-purpose flour
- 1 cup mini marshmallows
- 1 teaspoon vanilla extract
- 2 tablespoons coconut oil
- 2 tablespoons whole milk

Directions:

1. Mix the butter, coconut oil, sugar and vanilla in a container until pale and fluffy.
2. Stir in the milk then put in the flour, baking soda and salt then fold in the cornflakes, chocolate chips and marshmallows.
3. Drop spoonfuls of batter on a baking sheet coated with baking paper.
4. Preheat your oven and bake the cookies at 350F for about fifteen minutes or until a golden-brown colour is achieved on the edges.
5. These cookies taste best chilled.

Nutritional Content of One Serving:

Calories: 130 ‖ Fat: 6.9g ‖ Protein: 1.3g ‖ Carbohydrates: 16.3g

MAPLE SESAME COOKIES

Total Time Taken: 1 ½ hours
Yield: 25 Servings

Ingredients:

- ¼ cup sesame seeds
- ¼ teaspoon salt
- ½ cup butter, softened
- ½ cup maple syrup
- 1 ½ cups all-purpose flour
- 1 egg
- 1 teaspoon baking powder
- 2 tablespoons dark brown sugar

Directions:

1. Mix the butter, maple syrup and egg in a container until creamy and pale.
2. Stir in the sugar and mix thoroughly then put in the flour, salt, baking powder and sesame seeds.
3. Spoon the batter in a plastic wrap and shape it into a log. Put it in your freezer for about half an hour.
4. Take out of the freezer and cut into thin slices. Position the slices on a baking sheet coated with baking paper with the cut facing up.
5. Pre-heat the oven and bake at 350F for about ten minutes or until mildly golden-brown on the edges.
6. These cookies taste best chilled.

Nutritional Content of One Serving:

Calories: 90 ‖ Fat: 4.6g ‖ Protein: 1.3g ‖ Carbohydrates: 11.1g

MAPLE FLAVORED COOKIES

Total Time Taken: 1 ¼ hours
Yield: 30 Servings

Ingredients:

- ½ cup butter, softened
- 1 teaspoon vanilla extract
- 1 egg
- ½ cup maple syrup
- 2 cups all-purpose flour
- ¼ teaspoon salt

- 1 teaspoon baking powder
- 1 cup walnuts, chopped
- 1/2 cup light brown sugar

Directions:

1. Mix the butter, sugar and maple syrup in a container until fluffy and creamy.
2. Put in the vanilla and eggs and mix thoroughly then mix in the rest of the ingredients.
3. Drop spoonfuls of batter on baking trays coated with baking paper.
4. Preheat your oven and bake the cookies at 350F for about fifteen minutes or until a golden-brown colour is achieved on the edges.
5. These cookies taste best chilled.

Nutritional Content of One Serving:

Calories: 109 ‖ Fat: 5.8g ‖ Protein: 2.1g ‖ Carbohydrates: 12.8g

MANGO CRUNCH COOKIES

Total Time Taken: 1 ¼ hours

Yield: 20 Servings

Ingredients:

- ¼ cup white sugar
- ¼ teaspoon salt
- ½ cup butter, softened
- ½ teaspoon baking soda
- 1 ½ cups all-purpose flour
- 1 cup dried mango, chopped
- 1 egg
- 1 teaspoon vanilla extract

Directions:

1. Mix the butter, sugar and egg in a container until creamy. Put in the vanilla and mix thoroughly then fold in the flour, salt and baking soda.
2. Put in the mango and mix using a spatula.
3. Drop spoonfuls of batter on a baking tray coated with baking paper.
4. Pre-heat the oven and bake at 350F for about fifteen minutes or until a golden-brown colour is achieved on the edges.

5. These cookies taste best chilled.

Nutritional Content of One Serving:

Calories: 95 ‖ Fat: 5.0g ‖ Protein: 1.4g ‖ Carbohydrates: 11.5g

MACADAMIA COOKIES

Total Time Taken: 1 ¼ hours
Yield: 20 Servings

Ingredients:

- ¼ cup golden syrup
- ¼ cup light brown sugar
- ½ cup butter, softened
- ½ cup shredded coconut
- ½ teaspoon salt
- 1 cup all-purpose flour
- 1 cup rolled oats
- 1 teaspoon baking powder
- 2/3 cup macadamia nuts, chopped

Directions:

1. Mix the oats, flour, baking powder, salt, coconut and macadamia nuts in a container.
2. Mix the butter and syrup and sugar in a container until creamy and pale.
3. Fold in the remaining ingredients then drop spoonfuls of batter on a baking sheet coated with baking paper.
4. Pre-heat the oven and bake at 350F for about fifteen minutes or until a golden-brown colour is achieved on the edges.
5. These cookies taste best chilled.

Nutritional Content of One Serving:

Calories: 137 ‖ Fat: 9.0g ‖ Protein: 1.7g ‖ Carbohydrates: 13.5g

M&M COOKIES

Total Time Taken: 1 ¼ hours

Yield: 30 Servings

Ingredients:

- 1 cup butter, softened
- 2/3 cup light brown sugar
- 2 eggs
- 2 cups all-purpose flour
- 1 teaspoon baking powder
- ¼ teaspoon salt
- 1 cup M&M candies

Directions:

1. Mix the butter and sugar in a container until creamy and fluffy.
2. Stir in the eggs, one at a time, then put in the flour, baking powder and salt.
3. Fold in the candies then drop spoonfuls of batter on a baking tray coated with baking paper.
4. Preheat your oven and bake the cookies at 350F for fifteen minutes or until a golden-brown colour is achieved on the edges.
5. These cookies taste best chilled.

Nutritional Content of One Serving:

Calories: 102 ‖ Fat: 6.5g ‖ Protein: 1.3g ‖ Carbohydrates: 9.8g

LENTIL COOKIES

Total Time Taken: 1 ¼ hours

Yield: 30 Servings

Ingredients:

- ¼ teaspoon salt
- ½ cup butter, melted
- ½ cup walnuts, chopped
- ½ teaspoon baking powder
- ½ teaspoon cinnamon powder
- ½ teaspoon ground ginger
- ¾ cup light brown sugar
- 1 ½ cups all-purpose flour

- 1 egg
- 1 teaspoon vanilla extract
- 4 oz. lentil, cooked and pureed

Directions:

1. Mix the lentil puree, butter, egg, vanilla and sugar in a container until creamy and light.
2. Put in the rest of the ingredients and mix thoroughly.
3. Make small balls of mixture and place them on a baking tray coated with baking paper.
4. Preheat your oven and bake the cookies at 350F for about fifteen minutes or until a golden-brown colour is achieved and fragrant.
5. These cookies taste best chilled.

Nutritional Content of One Serving:

Calories: 93 ‖ Fat: 4.5g ‖ Protein: 2.3g ‖ Carbohydrates: 10.9g

BONUS: CAKE RECIPES

Cakes hardly need an explanation. Just remember to sift the flour before using in a recipe as it aerates the flour before it is added to the batter. Also, the toothpick is one of the most popular methods to tell if a cake is cooked. Basically you insert a toothpick into the center of the cake, and if the toothpick comes out dry, your cake is done!

All righty then, let us jump straight into the recipes!

YOGURT STRAWBERRY CAKE

Total Time Taken: 1 hour
Yield: 8 Servings
Ingredients:

- ½ cup cornstarch
- ½ teaspoon salt
- ¾ cup canola oil
- ¾ cup white sugar
- 1 ½ cups all-purpose flour

- 1 cup plain yogurt
- 1 cup strawberries, sliced
- 1 teaspoon baking powder
- 1 teaspoon vanilla extract
- 2 eggs

Directions:

1. Mix the canola oil, sugar, eggs and vanilla in a container until fluffy.
2. Stir in the yogurt and mix thoroughly then fold in the flour, cornstarch, baking powder and salt then pour the batter in a 9-inch round cake pan covered with parchment paper.
3. Top the cake with fresh strawberries and preheat your oven and bake at 350F for about forty minutes or until a toothpick inserted in the center comes out cleans.
4. Let the cake cool in the pan before you serve.

Nutritional Content of One Serving:

Calories: 412 ‖ Fat: 22.2g ‖ Protein: 5.7g ‖ Carbohydrates: 47.9g

YOGURT BUNDT CAKE

Total Time Taken: 1 ¼ hours

Yield: 12 Servings

Ingredients:

- ½ teaspoon salt
- 1 ½ cups plain yogurt
- 1 ½ cups white sugar
- 1 cup butter, softened
- 1 teaspoon baking powder
- 1 teaspoon baking soda
- 2 tablespoons lemon juice
- 2 tablespoons lemon zest
- 3 cups all-purpose flour
- 6 eggs, separated

Directions:

1. Mix the egg yolks with sugar until pale and fluffy. Stir in the butter and mix thoroughly.
2. Put in the lemon zest and juice then mix in the yogurt.
3. Fold in the flour, baking powder, baking soda and salt.
4. Spoon the batter in a greased Bundt cake pan and preheat your oven and bake at 350F for about forty minutes or until a toothpick inserted into the center of the cake comes out clean.
5. Let the cake cool in the pan before transferring on a platter.

Nutritional Content of One Serving:

Calories: 398 ‖ Fat: 18.2g ‖ Protein: 7.9g ‖ Carbohydrates: 51.7g

YEASTED PLUM CAKE

Total Time Taken: 2 hours

Yield: 16 Servings

Ingredients:

- ¼ cup butter, melted
- ½ cup light brown sugar

- ½ cup warm milk
- ½ teaspoon salt
- 1 ¼ teaspoons instant yeast
- 1 cup warm water
- 1 pound plums, pitted and sliced
- 1 tablespoon lemon zest
- 1 teaspoon vanilla extract
- 2 eggs
- 3 cups all-purpose flour

Directions:

1. Mix the flour, salt and yeast in a container.
2. Put in the water, milk, butter, eggs, vanilla and lemon zest and knead the dough minimum ten minutes until it looks and feels elastic.
3. Allow the dough to rest for an hour then roll it into a rectangle and move it to a sheet cake pan coated with baking paper.
4. Top with plums and drizzle with brown sugar.
5. Pre-heat the oven and bake at 350F for about forty minutes or until it rises significantly and starts to appear golden-brown.
6. Let the cake cool in the pan before you serve.

Nutritional Content of One Serving:

Calories: 150 ‖ Fat: 3.9g ‖ Protein: 3.7g ‖ Carbohydrates: 25.1g

WHOLE PEAR SPONGE CAKE

Total Time Taken: 2 hours
Yield: 14 Servings
Ingredients:

- ¼ cup canola oil
- ¼ cup honey
- ¼ teaspoon salt
- ½ cup butter, softened
- ½ cup cocoa powder
- ½ cup sour cream
- 1 ½ cups all-purpose flour
- 1 cinnamon stick

- 1 teaspoon baking soda
- 2 cups white wine
- 2 eggs
- 2 star anise
- 4 pears

Directions:

1. Peel the pears and place them in a saucepan. Put in the star anise, cinnamon, honey and wine and cook over low heat for about half an hour. Let cool and then position the pears in a 9-inch round cake pan coated with baking paper.
2. Mix the butter, canola oil and eggs in a container until creamy.
3. Put in the sour cream and mix thoroughly then fold in the flour, cocoa powder, baking soda and salt.
4. Spoon the batter over the pears.
5. Preheat your oven and bake the cake for 45 minutes or until a toothpick inserted into the center of the cake comes out clean.
6. Let the cake cool before you serve.

Nutritional Content of One Serving:

Calories: 257 ‖ Fat: 13.5g ‖ Protein: 3.4g ‖ Carbohydrates: 27.6g

WHITE CHOCOLATE BLACKBERRY CAKE

Total Time Taken: 2 hours
Yield: 10 Servings
Ingredients:

Sponge cake:

- ¼ teaspoon salt
- ½ cup white sugar
- ½ teaspoon baking powder
- 1 cup all-purpose flour
- 5 eggs

Filling:

- 1 ½ cups heavy cream
- 2 ½ cups white chocolate chips

- 2 cups fresh blackberries

Directions:

1. For the sponge cake, whip the eggs, sugar and salt in a container until volume increases to twice what it was.
2. Fold in the flour and baking powder then spoon the batter in a 8-inch round cake pan coated with baking paper.
3. Pre-heat the oven and bake at 350F for around forty minutes then allow the cake to cool in the pan.
4. Slice the cake in half along the length.
5. For the filling, bring the cream to the boiling point in a saucepan. Turn off the heat and put in the chocolate. Stir until melted then let cool in your refrigerator.
6. Whip the white chocolate cream for at least two minutes until fluffy.
7. Fill the cake with half of the cream and half of the blackberries. Cover the cake with the rest of the cream and garnish with blackberries.
8. The cake tastes best chilled.

Nutritional Content of One Serving:

Calories: 418 ‖ Fat: 22.8g ‖ Protein: 7.3g ‖ Carbohydrates: 48.3g

WALNUT HONEY POUND CAKE

Total Time Taken: 1 ¼ hours

Yield: 12 Servings

Ingredients:

- ½ cup butter, softened
- ½ teaspoon salt
- 1 ½ cups walnuts, chopped
- 1 cup honey
- 1 cup whole milk
- 1 teaspoon vanilla extract
- 2 cups all-purpose flour
- 2 eggs
- 2 teaspoons baking powder

Directions:

1. Sift the flour, baking powder and salt in a container.
2. In a separate container, combine the butter and honey until fluffy. Stir in the eggs and vanilla and mix thoroughly.
3. Put in the flour mixture, alternating it with the milk.
4. Fold in the walnuts then spoon the batter in a 9-inch round cake pan coated with baking paper.
5. Pre-heat the oven and bake at 350F for about forty minutes or until it rises significantly and starts to appear golden-brown.
6. Let the cake cool in the pan and serve, sliced.

Nutritional Content of One Serving:

Calories: 351 ‖ Fat: 18.5g ‖ Protein: 7.6g ‖ Carbohydrates: 42.1g

WALNUT COFFEE CAKE

Total Time Taken: 2 hours
Yield: 16 Servings
Ingredients:

Walnut cake:

- ¼ cup whole milk
- ½ teaspoon salt
- 1 cup butter, softened
- 1 cup ground walnuts
- 1 cup white sugar
- 1 teaspoon vanilla extract
- 2 cups all-purpose flour
- 2 teaspoons baking powder
- 4 eggs

Coffee buttercream:

- 1 cup butter, softened
- 1 teaspoon vanilla extract
- 2 ½ cups powdered sugar
- 2 teaspoons instant coffee

Directions:

1. For the cake, combine the flour, baking powder, walnuts and salt in a container.
2. In a separate container, combine the butter and sugar until creamy. Stir in the eggs, one at a time, then put in the milk and vanilla.
3. Fold in the flour and stir lightly using a spatula.
4. Pour the batter in a round cake pan coated with baking paper and preheat your oven and bake at 350F for around forty minutes.
5. Let the cake cool in the pan then move to a platter.
6. For the buttercream, combine the butter until creamy and light. Put in the sugar, progressively and stir thoroughly for a few minutes until firm.
7. Mix the vanilla with the coffee then add it into the buttercream. Stir thoroughly to mix.
8. Cover the cake with the buttercream and serve it fresh.

Nutritional Content of One Serving:

Calories: 449 ‖ Fat: 29.0g ‖ Protein: 5.2g ‖ Carbohydrates: 44.5g

WALNUT CARROT CAKE

Total Time Taken: 1 ½ hours
Yield: 16 Servings
Ingredients:

Cake:

- ½ cup ground walnuts
- ½ teaspoon salt
- 1 cup canola oil
- 1 cup chopped walnuts
- 1 cup crushed pineapple
- 1 cup white sugar
- 1 teaspoon all-spice powder
- 1 teaspoon baking powder
- 1 teaspoon baking soda
- 1 teaspoon cinnamon powder
- 2 cups all-purpose flour
- 2 cups grated carrots
- 3 eggs

Frosting:

- ¼ cup butter
- 1 cup cream cheese, softened
- 3 cups powdered sugar

Directions:

1. To prepare the cake, combine the dry ingredients in a container and the wet ingredients in another container.
2. Pour the wet ingredients over the dry ones and mix using a spatula.
3. Pour the batter in 9-inch round cake pan coated with baking paper.
4. Preheat your oven and bake the cake at 350F for about forty minutes or until they pass the toothpick test.
5. Let the cakes cool completely.
6. For the frosting, combine the cream cheese and butter in a container until creamy.
7. Put in the sugar, progressively, stirring thoroughly after each addition.
8. Whip the frosting thoroughly until fluffy.
9. Fill the cake with 1/3 of the frosting and cover it with the rest of the cream cheese frosting.
10. Serve the cake fresh or place in your refrigerator.

Nutritional Content of One Serving:

Calories: 483 ‖ Fat: 29.5g ‖ Protein: 6.8g ‖ Carbohydrates: 51.3g

WALNUT BANANA CAKE

Total Time Taken: 1 ¼ hours
Yield: 10 Servings

Ingredients:

- ¼ cup whole milk
- ½ teaspoon salt
- 1 cup butter, softened
- 1 cup ground walnuts
- 1 cup light brown sugar
- 1 teaspoon cinnamon powder
- 2 cups all-purpose flour

- 2 teaspoons baking soda
- 3 ripe bananas, mashed
- 4 eggs

Directions:

1. Mix the flour, walnuts, baking soda, salt and cinnamon in a container.
2. In a separate container, combine the butter and sugar until creamy, then put in the eggs, one at a time.
3. Put in the milk and bananas then fold in the flour mixture.
4. Spoon the batter into a 10-inch round cake pan coated with baking paper.
5. Pre-heat the oven and bake at 350F or until a toothpick inserted into the center of the cake comes out clean.
6. Let the cake cool completely and serve, sliced.

Nutritional Content of One Serving:

Calories: 446 ‖ Fat: 28.1g ‖ Protein: 8.6g ‖ Carbohydrates: 43.1g

VICTORIA SPONGE CAKE WITH STRAWBERRIES

Total Time Taken: 1 ¼ hours
Yield: 8 Servings

Ingredients:

- ¼ teaspoon salt
- 1 ¼ cups all-purpose flour
- 1 cup butter, softened
- 1 cup fresh strawberries, sliced
- 1 cup heavy cream, whipped
- 1 cup white sugar
- 1 teaspoon baking powder
- 4 eggs

Directions:

1. Mix the butter and sugar in a container until light and creamy.
2. Stir in the eggs, one at a time, then fold in the flour, salt and baking powder.

3. Spoon the batter in a 9-inch round cake pan covered with parchment paper and preheat your oven and bake at 350F for about half an hour or until it rises significantly and starts to appear golden-brown.
4. Let the cake cool down then take it out of the pan and cut it in half along the length.
5. Fill the cake with whipped cream and strawberries and garnish it with a dust of powdered sugar.

Nutritional Content of One Serving:

Calories: 458 ‖ Fat: 31.0g ‖ Protein: 5.5g ‖ Carbohydrates: 42.2g

VANILLA WHITE CHOCOLATE CHIP CAKE

Total Time Taken: 1 ¼ hours

Yield: 12 Servings

Ingredients:

- ½ teaspoon salt
- 1 ½ teaspoons baking powder
- 1 cup butter, softened
- 1 cup white chocolate chips
- 1 cup white sugar
- 1 cup whole milk
- 1 tablespoon vanilla extract
- 2 cups all-purpose flour
- 4 eggs

Directions:

1. Mix the butter and sugar in a container until fluffy and pale.
2. Stir in the eggs, one at a time, then put in the vanilla and milk.
3. Stir in the flour, baking powder and salt then fold in the chocolate chips.
4. Spoon the batter in a 9-inch round cake pan coated with baking paper.
5. Pre-heat the oven and bake at 350F for about forty minutes.
6. Let the cake cool in the pan and serve, sliced.

Nutritional Content of One Serving:

Calories: 387 ‖ Fat: 22.2g ‖ Protein: 5.6g ‖ Carbohydrates: 42.4g

VANILLA STRAWBERRY CAKE

Total Time Taken: 1 ½ hours
Yield: 10 Servings
Ingredients:

Cake:

- ¼ cup sour cream
- ½ cup butter, softened
- ½ cup whole milk
- ½ teaspoon baking soda
- ½ teaspoon salt
- 1 ½ cups all-purpose flour
- 1 cup white sugar
- 1 teaspoon baking powder
- 1 teaspoon vanilla extract
- 4 egg whites

Filling:

- ½ cup butter, softened
- 1 cup fresh strawberries, sliced
- 2 cups powdered sugar
- 2 teaspoons vanilla extract

Directions:

1. For the cake, sift the flour with baking powder, baking soda and salt in a container.
2. Put in the sugar and butter and stir until grainy.
3. Combine the egg whites, milk and sour cream, as well as vanilla in a container. Pour this mixture over the dry ingredients and stir only until blended.
4. Spoon the batter in two 8-inch circular cake pans coated with baking paper.
5. For the filling, combine the butter with sugar for five minutes until fluffy and creamy. Put in the vanilla and mix thoroughly.
6. Fill the cake with the buttercream and strawberry slices.

7. Serve it fresh.

Nutritional Content of One Serving:

Calories: 435 ‖ Fat: 20.3g ‖ Protein: 4.2g ‖ Carbohydrates: 60.6g

VANILLA GENOISE CAKE

Total Time Taken: 1 hour
Yield: 8 Servings
Ingredients:

6 eggs

- ¼ teaspoon baking powder
- ¼ teaspoon salt
- ¾ cup white sugar
- 1 cup all-purpose flour
- 1 teaspoon vanilla extract

Directions:

1. Mix the eggs, sugar and vanilla in a container until fluffy and light.
2. Fold in the flour, salt and baking powder then spoon the batter in a 8-inch round cake pan coated with baking paper.
3. Pre-heat the oven and bake at 350F for about half an hour or until it rises significantly and starts to appear golden-brown.
4. Let the cake cool down before you serve.

Nutritional Content of One Serving:

Calories: 176 ‖ Fat: 3.4g ‖ Protein: 5.8g ‖ Carbohydrates: 31.1g

VANILLA FUNFETTI CAKE

Total Time Taken: 1 ½ hours
Yield: 12 Servings
Ingredients:

Cake:

- ½ cup sprinkles
- ½ teaspoon salt
- 1 ½ teaspoons baking powder
- 1 cup butter, softened
- 1 cup sour cream
- 1 cup white sugar
- 1 teaspoon vanilla extract
- 2 cups all-purpose flour
- 3 eggs

Frosting:

- ½ cup butter, softened
- 1 ½ cups powdered sugar
- 1 teaspoon vanilla extract

Directions:

1. For the cake, combine the butter and sugar in a container until fluffy and creamy.
2. Put in the eggs and vanilla and stir thoroughly for a few minutes.
3. Stir in the sour cream then fold in the flour, baking powder and salt, as well as sprinkles.
4. Spoon the batter in a 9-inch round cake pan coated with baking paper.
5. Pre-heat the oven and bake at 350F for about forty minutes or until it rises significantly and starts to appear golden-brown.
6. For the frosting, combine the butter, sugar and vanilla and stir thoroughly until fluffy and
7. pale.
8. Top the cake with frosting and serve it fresh.

Nutritional Content of One Serving:

Calories: 464 ‖ Fat: 28.3g ‖ Protein: 4.4g ‖ Carbohydrates: 50.0g

VANILLA CARDAMOM CAKE

Total Time Taken: 1 ¼ hours
Yield: 12 Servings
Ingredients:

Cake:

- ¼ teaspoon salt
- ½ cup canola oil
- 1 ½ cups all-purpose flour
- 1 cup white sugar
- 1 teaspoon baking powder
- 1 teaspoon cardamom powder
- 6 eggs

Frosting:

- ½ cup butter, softened
- 1 ½ cups powdered sugar
- 1 cup cream cheese
- 1 teaspoon vanilla extract

Directions:

1. For the cake, sift the flour with baking powder, salt and cardamom.
2. Mix the eggs with sugar until fluffy and pale.
3. Put in the oil and mix thoroughly then fold in the flour.
4. Pour the batter in a 9-inch round cake pan coated with baking paper.
5. Pre-heat the oven and bake at 350F for about forty minutes.
6. When finished, allow the cake to cool in the pan then cut it in half along the length.
7. For the frosting, combine the butter and cream cheese in a container until fluffy. Put in the vanilla and sugar and continue mixing for minimum five minutes until pale.
8. Use half of the frosting as filling and the second half to cover the cake.
9. Serve the cake fresh.

Nutritional Content of One Serving:

Calories: 427 ‖ Fat: 25.9g ‖ Protein: 5.9g ‖ Carbohydrates: 44.6g

TROPICAL CARROT CAKE

Total Time Taken: 1 ½ hours
Yield: 16 Servings
Ingredients:

Cake:

- ¼ cup dark brown sugar
- 1 cup vegetable oil
- ½ cup chopped walnuts
- 1 cup shredded coconut **Frosting:**
- ½ teaspoon ground cloves
- 1 cup white sugar
- ½ teaspoon ground ginger
- ½ teaspoon salt
- 1 cup butter, softened
- 1 cup cream cheese, softened
- 2 ½ cups powdered sugar
- 1 cup crushed pineapple (with juice)
- 1 teaspoon baking powder
- 1 teaspoon cinnamon powder
- 1 teaspoon vanilla extract
- 1 teaspoon vanilla extract
- 4 carrots, grated
- 2 cups all-purpose flour
- 1 teaspoon baking soda
- 4 eggs

Directions:

1. For the cake, combine the flour, baking soda, baking powder, spices and salt in a container.
2. Combine the sugars, oil, eggs and vanilla in a container and stir thoroughly until volume increases to twice what it was.
3. Stir in the carrots, pineapple, walnuts and coconut then put in the dry ingredients.
4. Pour the batter in two 9-inch cake pans and preheat your oven and bake at 350F for around forty minutes or until it rises and looks golden brown.
5. Let the cakes cool in the pans then level them and set aside for later.
6. For the frosting, combine the cream cheese, butter, sugar and vanilla in a container for minimum five minutes until firm and fluffy.
7. Use half of the frosting to fill the cakes and the second half to garnish them.

Nutritional Content of One Serving:

Calories: 529 ‖ Fat: 35.5g ‖ Protein: 5.5g ‖ Carbohydrates: 50.1g

TIRAMISU CAKE

Total Time Taken: 2 hours
Yield: 12 Servings
Ingredients:

- ¼ cup Grand Marnier
- 1 cup powdered sugar
- 1 tablespoon vanilla extract
- 10 oz. ladyfingers
- 2 cups brewed coffee
- 2 cups heavy cream, whipped
- 2 cups mascarpone cheese

Directions:

1. Coat a 9-inch round cake pan using plastic wrap.
2. Mix the mascarpone cheese with sugar then fold in the whipped cream.
3. Mix the coffee and Grand Marnier in a container.
4. Immerse the ladyfingers in the coffee mixture and layer them at the bottom of the pan.
5. Top with 1/3 of the cream, followed by an additional layer of ladyfingers.
6. Carry on until you run out of ingredients and place in your fridge at least an hour.
7. The cake tastes best chilled.

Nutritional Content of One Serving:

Calories: 285 ‖ Fat: 14.9g ‖ Protein: 7.6g ‖ Carbohydrates: 26.0g

THE ULTIMATE CHOCOLATE CAKE

Total Time Taken: 1 ¼ hours
Yield: 14 Servings
Ingredients:

Cake:

- ¼ cup canola oil
- ½ cup cocoa powder
- ½ teaspoon salt

- 1 ½ cups white sugar
- 1 cup butter, softened
- 1 cup buttermilk
- 2 ½ cups all-purpose flour
- 2 egg yolks
- 2 teaspoons baking powder
- 4 eggs

Frosting:

- 1 ½ cups dark chocolate chips
- 1 cup heavy cream

Directions:

1. Mix the butter and sugar in a container until creamy and fluffy.
2. Stir in the eggs and egg yolks and mix thoroughly.
3. Put in the buttermilk and oil and mix thoroughly then fold in the dry ingredients.
4. Pour the batter in a 10-inch round cake pan and preheat your oven and bake at 350F for 45 minutes or until the toothpick inserted in the center of the cake comes out clean.
5. Let the cake cool in the pan then move to a platter.
6. For the frosting, bring the cream to the boiling point then turn off the heat and put in the chocolate. let the frosting cool in your refrigerator for a few hours then whip it using an electric mixer until fluffy.
7. Sprinkle the chocolate frosting over the cake and serve it fresh.

Nutritional Content of One Serving:

Calories: 442 ‖ Fat: 26.3g ‖ Protein: 6.6g ‖ Carbohydrates: 50.3g

TAHINI CAKE

Total Time Taken: 1 ¼ hours
Yield: 10 Servings

Ingredients:

- ½ cup butter, softened
- ½ cup tahini paste
- ½ teaspoon baking soda

- ½ teaspoon salt
- 1 cup buttermilk
- 1 cup white sugar
- 1 teaspoon baking powder
- 1 teaspoon vanilla extract
- 2 cups all-purpose flour
- 2 eggs

Directions:

1. Mix the tahini paste, butter and sugar in a container and give it a good mix.

2. Stir in the eggs, one at a time, then put in the vanilla and buttermilk.

3. Fold in the flour, baking powder, baking soda and salt then spoon the batter in a round cake pan coated with baking paper.

4. Pre-heat the oven and bake at 350F for about forty minutes or until the cake is well risen and seems golden brown.

5. Let the cake cool in the pan and serve, sliced.

Nutritional Content of One Serving:

Calories: 343 ‖ Fat: 17.0g ‖ Protein: 6.6g ‖ Carbohydrates: 43.1g

SWEET POTATO BUNDT CAKE

Total Time Taken: 1 hour
Yield: 10 Servings
Ingredients:

- 1 cup sweet potato puree
- 2 eggs
- ½ cup sour cream
- ¼ cup canola oil
- 1 teaspoon vanilla extract
- 2 cups all-purpose flour
- 2 teaspoons baking powder
- ½ teaspoon salt
- ½ cup dark chocolate chips
- 3/4 cup maple syrup

Directions:

1. Mix the potato puree, maple syrup, eggs, sour cream, canola oil and vanilla in a container.
2. Stir in the remaining ingredients then spoon the batter in a greased Bundt cake pan.
3. Pre-heat the oven and bake at 350F for about forty minutes or until a toothpick comes out clean after being inserted into the center of the cake.
4. Let the cake cool in the pan then serve, sliced.

Nutritional Content of One Serving:

Calories: 294 ‖ Fat: 10.7g ‖ Protein: 5.0g ‖ Carbohydrates: 45.9g

SUMMER FRUIT CAKE

Total Time Taken: 1 ¼ hours
Yield: 12 Servings

Ingredients:

- ½ cup butter, softened
- ½ cup canola oil
- 1 cup all-purpose flour
- 1 cup cherries, pitted
- 1 cup ground almonds
- 1 cup mixed berries
- 1 cup white sugar
- 1 teaspoon baking powder
- 1 teaspoon vanilla extract
- 6 eggs

Directions:

1. Mix the butter, oil and sugar in a container until creamy and fluffy. Put in the vanilla and eggs, one at a time, and mix thoroughly.
2. Stir in the almonds, flour and baking powder then pour the batter in a 9-inch round cake pan coated with baking paper.
3. Top with berries and cherries and preheat your oven and bake at 350F for 40- 45 minutes or until it rises significantly and starts to appear golden-brown.

4. Let the cake cool in the pan and serve, sliced.

Nutritional Content of One Serving:

Calories: 341 ‖ Fat: 23.0g ‖ Protein: 5.7g ‖ Carbohydrates: 29.9g

SULTANA CAKE

Total Time Taken: 1 ½ hours
Yield: 10 Servings

Ingredients:

- ¼ cup orange marmalade
- ¼ teaspoon salt
- ½ cup brandy
- ½ cup butter, softened
- 1 ½ cups sultanas
- 1 cup all-purpose flour
- 1 cup white sugar
- 1 teaspoon baking soda
- 2 eggs
- 2 tablespoons dark brown sugar

Directions:

1. Mix the sultanas with the brandy and allow to soak up for about half an hour.
2. Mix the butter, sugars and marmalade in a container until creamy.
3. Put in the eggs and mix thoroughly.
4. Fold in the flour, salt and baking soda then put in the sultanas.
5. Spoon the batter in a 8-inch round cake pan coated with baking paper.
6. Pre-heat the oven and bake at 350F for about fifty minutes or until a toothpick inserted into the center of the cake comes out clean.
7. Let the cake cool down before you serve.

Nutritional Content of One Serving:

Calories: 262 ‖ Fat: 10.2g ‖ Protein: 2.7g ‖ Carbohydrates: 40.7g

STRAWBERRY YOGURT CAKE

Total Time Taken: 1 hour

Yield: 8 Servings

Ingredients:

- ½ cup butter, softened
- 1 cup all-purpose flour
- 1 cup strawberries, sliced
- 1 cup white sugar
- 1 teaspoon baking powder
- 1 teaspoon vanilla extract
- 1/2 cup plain yogurt
- 3 eggs

Directions:

1. Mix the butter and sugar until softened and creamy.
2. Put in the eggs, one at a time, then mix in the yogurt and vanilla.
3. Fold in the flour and baking powder using a spatula then put in the strawberries.
4. Pour the batter in a round cake pan coated with baking paper.
5. Pre-heat the oven and bake at 350F for about forty minutes or until a toothpick inserted into the center of the cake comes out clean.
6. Let the cake cool in the pan before you serve.

Nutritional Content of One Serving:

Calories: 295 ‖ Fat: 13.5g ‖ Protein: 4.8g ‖ Carbohydrates: 39.9g

STRAWBERRY POLENTA CAKE

Total Time Taken: 1 ¼ hours

Yield: 10 Servings

Ingredients:

- ¼ cup butter, melted
- ¼ teaspoon salt
- ½ cup white sugar
- 1 cup polenta flour

- 1 teaspoon baking soda
- 1 teaspoon vanilla extract
- 2 cups strawberries, sliced
- 2 cups water
- 2 cups whole milk
- 2 tablespoons all-purpose flour

Directions:

1. Mix the polenta flour, flour, salt and baking soda in a container.
2. Stir in the milk, water, sugar, vanilla and melted butter.
3. Pour the batter in a 8x8-inch and top with strawberry slices.
4. Pre-heat the oven and bake at 350F for around forty minutes or until a toothpick inserted into the center of the cake comes out clean.
5. When finished, take it out of the oven, let cool down then cut into small squares.
6. Serve immediately.

Nutritional Content of One Serving:

Calories: 147 ‖ Fat: 6.4g ‖ Protein: 2.4g ‖ Carbohydrates: 20.7g

STRAWBERRY LEMON OLIVE OIL CAKE

Total Time Taken: 1 ¼ hours
Yield: 10 Servings

Ingredients:

- ¼ teaspoon salt
- ¾ cup olive oil
- ¾ cup white sugar
- 1 ¼ cups all-purpose flour
- 1 ½ cups strawberries, sliced
- 1 lemon, zested and juiced
- 1 teaspoon baking powder
- 4 eggs

Directions:

1. Mix the eggs, oil and sugar in a container until fluffy and pale.
2. Put in the lemon zest and juice and mix thoroughly.

3. Fold in the flour, baking powder and salt then spoon the batter in a 9-inch round cake pan coated with baking paper.
4. Top with strawberries and preheat your oven and bake at 350F for about forty minutes.
5. Let the cake cool in the pan before you serve.

Nutritional Content of One Serving:

Calories: 277 ‖ Fat: 17.1g ‖ Protein: 4.0g ‖ Carbohydrates: 29.5g

STRAWBERRY CRUMBLE CAKE

Total Time Taken: 1 ¼ hours
Yield: 12 Servings
Ingredients:

Cake:

- ¼ cup canola oil
- ¼ teaspoon salt
- ½ teaspoon baking powder
- 1 ½ cups all-purpose flour
- 1 cup plain yogurt
- 1 cup white sugar
- 1 teaspoon vanilla extract
- 2 cups fresh strawberries, sliced
- 6 eggs

Crumble:

- ¼ cup chilled butter
- ½ cup all-purpose flour
- 2 tablespoons white sugar

Directions:

1. For the cake, combine the eggs, sugar and vanilla in a container until fluffy and twofold in volume at least.
2. Stir in the yogurt and oil then fold in the flour, baking powder and salt.
3. Pour the batter in a 9-inch round cake pan coated with baking paper.
4. Top with strawberries.
5. For the streusel, combine all the ingredients in a container until grainy.

6. Top the cake with streusel and preheat your oven and bake at 350F for 45 minutes or until a toothpick comes out clean after being inserted into the center of the cake.
7. The cake tastes best chilled.

Nutritional Content of One Serving:

Calories: 275 ‖ Fat: 11.1g ‖ Protein: 6.3g ‖ Carbohydrates: 38.2g

STRAWBERRY CAKE

Total Time Taken: 1 ½ hours
Yield: 12 Servings
Ingredients:

Cake:

- ½ cup canola oil
- ½ cup coconut milk
- ½ teaspoon salt
- 1 cup white sugar
- 1 teaspoon vanilla extract
- 2 cups all-purpose flour
- 2 teaspoons baking powder
- 4 eggs

Strawberry buttercream:

- ¼ cup strawberry puree
- 1 cup butter
- 3 cups powdered sugar

Directions:

1. For the cake, combine the flour, baking powder and salt in a container.
2. In a separate container, combine the sugar, canola oil and eggs in a container until volume increases to twice what it was.
3. Stir in the milk and vanilla then fold in the dry ingredients.
4. Spoon the batter in two 9-inch circular cake pans and preheat your oven and bake at 350F for half an hour.
5. Let the cakes cool in the pan then level them up.

6. For the buttercream, combine the butter and sugar in a container until firm and fluffy.
7. Stir in the strawberry puree and mix thoroughly.
8. Fill the cake with half of the buttercream then use the rest of the buttercream to cover the cake.
9. Serve immediately or place in your refrigerator.

Nutritional Content of One Serving:

Calories: 522 ‖ Fat: 28.6g ‖ Protein: 4.4g ‖ Carbohydrates: 64.6g

SPICY CHOCOLATE CAKE

Total Time Taken: 1 hour
Yield: Servings 6
Ingredients:

- ¼ cup canola oil
- ¼ teaspoon cinnamon powder
- ½ cup cocoa powder
- ½ teaspoon salt
- 1 ½ cups all-purpose flour
- 1 cup hot coffee
- 1 teaspoon baking soda
- 1 teaspoon vanilla extract
- 1/2 teaspoon chili powder
- 2 oz. dark chocolate, chopped

Directions:

1. Sift the flour with cocoa powder, chili, cinnamon, baking soda and salt.
2. Mix the canola oil with coffee and chocolate and stir until it melts completely.
3. Put in the vanilla, then fold in the flour mixture.
4. Pour the batter in a 9-inch round cake pan covered with parchment paper and preheat your oven and bake at 350F for around forty minutes or until a toothpick comes out clean after being inserted into the center of the cake.
5. The cake tastes best chilled.

Nutritional Content of One Serving:

Calories: 264 ‖ Fat: 13.2g ‖ Protein: 5.3g ‖ Carbohydrates: 33.6g

SPICED WALNUT CAKE

Total Time Taken: 1 hour
Yield: 8 Servings
Ingredients:

3 eggs

- ¼ cup canola oil
- ½ teaspoon ground cardamom
- ½ teaspoon ground ginger
- ½ teaspoon salt
- ¾ cup all-purpose flour
- 1 cup ground walnuts
- 1 cup white sugar
- 1 teaspoon baking soda
- 1 teaspoon cinnamon powder

Directions:

1. Mix the eggs and sugar in a container until fluffy and volume increases to twice what it was.
2. Stir in the canola oil then fold in the walnuts, cinnamon, ginger, cardamom, flour, salt and baking soda.
3. Pour the batter in a 8-inch round cake pan coated with baking paper.
4. Pre-heat the oven and bake at 350F for around forty minutes or until it rises completely and is aromatic.
5. Let the cake cool in the pan and serve, sliced.

Nutritional Content of One Serving:

Calories: 318 ‖ Fat: 17.8g ‖ Protein: 7.1g ‖ Carbohydrates: 35.8g

SPICED PUMPKIN SHEET CAKE

Total Time Taken: 1 ¼ hours

Yield: 16 Servings

Ingredients:

- ¼ teaspoon baking soda
- ½ cup walnuts, chopped
- ½ teaspoon ground cloves
- ½ teaspoon ground star anise
- ½ teaspoon salt
- 1 ½ cups pumpkin puree
- 1 ½ cups white sugar
- 1 cup canola oil
- 1 teaspoon cinnamon powder
- 1 teaspoon ground ginger
- 2 cups all-purpose flour
- 2 teaspoons baking powder
- 4 eggs

Directions:

1. Sift the flour, baking powder, baking soda, salt and spices in a container.
2. Mix the sugar, canola oil and eggs in a container until pale and fluffy.
3. Stir in the pumpkin puree then incorporate the flour, ½ cup at a time, mixing gently using a spatula.
4. Fold in the walnuts then spoon the batter in a 10x10 inch rectangle pan coated with baking paper.
5. Pre-heat the oven and bake at 350F for around forty minutes or until a toothpick inserted into the center of the cake comes out clean.
6. The cake tastes best chilled, cut into small squares.

Nutritional Content of One Serving:

Calories: 297 ‖ Fat: 17.3g ‖ Protein: 4.2g ‖ Carbohydrates: 33.5g

SOUR CHERRY CHOCOLATE CAKE

Total Time Taken: 1 ¼ hours

Yield: 10 Servings

Ingredients:

- ¼ cup whole milk
- ½ cup cocoa powder
- ½ teaspoon salt
- 1 cup all-purpose flour
- 1 cup butter, softened
- 1 cup heavy cream, whipped
- 1 cup sour cherries, pitted
- 1 cup white sugar
- 1 teaspoon baking powder
- 1 teaspoon vanilla extract
- 4 eggs

Directions:

1. Sift the flour with cocoa, salt and baking powder.
2. Mix the butter with sugar and vanilla until creamy. Put in the eggs, one at a time, then fold in the flour mixture.
3. Put in the cherries then spoon the batter in a 9-inch round cake pan coated with baking paper.
4. Pre-heat the oven and bake at 350F for around forty minutes or until a toothpick comes out clean after being inserted into the center of the cake.
5. Let the cake cool then move to a platter and cover it in whipped cream.
6. Serve fresh or place in your refrigerator.

Nutritional Content of One Serving:

Calories: 373 ‖ Fat: 25.5g ‖ Protein: 5.0g ‖ Carbohydrates: 35.0g

SNICKERDOODLE BUNDT CAKE

Total Time Taken: 1 ½ hours
Yield: 12 Servings
Ingredients:

Filling:

- 1 cup white sugar
- 1 tablespoon cinnamon powder

Cake:

- ½ teaspoon baking soda

- ½ teaspoon salt
- 1 cup butter, softened
- 1 cup sour cream
- 1 cup white sugar
- 1 teaspoon baking powder
- 1 teaspoon ground ginger
- 2 ½ cups all-purpose flour
- 2 tablespoons dark brown sugar
- 3 eggs

Directions:

1. For the filling, combine the sugar with cinnamon in a container.
2. For the cake, sift the flour, ginger, baking powder, baking soda and salt.
3. Mix the butter and sugars in a container until fluffy and light.
4. Put in the eggs, one at a time, then mix in the sour cream.
5. Fold in the flour then spoon half of the batter in a greased Bundt cake pan. Drizzle with the cinnamon sugar mixture then top with the rest of the batter.
6. Pre-heat the oven and bake at 350F for about forty-five minutes or until a golden-brown colour is achieved and a toothpick inserted into the center of the cake comes out clean.
7. The cake tastes best chilled.

Nutritional Content of One Serving:

Calories: 419 ‖ Fat: 20.7g ‖ Protein: 4.9g ‖ Carbohydrates: 55.9g

RUM PINEAPPLE UPSIDE DOWN CAKE

Total Time Taken: 1 ¼ hours

Yield: 10 Servings

Ingredients:

- ¼ cup butter, melted
- ¼ cup light rum
- ¼ teaspoon salt
- 1 ½ teaspoons baking powder
- 1 can pineapple rings, drained
- 1 cup white sugar

- 2 cups all-purpose flour
- 4 eggs

Directions:

1. Position the pineapple rings at the bottom of a 9-inch round cake pan coated with baking paper.
2. Mix the eggs and sugar in a container until volume increases to twice what it was.
3. Stir in the rum and melted butter then fold in the flour, baking powder and salt.
4. Pour the batter over the pineapple and preheat your oven and bake at 350F for around forty minutes.
5. When finished, flip it over on a platter and let cool before you serve.

Nutritional Content of One Serving:

Calories: 254 ‖ Fat: 6.6g ‖ Protein: 4.9g ‖ Carbohydrates: 41.7g

RICH VANILLA CAKE

Total Time Taken: 1 hour
Yield: 10 Servings
Ingredients:

- ½ teaspoon salt
- 1 cup butter, softened
- 1 cup white sugar
- 1 tablespoon vanilla extract
- 2 cups all-purpose flour
- 2 egg whites
- 2 teaspoons baking powder
- 6 egg yolks

Directions:

1. Mix the butter, sugar and vanilla in a container until fluffy and creamy.
2. Put in the egg yolks and whole eggs, one at a time, stirring thoroughly after each addition.
3. Fold in the flour, baking powder and salt then spoon the batter in a 9-inch round cake pan coated with baking paper.

4. Pre-heat the oven and bake at 350F for around forty minutes or until a toothpick inserted into the center of the cake comes out clean.
5. Let the cake cool in the pan before you serve.

Nutritional Content of One Serving:

Calories: 369 ‖ Fat: 21.4g ‖ Protein: 5.1g ‖ Carbohydrates: 40.1g

RHUBARB UPSIDE DOWN CAKE

Total Time Taken: 1 ¼ hours
Yield: 10 Servings

Ingredients:

- ½ cup sour cream
- ½ cup white sugar
- ½ teaspoon salt
- ¾ cup butter, softened
- ¾ cup white sugar
- 1 ½ teaspoons baking powder
- 1 teaspoon vanilla extract
- 2 cups all-purpose flour
- 3 eggs
- 4 rhubarb stalks, peeled and sliced

Directions:

1. Position the stalks of rhubarb in a 9-inch round cake pan coated with baking paper.
2. Top with ½ cup white sugar.
3. Mix the butter with
4. 1 cup sugar until fluffy and pale.
5. Put in the eggs and sour cream and mix thoroughly.
6. Stir in the vanilla then fold in the flour, baking powder and salt.
7. Pour the batter in the pan and preheat your oven and bake at 350F for about forty minutes.
8. When finished, flip the cake upside down on a platter.

Nutritional Content of One Serving:

Calories: 357 ‖ Fat: 17.8g ‖ Protein: 4.9g ‖ Carbohydrates: 46.0g

RASPBERRY RICOTTA CAKE

Total Time Taken: 1 hour
Yield: 10 Servings
Ingredients:

- ¼ cup cocoa powder
- ¼ teaspoon salt
- ½ cup butter, softened
- ¾ cup white sugar
- 1 cup hot water
- 1 cup raspberries
- 1 cup ricotta cheese
- 2 cups all-purpose flour
- 2 teaspoons baking powder

Directions:

1. Mix the ricotta cheese, butter and sugar in a container until creamy.
2. Put in the water and mix thoroughly.
3. Fold in the flour, cocoa powder, baking powder and salt.
4. Put in the raspberries then spoon the batter in a 9-inch round cake pan coated with baking paper.
5. Pre-heat the oven and bake at 350F for forty minutes or until a toothpick inserted into the center of the cake comes out clean.
6. The cake tastes best chilled.

Nutritional Content of One Serving:

Calories: 275 ‖ Fat: 11.8g ‖ Protein: 6.0g ‖ Carbohydrates: 38.5g

RASPBERRY MATCHA CAKE

Total Time Taken: 1 ¼ hours
Yield: 10 Servings

Ingredients:

- ½ teaspoon salt
- 1 ½ cups all-purpose flour
- 1 cup fresh raspberries

- 1 tablespoons matcha powder
- 1 teaspoon vanilla extract
- 2 teaspoons baking powder
- 2/3 cup butter, softened
- 2/3 cup white sugar
- 4 eggs

Directions:

1. Sift the flour, matcha powder, baking powder and salt in a container.
2. Mix the butter and sugar until fluffy and creamy.
3. Put in the eggs, one at a time, and mix thoroughly after each addition. Stir in the vanilla then fold in the flour.
4. Put in the raspberries then spoon the batter in a loaf cake pan coated with baking paper.
5. Pre-heat the oven and bake at 350F for around forty minutes or until a toothpick inserted into the center of the cake comes out clean.
6. The cake tastes best chilled.

Nutritional Content of One Serving:

Calories: 262 ‖ Fat: 14.3g ‖ Protein: 4.4g ‖ Carbohydrates: 30.3g

RASPBERRY LEMON OLIVE OIL CAKE

Total Time Taken: 1 hour
Yield: 10 Servings
Ingredients:

- ¼ cup butter, softened
- ¼ cup whole milk
- ¼ teaspoon baking soda
- ½ teaspoon salt
- ¾ cup extra virgin olive oil
- 1 ¾ cups all-purpose flour
- 1 cup fresh raspberries
- 1 cup white sugar
- 1 teaspoon baking powder
- 2 tablespoons lemon zest
- 4 eggs

Directions:

1. Mix the flour, baking powder, baking soda and salt in a container or platter.
2. In a separate container, mix the oil, butter and sugar and mix thoroughly. Stir in the eggs, one at a time, then put in the milk and lemon zest.
3. Fold in the dry ingredients then put in the raspberries.
4. Spoon the batter in a round cake pan coated with baking paper and preheat your oven and bake at 350F for around forty minutes or until a toothpick inserted into the center of the cake comes out clean.

The cake tastes best chilled.

Nutritional Content of One Serving:

Calories: 361 ‖ Fat: 22.0g ‖ Protein: 4.9g ‖ Carbohydrates: 39.1g

RASPBERRY GANACHE CAKE

Total Time Taken: 1 ¼ hours
Yield: 8 Servings
Ingredients:

Cake:

- ¼ teaspoon salt
- ½ cup butter, softened
- ½ cup white sugar
- 1 cup all-purpose flour
- 1 cup fresh raspberries
- 1 teaspoon baking powder
- 4 eggs

Ganache:

- ½ cup heavy cream
- 1 cup dark chocolate chips

Directions:

1. For the cake, combine the butter and sugar in a container until fluffy. Put in the eggs, one at a time, then mix in the flour, salt and baking powder.
2. Spoon the batter in a 8-inch round cake pan coated with baking paper.

3. Top with raspberries and preheat your oven and bake at 350F for around forty minutes or until it rises significantly and starts to appear golden-brown.
4. Let the cake cool in the pan then move to a platter.
5. For the ganache, bring the cream to the boiling point in a saucepan. Turn off the heat and mix in the chocolate. Combine until melted.
6. Sprinkle the ganache over the cake and serve the cake chilled.

Nutritional Content of One Serving:

Calories: 341 ‖ Fat: 20.7g ‖ Protein: 5.8g ‖ Carbohydrates: 37.0g

RASPBERRY CHOCOLATE MUD CAKE

Total Time Taken: 1 ½ hours

Yield: 12 Servings

Ingredients:

- ½ cup buttermilk
- ½ cup cocoa powder
- ½ cup heavy cream
- ½ teaspoon salt
- 1 ½ cups fresh raspberries
- 1 ½ cups white sugar
- 1 cup butter, softened
- 1 cup dark chocolate chips
- 1 cup hot water
- 2 cups all-purpose flour
- 2 tablespoons brandy
- 2 teaspoons baking powder
- 3 eggs

Directions:

1. Mix the butter and chocolate chips in a heatproof container and place over a hot water bath. Melt them together until the desired smoothness is achieved.
2. Stir in the sugar and hot water and mix thoroughly.
3. Put in the buttermilk, cream, eggs and brandy.
4. Fold in the dry ingredients and mix thoroughly.

5. Put in the raspberries and pour the batter in a 9-inch round cake pan coated with baking paper.
6. Pre-heat the oven and bake at 350F for 50 minutes.
7. Let the cake cool in the pan and serve, sliced.

Nutritional Content of One Serving:

Calories: 415 ‖ Fat: 21.8g ‖ Protein: 5.6g ‖ Carbohydrates: 52.5g

RASPBERRY CHOCOLATE CAKE

Total Time Taken: 1 ¼ hours
Yield: 10 Servings

Ingredients:

- ½ cup butter, melted
- ½ teaspoon baking powder
- ½ teaspoon salt
- 1 ¼ cups all-purpose flour
- 1 cup white sugar
- 1 teaspoon vanilla extract
- 2 cups fresh raspberries
- 3 oz. dark chocolate, melted
- 6 eggs

Directions:

1. Mix the eggs and sugar in a container until its volume increases to almost three times it was.
2. Stir in the melted butter and chocolate, as well as vanilla.
3. Fold in the baking powder and salt then put in the raspberries and stir lightly.
4. Pour the batter in a 9-inch round cake pan and preheat your oven and bake at 350F for around forty minutes or until a toothpick inserted into the center of the cake comes out clean.
5. Let cool in the pan then serve, sliced.

Nutritional Content of One Serving:

Calories: 311 ‖ Fat: 14.7g ‖ Protein: 6.0g ‖ Carbohydrates: 40.3g

RAINBOW CAKE

Total Time Taken: 1 hour
Yield: 10 Servings
Ingredients:

- ½ cup sour cream
- ½ teaspoon baking soda
- ½ teaspoon salt
- 1 ½ cups white sugar
- 1 cup butter, softened
- 1 teaspoon baking powder
- 1 teaspoon vanilla extract
- 2 ½ cups all-purpose flour
- 2 whole eggs
- 3 egg whites
- Red, green, blue and yellow food coloring

Directions:

1. Mix the butter and sugar in a container until fluffy and creamy.
2. Stir in the eggs, egg whites, vanilla and sour cream and stir thoroughly for a few minutes.
3. Mix the flour with baking powder, baking soda and salt then fold it in the batter.
4. Divide the batter into 4 smaller containers then add a drop of food colouring into each container and stir gently using a spoon in each batch of batter.
5. Spoon the colourful batter into a 9-inch cake pan coated with baking paper.
6. Use a toothpick to swirl the batter around until colours are blended.
7. Pre-heat the oven and bake at 350F for around forty minutes.
8. Let the cake cool in the pan then serve, sliced.

Nutritional Content of One Serving:

Calories: 433 ‖ Fat: 22.0g ‖ Protein: 6.0g ‖ Carbohydrates: 54.8g

POPPY SEED LEMON BUNDT CAKE

Total Time Taken: 1 ¼ hours
Yield: 12 Servings

Ingredients:

- ½ cup cornstarch
- ½ cup sour cream
- ½ teaspoon salt
- 1 cup butter, softened
- 1 cup white sugar
- 1 tablespoon lemon zest
- 1 teaspoon baking powder
- 1 teaspoon baking soda
- 1 teaspoon vanilla extract
- 2 cups all-purpose flour
- 2 tablespoons lemon juice
- 2 tablespoons poppy seeds
- 4 eggs

Directions:

1. Sift the flour, cornstarch, baking powder, baking soda and salt then mix it with the poppy seeds.
2. Mix the butter and sugar in a container until creamy and fluffy.
3. Stir in the eggs, lemon zest and lemon juice and mix thoroughly.
4. Fold in the flour mixture then put in the sour cream and mix thoroughly.
5. Spoon the batter in a greased Bundt cake pan and preheat your oven and bake at 350F for about forty minutes or until a toothpick comes out clean after being inserted into the center of the cake.
6. Let the cake cool in the pan before you serve.

Nutritional Content of One Serving:

Calories: 346 ‖ Fat: 19.7g ‖ Protein: 4.8g ‖ Carbohydrates: 38.7g

POMEGRANATE CAKE

Total Time Taken: 1 ½ hours
Yield: 10 Servings
Ingredients:

White cake:

- ½ teaspoon salt

- ¾ cup whole milk
- 1 ¼ cups butter, softened
- 1 ½ cups all-purpose flour
- 1 ½ teaspoons baking powder
- 1 cup white sugar
- 1 teaspoon lemon zest
- 1 teaspoon vanilla extract
- 4 eggs whites

Pomegranate frosting:

- ¼ cup pomegranate juice
- 1 cup white sugar 1 pinch salt
- 4 egg whites

Directions:

1. Mix the flour with sugar, baking powder, salt and butter in a container until grainy.
2. Combine the egg whites with milk, vanilla and lemon zest in a container then pour this mixture over the flour mixture.
3. Stir slowly until mixed then spoon the batter into two 7-inch circular cake pans coated with baking paper.
4. Pre-heat the oven and bake at 350F for about half an hour.
5. Let the cakes cool in the pan then level them and cut each cake in half along the length.
6. For the frosting, combine all the ingredients in a heatproof container and place over a hot water bath. Keep over heat, stirring constantly, until the mixture is hot.
7. Turn off the heat and whip using an electric mixer for minimum seven minutes until firm and shiny.
8. Use half of the frosting to fill the cake and the rest of the frosting to frost the cake.
9. Serve immediately or place in your refrigerator.

Nutritional Content of One Serving:

Calories: 449 ‖ Fat: 23.8g ‖ Protein: 5.7g ‖ Carbohydrates: 55.8g

PLUM POLENTA CAKE

Total Time Taken: 1 hour
Yield: 8 Servings
Ingredients:

- ½ cup butter, softened
- ½ cup honey
- ½ pound plums, pitted and sliced
- ½ teaspoon salt
- ½ teaspoon salt
- 1 cup instant polenta flour
- 1 tablespoon lemon zest
- 1 teaspoon baking soda
- 2 cups whole milk
- 4 eggs

Directions:

1. Mix the butter with honey until creamy and firm. Stir in the eggs, one at a time, then put in the milk and lemon zest.
2. Fold in the polenta flour, baking soda and salt then pour the batter in a 9-inch round cake pan coated with baking paper.
3. Top with plum slices and preheat your oven and bake at 350F for around forty minutes or until a golden-brown colour is achieved and it rises significantly.
4. Let the cake cool in the pan then serve, sliced.

Nutritional Content of One Serving:

Calories: 298 ‖ Fat: 15.7g ‖ Protein: 7.1g ‖ Carbohydrates: 33.7g

PISTACHIO CAKE

Total Time Taken: 1 hour
Yield: 8 Servings
Ingredients:

- ¼ cup whole milk
- ¼ teaspoon cinnamon powder
- ¼ teaspoon salt
- ½ cup all-purpose flour

- ½ cup butter, softened
- ½ cup white sugar
- ½ teaspoon ground cardamom
- 1 cup ground pistachio
- 1 teaspoon baking powder
- 1 teaspoon lemon zest
- 2 eggs

Directions:

1. Mix the pistachio, flour, salt, baking powder, cardamom and cinnamon in a container.
2. Mix the butter and sugar in a container until fluffy and light. Stir in the eggs and milk, as well as lemon zest.
3. Fold in the flour and pistachio mixture then spoon the batter in a 8-inch round cake pan coated with baking paper.
4. Pre-heat the oven and bake at 350F for around forty minutes.
5. The cake tastes best chilled, dusted with powdered sugar.

Nutritional Content of One Serving:

Calories: 214 ‖ Fat: 14.1g ‖ Protein: 3.2g ‖ Carbohydrates: 20.1g

PISTACHIO BUNDT CAKE

Total Time Taken: 1 hour
Yield: 10 Servings
Ingredients:

- ½ teaspoon salt
- ¾ cup butter, softened
- 1 ½ cups all-purpose flour
- 1 ½ teaspoons baking powder
- 1 cup ground pistachio
- 1 cup white sugar
- 1 teaspoon vanilla extract
- 4 eggs

Directions:

1. Mix the butter and sugar until pale and light. Stir in the eggs and vanilla and mix thoroughly.
2. Fold in the flour, pistachio, baking powder and salt then spoon the batter in a greased Bundt cake pan.
3. Pre-heat the oven and bake at 350F for about forty minutes or until it rises significantly and starts to appear golden-brown.
4. Let the cake cool in the pan before you serve.

Nutritional Content of One Serving:

Calories: 292 ‖ Fat: 15.7g ‖ Protein: 4.3g ‖ Carbohydrates: 34.9g

PEPPERMINT CHOCOLATE CAKE

Total Time Taken: 1 ¼ hours
Yield: 10 Servings
Ingredients:

Cake:

- ½ cup canola oil
- 1 cup buttermilk
- ½ cup cocoa powder
- ½ cup hot coffee
- ½ teaspoon baking soda
- ½ teaspoon salt
- 1 ½ cups all-purpose flour
- 1 teaspoon baking powder
- 1 teaspoon vanilla extract

Frosting:

- ½ cup butter, softened
- 1 ½ cups powdered sugar
- 1 teaspoon peppermint extract
- 3 oz. dark chocolate, melted and cooled

Directions:

1. To prepare the cake, combine the dry ingredients in a container and the wet ingredients in a separate container.

2. Combine the flour mixture with the wet ingredients and stir for a few seconds to mix.
3. Pour the batter in a 9-inch cake pan coated with baking paper.
4. Pre-heat the oven and bake at 350F for about 35 minutes.
5. Let the cake cool in the pan then move to a platter.
6. For the frosting, combine the butter with the sugar until creamy and fluffy.
7. Put in the peppermint extract and the melted chocolate and mix thoroughly.
8. Frost the top of the cake with this chocolate buttercream and serve immediately or place in your refrigerator.

Nutritional Content of One Serving:

Calories: 384 ‖ Fat: 23.6g ‖ Protein: 4.3g ‖ Carbohydrates: 41.2g

PECAN RUM CAKE

Total Time Taken: 1 ¼ hours
Yield: 12 Servings
Ingredients:

Cake:

- ¼ cup dark rum
- ½ cup whole milk
- ½ teaspoon salt
- 1 ¼ cups all-purpose flour
- 1 cup butter, softened
- 1 cup ground pecans
- 1 cup white sugar
- 1 teaspoon baking soda
- 1 teaspoon vanilla extract
- 3 eggs

Glaze:

- 1 cup powdered sugar
- 1 tablespoon dark rum

Directions:

1. For the cake, combine the flour with baking soda, salt and pecans.

2. In a separate container, combine the butter and sugar until fluffy and creamy.
3. Stir in the eggs, one after another, then put in the vanilla, rum and milk and mix thoroughly.
4. Fold in the pecan and flour mixture then spoon the batter in a 8-inch round cake pan coated with baking paper.
5. Pre-heat the oven and bake at 350F for around forty minutes or until well risen and fragrant.
6. Let the cake cool in the pan then move to a platter.
7. For the glaze, combine the ingredients in a container. Sprinkle the glaze over the cake and serve fresh.

Nutritional Content of One Serving:

Calories: 329 ‖ Fat: 17.8g ‖ Protein: 3.3g ‖ Carbohydrates: 37.3g

PECAN CARROT BUNDT CAKE

Total Time Taken: 1 ½ hours
Yield: 14 Servings

Ingredients:

- ¼ cup orange juice
- ½ cup dark brown sugar
- ½ teaspoon baking powder
- ½ teaspoon cardamom powder
- ½ teaspoon salt
- 1 cup butter, softened
- 1 cup crushed pineapple
- 1 cup white sugar
- 1 tablespoon lemon zest
- 1 tablespoon orange zest
- 1 teaspoon baking soda
- 1 teaspoon cinnamon powder
- 2 ½ cups all-purpose flour
- 2 cups grated carrots
- 4 eggs

Directions:

1. Sift the flour, baking soda, baking powder, salt and spices in a container.
2. In a separate container, combine the butter and sugars until creamy and fluffy.
3. Stir in the eggs, one at a time, then put in the citrus zest, carrots, orange juice and pineapple.
4. Fold in the flour and stir lightly using a spatula.
5. Pour the batter in a greased Bundt cake pan.
6. Pre-heat the oven and bake at 350F for about fifty minutes or until a toothpick inserted into the center of the cake comes out clean.
7. Let the cake cool in the pan before you serve.

Nutritional Content of One Serving:

Calories: 304 ‖ Fat: 14.6g ‖ Protein: 4.3g ‖ Carbohydrates: 40.4g

PECAN BUTTER CAKE

Total Time Taken: 1 ¼ hours

Yield: 12 Servings

Ingredients:

- ½ cup butter, softened
- ½ teaspoon salt
- 1 ½ cups pecans, chopped
- 1 ½ teaspoons baking powder
- 1 cup pecan butter
- 1 cup white sugar
- 1 teaspoon lemon zest
- 1 teaspoon vanilla extract
- 2 cups all-purpose flour
- 4 eggs

Directions:

1. Mix the two types of butter with sugar until creamy and light.
2. Stir in the eggs, one at a time, then put in the vanilla and lemon zest then fold in the dry ingredients.
3. Spoon the batter in a 9-inch round cake pan coated with baking paper.
4. Pre-heat the oven and bake at 350F for about forty minutes or until it rises significantly and starts to appear golden-brown.

5. Let the cake cool in the pan then sprinkle it with powdered sugar and serve.

Nutritional Content of One Serving:

Calories: 377 ‖ Fat: 24.2g ‖ Protein: 6.2g ‖ Carbohydrates: 37.9g

PEAR CINNAMON BUNDT CAKE

Total Time Taken: 1 ¼ hours
Yield: 10 Servings

Ingredients:

- ½ cup buttermilk
- ½ teaspoon ground ginger
- ½ teaspoon salt
- 1 ½ cups light brown sugar
- 1 cup butter, melted
- 1 teaspoon cinnamon powder
- 2 cups all-purpose flour
- 2 pears, peeled, cored and diced
- 2 teaspoons baking powder
- 4 eggs

Directions:

1. Mix the flour, cinnamon, ginger, baking powder and salt in a container.
2. In a separate container, mix the butter, sugar, eggs and buttermilk and mix thoroughly. Pour this mixture over the dry ingredients then fold in the pears.
3. Spoon the batter in a Bundt cake pan lined using butter.
4. Pre-heat the oven and bake at 350F for around forty minutes or until golden and it rises significantly.
5. Let the cake cool in the pan before you serve.

Nutritional Content of One Serving:

Calories: 392 ‖ Fat: 20.6g ‖ Protein: 5.6g ‖ Carbohydrates: 48.0g

PEAR BROWNIE CAKE

Total Time Taken: 1 ¼ hours

Yield: 10 Servings

Ingredients:

- ¼ cup cocoa powder
- ¼ teaspoon salt
- ½ cup all-purpose flour
- ½ cup butter, softened
- ½ cup white sugar
- 1 cup dark chocolate chips
- 2 pears, peeled, cored and diced
- 4 eggs

Directions:

1. Mix the butter and chocolate in a heatproof container over a hot water bath. Melt them together until the desired smoothness is achieved.
2. Put in the eggs, one at a time, then mix in the sugar.
3. Fold in the flour, cocoa powder and salt then spoon the batter in a 8-inch round cake pan coated with baking paper.
4. Top with pear dices and preheat your oven and bake at 350F for 25 minutes.
5. Let the cake cool in the pan before you serve.

Nutritional Content of One Serving:

Calories: 252 ‖ Fat: 14.6g ‖ Protein: 4.3g ‖ Carbohydrates: 30.5g

PEANUT BUTTER JELLY CAKE

Total Time Taken: 1 ½ hours

Yield: 12 Servings

Ingredients:

- ½ cup butter, softened
- ½ cup cranberry jelly
- ½ cup light brown sugar
- ½ cup peanut butter
- ½ cup whole milk
- ½ teaspoon salt
- 1 cup white sugar

- 1 teaspoon vanilla extract
- 2 cups all-purpose flour
- 2 eggs
- 2 tablespoons canola oil
- 2 teaspoons baking powder

Directions:

1. Sift the flour, baking powder and salt.
2. Mix the peanut butter, butter, canola oil and sugars in a container until creamy and fluffy.
3. Stir in the eggs and vanilla and mix thoroughly.
4. Fold in the flour mixture, alternating it with the milk. Begin and finish with flour.
5. Spoon the batter in a round cake pan coated with baking paper.
6. Pre-heat the oven and bake at 350F for about forty minutes or until a toothpick inserted into the center of the cake comes out clean.
7. When finished, brush the cake with cranberry jelly and serve it fresh.

Nutritional Content of One Serving:

Calories: 334 ‖ Fat: 16.7g ‖ Protein: 6.2g ‖ Carbohydrates: 42.0g

PEANUT BUTTER CHOCOLATE BUNDT CAKE

Total Time Taken: 1 ¼ hours
Yield: 10 Servings

Ingredients:

- ¼ cup butter, softened
- ½ cup cocoa powder
- ½ cup dark chocolate chips
- ½ teaspoon baking soda
- ½ teaspoon salt
- 1 cup buttermilk
- 1 cup light brown sugar
- 1 cup smooth peanut butter

- 1 teaspoon vanilla extract
- 2 cups all-purpose flour
- 2 teaspoons baking powder
- 3 eggs

Directions:

1. Sift the flour, baking powder, baking soda, salt and cocoa powder.
2. Mix the peanut butter, butter and sugar in a container until creamy and light.
3. Put in the eggs and mix thoroughly then mix in the vanilla.
4. Fold in the flour, alternating it with buttermilk. Begin and finish with flour.
5. Put in the chocolate chips then spoon the batter in a Bundt cake pan lined using butter.
6. Preheat your oven and bake the cake for about forty minutes or until it rises significantly and starts to appear golden-brown.
7. When finished, flip the cake upside down on a platter and serve chilled.

Nutritional Content of One Serving:

Calories: 407 ‖ Fat: 21.6g ‖ Protein: 12.8g ‖ Carbohydrates: 46.5g

PEACH UPSIDE DOWN CAKE

Total Time Taken: 1 hour
Yield: 8 Servings
Ingredients:

- ¼ cup butter, melted
- ¼ cup whole milk
- ¼ teaspoon salt
- 1 egg
- ½ cup light brown sugar
- ½ cup sour cream
- 1 cup all-purpose flour
- 1 teaspoon baking powder
- 2 tablespoons butter
- 4 peaches, sliced

Directions:

1. Position the peaches at the bottom of a 9-inch round cake pan coated with baking paper.
2. Drizzle with brown sugar and top with a few pieces of butter.
3. For the batter, combine the flour, baking powder and salt in a container. Put in the rest of the ingredients and stir for a few seconds to mix.
4. Spoon the batter over the peaches and preheat your oven and bake at 350F for about half an hour.
5. When finished, flip the cake upside down on a platter.
6. Serve chilled.

Nutritional Content of One Serving:

Calories: 231 ‖ Fat: 12.7g ‖ Protein: 3.6g ‖ Carbohydrates: 26.8g

PEACH MERINGUE CAKE

Total Time Taken: 1 ½ hours
Yield: 10 Servings
Ingredients:

Cake:

- ½ cup butter, softened
- ½ cup canola oil
- ½ cup plain yogurt
- ½ teaspoon salt
- ¾ cup white sugar
- 1 teaspoon baking soda
- 1 teaspoon vanilla extract
- 2 cups all-purpose flour
- 3 eggs
- 3 peaches, pitted and sliced

Meringue:

- ½ cup white sugar
- 1 teaspoon vanilla extract
- 3 egg whites

Directions:

1. For the cake, combine the butter, oil and sugar in a container until fluffy and creamy.
2. Stir in the egg, vanilla and yogurt and mix thoroughly.
3. Fold in the flour, baking soda and salt then spoon the batter in a round cake pan coated with baking paper.
4. Top with peach slices and preheat your oven and bake at 350F for about forty minutes or until it rises significantly and starts to appear golden-brown.
5. While the cake bakes, combine the egg whites and sugar in a heatproof container.
6. Place over a hot water bath and mix with a whisk until the mixture is hot.
7. Turn off the heat and continue mixing until firm and shiny. Put in the vanilla and mix thoroughly.
8. Spoon the meringue over the hot cake and allow to cool.
9. Serve immediately.

Nutritional Content of One Serving:

Calories: 411 ‖ Fat: 21.9g ‖ Protein: 6.4g ‖ Carbohydrates: 48.5g

PEACH BRANDY CAKE

Total Time Taken: 1 ½ hours
Yield: 10 Servings
Ingredients:

Cake:

- ½ cup butter, melted
- ½ teaspoon salt
- 1 cup sweet red win
- 1 cup white sugar
- 1 teaspoon baking powder
- 1 teaspoon ground cardamom
- 2 cups almond flour
- 4 peaches, pitted and sliced Brandy
- 5 eggs

Glaze:

- 1 cup powdered sugar
- 1 tablespoon brandy

Directions:

1. To prepare the cake, combine the almond flour, baking powder, salt and cinnamon.
2. In a separate container, combine the sugar and eggs until fluffy and pale. Put in the butter and mix thoroughly, then mix in the red wine.
3. Fold in the almond flour then pour the batter in a 9-inch round cake pan coated with baking paper.
4. Top with sliced peaches and preheat your oven and bake at 350F for 45 minutes or until a toothpick comes out clean after being inserted into the center of the cake.
5. Let the cake cool in the pan then move it to a platter.
6. For the glaze, combine the sugar with brandy. Sprinkle the glaze over the cake and serve it fresh.

Nutritional Content of One Serving:

Calories: 317 ║ Fat: 15.8g ║ Protein: 8.3g ║ Carbohydrates: 37.4g

PARSNIP CARROT CAKE

Total Time Taken: 1 ½ hours
Yield: 12 Servings

Ingredients:

- ¼ cup white sugar
- ½ cup walnuts, chopped
- ½ teaspoon salt
- 1 cup canola oil
- 1 cup crushed pineapple
- 1 cup grated carrots
- 1 cup grated parsnips
- 1 cup light brown sugar
- 1 teaspoon baking powder
- 1 teaspoon baking soda
- 1 teaspoon cinnamon powder
- 1 teaspoon ground ginger
- 2 cups all-purpose flour
- 4 eggs

Directions:

1. Mix the flour, salt, baking soda, baking powder and spices in a container.
2. In a separate container, combine the eggs with the sugars until fluffy and pale.
3. Put in the oil then mix in the carrots, parsnips, pineapple and walnuts.
4. Fold in the dry ingredients you readied a while back.
5. Pour the batter in a 9-inch round cake pan coated with baking paper.
6. Pre-heat the oven and bake at 350F for about forty minutes or until a toothpick inserted in the center comes out clean.
7. Sprinkle with powdered sugar and serve chilled.

Nutritional Content of One Serving:

Calories: 371 ‖ Fat: 23.0g ‖ Protein: 5.5g ‖ Carbohydrates: 37.6g

ORANGE RICOTTA CAKE

Total Time Taken: 1 ¼ hours

Yield: 10 Servings

Ingredients:

- ½ cup all-purpose flour
- ½ cup white chocolate, chopped
- ¾ cup white sugar
- 1 cup fresh raspberries
- 1 teaspoon baking powder
- 1 teaspoon orange zest
- 1 teaspoon vanilla extract
- 3 cups ricotta cheese
- 3 eggs

Directions:

1. Mix the ricotta cheese, vanilla, orange zest, sugar and eggs in a container.
2. Stir in rest of the ingredients then spoon the batter in a 9-inch round cake pan coated with baking paper.
3. Pre-heat the oven and bake at 350F for around forty minutes or until a golden-brown colour is achieved.
4. The cake tastes best chilled.

Nutritional Content of One Serving:

Calories: 255 ‖ Fat: 10.1g ‖ Protein: 11.4g ‖ Carbohydrates: 30.5g

ORANGE PUMPKIN BUNDT CAKE

Total Time Taken: 1 ¼ hours
Yield: 12 Servings

Ingredients:

- ½ teaspoon cinnamon powder
- ½ teaspoon ground cardamom
- ½ teaspoon ground ginger
- ½ teaspoon salt
- ¾ cup butter, softened
- 1 ¼ cups white sugar
- 1 ½ teaspoons baking soda
- 1 cup pumpkin puree
- 1 orange, zested and juiced
- 1 teaspoon vanilla extract
- 2 ½ cups all-purpose flour
- 4 eggs

Directions:

1. Mix the butter with sugar in a container until creamy and fluffy.
2. Stir in the eggs and vanilla and mix thoroughly then put in the orange zest and juice, as well as pumpkin puree.
3. Fold in the rest of the ingredients then spoon the batter in a loaf cake pan coated with baking paper.
4. Preheat your oven and bake the cake for about forty minutes.
5. Let the cake cool in the pan before you serve.

Nutritional Content of One Serving:

Calories: 311 ‖ Fat: 13.3g ‖ Protein: 5.0g ‖ Carbohydrates: 44.4g

ORANGE POUND CAKE

Total Time Taken: 1 ¼ hours

Yield: 16 Servings

Ingredients:

- ½ teaspoon salt
- 1 ½ cups butter, softened
- 1 cup sour cream
- 1 orange, zested and juiced
- 1 teaspoon vanilla extract
- 2 cups white sugar
- 2 teaspoons baking powder
- 3 cups all-purpose flour
- 6 eggs

Directions:

1. Sift the flour with salt and baking powder.
2. Mix the butter with sugar for five minutes until creamy and fluffy.
3. Put in the vanilla, orange zest and orange juice and mix thoroughly.
4. Stir in the sour cream then fold in the flour mixture.
5. Pour the batter in a large loaf cake pan coated with baking paper.
6. Pre-heat the oven and bake at 330F for forty minutes then turn the heat on 350F for another ten minutes.
7. Let the cake cool in the pan and serve, sliced.

Nutritional Content of One Serving:

Calories: 393 ‖ Fat: 22.2g ‖ Protein: 5.2g ‖ Carbohydrates: 45.3g

ORANGE CHOCOLATE MUD CAKE

Total Time Taken: 1 ¼ hours

Yield: 10 Servings

Ingredients:

- ½ cup brewed coffee
- ½ cup candied orange peel, chopped

- ½ teaspoon salt
- ¾ cup cocoa powder
- 1 ½ cups all-purpose flour
- 1 cup butter, softened
- 1 tablespoon orange zest
- 1 teaspoon baking soda
- 1 teaspoon vanilla extract
- 2 cups white sugar
- 2 tablespoons cornstarch
- 4 eggs

Directions:

1. Mix the sugar and butter in a container until fluffy and pale.
2. Put in the coffee, eggs, vanilla and orange zest.
3. Stir in the remaining ingredients and mix thoroughly.
4. Pour the batter in a 9-inch round cake pan coated with baking paper.
5. Preheat your oven and bake the cake for about fifty minutes or until the cake looks set.
6. The cake tastes best chilled.

Nutritional Content of One Serving:

Calories: 433 ‖ Fat: 21.2g ‖ Protein: 5.6g ‖ Carbohydrates: 60.9g

ORANGE CHOCOLATE CAKE

Total Time Taken: 1 ¼ hours
Yield: 12 Servings

Ingredients:

- ½ cup candied orange peel, chopped
- ½ teaspoon salt
- 1 cup white sugar
- 1 teaspoon baking soda
- 2 cups ground almonds
- 4 eggs
- 8 oz. dark chocolate, melted

Directions:

1. Mix the eggs with sugar until fluffy and pale.
2. Stir in the melted chocolate then put in the almonds, baking soda and salt.
3. Fold in the candied orange peel then pour the batter in 1 8-inch round cake pan coated with baking paper.
4. Pre-heat the oven and bake at 350F for about half an hour.
5. Let the cake cool in the pan before you serve.

Nutritional Content of One Serving:

Calories: 280 ‖ Fat: 15.0g ‖ Protein: 6.7g ‖ Carbohydrates: 32.4g

OLIVE OIL PISTACHIO CAKE

Total Time Taken: 1 hour
Yield: 10 Servings
Ingredients:

- ½ cup corn meal
- ½ cup extra virgin olive oil
- ½ cup ground pistachios
- ½ cup white sugar
- 3 eggs
- ½ cup whole milk
- ½ teaspoon salt
- 1 cup all-purpose flour
- 1 teaspoon baking powder
- 1 teaspoon baking soda
- 2 tablespoons orange zest

Directions:

1. Mix the dry ingredients in a container.
2. In a separate container, mix the oil, sugar, eggs and orange zest and stir thoroughly for a few minutes until volume increases to twice what it was.
3. Stir in the milk, followed by the dry ingredients.
4. Pour the batter in 10-inch round cake pan coated with baking paper.
5. Preheat your oven and bake the cake for around forty minutes.
6. The cake tastes best chilled.

Nutritional Content of One Serving:

Calories: 221 ‖ Fat: 12.1g ‖ Protein: 4.0g ‖ Carbohydrates: 26.1g

NATURAL RED VELVET CAKE

Total Time Taken: 1 ¼ hours
Yield: 10 Servings
Ingredients:

Cake:

- ¼ cup white sugar
- ½ cup canola oil
- ½ cup light brown sugar
- ½ teaspoon cinnamon powder
- ½ teaspoon salt
- 1 ¼ cups all-purpose flour
- 1 teaspoon baking powder
- 2 beetroots, peeled and pureed
- 2 eggs
- 2 tablespoons cornstarch

Frosting:

- ¼ cup butter, softened
- 1 cup cream cheese
- 1 cup powdered sugar

Directions:

1. For the cake, combine the beetroot puree, canola oil, eggs and sugar in a container.
2. Stir in the remaining ingredients and mix thoroughly.
3. Pour the batter in a 8-inch round cake pan coated with baking paper.
4. Pre-heat the oven and bake at 350F for forty minutes.
5. When finished, allow the cake to cool in the pan then transfer the cake on a platter.
6. For the frosting, combine all the ingredients in a container until fluffy.
7. Cover the cake with the frosting and serve it fresh.

Nutritional Content of One Serving:

Calories: 395 ‖ Fat: 24.7g ‖ Protein: 4.8g ‖ Carbohydrates: 40.1g

MORELLO CHERRY CAKE

Total Time Taken: 1 ¼ hours
Yield: 12 Servings

Ingredients:

- ¼ cup brandy
- ½ cup cocoa powder
- ½ cup cocoa powder
- ½ cup coconut oil, melted
- ½ cup white sugar
- ½ teaspoon salt
- ¾ cup all-purpose flour
- 1 cup almond flour
- 1 cup maple syrup
- 1 cup Morello cherries
- 3 eggs

Directions:

1. Mix the maple syrup, coconut oil, brandy and eggs in a container.
2. Stir in the sugar and mix thoroughly.
3. Fold in the cocoa powder, almond flour, all-purpose flour, salt and cocoa powder.
4. Spoon the batter in a 9-inch round cake pan and top with cherries.
5. Pre-heat the oven and bake at 350F for forty minutes.
6. The cake tastes best chilled.

Nutritional Content of One Serving:

Calories: 270 || Fat: 12.4g || Protein: 4.2g || Carbohydrates: 40.9g

MOLASSES PEAR BUNDT CAKE

Total Time Taken: 1 ¼ hours
Yield: 10 Servings

Ingredients:

- ½ cup light brown sugar

- ½ cup molasses
- ½ cup sour cream
- ½ cup whole milk
- ½ teaspoon ground ginger
- ½ teaspoon salt
- 1 cup butter, softened
- 1 teaspoon all-spice
- 1 teaspoon baking powder
- 1 teaspoon baking soda
- 1 teaspoon cinnamon powder
- 2 cups all-purpose flour
- 2 pears, peeled, cored and diced
- 3 eggs

Directions:

1. Mix the butter, molasses and sugar in a container until creamy and pale.
2. Stir in the eggs, one at a time, stirring thoroughly after each addition.
3. Mix the flour with baking powder, baking soda, salt and spices.
4. Mix the milk with cream.
5. Fold the flour into the butter mixture, alternating it with the milk and sour cream mix.
6. Put in the pears then spoon the batter in a greased Bundt cake pan.
7. Pre-heat the oven and bake at 350F for about forty minutes or until a toothpick inserted in the center comes out clean.
8. Let the cake cool in the pan for about ten minutes then flip over on a platter.
9. Serve chilled.

Nutritional Content of One Serving:

Calories: 405 ‖ Fat: 22.9g ‖ Protein: 5.3g ‖ Carbohydrates: 46.3g

MOIST PUMPKIN CAKE

Total Time Taken: 1 ¼ hours
Yield: 12 Servings

Ingredients:

- ¼ teaspoon ground nutmeg

- ½ teaspoon ground ginger
- ½ teaspoon salt
- 1 ½ cups pumpkin puree
- 1 cup canola oil
- 1 teaspoon cinnamon powder
- 2 cups white sugar
- 2 teaspoons baking powder
- 3 cups all-purpose flour
- 4 eggs

Directions:

1. Mix the sugar, canola oil and eggs in a container until creamy and volume increases to twice what it was.
2. Stir in the pumpkin puree, then fold in the remaining ingredients.
3. Pour the batter in a 9-inch round cake pan coated with baking paper.
4. Pre-heat the oven and bake at 350F for around forty minutes or until well risen and fragrant.
5. Let the cake cool in the pan and serve, sliced.

Nutritional Content of One Serving:

Calories: 432 ‖ Fat: 20.1g ‖ Protein: 5.4g ‖ Carbohydrates: 60.2g

MOIST CHOCOLATE CAKE

Total Time Taken: 1 ¼ hours

Yield: 12 Servings

Ingredients:

- ½ cup canola oil
- ½ cup cocoa powder
- ½ teaspoon salt
- 1 ½ teaspoon baking powder
- 1 cup buttermilk
- 1 cup hot coffee
- 1 teaspoon vanilla extract
- 2 cups all-purpose flour
- 2 cups white sugar

- 2 eggs

Directions:

1. Mix the sugar, eggs and canola oil in a container until creamy.
2. Stir in the vanilla, coffee and buttermilk then put in the remaining ingredients.
3. Pour the batter in a 9-inch round cake pan coated with baking paper.
4. Pre-heat the oven and bake at 350F for about forty-five minutes or until a toothpick comes out clean after being inserted into the center of the cake.
5. Let the cake cool in the pan before you serve.

Nutritional Content of One Serving:

Calories: 310 ‖ Fat: 10.7g ‖ Protein: 4.4g ‖ Carbohydrates: 52.6g

MOIST APPLE CAKE

Total Time Taken: 1 ½ hours
Yield: 14 Servings

Ingredients:

- ¼ cup maple syrup
- ½ teaspoon salt
- 1 ½ cups light brown sugar
- 1 cup butter, softened
- 1 teaspoon cinnamon powder
- 1 teaspoon ground cardamom
- 1 teaspoon ground ginger
- 2 cups applesauce
- 2 eggs
- 2 green apples, peeled, cored and diced
- 2 teaspoons baking soda
- 3 cups all-purpose flour

Directions:

1. Mix the flour, baking soda, salt and spices in a container.
2. In a separate container, mix the butter, sugar and maple syrup and stir thoroughly for a few minutes.
3. Stir in the eggs and applesauce then fold in the flour mixture.

4. Put in the apples then spoon the batter in a 10-inch round cake pan coated with baking paper.
5. Pre-heat the oven and bake at 350F for about fifty minutes or until a toothpick inserted into the center of the cake comes out clean.
6. Let the cake cool in the pan and serve, sliced.

Nutritional Content of One Serving:

Calories: 326 ‖ Fat: 14.1g ‖ Protein: 3.9g ‖ Carbohydrates: 47.2g

MISSISSIPPI MUD CAKE

Total Time Taken: 1 ¼ hours

Yield: 12 Servings

Ingredients:

- ½ cup cocoa powder
- ½ teaspoon salt
- 1 cup buttermilk
- 1 cup canola oil
- 1 cup hot coffee
- 1 teaspoon baking powder
- 1 teaspoon baking soda
- 2 ½ cups all-purpose flour
- 2 cups white sugar
- 2 eggs
- 2 teaspoons vanilla extract

Directions:

1. Mix the sugar, eggs, coffee, oil, vanilla and buttermilk in a container.
2. In a separate container, mix the cocoa powder, salt, flour, baking soda and baking powder then mix in the coffee mixture.
3. Pour the batter in a 10-inch round cake pan covered with parchment paper.
4. Pre-heat the oven and bake at 330F for about fifty minutes.
5. Let the cake cool in the pan and serve, sliced.

Nutritional Content of One Serving:

Calories: 410 ‖ Fat: 19.8g ‖ Protein: 5.0g ‖ Carbohydrates: 56.5g

MILK CHOCOLATE CHUNK CAKE

Total Time Taken: 1 1/5 hours

Yield: 12 Servings

Ingredients:

- ½ cup chocolate syrup
- ½ cup cocoa powder
- ½ teaspoon baking soda
- ½ teaspoon salt
- 1 cup butter, softened
- 1 cup buttermilk
- 1 cup white sugar
- 1 teaspoon baking powder
- 1 teaspoon vanilla extract
- 2 cups all-purpose flour
- 4 eggs
- 8 oz. milk chocolate, chopped

Directions:

1. Sift the flour, cocoa powder, baking powder, baking soda and salt.
2. Mix the butter with sugar until creamy and fluffy. Put in the chocolate syrup then mix in the eggs and vanilla.
3. Fold in the flour, alternating it with buttermilk. Begin and finish with flour.
4. Put in the chocolate chunks then spoon the batter in a round cake pan coated with baking paper.
5. Pre-heat the oven and bake at 350F for about forty minutes or until a toothpick comes out clean after being inserted into the center of the cake.

Nutritional Content of One Serving:

Calories: 449 ‖ Fat: 23.4g ‖ Protein: 7.2g ‖ Carbohydrates: 55.2g

MERINGUE BLACK FOREST CAKE

Total Time Taken: 2 ½ hours

Yield: 8 Servings

Ingredients:

- ¼ teaspoon salt
- ½ teaspoon cream of tartar
- 1 ½ cups dark chocolate chips
- 1 cup heavy cream
- 1 cup sour cherries, pitted
- 1 cup white sugar
- 1 teaspoon vanilla extract
- 2 tablespoons cocoa powder
- 4 egg whites

Directions:

1. Mix the egg whites, cream of tartar and salt in a container for minimum five minutes or until firm and fluffy.
2. Put in the sugar, progressively, whipping until shiny and firm.
3. Fold in the cocoa powder then spoon the meringue on a large baking sheet coated with baking paper, shaping it into two 8-inch rounds.
4. Pre-heat the oven and bake at 250F for about two hours.
5. Bring the cream to the boiling point in a saucepan. Put in the chocolate and stir until it melts completely. Allow this cream to cool down then put in the vanilla.
6. Layer the baked meringue with chocolate cream and sour cherries.
7. Serve the cake fresh.

Nutritional Content of One Serving:

Calories: 275 ‖ Fat: 11.8g ‖ Protein: 3.9g ‖ Carbohydrates: 44.1g

MATCHA POUND CAKE

Total Time Taken: 1 hour
Yield: 10 Servings
Ingredients:

- ¼ teaspoon salt
- ½ cup butter, softened
- ½ cup light brown sugar
- 1 cup all-purpose flour
- 1 tablespoon lemon juice
- 1 teaspoon baking powder

- 1 teaspoon lemon zest
- 2 teaspoons matcha powder
- 4 eggs, separated

Directions:

1. Sift the flour, salt, baking powder and matcha powder in a container.
2. Mix the butter with sugar until creamy and pale. Stir in the egg yolks and mix thoroughly. Put in the lemon zest and lemon juice and give it a good mix.
3. Fold in the flour.
4. Whip the egg whites until fluffy and firm. Fold the meringue into the cake batter.
5. Pour the batter in a loaf cake pan coated with baking paper.
6. Pre-heat the oven and bake at 350F for about forty minutes or until a toothpick inserted into the center of the cake comes out clean.
7. The cake tastes best chilled.

Nutritional Content of One Serving:

Calories: 185 ‖ Fat: 11.1g ‖ Protein: 3.6g ‖ Carbohydrates: 18.1g

MATCHA CHOCOLATE CAKE

Total Time Taken: 1 ¼ hours
Yield: 8 Servings
Ingredients:

Cake:

- ¼ cup butter, melted
- ½ teaspoon salt
- 1 ¼ cups all-purpose flour
- 1 ½ teaspoons matcha powder
- 1 cup white sugar
- 1 teaspoon baking powder Chocolate
- 4 eggs
- 4 tablespoons hot water

Glaze:

- ¼ cup butter
- 1 cup dark chocolate chips

Directions:

1. For the cake, sift the flour with salt, matcha powder and baking powder.
2. Mix the eggs and white sugar until volume increases to twice what it was.
3. Stir in the melted butter and hot water then fold in the flour mixture.
4. Spoon the batter in a 9-inch round cake pan coated with baking paper.
5. Preheat your oven and bake the cake for around forty minutes or until a toothpick inserted in the center comes out clean.
6. For the glaze, mix the chocolate chips and butter in a heatproof container and place over a hot water bath. Melt them together until the desired smoothness is achieved.
7. Sprinkle the glaze over the cake and serve immediately or place in your refrigerator.

Nutritional Content of One Serving:

Calories: 371 ‖ Fat: 17.9g ‖ Protein: 5.9g ‖ Carbohydrates: 51.0g

MARBLE CAKE

Total Time Taken: 1 hour
Yield: 10 Servings
Ingredients:

- ¼ cup cocoa powder
- ¼ cup hot water
- ½ cup butter, softened
- ½ teaspoon baking soda
- ½ teaspoon salt
- 1 cup white sugar
- 1 cup whole milk
- 1 teaspoon vanilla extract
- 2 ½ cups all-purpose flour
- 2 teaspoon baking powder
- 3 eggs

Directions:

1. Mix the cocoa powder with hot water in a small container.
2. Mix the butter and sugar in a container until creamy and firm. Put in the eggs, one at a time, then mix in the vanilla and milk.

3. Fold in the flour, baking powder, baking soda and salt.
4. Divide the batter in half. Spoon one half in a loaf pan coated with baking paper.
5. Mix the half that is left over of batter with the cocoa mixture.
6. Spoon the cocoa batter over the white one and swirl it around with a toothpick.
7. Preheat your oven and bake the cake at 350F for around forty minutes or until a toothpick inserted in the center comes out clean.
8. Let the cake cool in the pan and serve, sliced.

Nutritional Content of One Serving:

Calories: 311 ‖ Fat: 11.9g ‖ Protein: 6.2g ‖ Carbohydrates: 46.8g

MAPLE SYRUP APPLE CAKE

Total Time Taken: 1 ¼ hours
Yield: 10 Servings

Ingredients:

- ¼ cup butter, softened
- ½ cup walnuts, chopped
- ½ cup whole milk
- ½ teaspoon salt
- 1 cup maple syrup
- 1 teaspoon cinnamon powder
- 1 teaspoon ground ginger
- 2 cups all-purpose flour
- 2 red apples, peeled, cored and diced
- 2 teaspoons baking powder
- 4 eggs

Directions:

1. Mix the flour, baking powder, cinnamon, ginger and salt in a container.
1. In a separate container, combine the butter and maple syrup. Stir in the eggs and the milk then fold in the flour.
2. Put in the apples and walnuts then spoon the batter in a Bundt cake pan lined using butter.

3. Pre-heat the oven and bake at 350F for around forty minutes or until it rises significantly and starts to appear golden-brown.
4. Let the cake cool in the pan and serve, sliced.

Nutritional Content of One Serving:

Calories: 306 ‖ Fat: 10.8g ‖ Protein: 6.8g ‖ Carbohydrates: 47.1g

MANGO ICE BOX CAKE

Total Time Taken: 1 hour
Yield: 8 Servings
Ingredients:

- ½ cup white sugar
- 1 tablespoon lemon juice
- 1/3 cup sweetened condensed milk
- 15 graham crackers
- 2 cups heavy cream, whipped
- 2 ripe mangos, peeled and cubed

Directions:

1. Mix the mangos, sugar and lemon juice in a saucepan and place over low heat. Cook for about ten minutes until softened. Let cool completely.
2. To finish the cake, take a loaf pan and line it using plastic wrap.
3. Mix the cream and sweetened condensed milk.
4. Layer the crackers with the mango mixture and cream in the readied pan.
5. Wrap securely and store in the refrigerator for minimum an hour.
6. The cake tastes best chilled.

Nutritional Content of One Serving:

Calories: 303 ‖ Fat: 14.9g ‖ Protein: 3.5g ‖ Carbohydrates: 40.5g

MADEIRA CAKE

Total Time Taken: 1 hour
Yield: 8 Servings
Ingredients:

- ¼ cup whole milk
- ¼ teaspoon salt
- ¾ cup butter, softened
- ¾ cup white sugar
- 3 eggs
- 1 ½ cups all-purpose flour
- 1 teaspoon baking powder
- 1 teaspoon lemon zest

Directions:

1. Mix the butter and sugar in a container until creamy and firm. Put in the eggs, one at a time, then fold in the flour, baking powder and salt, alternating it with milk.
2. Put in the lemon zest then spoon the batter in a 9-inch round cake pan coated with baking paper.
3. Preheat your oven and bake the cake for around forty minutes or until it rises significantly and starts to appear golden-brown.
4. Let the cake cool in the pan and serve, sliced.

Nutritional Content of One Serving:

Calories: 337 ‖ Fat: 19.4g ‖ Protein: 4.9g ‖ Carbohydrates: 37.5g

LIME POUND CAKE

Total Time Taken: 1 ¼ hours
Yield: 12 Servings

Ingredients:

- ¼ cup canola oil
- ½ cup sour cream
- ½ teaspoon salt
- 1 ½ cups white sugar
- 1 cup butter, softened
- 1 lime, zested and juiced

- 1 teaspoon baking soda
- 2 cups all-purpose flour
- 4 eggs

Directions:

1. Mix the butter, oil and sugar in a container until pale and creamy.
2. Stir in the eggs and mix thoroughly then put in the lime zest and lime juice. Stir thoroughly to mix.
3. Fold in the dry ingredients then put in the sour cream.
4. Pulse using a mixer on high speed for a minute.
5. Spoon the batter in a loaf cake pan and preheat your oven and bake at 350F for about forty minutes or until it rises significantly and starts to appear golden-brown.
6. Let the cake cool in the pan and serve, sliced.

Nutritional Content of One Serving:

Calories: 389 ‖ Fat: 23.6g ‖ Protein: 4.5g ‖ Carbohydrates: 42.0g

LEMON SPRINKLE CAKE

Total Time Taken: 1 ¼ hours
Yield: 10 Servings
Ingredients:

Cake:

- ½ cup butter, melted
- ½ cup sour cream
- 1 ½ cups all-purpose flour
- 1 cup white sugar
- 1 teaspoon baking powder
- 2 tablespoons lemon juice
- 2 tablespoons lemon zest
- 5 eggs

Icing:

- 1 cup powdered sugar
- 1 tablespoon lemon juice
- 1 teaspoon lemon zest

Directions:

1. For the cake, combine the eggs and sugar in a container until twofold in volume and fluffy.
2. Put in the melted butter and stir lightly. Stir in the sour cream, lemon zest and lemon juice.
3. Fold in the flour, baking powder and salt then pour the batter in a 9-inch round cake pan covered with parchment paper.
4. Pre-heat the oven and bake at 350F for around forty minutes or until a golden-brown colour is achieved and it rises significantly.
5. Let the cake cool in the pan then move to a platter.
6. For the icing, combine all the ingredients then sprinkle it over the cake.
7. Serve immediately.

Nutritional Content of One Serving:

Calories: 330 ‖ Fat: 14.0g ‖ Protein: 5.2g ‖ Carbohydrates: 47.5g

LEMON RICOTTA CAKE

Total Time Taken: 1 hour
Yield: 8 Servings
Ingredients:

- ¼ cup butter, melted
- ¼ teaspoon salt
- ½ cup almond flour
- ¾ cup white sugar
- 1 ¼ cups all-purpose flour
- 1 cup ricotta cheese
- 1 teaspoon baking powder
- 2 eggs
- 2 tablespoons lemon zest

Directions:

1. Mix the cheese, eggs, sugar, butter and lemon zest in a container.
2. Fold in the flours, baking powder and salt then spoon the batter in a 8-inch round cake pan coated with baking paper.
3. Pre-heat the oven and bake at 350F for around forty minutes or until a toothpick comes out clean after being inserted into the center of the cake.

4. The cake tastes best chilled.

Nutritional Content of One Serving:

Calories: 262 ‖ Fat: 10.4g ‖ Protein: 7.4g ‖ Carbohydrates: 36.3g

LEMON RASPBERRY POUND CAKE

Total Time Taken: 1 ¼ hours
Yield: 10 Servings
Ingredients:

Cake:

- ½ cup cream cheese
- ½ teaspoon salt
- 1 ½ cups fresh raspberries
- 1 cup butter, softened
- 1 cup white sugar
- 1 teaspoon baking powder
- 1 teaspoon baking soda
- 1 teaspoon lemon zest
- 1 teaspoon vanilla extract
- 2 ¼ cups all-purpose flour
- 2 tablespoons lemon juice
- 4 eggs

Glaze:

- ½ cup cream cheese
- 1 teaspoon lemon zest
- 2 tablespoons lemon juice
- 2 tablespoons powdered sugar

Directions:

1. For the cake, sift the flour, baking soda, baking powder and salt in a container.
2. In a separate container, combine the butter, cream cheese, sugar, vanilla and lemon zest until creamy.
3. Stir in the eggs, one at a time, then put in the lemon juice.
4. Fold in the flour, mixing using a spatula.

5. Put in the raspberries then spoon the batter in a loaf cake pan coated with baking paper.
6. Pre-heat the oven and bake at 350F for about forty minutes or until a toothpick inserted into the center of the cake comes out clean.
7. When the cake is finished cooking, move it to a platter.
8. For the glaze, combine all the ingredients in a container.
9. Sprinkle the glaze over the cake and serve it fresh.

Nutritional Content of One Serving:

Calories: 466 ‖ Fat: 28.7g ‖ Protein: 7.3g ‖ Carbohydrates: 46.5g

LEMON GINGER CAKE

Total Time Taken: 1 ¼ hours
Yield: 10 Servings

Ingredients:

- ¼ cup lemon juice
- ¼ teaspoon salt
- ½ teaspoon baking powder
- 1 ½ cups white sugar
- 1 cup butter, softened
- 1 cup sour cream
- 1 tablespoon lemon zest
- 1 teaspoon baking soda
- 1 teaspoon grated ginger
- 2 ½ cups all-purpose flour
- 4 eggs

Directions:

1. Sift the flour, baking soda, baking powder and salt.
2. Mix the butter and sugar in a container until creamy and fluffy.
3. Put in the eggs, one at a time, then mix in the lemon juice, lemon zest and ginger, as well as the sour cream.
4. Fold in the sifted flour then spoon the batter in a 9-inch round cake pan coated with baking paper.
5. Pre-heat the oven and bake at 350F for around forty minutes or until a toothpick comes out clean after being inserted into the center of the cake.

6. Let the cake cool in the pan and serve, sliced.

Nutritional Content of One Serving:

Calories: 466 ‖ Fat: 25.4g ‖ Protein: 6.4g ‖ Carbohydrates: 55.5g

LEMON BLUEBERRY BUNDT CAKE

Total Time Taken: 1 ¼ hours
Yield: 10 Servings

Ingredients:

- ½ cup butter, softened
- ½ cup cream cheese
- ½ teaspoon salt
- 1 ½ teaspoons baking powder
- 1 cup fresh blueberries
- 1 cup plain yogurt
- 1 cup white sugar
- 1 tablespoon lemon zest
- 1 teaspoon vanilla extract
- 2 cups all-purpose flour
- 2 egg whites
- 2 eggs

Directions:

1. Mix the butter, cream cheese and sugar in a container until creamy.
2. Stir in the eggs, egg whites, lemon zest and vanilla.
3. Fold in the flour, baking powder and salt, alternating it with yogurt.
4. Put in the blueberries then spoon the batter in a greased Bundt cake pan.
5. Pre-heat the oven and bake at 350F for about forty minutes or until a toothpick inserted in the center comes out clean.
6. Let the cake cool in the pan and serve, sliced.

Nutritional Content of One Serving:

Calories: 332 ‖ Fat: 14.7g ‖ Protein: 6.9g ‖ Carbohydrates: 43.9g

JAM STUDDED CAKE

Total Time Taken: 1 hour

Yield: 8 Servings

Ingredients: 5 eggs

- ¼ cup canola oil
- ¼ teaspoon salt
- ¾ cup white sugar
- 1 cup all-purpose flour
- 1 cup apricot jam
- 1 teaspoon baking powder
- 1 teaspoon orange zest
- 1 teaspoon vanilla extract

Directions:

1. Mix the eggs and sugar in a container until its volume increases to almost three times it was.
2. Stir in the oil, vanilla and orange zest then fold in the flour, baking powder and salt.
3. Spoon the batter in 1 9-inch round cake pan coated with baking paper.
4. Drop spoonfuls of apricot jam over the batter and preheat your oven and bake at 350F for around forty minutes or until a golden-brown colour is achieved and it rises significantly.
5. Let the cake cool in the pan and serve, sliced.

Nutritional Content of One Serving:

Calories: 326 ‖ Fat: 9.8g ‖ Protein: 5.4g ‖ Carbohydrates: 57.1g

HOT CHOCOLATE BUNDT CAKE

Total Time Taken: 1 hour

Yield: 12 Servings

Ingredients:

Cake:

- ½ cup canola oil
- ½ teaspoon salt

- ¾ cup butter, softened
- ¾ cup cocoa powder
- 1 cup hot water
- 1 cup light brown sugar
- 1 teaspoon vanilla extract
- 2 cups all-purpose flour
- 2 teaspoons baking powder
- 3 eggs
- 4 oz. dark chocolate, melted

Glaze:

- ½ cup heavy cream
- 1 cup dark chocolate chips

Directions:

1. For the cake, combine the butter, oil and sugar in a container until creamy and light.
2. Stir in the eggs, vanilla and melted chocolate.
3. Sift the flour with cocoa powder, baking powder and salt and fold it in the butter mixture.
4. Progressively mix in the hot water then spoon the batter in a greased Bundt cake pan.
5. Pre-heat the oven and bake at 350F for about forty minutes or until a toothpick inserted into the center of the cake comes out clean.
6. When finished, take out of the pan on a platter.
7. For the glaze, bring the cream to the boiling point then mix in the chocolate. Stir until melted and smooth.
8. Sprinkle the glaze over the cake and serve chilled.

Nutritional Content of One Serving:

Calories: 448 ‖ Fat: 29.9g ‖ Protein: 6.1g ‖ Carbohydrates: 43.6g

HONEY FIG CAKE

Total Time Taken: 1 hour
Yield: 8 Servings
Ingredients:

- ½ cup butter, softened
- ½ cup honey
- ½ teaspoon salt
- 1 ½ cups all-purpose flour
- 1 teaspoon baking powder
- 1 teaspoon orange zest
- 1 teaspoon vanilla extract
- 1 whole egg
- 3 egg whites
- 6 fresh figs, quartered

Directions:

1. Mix the butter, honey, egg whites and egg in a container until creamy. Put in the vanilla and orange zest and mix thoroughly.
2. Fold in the flour, baking powder and salt then spoon the batter in a 9-inch round cake pan coated with baking paper.
3. Top the batter with fig slices and preheat your oven and bake at 350F for about forty minutes.
4. Let the cake cool in the pan and serve, sliced.

Nutritional Content of One Serving:

Calories: 304 ‖ Fat: 12.4g ‖ Protein: 5.1g ‖ Carbohydrates: 45.0g

HOLIDAY POUND CAKE

Total Time Taken: 1 ¼ hours
Yield: 16 Servings

Ingredients:

- ½ teaspoon salt
- 1 cup butter, softened
- 1 cup buttermilk
- 1 cup cream cheese
- 1 teaspoon lemon zest
- 1 teaspoon orange zest
- 1 teaspoon vanilla extract
- 2 cups white sugar

- 2 teaspoons baking powder
- 3 cups all-purpose flour
- 6 eggs

Directions:

1. Mix the butter and sugar in a container until pale and light. Stir in the cream cheese and mix thoroughly.
2. Put in the eggs, one after another, then mix in the flour, baking powder and salt, alternating it with buttermilk.
3. Fold in the citrus zest and vanilla extract then spoon the batter in a large loaf cake pan coated with baking paper.
4. Preheat your oven and bake the cake for about fifty minutes or until a toothpick inserted into the center of the cake comes out clean.
5. Let the cake cool in the pan and serve, sliced.

Nutritional Content of One Serving:

Calories: 363 ‖ Fat: 18.6g ‖ Protein: 6.2g ‖ Carbohydrates: 44.5g

HEALTHIER CARROT CAKE

Total Time Taken: 1 ½ hours
Yield: 10 Servings

Ingredients:

- ¼ cup orange juice
- ½ cup coconut oil, melted
- ½ cup grated apples
- ½ cup quinoa powder
- ½ cup raisins
- ½ cup rolled oats
- ½ teaspoon ground ginger
- ½ teaspoon salt
- 1 ½ cups grated carrots
- 1 cup low-fat yogurt cake
- 1 cup whole wheat flour
- 1 tablespoon orange zest
- 1 teaspoon cinnamon powder

- 2 teaspoons baking powder

Directions:

1. Mix the yogurt, orange juice, coconut oil, orange zest, carrots, apples and raisins.
2. Fold in the remaining ingredients and mix using a spatula.
3. Pour the batter in a 9-inch round cake pan coated with baking paper.
4. Pre-heat the oven and bake at 350F for about fifty minutes or until a toothpick inserted into the center of the cake comes out clean.
5. The cake tastes best chilled.

Nutritional Content of One Serving:

Calories: 215 ‖ Fat: 12.0g ‖ Protein: 2.9g ‖ Carbohydrates: 25.1g

HAZELNUT CHOCOLATE CAKE

Total Time Taken: 1 hour
Yield: 10 Servings
Ingredients:

- ½ cup butter
- ½ teaspoon salt
- 1 cup ground hazelnuts
- 1 cup Nutella
- 6 eggs, separated
- 6 oz. dark chocolate chips

Directions:

1. Combine the chocolate chips and butter in a heatproof container and place over a hot water bath.
2. Melt them together until smooth then turn off heat and fold in the egg yolks, followed by the Nutella and ground hazelnuts.
3. Whip the egg whites with a pinch of salt until firm then fold them in the batter using a spatula.
4. Pour the batter in a 9-inch round cake pan coated with baking paper.
5. Pre-heat the oven and bake at 350F for about half an hour.
6. Let the cake cool in the pan and serve, sliced.

Nutritional Content of One Serving:

Calories: 326 || Fat: 25.3g || Protein: 6.5g || Carbohydrates: 22.0g

GRANNY SMITH CAKE

Total Time Taken: 1 ½ hours

Yield: 12 Servings

Ingredients:

- ¼ teaspoon salt
- 1 ½ cups all-purpose flour
- 1 cup canola oil
- 1 cup white sugar
- 1 cup whole milk
- 1 tablespoon lemon zest
- 1 teaspoon cinnamon powder
- 2 eggs
- 2 teaspoons baking powder
- 3 Granny Smith apples, peeled and diced

Directions:

1. Sift the flour, baking powder, salt and cinnamon in a container.
2. In a separate container, combine the canola oil, eggs and sugar until fluffy and pale. Put in the milk and lemon zest and mix thoroughly.
3. Fold in the flour then mix in the apples.
4. Spoon the batter in a 9-inch round cake pan coated with baking paper.
5. Pre-heat the oven and bake at 350F for around forty minutes or until a toothpick comes out clean after being inserted into the center of the cake.
6. Serve chilled.

Nutritional Content of One Serving:

Calories: 328 || Fat: 19.8g || Protein: 3.3g || Carbohydrates: 36.4g

GRAND MARNIER INFUSED LOAF CAKE

Total Time Taken: 2 hours
Yield: 14 Servings
Ingredients:

- ¼ cup grand Marnier
- ½ cup butter, softened
- ½ cup whole milk
- ½ teaspoon baking soda
- ½ teaspoon salt
- 1 ½ cups white sugar
- 1 cup cream cheese
- 1 cup dried cranberries
- 1 teaspoon vanilla extract
- 2 teaspoons baking powder
- 3 cups all-purpose flour
- 4 eggs

Directions:

1. Mix the cranberries and Grand Marnier in a jar and allow to soak up for an hour.
2. Mix the flour with baking powder, baking soda and salt.
3. Mix the butter, cream cheese and sugar in a container until fluffy.
4. Stir in the eggs, one at a time, then put in the vanilla and milk.
5. Fold in the flour mixture and stir until incorporated.
6. Put in the cranberries.
7. Spoon the batter in a large loaf pan coated with baking paper.
8. Pre-heat the oven and bake at 350F for about fifty minutes or until a toothpick inserted in the center comes out clean.
9. Let the cake cool in the pan then serve, sliced.

Nutritional Content of One Serving:

Calories: 336 ‖ Fat: 14.1g ‖ Protein: 6.0g ‖ Carbohydrates: 43.9g

GRAND MARNIER INFUSED LOAF CAKE

Total Time Taken: 2 hours
Yield: 14 Servings
Ingredients:

- ¼ cup grand Marnier
- ½ cup butter, softened
- ½ cup whole milk
- ½ teaspoon baking soda
- ½ teaspoon salt
- 1 ½ cups white sugar
- 1 cup cream cheese
- 1 cup dried cranberries
- 1 teaspoon vanilla extract
- 2 teaspoons baking powder
- 3 cups all-purpose flour
- 4 eggs

Directions:

1. Mix the cranberries and Grand Marnier in a jar and allow to soak up for an hour.
2. Mix the flour with baking powder, baking soda and salt.
3. Mix the butter, cream cheese and sugar in a container until fluffy.
4. Stir in the eggs, one at a time, then put in the vanilla and milk.
5. Fold in the flour mixture and stir until incorporated.
6. Put in the cranberries.
7. Spoon the batter in a large loaf pan coated with baking paper.
8. Pre-heat the oven and bake at 350F for about fifty minutes or until a toothpick inserted in the center comes out clean.
9. Let the cake cool in the pan then serve, sliced.

Nutritional Content of One Serving:

Calories: 336 ‖ Fat: 14.1g ‖ Protein: 6.0g ‖ Carbohydrates: 43.9g

GRAHAM CRACKER PUMPKIN CAKE

Total Time Taken: 1 ¼ hours
Yield: 12 Servings

Ingredients:

- ¼ cup dark brown sugar
- ½ cup butter, softened

- ½ cup whole milk
- ½ teaspoon salt
- 1 ¼ cups pumpkin puree
- 1 ½ cups graham crackers
- 1 cup all-purpose flour
- 1 cup light brown sugar
- 2 teaspoons baking powder
- 4 eggs

Directions:

1. Mix the butter with the sugars in a container until creamy and fluffy.
2. Stir in the eggs, one at a time, then put in the pumpkin puree and milk.
3. Put in the rest of the ingredients and mix thoroughly using a spatula.
4. Pour the batter in a greased Bundt cake pan and preheat your oven and bake at 350F for forty minutes or until it rises significantly and starts to appear golden-brown.
5. Let the cake cool in the pan before you serve.

Nutritional Content of One Serving:

Calories: 244 ‖ Fat: 10.7g ‖ Protein: 4.4g ‖ Carbohydrates: 33.9g

GRAHAM CRACKER CAKE

Total Time Taken: 1 ¼ hours
Yield: 10 Servings

Ingredients:

- ¼ cup dark brown sugar
- ½ cup heavy cream
- ½ teaspoon baking powder
- ½ teaspoon cinnamon powder
- ½ teaspoon salt
- ¾ cup butter, softened
- 1 cup graham cracker crumbs
- 1 cup white sugar
- 2 cups all-purpose flour
- 2 teaspoons baking powder

- 3 eggs

Directions:

1. Mix the graham cracker crumbs, flour, baking powder, baking soda, salt and cinnamon in a container.
2. In another container, combine the butter and sugars until creamy and light.
3. Stir in the eggs, one after another, and mix thoroughly then put in the cream.
4. Fold in the flour mixture then pour the batter in a 10-inch round cake pan coated with baking paper.
5. Bake for about forty-five minutes in the preheated oven at 350F or until a toothpick comes out clean after being inserted into the center of the cake.
6. Let the cake cool in the pan and serve, sliced.

Nutritional Content of One Serving:

Calories: 380 ‖ Fat: 18.4g ‖ Protein: 5.0g ‖ Carbohydrates: 50.4g

GINGERSNAP PUMPKIN BUNDT CAKE

Total Time Taken: 1 ¼ hours
Yield: 12 Servings

Ingredients:

- ¼ cup canola oil
- ½ cup butter, softened
- ½ teaspoon salt
- 1 ½ cups pumpkin puree
- 1 cup white sugar
- 1 teaspoon vanilla extract
- 2 cups all-purpose flour
- 2 tablespoons dark brown sugar
- 2 teaspoons baking powder
- 3 eggs
- 6 gingersnaps, crushed

Directions:

1. Mix the butter, oil and sugars in a container until light and creamy.

2. Stir in the eggs, one at a time, then put in the pumpkin and vanilla and mix thoroughly.
3. Fold in the flour, baking powder and salt then put in the crushed gingersnaps.
4. Spoon the batter in a greased Bundt cake pan and preheat your oven and bake at 350F for 45 minutes or until a toothpick comes out clean after being inserted into the center of the cake.
5. Let cool in the pan then move to a platter.

Nutritional Content of One Serving:

Calories: 350 ‖ Fat: 16.1g ‖ Protein: 5.0g ‖ Carbohydrates: 48.0g

GINGERBREAD CHOCOLATE CAKE

Total Time Taken: 1 ¼ hours
Yield: 10 Servings

Ingredients:

- ½ cup butter, softened
- ½ cup cocoa powder
- ½ cup sour cream
- ½ teaspoon ground cloves
- ½ teaspoon ground ginger
- ½ teaspoon ground star anise
- ½ teaspoon salt
- 1 ½ cups white sugar
- 1 teaspoon cinnamon powder
- 1 teaspoon orange zest
- 2 cups all-purpose flour
- 2 teaspoons baking powder
- 3 eggs
- 4 oz. dark chocolate, melted

Directions:

1. Mix the butter with sugar until creamy. Put in the eggs, one at a time, then mix in the melted chocolate and sour cream.
2. Fold in the flour, cocoa powder, baking powder, salt and spices.

3. Spoon the batter in a 9-icnh round cake pan coated with baking paper.
4. Pre-heat the oven and bake at 350F for forty minutes or until it rises completely and is aromatic.
5. Let the cake cool in the pan and serve, sliced.

Nutritional Content of One Serving:

Calories: 402 ‖ Fat: 17.1g ‖ Protein: 6.4g ‖ Carbohydrates: 59.6g

GINGER WHOLE ORANGE CAKE

Total Time Taken: 1 ¼ hours
Yield: 10 Servings
Ingredients:

Cake:

- ½ teaspoon salt
- 1 cup butter, softened
- 1 cup powdered sugar
- 1 cup white sugar
- 1 tablespoon orange juice
- 1 teaspoon grated ginger **Icing:**
- 1 teaspoon orange zest
- 1 whole orange
- 2 cups all-purpose flour
- 2 tablespoons dark brown sugar
- 2 teaspoons baking powder
- 4 eggs

Directions:

1. To prepare the cake, place the orange in a saucepan and cover it with water. Cook for about half an hour then drain well and place in a food processor. Pulse until the desired smoothness is achieved. Put in the ginger and mix thoroughly. Place aside.
2. Mix the butter with the sugars in a container until creamy and fluffy. Stir in the eggs, one at a time and mix thoroughly.
3. Fold in the flour, baking powder and salt, alternating it with the orange mixture.

4. Spoon the batter in a 9-inch round cake pan coated with baking paper and preheat your oven and bake at 350F for about forty minutes or until a toothpick comes out clean after being inserted into the center of the cake.
5. Let the cake cool then move it to a platter.
6. For the icing, combine all the ingredients in a container and sprinkle it over the chilled cake. Serve immediately.

Nutritional Content of One Serving:

Calories: 430 ‖ Fat: 21.1g ‖ Protein: 5.8g ‖ Carbohydrates: 56.2g

GINGER SWEET POTATO CAKE

Total Time Taken: 1 ½ hours
Yield: 10 Servings

Ingredients:

- ½ teaspoon baking soda
- ½ teaspoon salt
- ¾ cup canola oil
- 1 3/4 cups all-purpose flour
- 1 cup light brown sugar
- 1 cup sweet potato puree
- 1 tablespoon orange zest
- 1 teaspoon baking powder
- 1 teaspoon cinnamon powder
- 1 teaspoon vanilla extract
- 4 eggs

Directions:

1. Mix the sweet potato puree with the orange zest, canola oil, eggs, brown sugar and vanilla in a container.
2. Fold in the remaining ingredients then spoon the batter in a 9-inch round cake pan coated with baking paper.
3. Preheat your oven and bake the cake for around forty minutes or until a toothpick comes out clean after being inserted into the center of the cake.
4. Let the cake cool in the pan and serve, sliced.

Nutritional Content of One Serving:

Calories: 332 ‖ Fat: 18.4g ‖ Protein: 5.0g ‖ Carbohydrates: 37.4g

GERMAN FRUIT BUNDT CAKE

Total Time Taken: 1 ¼ hours

Yield: 10 Servings

Ingredients:

- ¼ cup dark brown sugar
- ¼ cup dried cranberries
- ¼ cup golden raisins
- ½ teaspoon salt
- 1 cup butter, softened
- 1 cup white sugar
- 1 teaspoon cinnamon powder
- 2 cups all-purpose flour
- 2 eggs
- 2 pears, peeled, cored and diced
- 2 teaspoons baking powder

Directions:

1. Mix the flour, baking powder, salt and cinnamon in a container.
2. In a separate container, mix the butter with the sugars and mix thoroughly. Stir in the eggs, one at a time and mix thoroughly.
3. Fold in the flour mixture then put in the pears, raisins and cranberries.
4. Spoon the batter in a Bundt cake pan lined using butter and preheat your oven and bake the cake at 350F for around forty minutes or until a golden-brown colour is achieved and it passes the toothpick test.
5. Let the cake cool down and serve, sliced.

Nutritional Content of One Serving:

Calories: 393 ‖ Fat: 19.6g ‖ Protein: 4.1g ‖ Carbohydrates: 52.7g

GANACHE CHOCOLATE CAKE

Total Time Taken: 1 ¼ hours
Yield: 8 Servings
Ingredients:

Cake:

- ¼ cup butter, melted and cooled
- ¼ cup cocoa powder
- ¼ teaspoon salt
- ¾ cup all-purpose flour
- 1 teaspoon baking powder
- 1 teaspoon vanilla extract
- 6 eggs, room temperature
- 2/3 cup white sugar

Ganache:

- 1 cup dark chocolate, chopped
- 2/3 cup heavy cream

Directions:

1. To prepare the cake, combine the eggs, sugar and vanilla in the container of your stand mixer for about five to seven minutes until its volume increases to almost three times it was.
2. Fold in the flour, cocoa powder, salt and baking powder with the help of a wooden spoon or spatula, being cautious not to deflate the eggs.
3. Progressively fold in the melted butter.
4. Pour the batter in a 10-inch cake pan coated with baking paper and preheat your oven and bake at 350F for around forty minutes.
5. Let cool in the pan then move to a platter.
6. For the ganache, bring the cream to the boiling point then turn off heat and mix in the chocolate. Stir until melted and smooth then let cool to room temperature.
7. Spoon the ganache over the cake and serve immediately.

Nutritional Content of One Serving:

Calories: 358 ‖ Fat: 19.4g ‖ Protein: 7.7g ‖ Carbohydrates: 40.5g

FUNFETTI CAKE

Total Time Taken: 1 hour

Yield: 8 Servings

Ingredients:

- ¼ cup butter, melted
- ½ cup canola oil
- ½ cup funfetti sprinkles
- ½ cup whole milk
- ½ teaspoon salt
- 1 ½ cups all-purpose flour
- 1 ½ teaspoons baking powder
- 1 cup white sugar
- 1 teaspoon vanilla extract
- 3 eggs

Directions:

1. Mix the flour, baking powder, salt and sprinkles in a container.
2. In a separate container, mix the canola oil, butter and sugar and mix thoroughly. Put in the eggs and stir thoroughly for five minutes.
3. Stir in the vanilla and milk and mix thoroughly then pour this mixture over the dry ingredients and stir lightly.
4. Spoon the batter in a 9-inch cake pan coated with baking paper and preheat your oven and bake at 350F for around forty minutes.
5. Let the cake cool in the pan and serve, sliced.

Nutritional Content of One Serving:

Calories: 392 ‖ Fat: 21.8g ‖ Protein: 5.1g ‖ Carbohydrates: 46.0g

FUDGY CHOCOLATE CAKE

Total Time Taken: 1 hour

Yield: 10 Servings

Ingredients:

- ½ cup butter, melted
- ½ cup cocoa powder
- ½ cup sour cream
- ½ teaspoon baking soda

- ½ teaspoon salt
- 1 3/4 cups all-purpose flour
- 1 cup hot coffee
- 1 cup white sugar
- 1 teaspoon baking powder
- 2 eggs
- 4 oz. dark chocolate, melted

Directions:

1. Mix the butter and chocolate in a container. Stir in the coffee, eggs and sour cream, as well as sugar.
2. Stir thoroughly to mix then fold in the remaining ingredients.
3. Spoon the batter in a 9-inch round cake pan, preheat your oven and bake at 330F for about fifty minutes.
4. Let the cake cool in the pan before you serve.

Nutritional Content of One Serving:

Calories: 344 ‖ Fat: 16.6g ‖ Protein: 5.5g ‖ Carbohydrates: 46.6g

FUDGY CHOCOLATE CAKE

Total Time Taken: 1 hour
Yield: 10 Servings
Ingredients:

- ¼ teaspoon salt
- ½ cup cocoa powder
- ¾ cup all-purpose flour
- 1 cup butter
- 1 cup ground walnuts
- 1 cup white sugar
- 2 cups dark chocolate chips
- 3 eggs

Directions:

1. Mix the chocolate chips and butter in a container and place over a hot water bath. Melt it over heat until the desired smoothness is achieved.
2. Put in the sugar and mix thoroughly then mix in the eggs.

3. Fold in the flour, cocoa powder, salt and walnuts then spoon the batter in a 8- inch round cake pan coated with baking paper.
4. Pre-heat the oven and bake at 350F for a little more than half an hour.
5. Let the cake cool in the pan before you serve.

Nutritional Content of One Serving:

Calories: 490 ‖ Fat: 34.1g ‖ Protein: 8.2g ‖ Carbohydrates: 46.9g

FRUITY BUNDT CAKE

Total Time Taken: 1 ¼ hours
Yield: 12 Servings

Ingredients:

- ¼ cup dried apricots, chopped
- ¼ cup golden raisins
- ½ cup candied cherries, chopped
- ½ cup chopped almonds
- ½ cup chopped pecans
- 1 ½ cups white sugar
- 1 ½ teaspoons baking powder
- 1 cup butter, softened
- 1 cup cream cheese, room temperature
- 1 teaspoon vanilla extract
- 2 cups all-purpose flour
- 4 eggs

Directions:

1. Mix the cream cheese, butter and sugar in a container until fluffy and creamy.
2. Stir in the eggs, one at a time, then put in the eggs and vanilla.
3. Stir thoroughly to mix then fold in the rest of the ingredients.
4. Spoon the batter in a greased Bundt cake pan and preheat your oven and bake at 350F for about forty minutes or until it rises significantly and starts to appear golden-brown.
5. Let the cake cool in the pan before you serve.

Nutritional Content of One Serving:

Calories: 447 ‖ Fat: 26.6g ‖ Protein: 6.8g ‖ Carbohydrates: 48.0g

FRUIT AND BRANDY CAKE

Total Time Taken: 1 ½ hours
Yield: 16 Servings

Ingredients:

- ¼ cup black treacle
- ¼ cup candied ginger, chopped
- ¼ cup honey
- ½ cup dried apricots, chopped
- ½ cup dried pineapple, chopped
- ½ cup golden syrup
- 1 cup brandy
- 1 cup butter, softened
- 1 cup dark brown sugar
- 1 cup golden raisins
- 1 cup heavy cream
- 1 teaspoon baking soda
- 1 teaspoon lemon zest
- 1 teaspoon orange zest
- 11 cup dried black currants
- 3 cups all-purpose flour
- 6 eggs

Directions:

1. Mix the dried fruits with brandy in a container and allow to soak up for a few hours, preferably overnight.
2. Mix the golden syrup, treacle, honey, brown sugar, cream, butter, lemon zest and orange zest in a container until creamy.
3. Stir in the eggs, one at a time, then put in the flour. and baking soda.
4. Fold in the dried fruits and stir lightly using a spatula.
5. Spoon the batter in a 10-inch round cake pan , preheat your oven and bake at 330F for an hour or until a toothpick comes out clean after being inserted into the center of the cake. If the toothpick is not clean, continue baking for 10 additional minutes and check again.

6. Let the cake cool in the pan then move to a platter and slice.

Nutritional Content of One Serving:

Calories: 450 ‖ Fat: 16.3g ‖ Protein: 5.2g ‖ Carbohydrates: 73.3g

FRENCH APPLE CAKE

Total Time Taken: 1 ¼ hours
Yield: 8 Servings

Ingredients:

- ¼ cup brandy
- ¼ teaspoon salt
- ½ cup butter, softened
- ½ teaspoon cinnamon powder
- 1 ½ cups all-purpose flour
- 1 cup light brown sugar
- 1 teaspoon baking powder
- 2 eggs
- 3 red apples, peeled, cored and sliced

Directions:

1. Sift the flour, baking powder and salt in a container.
2. Mix the eggs, sugar, brandy and butter in a container until fluffy and pale.
3. Fold in the flour then spoon the batter in a 8-inch round cake pan.
4. Top with apple slices and preheat your oven and bake at 350F for around forty minutes or until a golden-brown colour is achieved and it rises significantly.
5. The cake tastes best chilled.

Nutritional Content of One Serving:

Calories: 315 ‖ Fat: 12.9g ‖ Protein: 4.1g ‖ Carbohydrates: 45.5g

FLUFFY PEAR BUNDT CAKE

Total Time Taken: 1 ¼ hours
Yield: 14 Servings

Ingredients:

- ½ cup whole milk
- ½ teaspoon salt
- 1 ½ cups white sugar
- 1 cup canola oil
- 1 teaspoon vanilla extract
- 2 teaspoons baking powder
- 2 teaspoons pumpkin pie spice
- 3 cups all-purpose flour
- 3 eggs
- 3 pears, peeled, cored and diced

Directions:

1. Mix the flour, baking powder, salt and pumpkin pie spice in a container.
2. In a separate container, combine the canola oil with sugar and eggs until volume increases to twice what it was.
3. Put in the vanilla extract and milk then fold in the flour, followed by the pears.
4. Spoon the batter in a greased Bundt cake pan and preheat your oven and bake at 350F for about fifty minutes or until a toothpick comes out clean after being inserted into the center of the cake.
5. Let the cake cool in the pan then serve, sliced.

Nutritional Content of One Serving:

Calories: 363 ‖ Fat: 17.1g ‖ Protein: 4.4g ‖ Carbohydrates: 49.7g

DUO BUNDT CAKE

Total Time Taken: 1 ¼ hours
Yield: 14 Servings

Ingredients:

- ¼ cup cocoa powder
- ¼ cup hot water
- ½ cup butter, softened

- ½ cup cream cheese
- ½ teaspoon baking soda
- ½ teaspoon salt
- 1 cup buttermilk
- 2 cups white sugar
- 2 teaspoons baking powder
- 3 cups all-purpose flour
- 3 eggs
- 4 oz. dark chocolate, melted

Directions:

1. Mix the butter and sugar in a container until creamy and fluffy.
2. Stir in the chocolate and eggs and mix thoroughly, then put in the cream cheese.
3. Sift the flour, baking powder, baking soda and salt then fold it in the batter.
4. Divide the batter in half. Combine one half with the cocoa powder and hot water.
5. Spoon the white batter in a greased Bundt cake pan.
6. Top with the cocoa batter and preheat your oven and bake at 350F for about fifty minutes or until well risen and it passes the toothpick test.
7. Let the cake cool in the pan then move to a platter.

Nutritional Content of One Serving:

Calories: 360 ‖ Fat: 13.4g ‖ Protein: 6.1g ‖ Carbohydrates: 56.1g

DEVILS BUNDT CAKE

Total Time Taken: 1 ¼ hours
Yield: 14 Servings
Ingredients:

Cake:

- ¼ teaspoon baking soda
- ½ teaspoon salt
- 1 ½ cups white sugar
- 1 cup butter, softened
- 1 cup cocoa powder

- 1 cup hot water
- 1 cup sour cream
- 1 cup white chocolate chips
- 2 ½ cups all-purpose flour
- 2 teaspoons baking powder
- 4 eggs

Glaze:

- ½ cup heavy cream
- ¾ cup dark chocolate chips

Directions:

1. For the cake, combine the cocoa powder, water and sour cream in a container.
2. In a separate container, sift the flour, baking powder, baking soda and salt.
3. Mix the butter and sugar in a container until fluffy. Put in the eggs, one at a time and mix thoroughly.
4. Stir in the cocoa powder mixture then fold in the flour.
5. Put in the chocolate chips then spoon the batter in a Bundt cake lined using butter.
6. Preheat your oven and bake the cake for about forty minutes or until a toothpick inserted in the center comes out clean.
7. Let the cake cool in the pan then move to a platter.
8. For the glaze, combine the two ingredients in a heatproof container and place over low heat. Melt them together then sprinkle the glaze over the cake.
9. Serve immediately or place in your refrigerator.

Nutritional Content of One Serving:

Calories: 456 ‖ Fat: 26.1g ‖ Protein: 6.9g ‖ Carbohydrates: 54.6g

DECADENT CHOCOLATE CAKE

Total Time Taken: 1 hour
Yield: 10 Servings
Ingredients:

- ¼ cup all-purpose flour

- ½ cup cocoa powder
- ½ teaspoon salt
- 1 cup butter, softened
- 2/3 cup white sugar
- 3 cups dark chocolate chips
- 6 eggs, separated

Directions:

1. Melt the butter and chocolate chips in a heatproof container over a hot water bath.
2. Mix the egg yolks and sugar in a container until fluffy and pale.
3. Stir in the melted chocolate, then put in the cocoa powder, flour and salt.
4. Whip the egg whites until fluffy and firm. Fold the meringue into the batter then pour the batter in a 9-inch round cake pan.
5. Pre-heat the oven and bake at 350F for around forty minutes or until well risen.
6. The cake tastes best chilled.

Nutritional Content of One Serving:

Calories: 439 ‖ Fat: 31.2g ‖ Protein: 7.0g ‖ Carbohydrates: 42.3g

DARK RUM PECAN CAKE

Total Time Taken: 1 ¼ hours
Yield: 10 Servings
Ingredients:

Cake:

- ¼ cup sour cream
- ½ cup light brown sugar
- ½ cup white sugar
- ½ teaspoon baking powder
- ½ teaspoon salt
- ¾ cup butter, softened
- 1 ½ cups all-purpose flour
- 1 cup ground pecans
- 1 teaspoon baking soda

- 3 eggs

Glaze:

- 1 cup powdered sugar
- 2 tablespoons dark rum

Directions:

1. To prepare the cake, combine the flour, pecans, baking soda, baking powder and salt in a container.
2. In a separate container, combine the butter and sugars until creamy. Put in the eggs, one after another, then mix in the sour cream and mix thoroughly.
3. Fold in the flour mixture then spoon the batter in a 9-inch round cake pan covered with parchment paper.
4. Pre-heat the oven and bake at 350F for around forty minutes until a golden-brown colour is achieved and well risen then transfer the cake on a platter and allow to cool.
5. For the glaze, combine the sugar with dark rum. Sprinkle the glaze over the chilled cake and serve immediately.

Nutritional Content of One Serving:

Calories: 350 ‖ Fat: 17.5g ‖ Protein: 4.1g ‖ Carbohydrates: 44.0g

DARK CHOCOLATE COFFEE CAKE

Total Time Taken: 1 ¼ hours
Yield: 8 Servings

Ingredients:

- ¼ cup cocoa powder
- ¼ cup sour cream
- ½ cup light brown sugar
- ½ teaspoon salt
- 1 ½ cups all-purpose flour
- 1 teaspoon baking powder
- 1 teaspoon vanilla extract
- 3 oz. dark chocolate, melted
- 4 eggs
- 4 tablespoons butter, softened

Directions:

1. Mix the butter and chocolate, then mix in the eggs, sugar, vanilla and sour cream.
2. Fold in the flour, cocoa powder, baking powder and salt and stir lightly using a spatula.
3. Spoon the batter in a 9-inch round cake pan and preheat your oven and bake at 350F for around forty minutes or until it passes the toothpicks test.
4. Let the cake cool in the pan before you serve.

Nutritional Content of One Serving:

Calories: 282 ‖ Fat: 13.2g ‖ Protein: 6.8g ‖ Carbohydrates: 35.4g

CREAM CHEESE PUMPKIN CAKE

Total Time Taken: 1 ¼ hours
Yield: 14 Servings
Ingredients:

Cake:

- ½ teaspoon ground cloves
- ½ teaspoon ground ginger
- ½ teaspoon salt
- 1 ½ cups pumpkin puree
- 1 cup canola oil
- 1 teaspoon cinnamon powder
- 1 teaspoon ground ginger
- 2 cups all-purpose flour
- 2 cups white sugar
- 2 teaspoons baking soda
- 4 eggs

Cream cheese frosting:

- ½ cup butter, softened
- 1 cup cream cheese
- 1 cup powdered sugar

Directions:

1. For the cake, combine the pumpkin puree, sugar, eggs and canola oil in a container.
2. Stir in the remaining ingredients and stir until incorporated, don't over mix it!
3. Pour the batter in a 10-inch round cake pan coated with baking paper.
4. Pre-heat the oven and bake at 350F for about forty-five minutes or until it rises significantly and starts to appear golden-brown.
5. Let the cake cool in the pan then move to a platter.
6. For the frosting, combine all the ingredients in a container. Spread the frosting over the cake and serve fresh or place in your refrigerator.

Nutritional Content of One Serving:

Calories: 487 ‖ Fat: 29.5g ‖ Protein: 5.0g ‖ Carbohydrates: 53.6g

CREAM CHEESE PUMPKIN CAKE

Total Time Taken: 1 ¼ hours
Yield: 14 Servings
Ingredients:

Cake:

- ½ teaspoon ground cloves
- ½ teaspoon ground ginger
- ½ teaspoon salt
- 1 ½ cups pumpkin puree
- 1 cup canola oil
- 1 teaspoon cinnamon powder
- 1 teaspoon ground ginger
- 2 cups all-purpose flour
- 2 cups white sugar
- 2 teaspoons baking soda
- 4 eggs

Cream cheese frosting:

- ½ cup butter, softened
- 1 cup cream cheese
- 1 cup powdered sugar

Directions:

1. For the cake, combine the pumpkin puree, sugar, eggs and canola oil in a container.
2. Stir in the remaining ingredients and stir until incorporated, don't over mix it!
3. Pour the batter in a 10-inch round cake pan coated with baking paper.
4. Pre-heat the oven and bake at 350F for about forty-five minutes or until it rises significantly and starts to appear golden-brown.
5. Let the cake cool in the pan then move to a platter.
6. For the frosting, combine all the ingredients in a container. Spread the frosting over the cake and serve fresh or place in your refrigerator.

Nutritional Content of One Serving:

Calories: 487 ‖ Fat: 29.5g ‖ Protein: 5.0g ‖ Carbohydrates: 53.6g

CREAM CHEESE APPLE CAKE

Total Time Taken: 1 ¼ hours

Yield: 10 Servings

Ingredients:

- ½ cup canola oil
- ½ teaspoon salt
- 1 ½ cups white sugar
- 1 cup cream cheese
- 1 teaspoon vanilla extract
- 2 cups all-purpose flour
- 2 red apples, peeled, cored and diced
- 2 teaspoons baking powder
- 3 eggs

Directions:

1. Mix the cream cheese, canola oil and sugar in a container until pale and creamy.
2. Put in the eggs and mix thoroughly then mix in the vanilla, followed by the rest of the dry ingredients.

3. Combine in the apples then spoon the batter in a 9-inch round cake pan coated with baking paper.
4. Pre-heat the oven and bake at 350F for about fifty minutes or until it rises significantly and starts to appear golden-brown.
5. Let the cake cool in the pan before you serve.

Nutritional Content of One Serving:

Calories: 421 ‖ Fat: 20.6g ‖ Protein: 6.1g ‖ Carbohydrates: 55.4g

CREAM BUNDT CAKE

Total Time Taken: 1 hour
Yield: 10 Servings
Ingredients:

- ½ teaspoon salt
- 1 ½ cups heavy cream
- 1 cup white sugar
- 1 teaspoon vanilla extract
- 2 cups all-purpose flour
- 2 teaspoons baking powder
- 3 eggs

Directions:

1. Sift the flour, baking powder and salt.
2. Whip the heavy cream on moderate speed until soft peaks form. Carry on whipping until firm.
3. Stir in the eggs, one at a time, then put in the sugar and mix thoroughly.
4. Fold in the flour then spoon the batter in a Bundt cake pan lined using butter.
5. Pre-heat the oven and bake at 350F for around forty minutes or until a toothpick inserted in the center comes out clean.
6. Let the cake cool in the pan for about ten minutes then move to a platter.

Nutritional Content of One Serving:

Calories: 249 ‖ Fat: 8.2g ‖ Protein: 4.6g ‖ Carbohydrates: 40.2g

CRANBERRY UPSIDE DOWN CAKE

Total Time Taken: 1 hour
Yield: 10 Servings
Ingredients:

- ¼ teaspoon salt
- ½ cup butter, melted and chilled
- 1 ½ cups all-purpose flour
- ½ cup light brown sugar
- ½ teaspoon baking powder
- 1 cup fresh cranberries
- 1 cup white sugar
- 1 teaspoon vanilla extract
- 6 eggs

Directions:

1. Position the cranberries at the bottom of a round cake pan. Drizzle with brown sugar.
2. Mix the eggs and sugar in a container until fluffy and volume increases to twice what it was.
3. Stir in the butter and stir lightly.
4. Fold in the flour, baking powder and salt.
5. Pour the batter over the cranberries and preheat your oven and bake at 350F for about forty minutes or until it rises significantly and starts to appear golden-brown.
6. When finished, flip the cake upside down on a platter and serve chilled.

Nutritional Content of One Serving:

Calories: 297 ‖ Fat: 12.0g ‖ Protein: 5.4g ‖ Carbohydrates: 42.8g

COCONUT RASPBERRY CAKE

Total Time Taken: 1 hour
Yield: 8 Servings
Ingredients:

- ¼ cup coconut milk

- ½ cup butter, softened
- ½ cup coconut oil, melted
- ½ teaspoon salt
- 1 3/4 cups all-purpose flour
- 1 cup fresh raspberries
- 1 cup shredded coconut
- 1 cup white sugar
- 1 teaspoon baking soda
- 4 eggs

Directions:

1. Mix the flour, shredded coconut, salt and baking soda in a container.

2. In a separate container, mix the butter, coconut oil and sugar in a container. Stir thoroughly to mix until fluffy then put in the eggs, one at a time, and mix thoroughly.

3. Stir in the coconut oil then fold in the dry ingredients.

4. Spoon the batter in a 9-inch cake pan coated with baking paper.

5. Top with fresh raspberries and preheat your oven and bake at 350F for around forty minutes or until a golden-brown colour is achieved and it rises significantly.

6. The cake tastes best chilled.

Nutritional Content of One Serving:

Calories: 505 ‖ Fat: 32.8g ‖ Protein: 6.4g ‖ Carbohydrates: 49.8g

COCONUT CARROT BUNDT CAKE

Total Time Taken: 1 ¼ hours
Yield: 10 Servings

Ingredients:

- ½ cup coconut milk
- ½ cup crushed pineapple
- ½ teaspoon salt
- 1 ¼ cups all-purpose flour
- 1 cup canola oil
- 1 cup coconut flakes
- 1 cup light brown sugar

- 1 cup shredded coconut
- 1 tablespoon orange zest
- 1 teaspoon vanilla extract
- 2 cups grated carrots
- 2 teaspoons baking powder
- 4 eggs

Directions:

1. Mix the eggs and sugar in a container until volume increases to twice what it was.
2. Stir in the oil and vanilla then put in the orange zest, coconut, carrots, pineapple and coconut milk.
3. Fold in the flour, baking powder and salt then pour the batter in a 9-inch round cake pan coated with baking paper.
4. Pre-heat the oven and bake at 350F for about forty minutes or until a toothpick inserted in the center comes out clean.
5. Let the cake cool in the pan and serve, sliced.

Nutritional Content of One Serving:

Calories: 430 ‖ Fat: 31.9g ‖ Protein: 4.9g ‖ Carbohydrates: 33.3g

CLASSIC FRUIT CAKE

Total Time Taken: 2 hours
Yield: 16 Servings
Ingredients:

- ½ cup dates, pitted and chopped
- ½ cup dried apricots, chopped
- ½ cup dried cranberries
- ½ cup dried pineapple, chopped
- ½ cup fresh orange juice
- ½ cup sliced almonds
- ½ teaspoon baking powder
- ½ teaspoon salt
- 1 cup brandy
- 1 cup butter, softened
- 1 cup golden raisins

- 1 cup light brown sugar
- 1 cup sultanas
- 1 teaspoon baking soda
- 2 cups all-purpose flour
- 2 tablespoons orange zest
- 4 eggs

Directions:

1. Mix the dried fruits and brandy in a container. Allow to soak up for minimum an hour.
2. Mix the butter and sugar in a container until creamy and pale.
3. Put in the orange zest and orange juice and mix thoroughly then mix in the eggs, one at a time.
4. Fold in the flour, almonds, baking soda, baking powder and salt.
5. Put in the fruits and stir lightly using a spatula.
6. Spoon the batter in a 9-inch round cake pan coated with baking paper.
7. Pre-heat the oven and bake at 350F for 55-60 minutes. The cake is done when a toothpick inserted in the center comes out clean.
8. Let the cake cool in the pan then serve, sliced.

Nutritional Content of One Serving:

Calories: 290 ‖ Fat: 14.4g ‖ Protein: 4.4g ‖ Carbohydrates: 37.2g

CITRUS POPPY SEED BUNDT CAKE

Total Time Taken: 1 ¼ hours
Yield: 12 Servings

Ingredients:

- ½ cup butter, softened
- ½ cup canola oil
- ½ teaspoon salt
- 1 cup sour cream
- 1 cup white sugar
- 1 lemon, zested and juiced
- 1 lime, zested and juiced
- 2 cups all-purpose flour

- 2 eggs
- 2 tablespoons poppy seeds
- 2 teaspoons baking powder

Directions:

1. Mix the canola oil, butter and sugar in a container until creamy and pale.
2. Stir in the eggs and mix thoroughly then put in the sour cream.
3. Combine in the lime zest and juice, as well as the lemon zest and juice.
4. Fold in the remaining ingredients then spoon the batter in a greased Bundt cake pan.
5. Pre-heat the oven and bake at 350F for about forty minutes or until it rises significantly and starts to appear golden-brown.
6. Let the cake cool in the pan before you serve.

Nutritional Content of One Serving:

Calories: 350 ‖ Fat: 22.4g ‖ Protein: 4.1g ‖ Carbohydrates: 35.2g

CINNAMON STREUSEL RASPBERRY CAKE

Total Time Taken: 1 ¼ hours
Yield: 12 Servings
Ingredients:

Cake:

- ¼ cup canola oil
- ½ cup butter, softened
- ½ teaspoon salt
- ¾ cup whole milk
- 1 cup fresh raspberries Cinnamon
- 1 teaspoon vanilla extract
- 2 cups all-purpose flour
- 2 eggs
- 2 teaspoons baking powder

Streusel:

- ¼ cup light brown sugar

- ½ cup all-purpose flour
- ½ cup butter, chilled
- 1 pinch salt
- 1 teaspoon cinnamon powder

Directions:

1. To prepare the cake, sift the flour, baking powder and salt in a container.
2. In a separate container, combine the butter, oil and eggs until creamy. Stir in the milk and vanilla then fold in the flour.
3. Put in the raspberries then spoon the batter in a 8x8-inch cake pan coated with baking paper.
4. Make the cinnamon by mixing all the ingredients in a container until grainy.
5. Spread the streusel over the cake and preheat your oven and bake at 350F for about forty minutes or until fragrant and golden brown.
6. Let the cake cool in the pan and serve, sliced.

Nutritional Content of One Serving:

Calories: 309 ‖ Fat: 21.4g ‖ Protein: 4.4g ‖ Carbohydrates: 25.3g

CINNAMON MAPLE PUMPKIN CAKE

Total Time Taken: 1 ¼ hours
Yield: 10 Servings

Ingredients:

- ¼ teaspoon salt
- ½ cup canola oil
- ½ cup maple syrup
- ½ cup whole milk
- ½ teaspoon baking soda
- 1 ½ cups pumpkin puree
- 1 tablespoon cinnamon powder
- 1 teaspoon vanilla extract
- 2 ½ cups all-purpose flour
- 2 eggs
- 2 teaspoons baking powder
- 3/4 cup white sugar

Directions:

1. Mix the flour, baking powder, salt, baking soda and cinnamon in a container.
2. Mix the oil and sugar in a container for 2 minutes. Put in the eggs and mix thoroughly.
3. Stir in the pumpkin puree, vanilla and milk and mix thoroughly.
4. Fold in the flour mixture and mix using a spatula. Pour the batter in a 9-inch round cake pan coated with baking paper.
5. Pre-heat the oven and bake at 350F for about forty-five minutes or until a toothpick inserted into the center of the cake comes out clean.
6. The cake tastes best chilled.

Nutritional Content of One Serving:

Calories: 342 ‖ Fat: 12.6g ‖ Protein: 5.1g ‖ Carbohydrates: 53.5g

CINNAMON FROSTED BANANA CAKE

Total Time Taken: 1 ½ hours
Yield: 16 Servings
Ingredients:

Cake:

- ½ cup dark chocolate chips
- ½ teaspoon salt
- 1 cup canola oil
- 1 cup light brown sugar
- 1 cup sour cream
- 2 cups all-purpose flour
- 2 eggs
- 2 teaspoons baking powder
- 3 bananas, mashed

Cinnamon cream:

- ½ cup butter, softened
- 1 cup cream cheese
- 1 cup powdered sugar

Directions:

1. For the cake, combine the flour, baking powder and salt in a container.
2. In a separate container, combine the oil, sugar and eggs until fluffy and pale. Put in the bananas and sour cream and mix thoroughly then fold in the flour. Put in the chocolate chips too.
3. Spoon the batter in a 9-inch round cake pan and preheat your oven and bake at 350F for around forty minutes.
4. Let the cake cool in the pan then move to a platter.
5. For the frosting, combine the butter, cream cheese and sugar in a container for 5
6. minutes.
7. Cover the cake in frosting and serve it fresh.

Nutritional Content of One Serving:

Calories: 419 ‖ Fat: 29.2g ‖ Protein: 4.4g ‖ Carbohydrates: 37.2g

CINNAMON CHOCOLATE CAKE

Total Time Taken: 1 hour
Yield: 10 Servings
Ingredients:

- ½ cup buttermilk
- ½ cup cocoa powder
- ½ teaspoon salt
- 1 ½ cups white sugar
- 1 cup butter, softened
- 1 cup hot coffee
- 1 teaspoon cinnamon powder
- 1 teaspoon vanilla extract
- 2 cups all-purpose flour
- 2 teaspoons baking powder
- 3 eggs

Directions:

1. Mix the butter, sugar and cocoa powder in a container until creamy.
2. Stir in the eggs and vanilla and mix thoroughly.
3. Fold in the flour, baking powder and salt then put in the cinnamon, coffee and buttermilk and stir lightly.

4. Pour the batter in a 9-inch round cake pan coated with baking paper and bake for around forty minutes or until well risen and fragrant.
5. Let the cake cool in the pan before you serve.

Nutritional Content of One Serving:

Calories: 402 ‖ Fat: 20.6g ‖ Protein: 5.7g ‖ Carbohydrates: 52.7g

CHOCOLATE PUMPKIN CAKE

Total Time Taken: 1 hour
Yield: 10 Servings
Ingredients:

- ½ cup buttermilk
- ½ cup cocoa powder
- ½ cup sour cream
- ½ teaspoon ground star anise
- ½ teaspoon salt
- 1 cup butter, softened
- 1 cup light brown sugar
- 1 cup pumpkin puree
- 1 teaspoon baking powder
- 1 teaspoon baking soda
- 1 teaspoon ground cinnamon
- 1 teaspoon ground ginger
- 1 teaspoon vanilla extract
- 2 cups all-purpose flour
- 4 eggs

Directions:

1. Mix the butter and sugar in a container until fluffy and creamy.
2. Stir in the eggs, one at a time, then put in the vanilla, pumpkin puree, sour cream and buttermilk and mix thoroughly.
3. Fold in the dry ingredients then spoon the batter in a 10-inch round cake pan coated with baking paper.
4. Preheat your oven and bake the cake for about fifty minutes or until a toothpick inserted in the center comes out clean.
5. Let the cake cool in the pan and serve, sliced.

Nutritional Content of One Serving:

Calories: 385 ‖ Fat: 23.6g ‖ Protein: 6.9g ‖ Carbohydrates: 39.6g

CHOCOLATE PEPPERMINT CAKE

Total Time Taken: 1 ½ hours
Yield: 8 Servings
Ingredients:

Cake:

- ¼ teaspoon salt
- ½ cup butter, cubed
- ½ cup light brown sugar
- 1 cup all-purpose flour
- 1 cup dark chocolate chips
- 1 teaspoon baking powder
- 2 eggs
- 2 tablespoons cocoa powder

Glaze:

- ¼ cup heavy cream
- ¼ cup whole milk
- 1 pinch salt
- 3 tablespoons cocoa powder

Directions:

1. For the cake, combine the chocolate chips and butter in a heatproof container and place over a hot water bath. Melt them together until the desired smoothness is achieved.
2. Put in the sugar and eggs and mix thoroughly.
3. Stir in the flour, cocoa powder, baking powder and salt. Pour the batter in a 8-inch round cake pan coated with baking paper.
4. Pre-heat the oven and bake at 350F for about half an hour.
5. For the glaze, combine all the ingredients in a saucepan and place over low heat. Cook until it becomes thick.
6. Sprinkle the glaze over the cake and serve chilled.

Nutritional Content of One Serving:

Calories: 304 ‖ Fat: 18.8g ‖ Protein: 5.1g ‖ Carbohydrates: 33.5g

CHOCOLATE PEANUT BUTTER BUNDT CAKE

Total Time Taken: 1 ¼ hours
Yield: 10 Servings

Ingredients:

- ¼ cup whole milk
- ½ cup cocoa powder
- ½ teaspoon salt
- 1 ½ cups all-purpose flour
- 1 cup butter, softened
- 1 cup light brown sugar
- 1 cup sour cream
- 1 teaspoon baking powder
- 1 teaspoon baking soda
- 1 teaspoon vanilla extract
- 2/3 cup smooth peanut butter
- 3 eggs

Directions:

1. Mix the butter, sugar and vanilla in a container until fluffy and creamy.
2. Put in the eggs, one at a time, then mix in the sour cream and milk.
3. Fold in the flour, cocoa powder, baking powder, baking soda and salt.
4. Spoon half of the batter in a greased Bundt cake pan. Top with spoonfuls of peanut butter then cover with the rest of the batter.
5. Pre-heat the oven and bake at 350F for about forty minutes or until a toothpick inserted into the center of the cake comes out clean.
6. The cake tastes best chilled.

Nutritional Content of One Serving:

Calories: 470 ‖ Fat: 34.1g ‖ Protein: 9.8g ‖ Carbohydrates: 35.9g

CHOCOLATE OLIVE OIL CAKE

Total Time Taken: 1 ¼ hours
Yield: 10 Servings

Ingredients:

- ¼ cup whole milk
- ¼ teaspoon salt
- ½ cup cocoa powder
- 1 cup all-purpose flour
- 1 cup white sugar
- 1 teaspoon baking powder
- 1 teaspoon orange zest
- 1 teaspoon vanilla extract
- 2 eggs
- 2/3 cup olive oil

Directions:

1. Mix the eggs with sugar until fluffy and pale. Stir in the vanilla and orange zest and mix thoroughly.
2. Put in the olive oil and milk then fold in the cocoa powder, flour, salt and baking powder.
3. Pour the batter in a 8-inch round cake pan coated with baking paper.
4. Pre-heat the oven and bake at 350F for forty minutes or until a toothpick inserted in the center comes out clean.
5. The cake tastes best chilled.

Nutritional Content of One Serving:

Calories: 263 ‖ Fat: 15.2g ‖ Protein: 3.4g ‖ Carbohydrates: 32.6g

CHOCOLATE NUTELLA CAKE

Total Time Taken: 1 ½ hours
Yield: 10 Servings

Ingredients:

- ½ cup brewed coffee

- ½ cup canola oil
- ½ teaspoon salt
- 1 cup ground hazelnuts
- 1 cup Nutella
- 1 cup whole milk
- 1 teaspoon vanilla extract
- 2 cups all-purpose flour
- 2 eggs
- 2 tablespoons Kahlua
- 2 teaspoons baking powder

Directions:

1. Mix the ground hazelnuts, flour, baking powder and salt in a container.
2. Mix the eggs, milk, canola oil, Kahlua, vanilla and coffee in a separate container. Stir in the flour mixture then spoon the batter in a 9-inch round cake pan coated with baking paper.
3. Drop spoonfuls of Nutella over the batter and preheat your oven and bake at 350F for about forty minutes or until a toothpick inserted into the center of the cake comes out clean.
4. The cake tastes best chilled.

Nutritional Content of One Serving:

Calories: 295 ‖ Fat: 18.5g ‖ Protein: 5.8g ‖ Carbohydrates: 25.4g

CHOCOLATE MOUSSE CAKE

Total Time Taken: 1 ½ hours
Yield: 10 Servings
Ingredients:

Cake:

- ¼ cup cocoa powder
- ¼ cup heavy cream
- ¼ teaspoon salt
- ½ cup dark chocolate chips
- 1 cup all-purpose flour
- 1 cup buttermilk

- 1 egg
- 1 teaspoon baking powder

Chocolate mousse:

- ½ cup heavy cream, heated
- 1 cup dark chocolate chips
- 1 cup heavy cream, whipped

Directions:

1. For the cake, melt the cream and chocolate together in a heatproof container.
2. Stir in the remaining ingredients and stir for a few seconds to mix.
3. Pour the batter in a 9-inch round cake pan coated with baking paper.
4. Pre-heat the oven and bake at 350F for around forty minutes or until well risen and fragrant.
5. When finished, move the cake to a cake ring and place it on a platter.
6. For the chocolate mousse, combine the cream and chocolate chips in a container. Stir until melted and smooth. Let cool down.
7. Fold in the whipped cream then pour the mousse over the cake.
8. Chill the cake before you serve.

Nutritional Content of One Serving:

Calories: 223 ‖ Fat: 13.6g ‖ Protein: 4.7g ‖ Carbohydrates: 24.7g

CHOCOLATE HAZELNUT CAKE

Total Time Taken: 1 ¼ hours
Yield: 10 Servings
Ingredients:

Cake:

- ½ cup cocoa powder
- ½ teaspoon baking powder
- ½ teaspoon salt
- 1 cup all-purpose flour
- 1 cup ground hazelnuts
- 1 cup white sugar
- 6 eggs

Glaze:

- ½ cup heavy cream
- 1 cup dark chocolate chips

Directions:

1. To prepare the cake, combine the eggs with sugar until fluffy, minimum volume increases to twice what it was.
2. Fold in the flour, cocoa powder, baking powder, salt and hazelnuts then pour the batter in a 9-inch round cake pan coated with baking paper.
3. Preheat your oven and bake the cake for forty minutes or until a toothpick inserted in the center comes out clean.
4. Let the cake cool in the pan then move to a platter.
5. For the glaze, bring the cream to the boiling point then put in the chocolate and mix thoroughly.
6. Pour the warm glaze over the cake. Serve immediately or place in your refrigerator.

Nutritional Content of One Serving:

Calories: 292 ‖ Fat: 13.3g ‖ Protein: 7.4g ‖ Carbohydrates: 41.6g

CHOCOLATE HAZELNUT CAKE

Total Time Taken: 1 ¼ hours
Yield: 10 Servings

Ingredients:

- ¼ cup heavy cream
- ½ cup cherry jam
- ½ cup cocoa powder
- ½ cup white sugar
- ½ teaspoon baking soda
- ½ teaspoon salt
- 1 cup all-purpose flour
- 1 cup ground hazelnuts
- 1 teaspoon baking powder
- 2 whole eggs
- 6 egg yolks

Directions:

1. Mix the hazelnuts, flour, baking powder, baking soda and salt in a container. Put in the cocoa powder as well.
2. Mix the eggs, egg yolks and sugar in a container until thickened and fluffy. Stir in the cream and cherry jam.
3. Fold in the flour then spoon the cake in a 8-inch round cake pan coated with baking paper.
4. Pre-heat the oven and bake at 350F for around forty minutes or until a toothpick inserted into the center of the cake comes out clean.
5. The cake tastes best chilled.

Nutritional Content of One Serving:

Calories: 240 ‖ Fat: 9.9g ‖ Protein: 6.0g ‖ Carbohydrates: 34.9g

CHOCOLATE FUDGE CAKE

Total Time Taken: 1 ½ hours
Yield: 12 Servings
Ingredients:

Cake:

- ¼ cup cocoa powder
- ¼ teaspoon salt
- ½ cup dark chocolate chips
- 1 cup hot water
- ½ cup sour cream
- ½ teaspoon baking soda
- ¾ cup butter, softened
- 1 ½ teaspoons baking powder
- 1 ¾ cups all-purpose flour
- 1 cup dark brown sugar
- 2 eggs
- 2 tablespoons vegetable oil
- 1 teaspoon vanilla extract

Frosting:

- ½ cup cocoa powder

- 1 pinch salt
- 1 cup butter, softened
- 2 cups powdered sugar
- 2 tablespoons whole milk

Directions:

1. To prepare the cake, combine the chocolate chips, hot water and cocoa powder in a container.
2. In a separate container, combine the butter and sugar until creamy and pale. Stir in the eggs, one at a time, then put in the sour cream, vanilla and oil.
3. Mix the flour with baking powder, baking soda and salt then mix it with the butter mixture alternating it with the chocolate mixture. Begin and finish with flour.
4. Split the batter between two 9-inch circular cake pans covered with parchment paper.
5. Pre-heat the oven and bake at 350F for about half an hour.
6. Let cool and then take the cakes out of the pans and let them sit on the side you perform the next few steps.
7. For the frosting: combine the butter and powdered sugar for minimum five minutes until creamy and fluffy.
8. Put in the cocoa powder, salt and milk and stir thoroughly for another five minutes.
9. Use half of the frosting to fill the cake then garnish it with the half that is left over.
10. Serve immediately or place in your fridge until it is time to serve.

Nutritional Content of One Serving:

Calories: 517 ‖ Fat: 34.2g ‖ Protein: 4.8g ‖ Carbohydrates: 52.9g

CHOCOLATE DULCE DE LECHE CAKE

Total Time Taken: 1 ¼ hours

Yield: 12 Servings

Ingredients:

- ½ cup butter, softened
- ½ cup canola oil
- ½ cup dulce de leche

- ½ cup sour cream
- ½ teaspoon salt
- 1 ¾ cups all-purpose flour
- 1 cup dark chocolate chips
- 1 cup white sugar
- 2 teaspoons baking powder
- 3 eggs

Directions:

1. Mix the butter and oil in a container. Put in the sugar and stir thoroughly until creamy.
2. Put in the eggs and sour cream and mix thoroughly.
3. Fold in the flour, baking powder and salt then put in the chocolate chips. Pour the batter in a 9-inch round cake pan coated with baking paper.
4. Drop spoonfuls of dulce de leche over the batter and preheat your oven and bake at 350F for about forty minutes or until a toothpick inserted into the center of the cake comes out clean.
5. The cake tastes best chilled.

Nutritional Content of One Serving:

Calories: 397 ‖ Fat: 23.2g ‖ Protein: 5.0g ‖ Carbohydrates: 45.8g

CHOCOLATE COFFEE CAKE

Total Time Taken: 1 hour
Yield: 12 Servings
Ingredients:

Cake:

- ½ cup canola oil
- ½ teaspoon salt
- 1 cup buttermilk
- 1 cup hot coffee
- 1 cup white sugar
- 2 cups all-purpose flour
- 2 teaspoons baking powder
- 2 teaspoons instant coffee

- 3 eggs

Frosting:
- 1 cup heavy cream
- 2 cups dark chocolate chips
- 2 teaspoons instant coffee

Directions:

1. For the cake, combine the buttermilk, canola oil, hot coffee and eggs in a container.
2. Stir in the dry ingredients and mix thoroughly.
3. Pour the batter in a 9-inch round cake pan coated with baking paper.
4. Pre-heat the oven and bake at 350F for about fifty minutes.
5. When finished, transfer the chilled cake on a platter.
6. For the frosting, bring the cream to the boiling point in a saucepan. Put in the chocolate and stir until it melts completely. Stir in the coffee.
7. Cover the cake with chocolate coffee frosting and serve it fresh.

Nutritional Content of One Serving:

Calories: 371 ‖ Fat: 19.6g ‖ Protein: 5.8g ‖ Carbohydrates: 47.6g

CHOCOLATE COCONUT CAKE

Total Time Taken: 1 ¼ hours
Yield: 10 Servings

Ingredients:

- ¼ cup cocoa powder
- ¼ teaspoon salt
- ½ cup butter
- ¾ cup milk
- 1 ½ cups all-purpose flour
- 1 cup shredded coconut
- 1 cup white sugar
- 1 teaspoon baking powder
- 2 eggs
- 2 tablespoons canola oil

Directions:

1. Mix the butter, oil and sugar in a container until fluffy and creamy.
2. Put in the eggs, one at a time, then mix in the milk.
3. Put in the dry ingredients and stir lightly using a spatula.
4. Spoon the batter in a 8-inch round cake pan coated with baking paper.
5. Pre-heat the oven and bake at 350F for around forty minutes or until a toothpick inserted into the center of the cake comes out clean.
6. The cake tastes best chilled.

Nutritional Content of One Serving:

Calories: 305 ‖ Fat: 16.4g ‖ Protein: 4.4g ‖ Carbohydrates: 37.9g

CHOCOLATE CHIP PUMPKIN BUNDT CAKE

Total Time Taken: 1 ¼ hours
Yield: 12 Servings

Ingredients:

- ½ teaspoon salt
- 1 ½ cups white sugar
- 1 ½ teaspoons baking powder
- 1 cup butter, softened
- 1 cup dark chocolate chips
- 1 cup pumpkin puree
- 1 teaspoon vanilla extract
- 2 cups all-purpose flour
- 2 eggs
- 2 tablespoons molasses

Directions:

1. Mix the butter, sugar and molasses in a container until creamy and light.
2. Stir in the vanilla and eggs, as well as the pumpkin puree.
3. Fold in the remaining ingredients and stir lightly.

4. Spoon the batter in a greased Bundt cake pan. Pre-heat the oven and bake at 350F for about forty-five minutes or until a toothpick inserted into the center of the cake comes out clean.
5. Let the cake cool in the pan before you serve.

Nutritional Content of One Serving:

Calories: 381 ‖ Fat: 19.0g ‖ Protein: 4.1g ‖ Carbohydrates: 52.1g

CHOCOLATE CHIP BUNDT CAKE

Total Time Taken: 1 ¼ hours
Yield: 12 Servings

Ingredients:

- ½ teaspoon salt
- ¾ cup dark chocolate chips
- 1 cup butter, softened
- 1 cup plain yogurt
- 1 cup white sugar
- 1 teaspoon vanilla extract
- 2 cups all-purpose flour
- 2 teaspoons baking powder
- 3 eggs

Directions:

1. Mix the flour with baking powder and salt.
2. Mix the butter with sugar until creamy. Put in the eggs, one at a time, then mix in the vanilla and mix thoroughly.
3. Put in the yogurt and mix thoroughly then fold in the flour, followed by the chocolate chips.
4. Spoon the batter in a greased Bundt cake pan.
5. Pre-heat the oven and bake at 350F for about forty minutes or until a toothpick inserted in the cake comes out clean.

Nutritional Content of One Serving:

Calories: 341 ‖ Fat: 18.9g ‖ Protein: 5.3g ‖ Carbohydrates: 39.5g

CHOCOLATE CHIP BLACKBERRY CAKE

Total Time Taken: 1 ¼ hours

Yield: 10 Servings

Ingredients:

- ¼ cup canola oil
- ¼ cup cornstarch
- ¼ teaspoon salt
- ½ cup butter, softened
- ½ cup dark chocolate chips
- ½ cup plain yogurt
- 1 ½ cups all-purpose flour
- 1 cup fresh blackberries
- 1 cup white sugar
- 1 teaspoon baking powder
- 3 eggs

Directions:

1. Mix the butter, oil and sugar in a container until creamy and fluffy.
2. Put in the eggs and yogurt and mix thoroughly.
3. Fold in the flour, cornstarch, baking powder and salt and mix using a spatula.
4. Put in the chocolate chips and blackberries then spoon the batter in a 9-inch round cake pan coated with baking paper.
5. Preheat your oven and bake the cake for about forty minutes or until it rises significantly and starts to appear golden-brown.
6. Let the cake cool in the pan before you serve.

Nutritional Content of One Serving:

Calories: 347 ‖ Fat: 18.0 ‖ Protein: 5.0g ‖ Carbohydrates: 43.8g

CHOCOLATE BUNDT CAKE

Total Time Taken: 1 ¼ hours

Yield: 10 Servings

Ingredients:

- ½ cup butter, softened
- ½ cup cocoa powder
- ½ cup dark chocolate chips
- ½ teaspoon baking soda
- ½ teaspoon salt
- 1 ½ cups all-purpose flour
- 1 cup white sugar
- 1 teaspoon baking powder
- 1 teaspoon vanilla extract
- 2 tablespoons canola oil
- 3 eggs

Directions:

1. Mix the butter, canola oil and sugar in a container until light and pale.
2. Stir in the eggs and vanilla and mix thoroughly.
3. Fold in the flour, cocoa powder, baking powder, baking soda and salt.
4. Put in the chocolate chips then spoon the batter in a greased Bundt cake pan.
5. Pre-heat the oven and bake at 350F for about forty minutes or until well risen and it passes the toothpick test.
6. Let the cake cool in the pan and serve, sliced.

Nutritional Content of One Serving:

Calories: 308 ‖ Fat: 15.7g ‖ Protein: 4.9g ‖ Carbohydrates: 41.1g

CHOCOLATE BISCUIT CAKE

Total Time Taken: 3 hours
Yield: 10 Servings
Ingredients:

- ¼ cup cocoa powder
- ¼ cup dried cranberries
- ½ cup butter
- ½ cup dark chocolate chips
- ½ cup golden syrup
- ½ cup milk chocolate chips
- ½ cup pecans, chopped

- 1 cup golden raisins
- 1 cup heavy cream
- 1 cup milk
- 10 oz. digestive biscuits, chopped

Directions:

1. Melt the chocolate chips and butter in a heatproof container over a hot water bath.
2. Mix the cream, milk and cocoa powder and place over low heat. Bring to a boil and cook just until slightly thickened. Turn off the heat and mix in the chocolate mixture.
3. Mix this mixture with the remaining ingredients in a container then transfer in a 8-inch cake pan coated with plastic wrap.
4. Place in your refrigerator to set for about two hours then serve, sliced.

Nutritional Content of One Serving:

Calories: 408 ‖ Fat: 24.0g ‖ Protein: 4.3g ‖ Carbohydrates: 49.1g

CHIA SEED CHOCOLATE CAKE

Total Time Taken: 1 ¼ hours
Yield: 10 Servings

Ingredients:

- ¼ cup cocoa powder
- ¼ teaspoon salt
- ½ cup butter
- ½ cup dark chocolate chips
- 1 ½ cups all-purpose flour
- 1 cup canola oil
- 1 cup white sugar
- 1 tablespoon orange zest
- 1 teaspoon baking powder
- 2 tablespoons chia seeds
- 3 eggs

Directions:

1. Melt the chocolate and butter in a container until the desired smoothness is achieved.
2. Turn off the heat and mix in the eggs, orange zest, sugar and canola oil.
3. Fold in the cocoa powder, chia seeds, flour, baking powder and salt then pour the batter in a 9-inch round cake pan coated with baking paper.
4. Pre-heat the oven and bake at 350F for around forty minutes or until a toothpick inserted into the center of the cake comes out clean.
5. The cake tastes best chilled.

Nutritional Content of One Serving:

Calories: 470 ‖ Fat: 34.4g ‖ Protein: 4.5g ‖ Carbohydrates: 40.0g

CHESTNUT PUREE CHOCOLATE CAKE

Total Time Taken: 1 ¼ hours
Yield: 10 Servings

Ingredients:

- ¼ cup butter
- ¼ teaspoon salt
- ½ cup canola oil
- ½ cup cocoa powder
- ½ cup ground almonds
- 1 cup all-purpose flour
- 1 cup chestnut puree
- 1 cup dark chocolate chips
- 1 cup white sugar
- 1 teaspoon baking powder

Directions:

1. Mix the canola oil, butter and chocolate chips in a heatproof container. Place over heatproof container and melt them together.
2. Turn off the heat and mix in the sugar and chestnut puree.
3. Fold in the cocoa powder, flour, almonds, salt and baking powder.
4. Spoon the batter in a 9-inch round cake pan coated with baking paper.
5. Pre-heat the oven and bake at 350F for around forty minutes or until a toothpick inserted into the center of the cake comes out clean.
6. The cake tastes best chilled.

Nutritional Content of One Serving:

Calories: 354 ‖ Fat: 21.8g ‖ Protein: 3.9g ‖ Carbohydrates: 41.6g

CHERRY LIQUEUR SOAKED CAKE

Total Time Taken: 1 ¼ hours

Yield: 8 Servings

Ingredients:

- ¼ cup cherry liqueurs
- ¼ cup dark brown sugar
- ¼ teaspoon salt
- ½ cup all-purpose flour
- ½ cup butter, melted
- ½ cup hot coffee
- ½ cup white sugar
- ½ teaspoon baking powder
- 1 ½ cups dark chocolate chips
- 1 cup almond flour
- 2 eggs

Directions:

1. Mix the coffee and chocolate in a container. Stir until melted and smooth.
2. Stir in the sugars, butter and eggs then fold in the almond flour, all-purpose flour, salt and baking powder.
3. Pour the batter in a 8-inch round cake pan coated with baking paper.
4. Pre-heat the oven and bake at 350F for a little more than half an hour.
5. Let the cake cool down then move to a platter.
6. Brush the cherry liqueur over the cake.
7. The cake tastes best chilled.

Nutritional Content of One Serving:

Calories: 343 ‖ Fat: 20.8g ‖ Protein: 4.6g ‖ Carbohydrates: 39.7g

CHERRY CHOCOLATE CAKE

Total Time Taken: 1 ¼ hours

Yield: 10 Servings

Ingredients:

- ¼ teaspoon salt
- ½ cup butter, melted
- ½ cup milk
- ½ cup pine nuts, ground
- 1 ½ cups all-purpose flour
- 1 cup white sugar
- 1 teaspoon baking powder
- 1 teaspoon vanilla extract
- 2 cups cherries, pitted
- 3 eggs

Directions:

1. Mix the eggs and sugar in a container until volume increases to twice what it was.
2. Stir in the milk then progressively pour in the butter, stirring thoroughly.
3. Put in the vanilla then fold in the flour, baking powder and salt.
4. Put in the ground pine nuts then fold in the cherries.
5. Pour the batter in a 9-inch round cake pan coated with baking paper.
6. Pre-heat the oven and bake at 350F for about forty minutes or until a toothpick inserted into the center of the cake comes out clean.
7. Let the cake cool in the pan before you serve.

Nutritional Content of One Serving:

Calories: 314 ‖ Fat: 15.6g ‖ Protein: 5.1g ‖ Carbohydrates: 40.3g

CHERRY BROWNIE CAKE

Total Time Taken: 1 hour

Yield: 8 Servings

Ingredients:

- ¼ teaspoon salt

- ¾ cup butter
- ¾ cup light brown sugar
- 1 cup all-purpose flour
- 1 cup cherries, pitted
- 1 cup dark chocolate chips
- 1 teaspoon vanilla extract
- 3 eggs

Directions:

1. Mix the butter and chocolate chips in a heatproof container. Place over a hot water bath and melt them until the desired smoothness is achieved.
2. Turn off the heat and mix in the eggs, vanilla and sugar.
3. Fold in the flour and salt then pour the batter in a 8-inch round cake pan coated with baking paper.
4. Top with cherries and preheat your oven and bake at 350F for 20 minutes.
5. The cake tastes best chilled.

Nutritional Content of One Serving:

Calories: 367 ‖ Fat: 23.1g ‖ Protein: 4.9g ‖ Carbohydrates: 38.1g

CHAI SPICED STREUSEL CAKE

Total Time Taken: 1 hour
Yield: 10 Servings
Ingredients:

Streusel:

- ¼ cup all-purpose flour
- ¼ cup butter, melted
- ¼ cup light brown sugar
- ½ teaspoon cardamom powder
- ½ teaspoon cinnamon powder
- ½ teaspoon ground cloves
- ½ teaspoon star anise
- 1 cup pecans, chopped

Cake:

- ¼ cup butter, melted

- ¼ cup whole milk
- ½ cup white sugar
- 1 ¼ cups all-purpose flour
- 1 pinch salt
- 1 teaspoon baking powder
- 6 eggs, room temperature

Directions:

1. Mix the eggs, sugar and salt for minimum five minutes until its volume increases to almost three times it was.
2. Put in the milk then fold in the flour and baking powder.
3. Progressively mix in the melted butter then pour the batter in a 9-inch cake pan coated with baking paper.
4. For the streusel, combine all the ingredients in a container and stir thoroughly until grainy.
5. Spread the streusel over the cake and preheat your oven and bake at 350F for about forty minutes or until a golden-brown colour is achieved and fragrant.
6. Let cool in the pan and serve, sliced.

Nutritional Content of One Serving:

Calories: 254 ‖ Fat: 13.3g ‖ Protein: 5.7g ‖ Carbohydrates: 29.0g

CHAI SPICED CAKE

Total Time Taken: 1 ½ hours
Yield: 10 Servings
Ingredients:

Cake:

- ¼ teaspoon ground cloves
- ½ teaspoon ground ginger
- ½ teaspoon salt
- ½ teaspoon turmeric
- 1 ½ cups white sugar
- 1 cup butter, softened
- 1 teaspoon cinnamon powder

- 1 teaspoon vanilla extract
- 2 cups all-purpose flour
- 2 teaspoons baking powder
- 6 eggs

Frosting:

- ¼ cup light brown sugar
- ½ cup butter, softened
- 1 cup cream cheese
- 1 teaspoon grated ginger
- 2 cups powdered sugar

Directions:

1. For the cake, sift the flour with baking powder, salt and spices on a platter.
2. Mix the butter and sugar in a container until pale and thick.
3. Put in the eggs, one at a time, then mix in the dry ingredients, mixing gently using a spatula.
4. Spoon the batter in a 9-inch round cake pan coated with baking paper.
5. For the frosting, combine the cream cheese, butter and brown sugar in a container for minimum five minutes.
6. Put in the rest of the ingredients and mix thoroughly. Cover the cake with buttercream and serve fresh.

Nutritional Content of One Serving:

Calories: 484 ‖ Fat: 27.6g ‖ Protein: 5.7g ‖ Carbohydrates: 55.8g

CARDAMOM CARROT CAKE

Total Time Taken: 1 ¼ hours
Yield: 16 Servings
Ingredients:

Cake:

- ¼ cup dark brown sugar
- ½ teaspoon baking powder
- ½ teaspoon salt
- 1 cup crushed pineapple
- 1 cup pecans, chopped

- 1 cup shredded coconut
- 1 cup vegetable oil
- 1 cup white sugar
- 1 teaspoon baking soda
- 1 teaspoon ground cardamom
- 1 teaspoon vanilla extract
- 2 cups all-purpose flour
- 2 cups grated carrots
- 4 eggs

Frosting:

- ½ cup butter, softened
- 1 cup cream cheese
- 1 cup powdered sugar
- 1 teaspoon vanilla extract

Directions:

1. For the cake, sift the flour, baking soda, baking powder, salt and cardamom in a container.
2. In a separate container, combine the eggs and sugars until creamy and fluffy.
3. Put in the vanilla, carrots, pineapple, coconut and pecans and mix thoroughly.
4. Fold in the dry ingredients then pour the batter into a 10-inch round cake pan coated with baking paper.
5. Preheat your oven and bake the cake for about fifty minutes or until it rises completely and is aromatic.
6. For the frosting, combine all the ingredients in a container for minimum five minutes.
7. Frost the chilled cake with the cream cheese buttercream and serve fresh or place in your refrigerator.

Nutritional Content of One Serving:

Calories: 416 ‖ Fat: 28.0g ‖ Protein: 4.6g ‖ Carbohydrates: 38.4g

CARAMEL SPICE CAKE

Total Time Taken: 1 ¼ hours
Yield: 8 Servings
Ingredients:

Cake:

- ¼ teaspoon ground nutmeg
- ½ cup butter, softened
- ½ cup sour cream
- ½ teaspoon ground cardamom
- ½ teaspoon ground ginger
- ¾ cup light brown sugar
- 1 1/4 cups all-purpose flour
- 1 teaspoon baking soda
- 1 teaspoon cinnamon powder
- 3 eggs

Glaze:

- ½ cup heavy cream
- ½ teaspoon salt
- 1 cup white sugar

Directions:

1. For the cake, sift the flour, baking soda, spices and salt in a container.
2. In a separate container, combine the butter and sugar until creamy. Stir in the eggs and mix thoroughly then put in the sour cream and mix thoroughly.
3. Fold in the flour mixture then pour the batter in a 9-inch round cake pan covered with parchment paper.
4. Pre-heat the oven and bake at 350F for around forty minutes or until a toothpick inserted in the center comes out clean.
5. Let the cake cool in the pan.
6. For the glaze, melt the sugar in a heavy saucepan until it sppears amber in colour.
7. Stir in the cream and salt and mix thoroughly. Keep over low heat until the desired smoothness is achieved.
8. Let the glaze cool down then sprinkle it over the cake just before you serve.

Nutritional Content of One Serving:

Calories: 400 ‖ Fat: 19.2g ‖ Protein: 4.9g ‖ Carbohydrates: 54.4g

CARAMEL PUMPKIN CAKE

Total Time Taken: 1 ½ hours
Yield: 12 Servings
Ingredients:

Cake:

- ¼ cup white sugar
- ¼ cup whole milk
- ½ cup coconut oil, melted
- 1 cup dark brown sugar
- 1 cup pumpkin puree
- 1 pinch salt
- 1 teaspoon baking powder
- 1 teaspoon baking soda
- 1 teaspoon cinnamon powder
- 1 teaspoon ground ginger
- 2 cups all-purpose flour
- 4 eggs

Caramel frosting:

1. 1 cup butter, softened
2. 2 cups powdered sugar
3. 1 pinch salt
4. ½ cup caramel sauce

Directions:

1. For the cake, combine the flour, baking powder, baking soda, spices and salt in a container.
2. In a separate container, mix the coconut oil, pumpkin puree, eggs, sugars and milk.
3. Pour this mixture over the dry ingredients and mix thoroughly.
4. Pour the batter in 2 circular cake pans coated with baking paper.
5. Preheat your oven and bake the cake at 350F for 35 minutes or until it rises completely and is aromatic.
6. Let the cakes cool in the pans then level them and set aside for later.
7. For the frosting, combine the butter, sugar and salt in a container for about five to seven minutes or until twofold in volume and firm.
8. Stir in the caramel sauce.

9. Use half of the frosting to fill the cake and the half that is left over to garnish the cake.
10. Serve fresh.

Nutritional Content of One Serving:

Calories: 495 ‖ Fat: 26.4g ‖ Protein: 4.8g ‖ Carbohydrates: 63.2g

CARAMEL PINEAPPLE UPSIDE DOWN CAKE

Total Time Taken: 1 ½ hours
Yield: 14 Servings

Ingredients:

- ¼ cup whole milk
- ¼ teaspoon salt
- ½ cup butter, softened
- ½ cup canola oil
- ½ cup cornstarch
- ½ cup light brown sugar
- ½ cup white sugar
- 1 cup all-purpose flour
- 1 cup shredded coconut
- 1 teaspoon baking soda
- 2 tablespoons butter
- 3 eggs
- 6 slices pineapple

Directions:

1. Melt the white sugar in a saucepan until it sppears amber in colour.
2. Sprinkle the melted sugar on the bottom of a 9-inch round cake pan coated with baking paper.
3. Top the caramelized sugar with butter and set aside for later.
4. For the batter, combine the butter, oil and brown sugar until fluffy and creamy.
5. Fold in the eggs and milk then put in the remaining ingredients and mix using a spatula.

6. Spoon the batter over the pineapple slices and preheat your oven and bake at 350F for about forty minutes or until a toothpick inserted in the center comes out clean.
7. Let the cake cool in the pan for about ten minutes then flip it over on a platter.
8. Serve chilled.

Nutritional Content of One Serving:

Calories: 309 ‖ Fat: 19.2g ‖ Protein: 2.9g ‖ Carbohydrates: 33.6g

CARAMEL BANANA CAKE

Total Time Taken: 1 hour
Yield: 12 Servings
Ingredients:

- ¼ cup dark brown sugar
- ½ cup caramel sauce
- ½ teaspoon ground cardamom
- ½ teaspoon salt
- ¾ cup butter, softened
- 1 cup buttermilk
- 1 cup white sugar
- 1 teaspoon cinnamon powder
- 2 cups all-purpose flour
- 2 ripe bananas, mashed
- 2 teaspoons baking powder
- 4 eggs

Directions:

1. Mix the butter with sugars for five minutes until creamy. Put in the eggs, one at a time, then mix in the bananas.
2. Fold in the flour, spices, baking powder and salt, alternating it with buttermilk.
3. Pour the batter in a 9-inch round cake pan.
4. Sprinkle the batter with caramel sauce and preheat your oven and bake the cake at 350F for about forty-five minutes or until a toothpick inserted in the center comes out clean.

5. Let the cake cool in the pan and serve, sliced.

Nutritional Content of One Serving:

Calories: 334 ‖ Fat: 13.4g ‖ Protein: 5.2g ‖ Carbohydrates: 50.6g

CARAMEL APPLE CAKE

Total Time Taken: 1 ½ hours
Yield: 12 Servings
Ingredients:

Cake:

- ½ cup applesauce
- ½ teaspoon cinnamon powder
- ½ teaspoon ground ginger
- ½ teaspoon salt
- 1 ¼ cups white sugar
- 1 cup butter, softened
- 1 teaspoon baking soda
- 2 cups all-purpose flour
- 2 red apples, cored and diced
- 4 eggs

Glaze:

- ¼ teaspoon salt
- ½ cup heavy cream
- 1 cup white sugar

Directions:

1. For the cake, combine the sugar, butter and eggs in a container until creamy.
2. Stir in the applesauce then put in the flour, baking soda, salt and cinnamon, as well as ginger and apples.
3. Spoon the batter in a 9-inch round cake pan coated with baking paper.
4. Pre-heat the oven and bake at 350F for about forty-five minutes.
5. Let the cake cool in the pan then move to a platter.
6. For the glaze, melt the sugar in a heavy saucepan until it sppears amber in colour.
7. Put in the cream and salt and stir until melted and smooth.

8. let the glaze cool in the pan then sprinkle it over the cake.

Nutritional Content of One Serving:

Calories: 411 ‖ Fat: 18.9g ‖ Protein: 4.4g ‖ Carbohydrates: 59.1g

CANDIED GINGER APPLESAUCE CAKE

Total Time Taken: 1 ¼ hours
Yield: 10 Servings

Ingredients:

- ¼ cup candied ginger, chopped
- ¼ teaspoon baking soda
- ½ cup butter, room temperature
- ½ cup golden raisins
- ½ teaspoon cinnamon powder
- ½ teaspoon ground star anise
- ½ teaspoon salt
- 1 ¼ cups applesauce
- 1 cup white sugar
- 1 teaspoon vanilla extract
- 2 cups all-purpose flour
- 2 eggs
- 2 tablespoons molasses
- 2 teaspoons baking powder

Directions:

1. Mix the flour, baking powder, baking soda, salt and spices in a container.
2. In a separate container, combine the butter, sugar and molasses until creamy and firm. Put in the eggs, one at a time, then the applesauce and vanilla and mix thoroughly.
3. Fold in the flour mixture then put in the raisins and ginger.
4. Spoon the batter in a 9-inch round cake pan coated with baking paper.
5. Pre-heat the oven and bake at 350F for about forty minutes or until a golden-brown colour is achieved and it rises significantly.
6. Let the cake cool in the pan and serve, sliced.

Nutritional Content of One Serving:

Calories: 310 || Fat: 10.4g || Protein: 4.1g || Carbohydrates: 52.1g

BUTTERY ZUCCHINI CAKE

Total Time Taken: 1 ½ hours

Yield: 10 Servings

Ingredients:

- ½ cup dark brown sugar
- ½ cup dark chocolate chips
- ½ teaspoon salt
- 1 cup butter, softened
- 1 cup grated zucchinis
- 1 teaspoon baking powder
- 1 teaspoon baking soda
- 1/2 cup white sugar
- 2 cups all-purpose flour
- 4 eggs

Directions:

1. Mix the butter, brown sugar and white sugar in a container until creamy and firm.
2. Stir in the eggs, one at a time, then put in the zucchinis.
3. Fold in the remaining ingredients then pour the batter in a round cake pan coated with baking paper.
4. Preheat your oven and bake the cake for about forty minutes or until a toothpick inserted in the center comes out clean.
5. Let the cake cool in the pan then serve, sliced.

Nutritional Content of One Serving:

Calories: 374 || Fat: 22.0g || Protein: 5.5g || Carbohydrates: 40.9g

BUTTERY ORANGE CAKE

Total Time Taken: 1 hour
Yield: 8 Servings
Ingredients:

- ¼ cup canola oil
- ½ cup butter, softened
- ½ teaspoon salt
- ¾ cup whole milk
- 1 cup white sugar Zest of
- 1 lemon
- 1 lemon Juice of
- 2 cups all-purpose flour
- 2 teaspoons baking powder
- 4 eggs

Directions:

1. Mix the flour with baking powder and salt.
2. Mix the butter and eggs in a container for five minutes until creamy then put in the eggs, one at a time, as well as lemon juice and zest.
3. Fold in the flour mixture, alternating it with milk. Begin with flour and finish with flour.
4. Spoon the batter in a 9-inch round cake pan coated with baking paper.
5. Pre-heat the oven and bake at 350F for around forty minutes or until a golden-brown colour is achieved and it rises significantly.
6. Let the cake cool in the pan and serve, sliced.

Nutritional Content of One Serving:

Calories: 417 ‖ Fat: 21.6g ‖ Protein: 6.9g ‖ Carbohydrates: 50.8g

BUTTERSCOTCH SWEET POTATO CAKE

Total Time Taken: 1 ½ hours
Yield: 10 Servings
Ingredients:

Cake:

- ½ cup canola oil
- ½ cup coconut milk

- ½ cup dark brown sugar
- ½ cup white sugar
- ½ teaspoon salt
- 1 cup sweet potato puree
- 1 teaspoon baking powder
- 1 teaspoon baking soda
- 1 teaspoon cinnamon powder
- 2 cups all-purpose flour
- 3 eggs

Butterscotch sauce:

- ¼ cup butter
- ¼ cup heavy cream
- ¼ cup light corn syrup
- ¼ teaspoon salt
- ½ cup dark brown sugar

Directions:

1. To prepare the cake, combine the dry ingredients in a container and the wet ingredients in a separate container.
2. Combine the dry ingredients with the wet ingredients and give it a good mix.
3. Pour the batter in a 10-inch round cake pan coated with baking paper and preheat your oven and bake at 350F for around forty minutes.
4. Let the cake cool in the pan then move to a platter.
5. For the butterscotch sauce, combine all the ingredients in a saucepan and cook for about five to eight minutes until it becomes thick.
6. Let cool and then pour the sauce over each slice of cake before you serve.

Nutritional Content of One Serving:

Calories: 426 ‖ Fat: 21.1g ‖ Protein: 5.1g ‖ Carbohydrates: 56.2g

BUTTERSCOTCH PECAN CAKE

Total Time Taken: 1 ½ hours
Yield: 10 Servings

Ingredients:

- ¼ cup canola oil

- ¼ cup cocoa powder
- ¼ cup plain yogurt
- ¼ teaspoon salt
- ½ cup butter, softened
- ½ cup caramel sauce
- 1 ½ cups all-purpose flour
- 1 teaspoon baking powder
- 2 cups pecans
- 2 eggs

Directions:

1. Mix the butter, canola oil, eggs and yogurt in a container until fluffy.
2. Put in the flour, salt, baking powder and cocoa and stir lightly using a spatula.
3. Pour the batter in a 9-inch round cake pan and cover with half of the walnuts.
4. Mix the remaining pecans with caramel and set aside for later.
5. Preheat your oven and bake the cake for around forty minutes.
6. Let cool and then top with butterscotch pecans and serve fresh.

Nutritional Content of One Serving:

Calories: 281 ‖ Fat: 18.1g ‖ Protein: 4.4g ‖ Carbohydrates: 27.4g

BUTTERMILK CHOCOLATE CAKE

Total Time Taken: 50 minutes
Yield: 8 Servings
Ingredients:

- ½ cup butter, melted
- ½ cup cocoa powder
- ½ teaspoon salt
- 1 ½ cups all-purpose flour
- 1 cup buttermilk
- 1 cup sugar
- 1 teaspoon baking powder
- 1 teaspoon vanilla extract
- 2 eggs

Directions:

1. Mix the dry ingredients in a container and the wet ingredients in a separate container.
2. Pour the wet ingredients over the dry ones and stir for a few seconds to mix.
3. Pour the batter in a 9-inch cake pan coated with baking paper.
4. Pre-heat the oven and bake at 350F for about half an hour.
5. Let cool in the pan and serve, sliced.

Nutritional Content of One Serving:

Calories: 323 ‖ Fat: 13.8g ‖ Protein: 5.9g ‖ Carbohydrates: 47.8g

BUTTERMILK CHOCOLATE CAKE

Total Time Taken: 1 ¼ hours
Yield: 10 Servings

Ingredients:

- ½ cup cocoa powder
- ½ teaspoon salt
- 1 ¼ cups buttermilk
- 1 cup butter, melted
- 1 cup white sugar
- 1 teaspoon vanilla extract
- 2 cups all-purpose flour
- 2 eggs
- 2 teaspoons baking powder

Directions:

1. Mix all the ingredients in a container.
2. Give it a quick stir until incorporated.
3. Pour the batter in a 9-inch round cake pan coated with baking paper.
4. Preheat your oven and bake the cake for about forty minutes or until the cake is well risen and it passes the toothpick test.
5. Let the cake cool in the pan then serve it chilled.

Nutritional Content of One Serving:

Calories: 365 ‖ Fat: 20.4g ‖ Protein: 5.7g ‖ Carbohydrates: 43.5g

BUTTER CAKE

Total Time Taken: 1 hour

Yield: 8 Servings

Ingredients:

- ¼ teaspoon salt
- ½ cup butter, softened
- ½ cup whole milk
- ¾ cup white sugar
- 1 cup all-purpose flour
- 1 teaspoon baking powder
- 1 teaspoon vanilla extract
- 2 eggs

Directions:

1. Mix the butter, sugar and vanilla in a container until fluffy and pale.
2. Stir in the eggs and mix thoroughly.
3. Fold in the flour, baking powder and salt, alternating it with milk. Begin and finish with flour.
4. Spoon the batter in a 6-inch round cake pan coated with baking paper.
5. Pre-heat the oven and bake at 350F for about half an hour or until a golden-brown colour is achieved.
6. Let the cake cool in the pan before you serve.

Nutritional Content of One Serving:

Calories: 256 ‖ Fat: 13.2g ‖ Protein: 3.6g ‖ Carbohydrates: 31.8g

BROWN SUGAR PINEAPPLE BUNDT CAKE

Total Time Taken: 1 ¼ hours

Yield: 12 Servings

Ingredients:

- ½ cup buttermilk
- ½ cup cornstarch

- ½ cup light brown sugar
- ½ teaspoon salt
- ¾ cup butter, softened
- 1 cup white sugar
- 1 tablespoon lemon zest
- 1 teaspoon baking powder
- 1 teaspoon baking soda
- 1 teaspoon vanilla extract
- 2 cups all-purpose flour
- 3 eggs
- 4 pineapple slices, cubed

Directions:

1. Position the pineapple slices at the bottom of a greased Bundt cake pan and drizzle with brown sugar.
2. Sift the flour with cornstarch, baking soda, baking powder and salt.
3. Mix the butter with sugar in a container until light and creamy then mix in the eggs and vanilla, as well as the lemon zest and buttermilk.
4. Fold in the flour then pour the batter over the pineapple.
5. Pre-heat the oven and bake at 350F for about forty minutes or until it rises significantly and starts to appear golden-brown.
6. Let the cake cool in the pan for about ten minutes then flip it over on a platter.

Nutritional Content of One Serving:

Calories: 332 ‖ Fat: 13.0g ‖ Protein: 4.3g ‖ Carbohydrates: 51.5g

BROWN SUGAR CAKE

Total Time Taken: 1 ¼ hours
Yield: 10 Servings

Ingredients:

- ½ cup dark brown sugar
- ½ teaspoon salt
- 1 cup butter, softened
- 1 cup light brown sugar

- 1 teaspoon vanilla extract
- 2 cups all-purpose flour
- 2 teaspoons baking powder
- 4 eggs
- ½ cup milk

Directions:

1. Sift the flour, baking powder and salt in a container.
2. In another container, combine the butter and sugars until creamy and light.
3. Stir in the eggs, one at a time, then put in the vanilla and milk.
4. Fold in the flour then spoon the batter in a 9-inch round cake pan covered with parchment paper.
5. Pre-heat the oven and bake at 350F for forty minutes or until it rises significantly and starts to appear golden-brown.
6. Let the cake cool in the pan and serve, sliced.

Nutritional Content of One Serving:

Calories: 370 ‖ Fat: 20.7g ‖ Protein: 5.4g ‖ Carbohydrates: 41.7g

BROWN BUTTER WALNUT CAKE

Total Time Taken: 1 ¼ hours
Yield: 12 Servings

Ingredients:

- ½ teaspoon salt
- 1 ½ cups all-purpose flour
- 1 ½ cups white sugar
- 1 cup butter
- 1 cup ground walnuts
- 1 cup sour cream
- 1 cup walnuts, chopped
- 1 teaspoon baking powder
- 1 teaspoon vanilla extract
- 2 eggs

Directions:

1. Place the butter in a saucepan and melt it. Keep on heat until mildly browned and caramelized. Let the butter cool then move it to a container.
2. Put in the sugar and mix thoroughly.
3. Stir in the eggs and mix thoroughly then put in the sour cream and vanilla.
4. Fold in the flour, baking powder, salt and ground walnuts.
5. Spoon the batter in a 9-inch round cake pan and top with chopped walnuts.
6. Pre-heat the oven and bake at 350F for about forty-five minutes or until a toothpick inserted into the center of the cake comes out clean.
7. The cake tastes best chilled.

Nutritional Content of One Serving:

Calories: 468 ‖ Fat: 32.5g ‖ Protein: 8.3g ‖ Carbohydrates: 40.1g

BOOZY RAISIN BUNDT CAKE

Total Time Taken: 2 hours
Yield: 12 Servings
Ingredients:

- ½ cup brandy
- ½ cup whole milk
- ½ teaspoon salt
- 1 ½ cups white sugar
- 1 cup apricot jam
- 1 cup butter, softened
- 1 cup buttermilk
- 1 cup golden raisins
- 2 eggs
- 2 teaspoons baking powder
- 3 cups all-purpose flour

Directions:

1. Sift the flour, salt and baking powder.
2. Mix the butter, sugar and jam in a container until creamy and light.
3. Stir in the eggs, one at a time, then begin incorporating the flour mixture, alternating it with the buttermilk and milk.

4. Spoon the batter in a greased Bundt cake pan and preheat your oven and bake at 350F for about fifty minutes or until a toothpick inserted in the center comes out clean.
5. Let the cake cool in the pan before you serve.

Nutritional Content of One Serving:

Calories: 474 ‖ Fat: 17.0g ‖ Protein: 5.9g ‖ Carbohydrates: 77.5g

BOOZY CHOCOLATE CAKE

Total Time Taken: 1 ¼ hours
Yield: 14 Servings
Ingredients:

Cake:

- ¼ cup brandy
- ½ cup canola oil
- ½ cup cocoa powder
- ½ cup hot coffee
- ½ teaspoon salt
- 1 cup buttermilk
- 1 teaspoon baking powder
- 1 teaspoon baking soda
- 2 cups all-purpose flour
- 2 eggs

Frosting:

- ¼ cup brandy
- 1 cup heavy cream
- 2 cups dark chocolate chips
- 2 tablespoons butter

Directions:

1. For the cake, combine the flour, cocoa powder, baking soda, baking powder and salt in a container.
2. Put in the rest of the ingredients and mix thoroughly.
3. Pour the batter in a 9-inch round cake pan, preheat your oven and bake at 330F for 50 minutes.

4. When finished, allow the cake to cool in the pan then move to a platter.
5. For the frosting, bring the cream to the boiling point in a saucepan. Turn off the heat and put in the chocolate. Stir thoroughly to mix until melted and smooth.
6. let the frosting cool down then cover the cake with it.
7. Serve fresh or chilled.

Nutritional Content of One Serving:

Calories: 281 ‖ Fat: 18.5g ‖ Protein: 5.1g ‖ Carbohydrates: 28.0g

BLUEBERRY STREUSEL CAKE

Total Time Taken: 1 ¼ hours
Yield: 10 Servings
Ingredients:

Cake:

- ½ cup sour cream
- ½ teaspoon salt
- ¾ cup butter, softened
- 1 ½ cups fresh blueberries
- 1 cup white sugar
- 1 tablespoon lemon zest
- 1 teaspoon baking soda
- 2 cups all-purpose flour
- 2 tablespoons lemon juice
- 4 eggs

Streusel:

- ¼ cup butter, chilled
- ½ cup all-purpose flour
- 1 pinch salt
- 2 tablespoons powdered sugar

Directions:

1. To prepare the cake, combine the butter, sugar, eggs and sour cream in a container for five minutes until creamy.

2. Put in the lemon zest, lemon juice, flour, baking soda and salt and mix using a spatula.
3. Fold in the fruits then spoon the batter in a 9-inch round cake pan.
4. For the streusel, combine all the ingredients in a container until grainy.
5. Spread the streusel over the cake and preheat your oven and bake at 350F for about forty minutes or until a toothpick inserted in the center comes out clean.
6. Let the cake cool in the pan before you serve.

Nutritional Content of One Serving:

Calories: 421 ‖ Fat: 23.0g ‖ Protein: 6.2g ‖ Carbohydrates: 49.4g

BLUEBERRY CAKE

Total Time Taken: 1 hour
Yield: 12 Servings
Ingredients:

- ½ teaspoon salt
- 1 cup butter, softened
- 1 cup buttermilk
- 1 cup fresh blueberries
- 1 cup white sugar
- 1/4 cup light brown sugar
- 2 tablespoons lemon juice
- 2 tablespoons lemon zest
- 2 teaspoons baking powder
- 3 ½ cups all-purpose flour
- 4 eggs

Directions:

1. Mix the butter and sugars in a container until creamy and fluffy.
2. Stir in the eggs, one at a time, then put in the lemon juice, buttermilk and lemon zest.
3. Fold in the flour, baking powder and salt, followed by the fresh blueberries.
4. Spoon the batter in a 10-inch round cake pan coated with baking paper.
5. Pre-heat the oven and bake at 350F for about forty minutes or until the cake is well risen and golden brown.

6. Let the cake cool in the pan and serve, sliced.

Nutritional Content of One Serving:

Calories: 380 ‖ Fat: 17.4g ‖ Protein: 6.6g ‖ Carbohydrates: 50.9g

BLOOD ORANGE OLIVE OIL CAKE

Total Time Taken: 1 ¼ hours
Yield: 12 Servings

Ingredients:

- ½ cup corn meal
- ½ cup light brown sugar
- ½ teaspoon baking soda
- ½ teaspoon salt
- ¾ cup olive oil
- 1 ½ cups all-purpose flour
- 1 ½ cups white sugar
- 1 cup buttermilk
- 1 teaspoon baking powder
- 2 eggs
- 3 blood oranges, sliced

Directions:

1. Position the blood orange slices in a 10-inch baking tray covered with parchment paper and drizzle them with brown sugar.
2. Mix the oil with eggs and sugar in a container until volume increases to twice what it was.
3. Stir in the flour, baking powder, cornmeal, baking soda and salt then put in the buttermilk and stir for a few seconds to mix.
4. Pour the batter over the orange slices and preheat your oven and bake at 350F for around forty minutes or until a golden-brown colour is achieved and it rises significantly.
5. The cake tastes best chilled, turned upside down on a platter.

Nutritional Content of One Serving:

Calories: 342 ‖ Fat: 13.9g ‖ Protein: 4.2g ‖ Carbohydrates: 54.0g

BLOOD ORANGE CORNMEAL CAKE

Total Time Taken: 1 ½ hours

Yield: 12 Servings

Ingredients:

- ½ teaspoon salt
- 1 cup all-purpose flour
- 1 cup butter, softened
- 1 cup cornmeal
- 1 cup fresh blood orange juice
- 1 cup white sugar
- 2 blood oranges, sliced
- 2 tablespoons blood orange zest
- 2 teaspoons baking powder

Directions:

1. Mix the butter, sugar and orange zest in a container until creamy and fluffy.
2. Mix the flour, cornmeal, baking powder and salt.
3. Stir the flour into the butter mixture, alternating it with the orange juice.
4. Position the orange slices at the bottom of a 9-inch round cake pan coated with baking paper.
5. Pour the batter over the orange slices and preheat your oven and bake at 350F for 45 minutes or until a toothpick inserted into the center of the cake comes out clean.
6. When finished, flip the cake upside down on a platter and serve it chilled.

Nutritional Content of One Serving:

Calories: 298 ‖ Fat: 15.9g ‖ Protein: 2.5g ‖ Carbohydrates: 38.8g

BLACKBERRY BUNDT CAKE

Total Time Taken: 1 ¼ hours

Yield: 10 Servings

Ingredients:

- ½ cup butter, softened

- ½ teaspoon ground cardamom
- ½ teaspoon salt
- 1 cup fresh blackberries
- 1 cup white sugar
- 1 cup whole milk
- 1 teaspoon vanilla extract
- 2 cups all-purpose flour
- 2 eggs
- 2 teaspoons baking powder

Directions:

1. Mix the butter with sugar until creamy, at least five minutes.
2. Put in the eggs and mix thoroughly then mix in the milk and vanilla.
3. Fold in the flour, baking powder, salt and cardamom then put in the blackberries.
4. Spoon the batter in a Bundt cake pan lined using butter.
5. Pre-heat the oven and bake at 350F for around forty minutes or until a toothpick inserted in the center comes out clean.
6. Let the cake cool in the pan for about ten minutes then flip it over on a platter.

Nutritional Content of One Serving:

Calories: 283 ‖ Fat: 11.2g ‖ Protein: 4.8g ‖ Carbohydrates: 42.2g

BLACK PEPPER CHOCOLATE CAKE

Total Time Taken: 1 ¼ hours
Yield: 16 Servings

Ingredients:

- ½ teaspoon salt
- 1 ½ cups white sugar
- 1 ½ teaspoons baking powder
- 1 cup butter
- 1 cup sour cream
- 1 teaspoon ground black pepper
- 1 teaspoon lemon zest

- 2 cups all-purpose flour
- 4 eggs

Directions:

1. Mix the flour with baking powder and salt in a container.
2. In a separate container, combine the butter and sugar until fluffy and pale.
3. Stir in the black pepper, lemon zest and eggs and mix thoroughly.
4. Put in the sour cream and give it a good mix.
5. Fold in the flour, baking powder and salt then spoon the batter in a 9-inch round cake pan coated with baking paper.
6. Pre-heat the oven and bake at 350F for about forty minutes or until a toothpick inserted into the center of the cake comes out clean.
7. Let the cake cool in the pan before you serve.

Nutritional Content of One Serving:

Calories: 276 ‖ Fat: 15.8g ‖ Protein: 3.6g ‖ Carbohydrates: 31.7g

BERRY MERINGUE CAKE

Total Time Taken: 2 ½ hours
Yield: 8 Servings

Ingredients:

- ½ teaspoon salt
- 1 ½ cups fresh berries
- 1 cup heavy cream, whipped
- 1 cup white sugar
- 1 teaspoon vanilla extract
- 2 tablespoons cornstarch
- 4 egg whites

Directions:

1. Mix the egg whites, salt and sugar in a container. Place over a hot water bath and keep over heat until the sugar is melted.
2. Turn off the heat and whip the egg whites until shiny and fluffy.
3. Fold in the cornstarch then spoon the meringue on a baking sheet coated with baking paper, shaping it into 2 rounds.
4. Pre-heat the oven and bake at 250F for about two hours.

5. Fill and cover the cake with whipped cream and fresh berries.
6. Serve immediately.

Nutritional Content of One Serving:

Calories: 178 ‖ Fat: 5.7g ‖ Protein: 2.3g ‖ Carbohydrates: 30.6g

BERRY LEMON CAKE

Total Time Taken: 1 ¼ hours
Yield: 10 Servings

Ingredients:

- ½ cup butter, softened
- ½ cup plain yogurt
- ½ teaspoon salt
- 1 ½ teaspoons baking powder
- 1 cup mixed berries
- 1 cup white sugar
- 1 tablespoon lemon zest
- 2 cups all-purpose flour
- 2 tablespoons lemon juice
- 3 eggs

Directions:

1. Mix the butter and sugar in a container until creamy and fluffy.
2. Stir in the eggs, one at a time, then put in the lemon zest and lemon juice, as well as the yogurt.
3. Fold in the flour, baking powder and salt then put in the berries.
4. Pour the batter in a 8-inch round cake pan and preheat your oven and bake at 350F for around forty minutes or until it rises significantly and starts to appear golden-brown.
5. Let the cake cool in the pan before you serve.

Nutritional Content of One Serving:

Calories: 285 ‖ Fat: 11.0g ‖ Protein: 5.2g ‖ Carbohydrates: 42.3g

BEETROOT CHOCOLATE FUDGE CAKE

Total Time Taken: 1 ¼ hours

Yield: 10 Servings

Ingredients:

- ¼ cup canola oil
- ¼ teaspoon salt
- ½ cup almond flour
- ½ cup cocoa powder
- 1 ½ cups grated beetroot
- 1 cup all-purpose flour
- 1 cup light brown sugar
- 1 teaspoon baking soda
- 2 tablespoons honey
- 3 eggs

Directions:

1. Mix the eggs with sugar until fluffy and pale. Put in the oil and honey and mix thoroughly.
2. Fold in the flour, cocoa powder, baking soda, almond flour and salt.
3. Put in the beetroot and stir lightly using a spatula.
4. Pour the batter in a 9-inch round cake pan coated with baking paper.
5. Pre-heat the oven and bake at 350F for about half an hour.
6. Let the cake cool in the pan before you serve.

Nutritional Content of One Serving:

Calories: 209 ‖ Fat: 8.2g ‖ Protein: 4.5g ‖ Carbohydrates: 32.5g

BEETROOT CARROT CAKE

Total Time Taken: 1 ½ hours

Yield: 10 Servings

Ingredients:

- ¼ cup maple syrup
- ½ cup grated beetroots

- ½ cup light brown sugar
- 3 eggs
- ½ cup pecans, chopped
- ½ teaspoon ground cardamom
- ½ teaspoon ground ginger
- ½ teaspoon salt
- ¾ cup vegetable oil
- 1 ½ cups all-purpose flour
- 1 teaspoon baking powder
- 1 teaspoon cinnamon powder
- 1 teaspoon vanilla extract
- 2 cups grated carrots

Directions:

1. Mix the flour, salt, baking powder, cinnamon, ginger and cardamom in a container.
2. In a separate container, combine the oil, maple syrup, sugar, eggs and vanilla until fluffy.
3. Stir in the carrots and beetroots, as well as pecans then fold in the flour.
4. Spoon the batter in a 9-inch round cake pan coated with baking paper.
5. Pre-heat the oven and bake at 350F for about forty minutes or until a toothpick inserted into the center of the cake comes out clean.
6. The cake tastes best chilled.

Nutritional Content of One Serving:

Calories: 305 ‖ Fat: 18.9g ‖ Protein: 4.1g ‖ Carbohydrates: 30.4g

BANANA PEANUT BUTTER CAKE

Total Time Taken: 1 hour
Yield: 8 Servings
Ingredients:

- ¼ cup whole milk
- ½ cup smooth peanut butter
- ½ teaspoon salt
- 1 ½ cups all-purpose flour
- 1 teaspoon baking soda

- 1 teaspoon vanilla extract
- 2 eggs
- 2 ripe bananas, mashed
- 2/3 cup white sugar
- 4 tablespoons butter, softened

Directions:

1. Mix the butter with sugar until creamy and smooth.
2. Stir in the eggs one at a time, then mix in the vanilla and bananas, as well as milk.
3. Fold in the flour, baking soda and salt and mix thoroughly.
4. Spoon the batter in a 9pinch round cake pan coated with baking paper and preheat your oven and bake at 350F for about half an hour or until a golden-brown colour is achieved and it rises significantly.
5. Let the cake cool completely before you serve.

Nutritional Content of One Serving:

Calories: 342 ‖ Fat: 15.6g ‖ Protein: 8.5g ‖ Carbohydrates: 45.0g

BANANA MARS BAR CAKE

Total Time Taken: 1 ¼ hours
Yield: 10 Servings

Ingredients:

- ½ cup butter, softened
- ½ cup light brown sugar
- ½ cup whole milk
- ½ teaspoon salt
- 2 bananas, mashed
- 2 cups all-purpose flour
- 2 eggs
- 2 Mars bars, chopped
- 2 tablespoons maple syrup
- 2 teaspoons baking powder

Directions:

1. Mix the butter, sugar and maple syrup in a container until fluffy and pale.

2. Put in the eggs and mix thoroughly then mix in the mashed bananas and milk.
3. Fold in the remaining ingredients then spoon the batter in a loaf cake pan coated with baking paper.
4. Pre-heat the oven and bake at 350F for about forty minutes or until a golden-brown colour is achieved and it rises significantly.
5. The cake tastes best chilled.

Nutritional Content of One Serving:

Calories: 299 ‖ Fat: 13.1g ‖ Protein: 5.3g ‖ Carbohydrates: 41.6g

BANANA CHOCOLATE CHIP CAKE

Total Time Taken: 1 ¼ hours
Yield: 12 Servings

Ingredients:

- ¼ teaspoon salt
- ½ cup butter, softened
- ½ cup dark chocolate chips
- ½ cup walnuts, chopped
- 1 ¾ cups all-purpose flour
- 1 cup white sugar
- 1 teaspoon baking soda
- 1 teaspoon vanilla extract
- 3 eggs
- 3 ripe bananas, mashed

Directions:

1. Sift the flour, baking soda and salt on a platter.
2. Mix the butter with sugar until creamy and fluffy.
3. Stir in the eggs, one at a time, then put in the vanilla and bananas.
4. Stir thoroughly to mix then fold in the flour, followed by the walnuts and chocolate chips.
5. Spoon the batter in a 9-inch round cake pan covered with parchment paper.
6. Pre-heat the oven and bake at 350F for about forty minutes or until a toothpick inserted into the center of the cake comes out clean.
7. Let the cake cool in the pan and serve, sliced.

Nutritional Content of One Serving:

Calories: 295 ‖ Fat: 13.4g ‖ Protein: 5.2g ‖ Carbohydrates: 41.3g

BANANA CAKE

Total Time Taken: 55 minutes
Yield: 8 Servings
Ingredients:

- ¼ cup butter, softened
- ¼ cup whole milk
- ¼ teaspoon salt
- ½ cup dark chocolate chips
- ½ cup white sugar
- 1 ½ cups all-purpose flour
- 1 teaspoon baking soda
- 2 eggs
- 2 ripe bananas, mashed
- 2 tablespoons dark brown sugar

Directions:

1. Sift the flour, baking soda and salt in a container.
2. Combine the butter, sugars and eggs in a container and stir thoroughly for five minutes.
3. Put in the mashed bananas and milk then fold in the flour, followed by the chocolate chips.
4. Spoon the batter in a round cake pan coated with baking paper and preheat your oven and bake at 350F for about half an hour or until a golden-brown colour is achieved and it rises significantly.
5. Let the cake cool in the pan and serve, sliced.

Nutritional Content of One Serving:

Calories: 273 ‖ Fat: 9.4g ‖ Protein: 4.9g ‖ Carbohydrates: 44.8g

BANANA BUNDT CAKE WITH PEANUT BUTTER FROSTING

Total Time Taken: 1 ¼ hours
Yield: 12 Servings
Ingredients:

Cake:

- ½ teaspoon salt
- 1 cup buttermilk
- 1 cup canola oil
- 1 cup white sugar
- 1 teaspoon vanilla extract
- 2 cups all-purpose flour
- 2 eggs
- 2 ripe bananas, mashed
- 2 teaspoons baking powder

Frosting:

- ½ cup cream cheese
- ½ cup peanut butter, softened
- ½ cup powdered sugar

Directions:

1. To prepare the cake, combine the oil and sugar in a container then mix in the eggs and vanilla. Stir thoroughly to mix then put in the buttermilk and bananas.
2. Fold in the flour, baking powder and salt then spoon the batter in a greased Bundt cake pan.
3. Pre-heat the oven and bake at 350F for about forty minutes or until a toothpick inserted into the center of the cake comes out clean.
4. Move the cake to a platter.
5. For the frosting, combine the ingredients in a container until creamy.
6. Cover the cake with peanut butter frosting and serve fresh.

Nutritional Content of One Serving:

Calories: 453 ‖ Fat: 28.1g ‖ Protein: 7.4g ‖ Carbohydrates: 45.9g

APRICOT YOGURT LOAF CAKE

Total Time Taken: 1 ¼ hours
Yield: 10 Servings

Ingredients:

- ¼ cup sliced almonds
- ¼ teaspoon salt
- ½ cup butter, softened
- ¾ cup white sugar
- 1 ¼ cups all-purpose flour
- 1 cup plain yogurt
- 1 teaspoon baking powder
- 1 teaspoon vanilla extract
- 2 eggs
- 4 apricots, pitted and sliced

Directions:

1. Mix the butter and sugar in a container until fluffy and pale. Stir in the eggs, one at a time, then put in the yogurt and vanilla and mix thoroughly.
2. Fold in the flour, baking powder and salt.
3. Spoon the batter in a loaf cake pan coated with baking paper.
4. Top with apricots and drizzle with sliced almonds.
5. Pre-heat the oven and bake at 350F for around forty minutes or until it rises significantly and starts to appear golden-brown.
6. Let the cake cool in the pan before you serve.

Nutritional Content of One Serving:

Calories: 247 ‖ Fat: 11.8g ‖ Protein: 4.9g ‖ Carbohydrates: 31.1g

APRICOT CAKE

Total Time Taken: 1 hour
Yield: 10 Servings
Ingredients:

6 eggs

- ½ cup canola oil
- ½ cup sour cream
- ½ teaspoon salt
- 1 ½ teaspoons baking powder
- 1 cup white sugar
- 1 tablespoon lemon zest
- 1 teaspoon vanilla extract
- 2 cups all-purpose flour
- 6 apricots, halved and sliced

Directions:

1. Mix the eggs with sugar, vanilla and lemon zest in a container until fluffy and creamy.
2. Put in the canola oil and sour cream and mix thoroughly.
3. Fold in the remaining ingredients then pour the batter in a 9-inch round cake pan coated with baking paper.
4. Pre-heat the oven and bake at 350F for about forty minutes or until a toothpick inserted in the center comes out clean.
5. Let the cake cool in the pan before you serve.

Nutritional Content of One Serving:

Calories: 337 ‖ Fat: 16.3g ‖ Protein: 6.5g ‖ Carbohydrates: 42.6g

APPLESAUCE CARROT CAKE

Total Time Taken: 1 ½ hours
Yield: 12 Servings

Ingredients:

- ¼ cup dark brown sugar
- ½ cup canola oil
- ½ cup shredded coconut
- ½ teaspoon baking powder
- ½ teaspoon salt
- 1 cup applesauce
- 1 cup grated carrots
- 1 cup white sugar

- 1 egg white
- 1 teaspoon baking soda
- 1 teaspoon vanilla extract
- 2 ½ cups all-purpose flour
- 2 apples, peeled, cored and diced
- 3 eggs

Directions:

1. Mix the eggs, egg white, sugars and vanilla in a container until fluffy and pale.
2. Stir in the canola oil and applesauce and mix thoroughly then put in the carrots, coconut and apples, as well as the flour, baking soda, baking powder and salt.
3. Stir slowly until mixed using a spatula just until incorporated.
4. Pour the batter in a 9-inch round cake pan and preheat your oven and bake at 350F for about fifty minutes or until fragrant and a toothpick inserted into the center of the cake comes out clean.
5. Let the cake cool in the pan before you serve.

Nutritional Content of One Serving:

Calories: 307 ‖ Fat: 11.6g ‖ Protein: 4.7g ‖ Carbohydrates: 47.6g

APPLE VANILLA LOAF CAKE

Total Time Taken: 1 ¼ hours
Yield: 10 Servings

Ingredients:

- ¼ teaspoon salt
- ½ cup butter, softened
- ½ cup canola oil
- ½ cup cornstarch
- ½ cup whole milk
- ¾ cup white sugar
- 1 cup all-purpose flour
- 1 tablespoon vanilla extract
- 1 teaspoon baking powder

- 2 red apples, cored and diced
- 3 eggs

Directions:

1. Mix the butter, oil and sugar in a container. Stir thoroughly to mix until creamy.
2. Put in the eggs, one at a time, then mix in the milk and vanilla.
3. Fold in the flour, cornstarch, baking powder and salt, then incorporate the apples.
4. Spoon the batter in a loaf cake pan coated with baking paper.
5. Pre-heat the oven and bake at 350F for around forty minutes or until a toothpick inserted into the center of the cake comes out clean.
6. The cake tastes best chilled.

Nutritional Content of One Serving:

Calories: 353 ‖ Fat: 22.0g ‖ Protein: 3.6g ‖ Carbohydrates: 36.5g

APPLE POUND CAKE

Total Time Taken: 1 ¼ hours
Yield: 10 Servings

Ingredients:

- ¼ teaspoon salt
- ½ cup cream cheese, softened
- ½ teaspoon baking soda
- ½ teaspoon cinnamon powder
- ¾ cup butter, softened
- 1 ½ cups all-purpose flour
- 1 cup white sugar
- 1 teaspoon baking powder
- 1 teaspoon vanilla extract
- 2 granny Smith apples, peeled, cored and diced
- 3 eggs

Directions:

1. Mix the butter, cream cheese and sugar in a container until creamy and fluffy.
2. Stir in the eggs and vanilla and mix thoroughly.
3. Fold in the flour, baking powder, baking soda, salt and cinnamon.
4. Put in the apple dices then spoon the batter in a loaf cake pan coated with baking paper.
5. Pre-heat the oven and bake at 350F for forty minutes or until a toothpick inserted into the center of the cake comes out clean.
6. The cake tastes best chilled.

Nutritional Content of One Serving:

Calories: 345 ‖ Fat: 19.4g ‖ Protein: 4.7g ‖ Carbohydrates: 40.0g

APPLE AND PEAR MOLASSES CAKE

Total Time Taken: 1 ¼ hours
Yield: 10 Servings

Ingredients:

- ¼ cup butter, softened
- ½ cup canola oil
- ½ cup light molasses
- ½ cup white sugar
- 1 egg
- ½ cup whole milk
- 1 pear, peeled, cored and diced
- 1 red apple, peeled, cored and diced
- 1 teaspoon baking powder
- 1 teaspoon baking soda
- 1 teaspoon cinnamon powder
- 1 teaspoon grated ginger
- 2 cups all-purpose flour

Directions:

1. Mix the canola oil, butter, molasses and sugar in a container until creamy. Put in the egg, ginger and cinnamon and mix thoroughly then mix in the milk.

2. Fold in the remaining ingredients then spoon the batter in a 9-inch round cake pan covered with parchment paper.
3. Pre-heat the oven and bake at 350F for about forty minutes or until a toothpick comes out clean after being inserted into the center of the cake.
4. Let cool in the pan then cut and serve.

Nutritional Content of One Serving:

Calories: 345 ‖ Fat: 16.7g ‖ Protein: 3.7g ‖ Carbohydrates: 46.9g

AMARETTO ALMOND CAKE

Total Time Taken: 1 hour
Yield: 8 Servings
Ingredients:

- ¼ cup cocoa powder
- ¼ teaspoon salt
- ½ cup butter, softened
- ½ cup light brown sugar
- 1 ½ cups almond flour
- 1 teaspoon baking powder
- 1 teaspoon lemon zest
- 1 teaspoon orange zest
- 2 tablespoons Amaretto
- 3 eggs

Directions:

1. Mix the butter, sugar, orange zest and lemon zest in a container until fluffy and creamy.
2. Put in the eggs, one at a time, then mix in the almond flour, cocoa, salt and baking powder, preferably using a spatula.
3. Spoon the batter in a 8-inch round cake pan and preheat your oven and bake at 350F for 35 minutes or until a toothpick comes out clean after being inserted into the center of the cake.
4. Immediately after you take it out of the oven, sprinkle it with Amaretto.
5. Serve chilled.

Nutritional Content of One Serving:

Calories: 208 ‖ Fat: 16.1g ‖ Protein: 3.8g ‖ Carbohydrates: 12.0g

ALMOND WHITE CHOCOLATE CAKE

Total Time Taken: 1 ½ hours

Yield: 10 Servings

Ingredients:

- ½ cup dried cranberries
- ½ cup sliced almonds
- ½ cup sour cream
- ½ teaspoon salt
- 1 ½ teaspoons baking soda
- 1 cup all-purpose flour
- 1 cup butter, softened
- 1 cup ground almonds
- 1 cup light brown sugar
- 1 cup white chocolate chips
- 1 tablespoon orange zest
- 3 eggs

Directions:

1. Mix the butter and sugar in a container until creamy and fluffy.
2. Stir in the eggs, one at a time, then put in the orange zest and sour cream.
3. Fold in the flour, almonds, baking soda and salt then put in the cranberries and chocolate chips.
4. Spoon the batter in a 9-inch round cake pan and top with sliced almonds.
5. Pre-heat the oven and bake at 350F for about forty minutes or until it rises significantly and starts to appear golden-brown.
6. Let the cake cool in the pan and serve, sliced.

Nutritional Content of One Serving:

Calories: 485 ‖ Fat: 34.8g ‖ Protein: 7.5g ‖ Carbohydrates: 38.1g

ALMOND STRAWBERRY CAKE

Total Time Taken: 1 ¼ hours
Yield: 8 Servings

Ingredients:

- ½ cup butter, softened
- ½ cup white sugar
- ½ cup whole milk
- ½ teaspoon salt
- 1 cup all-purpose flour
- 1 cup fresh strawberries, sliced
- 1 cup ground almonds
- 1 teaspoon baking soda
- 1 teaspoon vanilla extract
- 2 eggs

Directions:

1. Mix the butter and sugar in a container until creamy. Stir in the eggs, one at a time, then put in the milk and vanilla.
2. Fold in the flour, almonds, baking soda and salt and stir lightly.
3. Fold in the strawberries then spoon the batter in a round cake pan coated with baking paper.
4. Preheat your oven and bake the cake for about half an hour or until a golden-brown colour is achieved and it rises significantly.
5. Let the cake cool in the pan before you serve.

Nutritional Content of One Serving:

Calories: 306 ‖ Fat: 19.2g ‖ Protein: 6.2g ‖ Carbohydrates: 29.2g

ALMOND STRAWBERRY CAKE

Total Time Taken: 1 ¼ hours
Yield: 10 Servings

Ingredients:

- ½ cup plain yogurt
- 1 cup all-purpose flour
- 1 cup almond flour
- 1 cup butter, softened

- 1 cup white sugar
- 1 teaspoon baking soda
- 1 teaspoon vanilla
- 2 cups fresh strawberries
- 4 eggs

Directions:

1. Mix the butter with sugar and vanilla in a container until creamy.
2. Stir in the eggs, one at a time, then put in the yogurt and mix thoroughly.
3. Fold in the almond flour, all-purpose flour, baking soda and a pinch of salt and stir lightly using a spatula.
4. Pour the batter in a 9-inch round cake pan and top with strawberries.
5. Pre-heat the oven and bake at 350F for about forty-five minutes or until a toothpick comes out clean after being inserted into the center of the cake.
6. The cake tastes best chilled.

Nutritional Content of One Serving:

Calories: 344 ‖ Fat: 21.9g ‖ Protein: 5.2g ‖ Carbohydrates: 33.4g

ALMOND HONEY CAKE

Total Time Taken: 1 ¼ hours
Yield: 10 Servings

Ingredients:

- ¼ cup light brown sugar
- ¼ teaspoon cinnamon powder
- ¼ teaspoon salt
- ½ cup ground almonds
- ½ cup honey
- ½ cup sliced almonds
- ¾ cup butter, softened
- 1 ½ cups all-purpose flour
- 1 teaspoon baking powder
- 3 eggs

Directions:

1. Mix the butter, honey and sugar in a container until creamy and pale.

2. Put in the eggs and mix thoroughly.
3. Fold in the flour, almonds, baking powder, salt and cinnamon powder.
4. Spoon the batter in a loaf cake pan coated with baking paper.
5. Top with sliced almonds and preheat your oven and bake at 350F for forty minutes or until a toothpick inserted into the center of the cake comes out clean.
6. The cake tastes best chilled.

Nutritional Content of One Serving:

Calories: 330 ‖ Fat: 20.1g ‖ Protein: 5.8g ‖ Carbohydrates: 34.2g

ALMOND FIG CAKE

Total Time Taken: 1 ¼ hours
Yield: 10 Servings

Ingredients:

- 2 eggs
- 4 egg whites
- 1 cup white sugar
- ½ cup butter, melted
- 1 cup all-purpose flour
- 1 teaspoon baking powder
- ¼ teaspoon salt
- 1 cup ground almonds
- 6 figs, sliced

Directions:

1. Mix the eggs, egg whites and sugar in a container until creamy and volume increases to twice what it was.
2. Put in the melted butter, progressively, then fold in the flour, baking powder, salt and almonds.
3. Pour the batter in a 8-inch round cake pan coated with baking paper.
4. Top with figs and preheat your oven and bake at 350F for around forty minutes or until it rises significantly and starts to appear golden-brown.
5. Let the cake cool in the pan and serve, sliced.

Nutritional Content of One Serving:

Calories: 305 ‖ Fat: 15.1g ‖ Protein: 6.3g ‖ Carbohydrates: 39.3g

ALMOND DATE CAKE

Total Time Taken: 1 hour
Yield: 8 Servings
Ingredients:

2 eggs

- ¼ cup cocoa powder
- ¼ cup rice flour
- ¼ teaspoon salt
- ½ cup white sugar
- ½ lemon, zested and juiced
- 1 ½ cups almond flour
- 1 cup dates, pitted
- 1 teaspoon baking soda
- 4 egg whites

Directions:

1. Mix the eggs, egg whites, lemon zest, lemon juice, sugar and dates in a food processor.
2. Put in the almond flour, rice flour, cocoa powder, baking soda and salt and stir lightly using a spatula.
3. Pour the batter in a 8-inch round cake pan coated with baking paper.
4. Pre-heat the oven and bake at 350F for around forty minutes.
5. Let the cake cool in the pan before you serve.

Nutritional Content of One Serving:

Calories: 188 ‖ Fat: 4.3g ‖ Protein: 5.6g ‖ Carbohydrates: 35.9g

ALMOND BUTTER BANANA CAKE

Total Time Taken: 1 ¼ hours
Yield: 12 Servings

Ingredients:

- ¼ cup canola oil
- ½ cup shredded coconut
- ½ teaspoon ground ginger
- ½ teaspoon salt
- 1 ½ cups white sugar
- 1 cup almond butter
- 1 teaspoon baking soda
- 1 teaspoon cinnamon powder
- 1 teaspoon vanilla extract
- 2 bananas, mashed
- 2 cups all-purpose flour
- 3 eggs

Directions:

1. Sift the flour, baking soda, salt, cinnamon and ginger. Combine it with the shredded coconut.
2. Mix the almond butter and sugar in a container until creamy.
3. Stir in the eggs, one at a time, then put in the vanilla, bananas and canola oil. Stir thoroughly to mix.
4. Fold in the flour mixture then pour the batter in a 9-inch round cake pan coated with baking paper.
5. Pre-heat the oven and bake at 350F for about forty-five minutes or until it rises significantly and starts to appear golden-brown.
6. Let the cake cool in the pan before you serve.

Nutritional Content of One Serving:

Calories: 388 ‖ Fat: 18.8g ‖ Protein: 8.3g ‖ Carbohydrates: 49.8g

ALMOND APPLE CAKE

Total Time Taken: 1 ¼ hours
Yield: 10 Servings

Ingredients:

- ¼ teaspoon salt
- ½ cup whole milk

- ¾ cup all-purpose flour
- ¾ cup butter, softened
- 1 cup almond flour
- 1 cup white sugar
- 1 teaspoon baking powder
- 1 teaspoon vanilla extract
- 2 red apples, cored and diced
- 3 eggs

Directions:

1. Mix the butter with sugar in a container until creamy.
2. Put in the vanilla and eggs and mix thoroughly then fold in the almond flour, flour, salt and baking powder.
3. Put in the milk and stir lightly then fold in the apples.
4. Spoon the batter in a 8-inch round cake pan coated with baking paper and preheat your oven and bake at 350F for forty minutes or until it rises significantly and seems golden.
5. Let the cake cool in the pan before you serve.

Nutritional Content of One Serving:

Calories: 294 ‖ Fat: 17.1g ‖ Protein: 3.9g ‖ Carbohydrates: 33.7g

ALL BUTTER CAKE

Total Time Taken: 1 ½ hours
Yield: 14 Servings
Ingredients:

Cake:

- ¼ teaspoon salt
- ½ cup whole milk
- 1 cup butter, softened
- 1 cup white sugar
- 1 teaspoon vanilla extract
- 2 cups all-purpose flour
- 2 teaspoons baking powder
- 4 eggs

Frosting:

- 1 cup butter, softened
- 1 teaspoon vanilla extract
- 2 cups powdered sugar

Directions:

1. To prepare the cake, combine the butter, sugar and vanilla in a container until fluffy and creamy.
2. Put in the eggs, one at a time then mix in the milk.
3. Fold in the flour, baking powder and salt then spoon the batter in a 9-inch round cake pan coated with baking paper.
4. Pre-heat the oven and bake at 350F for about forty minutes.
5. Let the cake cool in the pan then cut it in half along the length.
6. For the frosting, combine the butter, sugar and vanilla in a container until fluffy and pale.
7. Use half of the buttercream to fill the cake and the half that is left over to frost the cake.
8. Serve the cake fresh or chilled.

Nutritional Content of One Serving:

Calories: 443 ‖ Fat: 28.0g ‖ Protein: 4.0g ‖ Carbohydrates: 45.9g

BONUS: MUFFINS AND CUPCAKES

ZUCCHINI CHOCOLATE MUFFINS

Total Time Taken: 1 hour
Yield: 12 Servings
Ingredients:

- 1 teaspoon baking soda
- 1 egg
- 1 cup grated zucchinis
- 1 ½ cups all-purpose flour
- ¾ cup white sugar
- ½ teaspoon salt
- ½ teaspoon cinnamon powder
- ½ cup walnuts, chopped
- ½ cup cocoa powder
- ½ cup canola oil
- ¼ cup buttermilk

Directions:

1. Mix the flour, cocoa powder, sugar, baking soda, cinnamon and salt in a container.
2. Stir in the egg, canola oil, buttermilk and zucchinis then fold in the walnuts.
3. Pour the batter in a muffin tin lined using muffin papers of your choice and preheat your oven and bake at 350F for about twenty minutes or until it rises significantly and becomes aromatic.
4. Let the muffins cool in the pan before you serve.

Nutritional Content of One Serving:

Calories: 233 ‖ Fat: 13.2g ‖ Protein: 4.2g ‖ Carbohydrates: 27.5g

ZUCCHINI CARROT MUFFINS

Total Time Taken: 1 hour
Yield: 12 Servings
Ingredients:

- ¼ cup maple syrup
- ¼ teaspoon salt
- ½ cup brown rice flour
- ½ cup canola oil
- ½ cup golden raisins
- ½ teaspoon cinnamon powder
- 1 ½ teaspoons baking powder
- 1 cup almond flour
- 1 cup grated carrots
- 1 cup grated zucchinis
- 1 egg

Directions:

1. Mix the flours, salt, baking powder and cinnamon in a container.
2. Stir in the canola oil, maple syrup and egg and stir for a few seconds to mix.
3. Fold in the carrots, zucchinis and raisins then spoon the batter in a muffin tin covered with muffin papers.
4. Pre-heat the oven and bake at 350F for about twenty minutes or until a toothpick inserted into them comes out dry.

These muffins taste best chilled.

Nutritional Content of One Serving:

Calories: 164 ‖ Fat: 10.8g ‖ Protein: 1.8g ‖ Carbohydrates: 16.3g

ZESTY PISTACHIO MUFFINS

Total Time Taken: 1 hour
Yield: 12 Servings
Ingredients:

- ¼ cup canola oil

- ¼ cup plain yogurt
- ¼ teaspoon salt
- 1 cup all-purpose flour
- 1 cup fresh raspberries
- 1 cup ground pistachio
- 1 cup white sugar
- 1 teaspoon baking powder
- 1 teaspoon vanilla extract
- 3 eggs

Directions:

1. Mix the eggs and sugar in a container until volume increases to twice what it was.
2. Put in the oil, vanilla and yogurt and mix thoroughly.
3. Fold in the remaining ingredients then spoon the batter in a muffin tin covered with muffin papers.
4. Preheat your oven and bake the muffins at 350F for about twenty minutes or until it rises significantly and starts to appear golden-brown.
5. Let cool in the pan before you serve.

Nutritional Content of One Serving:

Calories: 184 ‖ Fat: 6.7g ‖ Protein: 3.3g ‖ Carbohydrates: 28.8g

YOGURT VANILLA BERRY MUFFINS

Total Time Taken: 1 hour
Yield: 12 Servings
Ingredients:

- ¼ cup canola oil
- ¼ teaspoon salt
- ½ teaspoon baking soda
- 1 ¾ cups all-purpose flour
- 1 cup Greek yogurt
- 1 cup mixed berries
- 1 tablespoon vanilla extract
- 1 teaspoon baking powder
- 2 eggs

Directions:

1. Mix the eggs, oil, yogurt and vanilla in a container.
2. Put in the flour, salt, baking powder and baking soda and stir for a few seconds to mix just until incorporated.
3. Fold in the berries then spoon the batter in a muffin tin covered with muffin papers.
4. Pre-heat the oven and bake at 350F for about twenty minutes or until a toothpick inserted into them comes out dry.
5. Let cool in the pan before you serve.

Nutritional Content of One Serving:

Calories: 140 ‖ Fat: 5.8g ‖ Protein: 4.6g ‖ Carbohydrates: 16.4g

YOGURT BLACKBERRY MUFFINS

Total Time Taken: 1 hour
Yield: 12 Servings
Ingredients:

- ¼ teaspoon salt
- ½ cup butter, melted
- ½ cup heavy cream
- 1 cup blackberries
- 1 cup white sugar
- 1 teaspoon vanilla extract
- 2 cups all-purpose flour
- 2 egg whites
- 2 eggs
- 2 teaspoons baking powder

Directions:

1. Mix the flour, baking powder and salt in a container.
2. Whip the eggs, egg whites, vanilla and sugar until fluffy and pale.
3. Put in the butter and mix thoroughly then mix in the cream.
4. Fold in the flour then put in the blackberries.
5. Spoon the batter in a muffin tin covered with muffin papers.
6. Pre-heat the oven and bake at 350F for about twenty minutes or until it rises significantly and starts to appear golden-brown.

7. Let the muffins cool to room temperature before you serve.

Nutritional Content of One Serving:

Calories: 244 ‖ Fat: 10.5g ‖ Protein: 4.0g ‖ Carbohydrates: 34.4g

WHOLESOME BLUEBERRY MUFFINS

Total Time Taken: 1 hour
Yield: 12 Servings
Ingredients:

- ¼ cup wheat bran
- ½ cup butter, melted
- ½ cup milk
- ½ teaspoon salt
- 1 cup all-purpose flour
- 1 cup fresh blueberries
- 1 cup whole wheat flour
- 2 eggs
- 2 tablespoons orange marmalade
- 2 teaspoons baking powder

Directions:

1. Mix the flours, bran, baking powder and salt in a container.
2. Put in the butter, eggs, milk and marmalade then fold in blueberries.
3. Spoon the batter in a muffin tin covered with muffin papers and preheat your oven and bake at 350F for about twenty minutes or until it rises significantly and starts to appear golden-brown.

These muffins taste best chilled.

Nutritional Content of One Serving:

Calories: 213 ‖ Fat: 10.7g ‖ Protein: 4.5g ‖ Carbohydrates: 25.9g

WHOLEMEAL MUFFINS

Total Time Taken: 1 hour
Yield: 12 Servings
Ingredients:

- ¼ cup canola oil
- ½ cup white sugar
- ½ cup whole wheat flour
- ½ teaspoon salt
- 1 ½ cups all-purpose flour
- 1 cup milk
- 1 egg
- 2 tablespoons chia seeds
- 2 tablespoons hemp seeds
- 2 teaspoons baking powder

Directions:

1. Mix the flour, wheat flour, baking powder, salt, chia seeds and hemp seeds.
2. Put in the sugar, egg, milk and canola oil and stir for a few seconds to mix.
3. Spoon the batter into a muffin tin covered with muffin papers and preheat your oven and bake at 350F for about twenty minutes or until a golden-brown colour is achieved and it rises significantly.

These muffins taste best chilled.

Nutritional Content of One Serving:

Calories: 182 ‖ Fat: 6.9g ‖ Protein: 4.2g ‖ Carbohydrates: 25.9g

WHOLE WHEAT STRAWBERRY MUFFINS

Total Time Taken: 1 hour
Yield: 12 Servings
Ingredients:

- 2 eggs
- 2 cups whole wheat flour
- 2 bananas, mashed
- 1 teaspoon vanilla extract

- 1 teaspoon baking soda
- 1 teaspoon baking powder
- 1 cup strawberries, sliced
- ½ cup light brown sugar
- ½ cup canola oil
- ½ cup applesauce

Directions:

1. Mix the eggs, applesauce, canola oil, bananas, sugar and vanilla in a container.
2. Put in the flour, baking soda and baking powder and stir swiftly to combine.
3. Fold in the strawberries then spoon the batter in a muffin tin coated with baking muffin papers.
4. Preheat your oven and bake the muffins at 350F for about twenty minutes or until a toothpick inserted into them comes out dry.

These muffins taste best chilled.

Nutritional Content of One Serving:

Calories: 217 ‖ Fat: 10.1g ‖ Protein: 3.4g ‖ Carbohydrates: 28.7g

WHOLE WHEAT BANANA MUFFINS

Total Time Taken: 1 hour
Yield: 12 Servings
Ingredients:

- ¼ cup canola oil
- ¼ teaspoon cinnamon powder
- ¼ teaspoon salt
- ½ cup light brown sugar
- 1 cup buttermilk
- 2 bananas, mashed
- 2 cups whole wheat flour
- 2 eggs
- 2 teaspoons baking powder

Directions:

1. Mix the dry ingredients in a container.
2. Put in the remaining ingredients, all at once, and stir for a few seconds to mix with a whisk.
3. Pour the batter in a muffin tin coated with baking muffin papers and preheat your oven and bake at 350F for about twenty minutes or until a toothpick inserted into them comes out dry.
4. Let cool down before you serve.

Nutritional Content of One Serving:

Calories: 176 ‖ Fat: 5.7g ‖ Protein: 4.0g ‖ Carbohydrates: 27.7g

WHITE CHOCOLATE PUMPKIN CUPCAKES

Total Time Taken: 1 ½ hours
Yield: 14 Servings
Ingredients:

Cupcakes:

- ¼ cup canola oil
- ½ cup dark chocolate chips
- ½ cup light brown sugar
- ½ cup milk
- ½ teaspoon baking soda
- ½ teaspoon cinnamon powder
- ½ teaspoon ground cardamom
- ½ teaspoon ground ginger
- ½ teaspoon salt
- 1 cup pumpkin puree
- 1 teaspoon baking powder
- 1 teaspoon vanilla extract
- 2 cups all-purpose flour
- 2 eggs

Frosting:

- 1 cup heavy cream

- 1 teaspoon vanilla extract
- 2 cups white chocolate chips
- 2 tablespoons butter

Directions:

1. To make the cupcakes, combine the flour, baking powder, baking soda, spices and salt in a container.
2. Mix the eggs and sugar in a container until fluffy and pale.
3. Put in the milk, pumpkin puree, canola oil and vanilla and mix thoroughly.
4. Fold in the flour mixture then spoon the batter in a muffin tin covered with muffin papers.
5. Pre-heat the oven and bake at 350F for about twenty minutes or until the cupcakes pass the toothpick test.
6. Let them cool in the pan.
7. To make the frosting, bring the cream to a boil. Turn off the heat and mix in the chocolate. Stir until melted and smooth.
8. Put in the vanilla and butter and mix thoroughly.
9. Let cool completely then whip the cream until fluffy and pale.
10. Top the cupcakes with the frosting and garnish with a dusting of cinnamon powder.

Nutritional Content of One Serving:

Calories: 336 ‖ Fat: 18.7g ‖ Protein: 5.1g ‖ Carbohydrates: 38.4g

WHITE CHOCOLATE PUMPKIN CUPCAKES

Total Time Taken: 1 ½ hours
Yield: 12 Servings
Ingredients:

Cupcakes:

- ¼ teaspoon ground cardamom
- ¼ teaspoon salt
- ½ cup butter, softened
- ½ cup buttermilk
- ½ teaspoon ground ginger

- 1 ½ cups all-purpose flour
- 1 cup pumpkin puree
- 1 teaspoon cinnamon powder
- 2 eggs
- 2 tablespoons canola oil
- 2/3 cup light brown sugar

Frosting:

- 1 cup heavy cream
- 2 cups white chocolate chips

Directions:

1. To make the cupcakes, combine the butter, oil and sugar in a container until fluffy and pale.
2. Put in the eggs and mix thoroughly then mix in the pumpkin puree and buttermilk.
3. Fold in the remaining ingredients then spoon the batter in a muffin tin covered with muffin papers.
4. Pre-heat the oven and bake at 350F for about twenty minutes or until it rises significantly and becomes aromatic.
5. Let cool in the pan completely.
6. To make the frosting, bring the cream to a boil in a saucepan. Turn off the heat and put in the chocolate. Stir until melted then let cool down.
7. Pipe the frosting over each cupcake and serve them fresh.

Nutritional Content of One Serving:

Calories: 385 ‖ Fat: 23.8g ‖ Protein: 5.1g ‖ Carbohydrates: 39.2g

WHITE CHOCOLATE LIME CUPCAKES

Total Time Taken: 1 ½ hours
Yield: 12 Servings
Ingredients:

Cupcakes:

- 3 eggs
- 1 teaspoon vanilla extract
- 1 tablespoon lime zest

- 1 tablespoon lime juice
- ½ cup buttermilk
- 1 ½ cups all-purpose flour
- ¼ cup cornstarch
- ½ teaspoon salt
- 1 teaspoon baking soda
- ½ cup white chocolate chips
- 2/3 cup butter, softened
- 2/3 cup light brown sugar

Frosting:

- ½ cup butter, softened
- 1 cup cream cheese, softened
- 1 tablespoon lime zest
- 2 cups powdered sugar

Directions:

1. To make the cupcakes, combine the butter and sugar in a container until pale and fluffy.
2. Put in the eggs, one at a time, then mix in the vanilla, lime zest and juice and buttermilk.
3. Fold in the flour, cornstarch, salt and baking soda then put in the chocolate chips.
4. Spoon the batter in a muffin tin covered with muffin papers and preheat your oven and bake at 350F for about twenty minutes until it rises significantly and starts to appear golden-brown.
5. Let them cool in the pan.
6. To make the frosting, combine the cream cheese and butter in a container until pale.
7. Put in the sugar and stir thoroughly until airy and light.
8. Stir in the lime zest then spoon the frosting over each cupcake.

These cupcakes taste best when fresh.

Nutritional Content of One Serving:

Calories: 462 || Fat: 28.3g || Protein: 5.5g || Carbohydrates: 48.0g

WALNUT BANANA MUFFINS

Total Time Taken: 1 hour
Yield: 12 Servings
Ingredients:

- ¼ cup butter, melted
- ½ cup light brown sugar
- ½ cup plain yogurt
- ½ cup walnuts, chopped
- ½ teaspoon salt
- 1 ½ teaspoons baking powder
- 1 cup all-purpose flour
- 1 cup ground walnuts
- 2 eggs
- 3 bananas, mashed

Directions:

1. Mix the bananas, sugar, eggs, yogurt and butter and mix thoroughly.
2. Fold in the flour, walnuts, salt and baking powder.
3. Fold in the walnuts then spoon the batter in a muffin tin covered with muffin papers and preheat your oven and bake at 350F for about twenty minutes or until it rises significantly and seems golden.

These muffins taste best chilled.

Nutritional Content of One Serving:

Calories: 236 ‖ Fat: 14.1g ‖ Protein: 6.7g ‖ Carbohydrates: 23.2g

VODKA CUPCAKES

Total Time Taken: 1 ½ hours
Yield: 12 Servings
Ingredients:

Cupcakes:

- ¼ cup vodka
- ¼ teaspoon salt

- ½ cup white sugar
- 1 cup heavy cream
- 1 teaspoon vanilla extract
- 2 cups all-purpose flour
- 2 eggs
- 2 teaspoons baking powder

Frosting:

- 1 cup butter, softened
- 1 tablespoon heavy cream
- 2 ½ cups powdered sugar

Topping:

- ¼ cup heavy cream
- ½ cup dark chocolate chips
- 2 tablespoons vodka

Directions:

1. To make the cupcakes, combine the cream, eggs, vodka, sugar and vanilla in a container.
2. Stir in the flour, baking powder and salt and stir swiftly to combine.
3. Spoon the batter in a muffin tin covered with muffin papers and preheat your oven and bake at 350F for about twenty minutes or until it rises significantly and starts to appear golden-brown.
4. Let cool down in the pan.
5. To make the frosting, combine the butter in a container until pale. Put in the sugar and mix on high speed until fluffy and light.
6. Stir in the cream and mix for a few more minutes.
7. Pipe the frosting over each cupcake.
8. For the topping, melt the chocolate and cream together in a heatproof container over a hot water bath.
9. Turn off the heat and put in the vodka. Let cool down then sprinkle it over the frosted cupcakes.

These cupcakes taste best when fresh.

Nutritional Content of One Serving:

Calories: 439 ‖ Fat: 22.7g ‖ Protein: 3.9g ‖ Carbohydrates: 53.3g

VEGAN CHOCOLATE MUFFINS

Total Time Taken: 1 hour
Yield: 12 Servings
Ingredients:

- ¼ cup cocoa powder
- ½ cup almond flour
- ½ cup dark chocolate chips
- 1 ½ cups all-purpose flour
- 1 ½ teaspoons baking powder
- 1 cup coconut milk
- 1 cup coconut sugar
- 1 teaspoon vanilla extract
- 1/3 cup coconut oil, melted

Directions:

1. Mix the flours, cocoa powder, baking powder and sugar in a container.
2. Put in the rest of the ingredient and stir for a few seconds to mix.
3. Fold in the chocolate chips then spoon the batter in a muffin tin coated with baking muffin papers.
4. Pre-heat the oven and bake at 350F for about twenty minutes or until a toothpick inserted into the center of a muffin comes out clean.

These muffins taste best chilled.

Nutritional Content of One Serving:

Calories: 251 ‖ Fat: 13.1g ‖ Protein: 3.0g ‖ Carbohydrates: 33.9g

VEGAN BLUEBERRIES MUFFINS

Total Time Taken: 1 hour
Yield: 12 Servings
Ingredients:

- ¼ teaspoon salt
- ½ cup canola oil
- ½ cup soy yogurt

- ¾ cup light brown sugar
- 1 cup almond milk
- 1 cup blueberries
- 1 teaspoon vanilla extract
- 2 cups all-purpose flour
- 2 tablespoons ground flaxseeds
- 2 teaspoons baking powder

Directions:

1. Mix the flour, baking powder, salt and sugar in a container.
2. Stir in the flaxseeds then put in the canola oil, almond milk, soy yogurt and vanilla.
3. Fold in the blueberries then spoon the batter in a muffin tin covered with muffin papers.
4. Pre-heat the oven and bake at 350F for about twenty minutes or until a toothpick inserted into them comes out dry.

These muffins taste best chilled.

Nutritional Content of One Serving:

Calories: 259 ‖ Fat: 14.7g ‖ Protein: 3.3g ‖ Carbohydrates: 29.4g

VANILLA CUPCAKES WITH MAPLE FROSTING

Total Time Taken: 1 ½ hours
Yield: 10 Servings
Ingredients:

Cupcakes:

- ½ cup butter, softened
- ½ cup whole milk
- ½ teaspoon salt
- ¾ cup white sugar
- 1 ½ cups all-purpose flour
- 1 teaspoon baking powder
- 1 teaspoon vanilla extract

- 3 eggs

Frosting:

- 1 cup butter, softened
- 1 teaspoon vanilla extract
- 2 cups powdered sugar

Directions:

1. To make the cupcakes, combine the butter and sugar until fluffy and pale.
2. Put in the vanilla then mix in the eggs and mix thoroughly.
3. Fold in the flour, salt and baking powder, alternating it with the milk.
4. Spoon the batter in a muffin tin covered with muffin papers.
5. Pre-heat the oven and bake at 350F for about twenty minutes or until a toothpick inserted into them comes out dry.
6. To make the frosting, combine the butter in a container until fluffy. Put in the sugar and continue mixing until airy and pale.
7. Put in the vanilla then spoon the frosting in a pastry bag and top the cupcakes with it.

Nutritional Content of One Serving:

Calories: 491 ‖ Fat: 29.5g ‖ Protein: 4.3g ‖ Carbohydrates: 54.2g

VANILLA CUPCAKES WITH CHOCOLATE BUTTERCREAM

Total Time Taken: 1 ½ hours
Yield: 14 Servings
Ingredients:

Cupcakes:

- 2 cups all-purpose flour
- ¼ teaspoon salt
- 2 teaspoons baking powder
- 1 cup butter, softened
- 2 eggs
- 1 cup milk
- 1 tablespoon vanilla extract

- 2/3 cup white sugar

Frosting:

- ½ cup white sugar
- 1 cup butter, softened
- 1 cup dark chocolate chips, melted
- 1 teaspoon vanilla extract
- 2 egg whites

Directions:

1. To make the cupcakes, combine the flour, sugar, salt and baking powder in a container. Put in the butter and stir until grainy.
2. Stir in the eggs, milk and vanilla and stir for a few seconds to mix.
3. Spoon the batter in a muffin tin covered with muffin papers and preheat your oven and bake at 350F for about twenty minutes or until a toothpick inserted into them comes out dry.
4. Let the cupcakes cool in the pan.
5. To make the frosting, combine the egg whites and sugar in a container. Place over a hot
6. water bath and keep over heat until the sugar has melted.
7. Turn off the heat and whip for about five to seven minutes until shiny and fluffy.
8. Put in the butter and mix for at least two minutes until fluffy and creamy.
9. Stir in the chocolate and mix briefly then pipe the buttercream over each cupcake.

These cupcakes taste best when fresh.

Nutritional Content of One Serving:

Calories: 424 ‖ Fat: 29.8g ‖ Protein: 4.6g ‖ Carbohydrates: 37.5g

TURKISH DELIGHT MUFFINS

Total Time Taken: 1 hour
Yield: 12 Servings
Ingredients:

- ¼ teaspoon salt
- ½ cup canola oil

- ½ cup sour cream
- ½ cup white sugar
- 1 cup Turkish delight, diced
- 1 teaspoon baking powder
- 1 teaspoon vanilla extract
- 2 cups all-purpose flour
- 4 eggs

Directions:

1. Mix the eggs and sugar in a container until fluffy and light.
2. Put in the vanilla, oil and sour cream and mix thoroughly.
3. Fold in the flour, salt and baking powder then mix in the Turkish delight.
4. Spoon the batter in a muffin tin covered with muffin papers.
5. Pre-heat the oven and bake at 350F for about twenty minutes or until a golden-brown colour is achieved and it rises significantly.

These muffins taste best chilled.

Nutritional Content of One Serving:

Calories: 239 ‖ Fat: 13.0g ‖ Protein: 4.3g ‖ Carbohydrates: 27.0g

THE ULTIMATE VANILLA CUPCAKES

Total Time Taken: 1 ½ hours
Yield: 12 Servings
Ingredients:

Cupcakes:

- ½ teaspoon salt
- 1 cup buttermilk
- 1 tablespoon vanilla extract
- 2 cups all-purpose flour
- 2 eggs
- 2 teaspoons baking powder
- 2/3 cup butter, softened
- 2/3 cup white sugar

Frosting:

- ½ teaspoon salt
- 1 cup butter, softened
- 1 cup white sugar
- 1 teaspoon vanilla extract
- 4 egg whites

Directions:

1. To make the cupcakes, combine the flour, salt, baking powder and sugar in a container.
2. Put in the butter and stir until grainy.
3. In a container, mix the eggs, buttermilk and vanilla and mix thoroughly. Pour over the flour and mix for a minute on high speed.
4. Spoon the batter in a muffin tin lined with baking muffins papers.
5. Pre-heat the oven and bake at 350F for about twenty minutes or until it rises significantly and starts to appear golden-brown.
6. Let cool in the pan.
7. To make the frosting, combine the egg whites and sugar in a container and place over hot water bath. Keep on heat and stir until heated and the sugar has melted.
8. Turn off the heat and mix for about five to seven minutes until fluffy and thickened, shiny and firm.
9. Put in the butter, all at once, and stir thoroughly for a couple of minutes. It will curdle up at first then it will come back together.
10. Put in the vanilla and mix thoroughly.
11. Spoon the frosting in a pastry bag and top the cupcakes with it.

These are best enjoyed fresh.

Nutritional Content of One Serving:

Calories: 435 ‖ Fat: 26.7g ‖ Protein: 5.2g ‖ Carbohydrates: 45.4g

THE ULTIMATE BLUEBERRY MUFFINS

Total Time Taken: 1 hour
Yield: 12 Servings
Ingredients:

- 2 eggs

- ½ cup canola oil
- 1 teaspoon lemon zest
- 1 teaspoon vanilla extract
- 2 cups all-purpose flour
- ½ teaspoon salt
- 2 teaspoons baking powder
- 1 cup sour cream
- 1 cup fresh blueberries
- 2/3 cup white sugar

Directions:

1. Mix the eggs and sugar in a container until fluffy and pale.
2. Put in the oil and vanilla and mix thoroughly.
3. Fold in the flour, salt and baking powder then put in the sour cream and mix for a minute on high speed.
4. Fold in the blueberries then spoon the batter in a muffin tin covered with muffin papers.
5. Preheat your oven and bake the muffins at 350F for about twenty minutes or until it rises significantly and seems golden.
6. Let them cool before you serve or storing.

Nutritional Content of One Serving:

Calories: 258 ‖ Fat: 14.1g ‖ Protein: 3.8g ‖ Carbohydrates: 30.1g

SWEET RASPBERRY CORN MUFFINS

Total Time Taken: 1 hour
Yield: 12 Servings
Ingredients:

- ¼ cup canola oil
- ¼ teaspoon salt
- ½ cup apricot jam
- ½ cup white sugar
- 1 ½ cups all-purpose flour
- 1 cup buttermilk
- 1 cup raspberries
- 1 cup yellow cornmeal

- 1 tablespoon orange zest
- 2 eggs
- 2 teaspoons baking powder

Directions:

1. Mix the flour, cornmeal, sugar, baking powder and salt in a container.
2. Stir in the buttermilk, apricot jam, oil, orange zest and eggs and mix thoroughly.
3. Fold in the raspberries then spoon the batter in a muffin tin coated with baking muffin papers.
4. Preheat your oven and bake the muffins at 350F for about twenty minutes or until it rises significantly and starts to appear golden-brown.
5. Let the muffins cool in the pan before you serve.

Nutritional Content of One Serving:

Calories: 223 ‖ Fat: 6.1g ‖ Protein: 4.3g ‖ Carbohydrates: 39.4g

SWEET POTATO ZUCCHINI MUFFINS

Total Time Taken: 1 hour
Yield: 12 Servings
Ingredients:

- ¼ cup canola oil
- ¼ cup heavy cream
- ¼ cup light brown sugar
- ¼ teaspoon salt
- ½ teaspoon baking soda
- 1 cup grated zucchinis
- 1 cup sweet potato puree
- 1 teaspoon baking powder
- 1 teaspoon orange zest
- 2 cups all-purpose flour
- 2 eggs

Directions:

1. Mix the sweet potato puree, zucchinis, sugar, cream, eggs, oil and orange zest in a container.

2. Put in the dry ingredients and stir for a few seconds to mix using a spatula.
3. Spoon the batter in a muffin tin lined using muffin papers of your choice.
4. Pre-heat the oven and bake at 350F for about twenty minutes or until well risen and a toothpick inserted into the center of a muffin comes out clean.
5. Let cool in the pan before you serve.

Nutritional Content of One Serving:

Calories: 170 ‖ Fat: 6.5g ‖ Protein: 3.6g ‖ Carbohydrates: 24.5g

SWEET POTATO MAPLE MUFFINS

Total Time Taken: 1 hour
Yield: 12 Servings
Ingredients:

- ¼ teaspoon salt
- ½ teaspoon all-spice powder
- ½ teaspoon cinnamon powder
- ½ teaspoon ground ginger
- 1 ½ teaspoons baking powder
- 1 cup light brown sugar
- 1 cup milk
- 1 cup sweet potato puree
- 1 teaspoon vanilla extract
- 2 cups all-purpose flour
- 2/3 cup canola oil
- 3 eggs

Directions:

1. Mix the flour, salt, baking powder, cinnamon, ginger and all-spice powder in a container.
2. Put in the remaining ingredients and mix thoroughly then pour the batter in a muffin tin covered with muffin papers.
3. Preheat your oven and bake the muffins at 350F for about twenty minutes or until a golden-brown colour is achieved and fragrant.
4. Let cool down before you serve.

Nutritional Content of One Serving:

Calories: 278 ‖ Fat: 13.9g ‖ Protein: 4.6g ‖ Carbohydrates: 34.2g

SWEET POTATO CUPCAKES

Total Time Taken: 1 ½ hours
Yield: 16 Servings
Ingredients:

Cupcakes:

- ½ cup mini marshmallows
- ½ teaspoon ground ginger
- ½ teaspoon salt
- 1 ½ cups sweet potato puree
- 1 cup butter, softened
- 1 cup white sugar
- 1 teaspoon cinnamon powder
- 1 teaspoon vanilla extract
- 2 cups all-purpose flour
- 2 teaspoons baking powder
- 3 eggs

Frosting:

- ½ cup butter, softened
- 1 cup cream cheese
- 2 cups powdered sugar

Directions:

1. To make the cupcakes, sift the flour, baking powder, salt, cinnamon and ginger in a container.
2. In a separate container, combine the butter and sugar until fluffy and pale.
3. Put in the eggs and mix thoroughly then mix in the pumpkin puree and vanilla.
4. Fold in the flour then spoon the batter in 12 muffin cups coated with baking muffin papers.
5. Preheat your oven and bake the cupcakes at 350F for about twenty minutes or until it rises significantly and becomes aromatic.

6. To make the frosting, combine all the ingredients in a container until pale and fluffy.
7. Spoon the frosting in a pastry bag and top the cupcakes with it.

Nutritional Content of One Serving:

Calories: 408 ‖ Fat: 23.4g ‖ Protein: 4.5g ‖ Carbohydrates: 47.1g

SWEET POTATO CINNAMON CUPCAKES

Total Time Taken: 1 ½ hours
Yield: 16 Servings
Ingredients:

Cupcakes:

- ¼ teaspoon salt
- ½ cup crushed pineapple
- ½ teaspoon baking powder
- ½ teaspoon baking soda
- ½ teaspoon ground ginger
- 1 cup butter, softened
- 1 cup light brown sugar
- 1 teaspoon cinnamon powder
- 2 cups all-purpose flour
- 2 cups sweet potato puree

Frosting:

- 1 cup butter, softened
- 1 teaspoon cinnamon powder
- 2 cups powdered sugar, sifted

Directions:

1. To make the cupcakes, sift the flour, spices, baking soda, baking powder and salt in a container.
2. Mix the butter and sugar in a separate container until fluffy and creamy. Put in the sweet potato puree and pineapple then fold in the flour.
3. Spoon the batter in a muffin tin lined with paper liners.
4. Pre-heat the oven and bake at 350F for about twenty minutes or until a toothpick inserted into them comes out dry.

5. Let the cupcakes cool down.
6. To make the frosting, combine the butter in a container until creamy.
7. Put in the sugar, ½ cup at a time, and stir thoroughly until fluffy and pale.
8. Pipe the frosting on top of each cupcake and drizzle with cinnamon powder.

These cupcakes taste best when fresh.

Nutritional Content of One Serving:

Calories: 388 ‖ Fat: 23.3g ‖ Protein: 2.5g ‖ Carbohydrates: 44.0g

SULTANA BRAN MUFFINS

Total Time Taken: 1 hour
Yield: 12 Servings
Ingredients:

- ¼ cup olive oil
- ¼ cup shredded coconut
- ½ cup sultanas
- ½ teaspoon cinnamon powder
- ½ teaspoon salt
- ¾ cup plain yogurt
- ¾ cup wheat bran
- 1 ¼ cups all-purpose flour
- 1 egg
- 1 teaspoon vanilla extract
- 2 bananas, mashed
- 2 teaspoons baking powder

Directions:

1. Mix the wheat bran, flour, baking powder, coconut, cinnamon and salt in a container.
2. Stir in the bananas, egg, yogurt, olive oil and vanilla.
3. Fold in the sultanas then spoon the batter in a muffin tin covered with muffin papers.
4. Pre-heat the oven and bake at 350F for about twenty minutes or until it rises significantly and starts to appear golden-brown.

These muffins taste best chilled.

Nutritional Content of One Serving:

Calories: 137 ‖ Fat: 5.7g ‖ Protein: 3.5g ‖ Carbohydrates: 19.7g

SUGARY PUMPKIN MUFFINS

Total Time Taken: 1 hour
Yield: 12 Servings
Ingredients:

- 2 teaspoons baking powder
- 2 eggs
- 2 cups all-purpose flour
- 1 teaspoon ground ginger
- 1 teaspoon cinnamon powder
- ¾ cup light brown sugar
- ¾ cup butter, softened
- ½ teaspoon salt
- ½ cup white sugar
- ½ cup pumpkin puree
- ¼ cup buttermilk

Directions:

1. Mix the butter and brown sugar in a container until pale and light.
2. Put in the eggs, buttermilk and pumpkin puree and mix thoroughly.
3. Fold in the flour, salt, baking powder and ginger then spoon the batter in a muffin tin lined using muffin papers of your choice.
4. Mix the sugar and cinnamon in a container. Top each muffin with the cinnamon sugar and preheat your oven and bake at 350F for about twenty minutes or until it rises significantly and starts to appear golden-brown.

These muffins taste best chilled.

Nutritional Content of One Serving:

Calories: 261 ‖ Fat: 12.5g ‖ Protein: 3.5g ‖ Carbohydrates: 34.8g

SUGARY BLUEBERRY MUFFINS

Total Time Taken: 1 hour
Yield: 12 Servings
Ingredients:

- ¼ cup milk
- ¼ teaspoon salt
- ½ cup butter, melted
- ½ cup Demerara sugar
- ½ cup white sugar
- 1 ½ cups blueberries
- 1 teaspoon vanilla extract
- 2 cups all-purpose flour
- 2 eggs
- 2 teaspoons baking powder

Directions:

1. Mix the butter and sugar in a container. Put in the eggs and mix thoroughly then mix in the milk and vanilla.
2. Fold in the flour, baking powder and salt then put in the blueberries.
3. Spoon the batter in a muffin tin covered with muffin papers.
4. Top each muffin with Demerara sugar and preheat your oven and bake at 350F for about twenty minutes or until it rises significantly and starts to appear golden-brown.
5. Let cool down before you serve.

Nutritional Content of One Serving:

Calories: 223 ‖ Fat: 8.8g ‖ Protein: 3.5g ‖ Carbohydrates: 33.5g

SUGARLESS MUFFINS

Total Time Taken: 1 hour
Yield: 12 Servings
Ingredients:

- 3 bananas, mashed
- 2 eggs

- 1 teaspoon baking soda
- 1 ½ cups all-purpose flour
- ½ cup walnuts, chopped
- ½ cup applesauce
- ¼ teaspoon salt

Directions:

1. Mix the eggs, bananas and applesauce in a container.
2. Put in the flour, salt and baking soda then mix in the walnuts.
3. Spoon the batter in a muffin tin lined using muffin papers of your choice and preheat your oven and bake at 350F for about twenty minutes.

These muffins taste best chilled.

Nutritional Content of One Serving:

Calories: 130 ‖ Fat: 4.1g ‖ Protein: 4.1g ‖ Carbohydrates: 20.4g

STREUSEL CRANBERRY MUFFINS

Total Time Taken: 1 hour
Yield: 12 Servings
Ingredients:

Muffins:

- ¼ teaspoon salt
- ½ cup butter, melted
- ½ cup milk
- 1 ½ cups all-purpose flour
- 1 ½ teaspoons baking powder
- 1 cup fresh cranberries
- 1 cup ground pecans
- 1 cup white sugar
- 1 teaspoon vanilla extract
- 2 eggs

Streusel:

- ¼ cup butter, chilled
- ½ cup whole wheat flour

- 2 tablespoons brown sugar

Directions:

1. For the muffins, combine the butter, eggs, milk, sugar and vanilla in a container.
2. Stir in the flour, salt, pecans and baking powder then fold in the cranberries.
3. Spoon the batter in a muffin tin covered with muffin papers.
4. For the streusel, combine all the ingredients in a container until grainy.
5. Top each muffin with streusel and preheat your oven and bake at 350F for about twenty minutes or until a golden-brown colour is achieved and it rises significantly.

These muffins taste best chilled.

Nutritional Content of One Serving:

Calories: 276 ‖ Fat: 13.5g ‖ Protein: 3.7g ‖ Carbohydrates: 36.0g

STREUSEL BANANA MUFFINS

Total Time Taken: 1 ¼ hours
Yield: 12 Servings
Ingredients:

Muffins:

- 2 tablespoons wheat bran
- 2 eggs
- 2 bananas, mashed
- 1 teaspoon vanilla extract
- 1 teaspoon baking soda
- 1 ¾ cups all-purpose flour
- ½ teaspoon cinnamon powder
- ½ cup buttermilk
- ¼ teaspoon salt

Streusel:

- 2 tablespoons dark brown sugar
- 1 cup all-purpose flour
- ½ cup butter, chilled

- ¼ teaspoon salt

Directions:

1. For the muffins, combine the bananas, eggs and buttermilk in a container.
2. Stir in the flour, wheat bran, baking soda, salt and cinnamon and stir for a few seconds to mix.
3. Spoon the batter in a muffin tin covered with muffin papers.
4. For the streusel, combine all the ingredients in a container until grainy.
5. Top each muffin with the streusel and preheat your oven and bake at 350F for about twenty minutes or until a golden-brown colour is achieved and it rises significantly.

These muffins taste best chilled.

Nutritional Content of One Serving:

Calories: 212 ‖ Fat: 8.9g ‖ Protein: 4.6g ‖ Carbohydrates: 28.8g

STRAWBERRY MUFFINS

Total Time Taken: 1 hour
Yield: 12 Servings
Ingredients:

- ½ cup canola oil
- ½ cup milk
- ½ teaspoon salt
- ¾ cup white sugar
- ¾ cup whole wheat flour
- 1 ½ cups strawberries, sliced
- 1 cup all-purpose flour
- 1 teaspoon baking soda
- 2 eggs

Directions:

1. Mix the flours, baking soda and salt in a container.
2. Put in the canola oil, sugar, eggs and mix and stir for a few seconds to mix.
3. Fold in the strawberries then spoon the batter in 12 muffin cups covered with muffin papers.

4. Preheat your oven and bake the muffins at 350F for about twenty minutes or until a golden-brown colour is achieved and it rises significantly.
5. Let cool down before you serve.

Nutritional Content of One Serving:

Calories: 215 ‖ Fat: 10.3g ‖ Protein: 3.3g ‖ Carbohydrates: 28.3g

STRAWBERRY MATCHA MUFFINS

Total Time Taken: 1 hour
Yield: 12 Servings
Ingredients:

- 2 eggs
- 2 cups all-purpose flour
- 1 teaspoon baking powder
- 1 tablespoon matcha powder
- 1 cup white sugar
- 1 cup strawberries, sliced
- 1 cup milk
- ½ teaspoon baking soda
- ½ cup butter, melted
- ¼ teaspoon salt

Directions:

1. Mix the flour, matcha powder, baking powder, baking soda and salt in a container.
2. Stir in the butter, eggs, milk and sugar and give it a quick whisk.
3. Fold in the strawberries then spoon the batter in a muffin tin lined using muffin papers of your choice.
4. Pre-heat the oven and bake at 350F for about twenty minutes or until a toothpick inserted into them comes out dry.
5. Serve the muffins chilled or store them in an airtight container.

Nutritional Content of One Serving:

Calories: 233 ‖ Fat: 9.1g ‖ Protein: 3.9g ‖ Carbohydrates: 35.2g

STRAWBERRY CHIA SEED MUFFINS

Total Time Taken: 1 hour
Yield: 12 Servings
Ingredients:

- ½ teaspoon salt
- 1 ¾ cups all-purpose flour
- 1 cup plain yogurt
- 1 cup strawberries, sliced
- 1/3 cup canola oil
- 2 eggs
- 2 tablespoons chia seeds
- 2 teaspoons baking powder
- 4 tablespoons milk

Directions:

1. Mix the dry ingredients in a container.
2. Put in the oil, yogurt, eggs and milk and stir for a few seconds to mix.
3. Fold in the strawberries then spoon the batter in 12 muffin cups covered with muffin papers.
4. Preheat your oven and bake the muffins at 350F for a couple of minutes or until it rises significantly and starts to appear golden-brown.
5. Let the muffins cool to room temperature before you serve.

Nutritional Content of One Serving:

Calories: 178 ‖ Fat: 9.0g ‖ Protein: 5.3g ‖ Carbohydrates: 18.7g

STRAWBERRY AND CREAM CUPCAKES

Total Time Taken: 1 ½ hours
Yield: 12 Servings

Ingredients:

- ½ cup butter, softened
- ½ teaspoon salt
- 1 ½ cups all-purpose flour
- 1 ½ cups heavy cream, whipped

- 1 ½ teaspoons baking powder
- 1 cup fresh strawberries, sliced
- 1 teaspoon vanilla extract
- 2/3 cup white sugar
- 3 eggs

Directions:

1. Mix the butter and sugar in a container until fluffy and pale.
2. Put in the eggs, one at a time, then mix in the vanilla.
3. Fold in the flour, salt and baking powder then put in the strawberries.
4. Spoon the batter into 12 muffin cups covered with muffin papers and preheat your oven and bake at 350F for about twenty minutes or until a golden-brown colour is achieved and it rises significantly.
5. Let cool down then put whipped cream on top of each cupcake.

The cupcakes taste best chilled.

Nutritional Content of One Serving:

Calories: 239 ‖ Fat: 14.5g ‖ Protein: 3.5g ‖ Carbohydrates: 24.8g

SPRINKLES CHOCOLATE CUPCAKES

Total Time Taken: 1 ½ hours
Yield: 12 Servings
Ingredients:

Cupcakes:

- ¼ cup cocoa powder
- ½ cup butter, softened
- ½ teaspoon salt
- 1 ½ cups all-purpose flour
- 1 ½ teaspoons baking powder
- 1 cup white sugar
- 1 cup whole milk
- 1 teaspoon vanilla extract
- 2 eggs

Frosting:

- ½ cup dark chocolate chips, melted
- 1 cup butter, softened
- 2 cups powdered sugar

Directions:

1. To make the cupcakes, combine the butter and sugar in a container until creamy and pale.
2. Put in the eggs and vanilla and mix thoroughly then mix in the flour, cocoa powder, salt and baking powder, alternating them with milk.
3. Spoon the batter in a muffin tin coated with baking muffin papers.
4. Preheat your oven and bake the cupcakes at 350F for about twenty minutes or until a toothpick inserted into them comes out dry.
5. To make the frosting, combine the butter and sugar in a container until fluffy and pale. Put in the melted and cooled chocolate.
6. Garnish the cupcakes with frosting and serve them fresh.

Nutritional Content of One Serving:

Calories: 452 ‖ Fat: 26.1g ‖ Protein: 4.1g ‖ Carbohydrates: 54.2g

SPICY PINEAPPLE MUFFINS

Total Time Taken: 1 hour
Yield: 12 Servings
Ingredients:

- ¼ teaspoon cayenne pepper
- ½ cup light brown sugar
- ½ cup sultanas
- ½ teaspoon ground ginger
- ½ teaspoon salt
- 1 ½ cups all-purpose flour
- 1 teaspoon baking soda
- 1/3 cup canola oil
- 2 cups crushed pineapple
- 2 eggs

Directions:

1. Mix the flour, salt, baking soda and sultanas in a container.

2. Put in the cayenne pepper and ginger then mix in the remaining ingredients and stir for a few seconds to mix.
3. Spoon the batter in a muffin tin covered with muffin papers.
4. Pre-heat the oven and bake at 350F for about twenty minutes or until it rises significantly and starts to appear golden-brown.
5. Serve the muffins chilled or store them in an airtight container.

Nutritional Content of One Serving:

Calories: 162 ‖ Fat: 7.0g ‖ Protein: 2.7g ‖ Carbohydrates: 22.7g

SPICED ZUCCHINI MUFFINS

Total Time Taken: 1 ¼ hours
Yield: 12 Servings

Ingredients:

- ¼ cup honey
- ¼ teaspoon salt
- ½ cup almond butter, softened
- ½ teaspoon cinnamon
- ½ teaspoon ground cardamom
- ½ teaspoon ground ginger
- 1 ½ cups all-purpose flour
- 1 ½ teaspoons baking powder
- 1 apple, cored and grated
- 1 cup grated zucchinis
- 1 teaspoon vanilla extract
- 2 eggs

Directions:

1. Mix the zucchinis, apples, almond butter, honey, eggs and vanilla in a container.
2. Stir in the flour, cinnamon, ginger, cardamom, salt and baking powder.
3. Spoon the batter in a muffin tin covered with muffin papers and preheat your oven and bake at 350F for about twenty minutes or until a toothpick inserted into them comes out dry.
4. Let cool down before you serve.

Nutritional Content of One Serving:

Calories: 167 ‖ Fat: 6.8g ‖ Protein: 4.9g ‖ Carbohydrates: 22.6g

SPICED STRAWBERRY CUPCAKES

Total Time Taken: 1 ½ hours
Yield: 12 Servings Ingredients

Cupcakes:

- ¼ teaspoon ground nutmeg
- ½ cup canola oil
- ½ teaspoon baking powder
- ½ teaspoon cinnamon powder
- ½ teaspoon ground ginger
- ½ teaspoon salt
- 1 cup all-purpose flour
- 1 cup milk
- 1 cup white sugar
- 1 egg
- 1 teaspoon apple cider vinegar
- 1 teaspoon baking soda

Frosting:

- ½ cup strawberry puree
- 1 cup butter, softened
- 2 ½ cups powdered sugar

Directions:

1. To make the cupcakes, combine all the ingredients in a container and stir for a few seconds to mix.
2. Pour the batter in a muffin tin coated with baking muffin papers.
3. Pre-heat the oven and bake at 350F for about twenty minutes or until it rises significantly and becomes aromatic.
4. Let cool in the pan.
5. To make the frosting, combine the butter in a container until fluffy. Put in the sugar and mix thoroughly then mix in the strawberry puree.
6. Top each cupcake with the frosting and serve them fresh.

Nutritional Content of One Serving:

Calories: 435 ‖ Fat: 25.4g ‖ Protein: 2.4g ‖ Carbohydrates: 51.8g

SPICED CUPCAKES WITH CREAM CHEESE CUPCAKES

Total Time Taken: 1 ½ hours
Yield: 16 Servings
Ingredients:

Cupcakes:

- ¼ teaspoon salt
- ½ cup butter, softened
- ½ teaspoon grated ginger
- ½ teaspoon ground cardamom
- ¾ cup plain yogurt
- 1 ½ teaspoons baking powder
- 1 cup white sugar
- 1 teaspoon cinnamon powder
- 1 teaspoon vanilla extract
- 2 cups all-purpose flour
- 2 eggs

Frosting:

- ½ cup butter, softened
- 1 cup cream cheese
- 3 cups powdered sugar

Directions:

1. To make the cupcakes, combine the butter and sugar in a container until fluffy and pale.
2. Put in the eggs and mix thoroughly then mix in the yogurt and vanilla.
3. Fold in the flour, spices, salt and baking powder then spoon the batter in a muffin tin covered with muffin papers.
4. Preheat your oven and bake the cupcakes at 350F for about twenty minutes.

5. To make the frosting, combine the cream cheese and butter in a container until creamy.
6. Put in the sugar, progressively, and stir thoroughly for a few minutes until fluffy.
7. Pipe the frosting over each cupcake and serve the cupcakes fresh.

Nutritional Content of One Serving:

Calories: 361 ‖ Fat: 17.4g ‖ Protein: 4.2g ‖ Carbohydrates: 48.4g

SPELT ZUCCHINI MUFFINS

Total Time Taken: 1 ¼ hours
Yield: 12 Servings

Ingredients:

- ¼ cup coconut oil, melted
- ¼ cup maple syrup
- ¼ teaspoon salt
- ½ cup plain yogurt
- 1 cup grated zucchinis
- 1 cup spelt flour
- 1 cup whole wheat flour
- 1 egg
- 1 teaspoon baking soda
- 1 teaspoon vanilla extract
- 2 tablespoons chia seeds

Directions:

1. Mix the spelt flour, wheat flour, salt and baking soda in a container.
2. Put in the remaining ingredients and stir for a few seconds to mix.
3. Spoon the batter in a muffin tin covered with muffin papers and preheat your oven and bake at 350F for about twenty minutes or until a toothpick inserted in the center comes out clean.
4. Let cool down before you serve.

Nutritional Content of One Serving:

Calories: 169 ‖ Fat: 6.9g ‖ Protein: 4.7g ‖ Carbohydrates: 22.5g

SOUR CREAM MUFFINS

Total Time Taken: 1 hour
Yield: 12 Servings
Ingredients:

- ¼ teaspoon salt
- 1 ½ cups sour cream
- 1 cup butter, softened
- 1 teaspoon vanilla extract
- 2 cups all-purpose flour
- 2 teaspoons baking powder

Directions:

1. Mix the butter, vanilla and sour cream in a container until creamy.
2. Put in the flour, salt and baking powder then spoon the batter in a muffin tin coated with baking muffin papers.
3. Pre-heat the oven and bake at 350F for about twenty minutes or until it rises significantly and starts to appear golden-brown.

These muffins taste best chilled.

Nutritional Content of One Serving:

Calories: 275 ‖ Fat: 21.6g ‖ Protein: 3.2g ‖ Carbohydrates: 17.6g

SNICKERS CUPCAKES

Total Time Taken: 1 ½ hours
Yield: 16 Servings
Ingredients:

Cupcakes:

- ¼ teaspoon salt
- ½ cup canola oil
- ½ cup cocoa powder
- 1 ½ cups all-purpose flour
- 1 ½ teaspoons baking powder
- 1 cup buttermilk

- 1 cup light brown sugar
- 1 teaspoon lemon juice
- 1 teaspoon vanilla extract
- 4 eggs

Frosting:

- ½ cup butter, softened
- ½ cup cocoa powder
- ½ cup smooth peanut butter
- 1 teaspoon vanilla extract
- 2 cups powdered sugar

Topping:

- 6 snickers, chopped

Directions:

1. To make the cupcakes, combine the eggs and sugar in a container until fluffy and pale. Put in the oil and mix thoroughly then mix in the buttermilk, lemon juice and vanilla.
2. Fold in the flour, cocoa powder, salt and baking powder then spoon the batter in a muffin tin covered with muffin papers.
3. Preheat your oven and bake the cupcakes at 350F for about twenty minutes or until a toothpick inserted into them comes out dry.
4. Let cool down in the pan.
5. To make the frosting, combine the butter and peanut butter in a container until fluffy.
6. Stir in the sugar, cocoa powder and vanilla and stir thoroughly for a few additional minutes until fluffy and well mixed.
7. Pipe the frosting over each cupcake and serve them fresh.

Nutritional Content of One Serving:

Calories: 399 ‖ Fat: 22.4g ‖ Protein: 7.4g ‖ Carbohydrates: 45.8g

SNICKERDOODLE MUFFINS

Total Time Taken: 1 hour
Yield: 12 Servings
Ingredients:

Muffins:

- ½ cup butter, softened
- ½ cup light brown sugar
- ½ teaspoon ground ginger
- ½ teaspoon salt
- 1 teaspoon vanilla extract
- 2 ¼ cups all-purpose flour
- 2 eggs
- 2 teaspoons baking powder
- 2/3 cup buttermilk

Topping:

- 1 teaspoon cinnamon powder
- 2/3 cup white sugar

Directions:

1. For the muffins, combine the butter and sugar in a container.
2. Put in the vanilla and eggs and mix thoroughly then mix in the buttermilk.
3. Fold in the flour, salt, baking powder and ginger then spoon the batter in a muffin tin covered with muffin papers.
4. Pre-heat the oven and bake at 350F for about twenty minutes or until a golden-brown colour is achieved and it rises significantly.
5. For the topping, combine the ingredients in a container.
6. While the muffins are still hot, immerse them in cinnamon sugar.

These muffins taste best chilled.

Nutritional Content of One Serving:

Calories: 236 ‖ Fat: 8.8g ‖ Protein: 3.9g ‖ Carbohydrates: 36.1g

SIMPLE LAVENDER CUPCAKES

Total Time Taken: 1 ½ hours
Yield: 12 Servings
Ingredients:

Cupcakes:

- ½ cup butter, softened

- 2 eggs
- 1 teaspoon vanilla extract
- 1 teaspoon lavender buds
- ½ cup heavy cream
- 1 ½ cups all-purpose flour
- ½ teaspoon salt
- 1 teaspoon baking powder
- 2/3 cup white sugar

Frosting:

- ¾ cup butter, softened
- 1 cup cream cheese
- 2 ½ cups powdered sugar

Directions:

1. To make the cupcakes, combine the butter and sugar in a container until creamy and pale.
2. Put in the eggs and vanilla and mix thoroughly. Stir in the lavender buds and cream and mix thoroughly.
3. Fold in the flour, salt and baking powder then spoon the batter in a muffin tin coated with baking muffin papers.
4. Pre-heat the oven and bake at 350F for about twenty minutes or until it rises significantly and starts to appear golden-brown.
5. Let them cool in the pan.
6. To make the frosting, combine the cream cheese and butter in a container until fluffy.
7. Put in the sugar and stir thoroughly for five minutes on high speed.
8. Top each cupcake with the frosting and serve them fresh.

Nutritional Content of One Serving:

Calories: 466 ‖ Fat: 28.8g ‖ Protein: 4.4g ‖ Carbohydrates: 49.8g

S'MORES CHOCOLATE CUPCAKES

Total Time Taken: 1 ½ hours
Yield: 12 Servings
Ingredients:

Cupcakes:

- ¼ cup cocoa powder
- ¼ teaspoon salt
- ½ cup butter, softened
- ½ cup buttermilk
- ½ cup white sugar
- ½ teaspoon baking soda
- 1 ½ cups all-purpose flour
- 1 teaspoon baking powder
- 1 teaspoon vanilla extract
- 2 eggs
- 2 tablespoons dark brown sugar

Frosting:

- ½ cup crushed graham crackers
- ½ cup dark chocolate chips
- ½ cup white sugar
- 1 teaspoon vanilla extract
- 2 egg whites

Directions:

1. To make the cupcakes, combine the flour, cocoa powder, baking soda, baking powder and salt in a container.
2. Mix the butter and sugars in a separate container until creamy and pale.
3. Put in the eggs, buttermilk and vanilla and mix thoroughly.
4. Fold in the flour mixture then spoon the batter in a muffin tin coated with baking muffin papers.
5. Pre-heat the oven and bake at 350F for about twenty minutes or until it is aromatic and appears golden brown.
6. Let cool in the pan.
7. To make the frosting, combine the egg whites, sugar and vanilla in a container and place over a hot water bath. Keep on heat until the sugar is melted.
8. Turn off the heat and whip using an electric mixer until fluffy, stiff and shiny.
9. Apply the frosting on top of each cupcake and drizzle with chocolate chips and graham crackers.

These cupcakes taste best when fresh.

Nutritional Content of One Serving:

Calories: 255 ‖ Fat: 10.6g ‖ Protein: 4.4g ‖ Carbohydrates: 37.9g

RICOTTA LEMON MUFFINS

Total Time Taken: 1 hour

Yield: 12 Servings

Ingredients:

- ¼ cup butter, melted
- ½ cup white sugar
- ½ teaspoon salt
- 1 ½ cups all-purpose flour
- 1 cup ricotta cheese
- 1 tablespoon lemon zest
- 1 teaspoon baking powder
- 1 teaspoon vanilla extract
- 2 eggs

Directions:

1. Mix the cheese, butter, eggs, vanilla and sugar in a container.
2. Put in the flour, salt and baking powder and mix using a spatula.
3. Spoon the batter in a muffin tin covered with muffin papers.
4. Preheat your oven and bake the muffins at 350F for about twenty minutes or until a golden-brown colour is achieved and it rises significantly.

These muffins taste best chilled.

Nutritional Content of One Serving:

Calories: 163 ‖ Fat: 6.3g ‖ Protein: 4.9g ‖ Carbohydrates: 21.7g

RICH CHOCOLATE MUFFINS

Total Time Taken: 1 hour

Yield: 12 Servings

Ingredients:

- ¼ teaspoon baking soda

- ½ cup canola oil
- ½ cup cocoa powder
- ½ teaspoon salt
- ¾ cup milk
- 1 ¾ cups all-purpose flour
- 1 cup white sugar
- 1 teaspoon baking powder
- 1 teaspoon vanilla extract
- 2 eggs

Directions:

1. Mix the flour, cocoa powder, salt, baking powder, baking soda and salt in a container.
2. Put in the remaining ingredients and mix thoroughly.
3. Pour the batter in a muffin tin covered with muffin papers.
4. Preheat your oven and bake the muffins at 350F for about twenty minutes.
5. Let them cool in the pan before you serve or storing.

Nutritional Content of One Serving:

Calories: 237 ‖ Fat: 10.8g ‖ Protein: 3.9g ‖ Carbohydrates: 33.6g

RHUBARB STREUSEL MUFFINS

Total Time Taken: 1 ¼ hours
Yield: 12 Servings
Ingredients: **Muffins:**

- 2 rhubarb stalks, sliced
- 2 eggs
- 2 cups all-purpose flour
- 1 teaspoon baking powder
- 1 cup buttermilk
- ½ teaspoon baking soda
- ½ cup light brown sugar
- ¼ teaspoon salt
- ¼ cup white sugar
- ¼ cup canola oil

Streusel:

- 2 tablespoons white sugar
- 1 pinch salt
- 1 cup all-purpose flour
- ½ cup butter, melted

Directions:

1. For the muffins, combine the flour, baking soda, baking powder, salt and sugars in a container.
2. Put in the eggs, buttermilk and oil and mix using a spatula.
3. Fold in the rhubarb then spoon the batter in a muffin tin coated with baking muffin papers.
4. For the streusel, combine the ingredients in a container until grainy. Spread the
5. streusel over each muffin.
6. Pre-heat the oven and bake at 350F for about twenty minutes or until a golden-brown colour is achieved and it rises significantly.

These muffins taste best chilled.

Nutritional Content of One Serving:

Calories: 289 ‖ Fat: 13.4g ‖ Protein: 5.0g ‖ Carbohydrates: 37.6g

RHUBARB STRAWBERRY MUFFINS

Total Time Taken: 1 hour
Yield: 12 Servings
Ingredients:

- ½ cup light brown sugar
- ½ cup milk
- ½ cup whole wheat flour
- ½ teaspoon salt
- 1 cup all-purpose flour
- 1 cup strawberries, sliced
- 1 rhubarb stalk, sliced
- 1 teaspoon baking soda
- 1 teaspoon vanilla extract

- 3 eggs

Directions:

1. Mix the flours, salt and baking soda in a container.
2. Whip the eggs and sugar in a container until pale and light.
3. Put in the milk and vanilla and mix thoroughly.
4. Fold in the flour mixture then put in the rhubarb and strawberries.
5. Spoon the batter in a muffin tin covered with muffin papers.
6. Preheat your oven and bake the muffins at 350F for about twenty minutes or until a golden-brown colour is achieved and fluffy.

These muffins taste best chilled.

Nutritional Content of One Serving:

Calories: 106 ‖ Fat: 1.5g ‖ Protein: 3.5g ‖ Carbohydrates: 19.6g

RED WINE FIG CUPCAKES

Total Time Taken: 1 ½ hours
Yield: 16 Servings
Ingredients:

Cupcakes:

- ½ cup red wine
- 1 teaspoon vanilla extract
- 2 eggs
- 1 ½ cups all-purpose flour
- ¼ cup cocoa powder
- ¼ teaspoon salt
- 1 ½ teaspoons baking powder
- 2/3 cup butter, softened
- 2/3 cup white sugar

Frosting:

- ½ cup butter, softened
- 1 cup cream cheese
- 2 cups powdered sugar

Fig compote:

- ¼ cup light brown sugar
- ½ cup red wine
- 1 cinnamon stick
- 6 figs, halved

Directions:

1. To make the cupcakes, combine the butter and sugar in a container until creamy. Put in the wine, vanilla and eggs and mix thoroughly.
2. Fold in the flour, cocoa powder, salt and baking powder and mix using a spatula.
3. Spoon the batter in a muffin tin covered with muffin papers.
4. Pre-heat the oven and bake at 350F for about twenty minutes or until it rises significantly and seems golden.
5. Let the muffins cool to room temperature in the pan.
6. To make the frosting, combine the butter and cream cheese in a container until fluffy and pale.
7. Put in the sugar, ½ cup at a time and stir thoroughly for 4-5 minutes until airy.
8. Pipe the frosting over each cupcake.
9. For the compote, mix the ingredients in a saucepan and cook for about five minutes just until softened.
10. Top rach cupcake with the compote and serve fresh.

Nutritional Content of One Serving:

Calories: 353 ‖ Fat: 19.4g ‖ Protein: 3.6g ‖ Carbohydrates: 40.9g

RED VELVET CUPCAKES

Total Time Taken: 1 ½ hours
Yield: 12 Servings
Ingredients:

Cupcakes:

- ½ cup buttermilk
- ½ teaspoon baking soda
- ½ teaspoon salt
- ½ teaspoon white wine vinegar
- ¾ cup canola oil

- ¾ cup white sugar
- 1 ½ cups all-purpose flour
- 1 egg
- 1 tablespoon cocoa powder
- 1 teaspoon baking powder
- 1 teaspoon red food coloring
- 1 teaspoon vanilla extract

Frosting:

- ½ cup butter, softened
- 1 cup cream cheese, softened
- 1 teaspoon vanilla extract
- 3 cups powdered sugar

Directions:

1. To make the cupcakes, sift the flour, baking soda, baking powder and cocoa powder in a container.
2. In a separate container, combine the oil, egg and sugar until creamy and pale.
3. Stir in the buttermilk, red food coloring, vinegar and vanilla extract.
4. Spoon the batter in a muffin tin covered with muffin papers.
5. Preheat your oven and bake the cupcakes at 350F for about twenty minutes or until well risen.
6. Let the cupcakes cool in the pan.
7. To make the frosting, combine the cream cheese and butter in a container. Put in the vanilla and mix thoroughly then mix in the sugar and continue mixing for five minutes until fluffy and airy.
8. Spoon the frosting in a pastry bag and top the cupcakes with it.

These cupcakes taste best when fresh.

Nutritional Content of One Serving:

Calories: 489 ‖ Fat: 28.7g ‖ Protein: 4.0g ‖ Carbohydrates: 55.9g

RED BERRIES CREAM CHEESE MUFFINS

Total Time Taken: 1 hour
Yield: 12 Servings
Ingredients:

- ¼ teaspoon salt
- ½ cup butter, softened
- ½ cup heavy cream
- ½ cup sliced almonds
- ¾ cup white sugar
- 1 ½ cups all-purpose flour
- 1 cup cream cheese
- 1 cup mixed berries
- 1 teaspoon vanilla extract
- 2 eggs
- 2 teaspoons baking powder

Directions:

1. Mix the cream cheese and butter in a container.
2. Put in the sugar and eggs and mix thoroughly. Stir in the cream and vanilla and stir thoroughly until blended.
3. Fold in the flour, salt and baking powder then put in the berries.
4. Spoon the batter in a muffin tin covered with muffin papers.
5. Top the muffins with sliced almonds and preheat your oven and bake at 350F for about twenty minutes or until it rises significantly and starts to appear golden-brown.
6. Let cool down before you serve.

Nutritional Content of One Serving:

Calories: 298 ‖ Fat: 19.2g ‖ Protein: 5.1g ‖ Carbohydrates: 27.9g

RASPBERRY WHITE CHOCOLATE MUFFINS

Total Time Taken: 1 hour
Yield: 12 Servings
Ingredients:

- ½ cup sour cream

- ½ cup white chocolate chips
- ½ cup white sugar
- ½ teaspoon salt
- 1 ½ cups all-purpose flour
- 1 cup fresh raspberries
- 1 teaspoon baking powder
- 1 teaspoon vanilla extract
- 2 eggs

Directions:

1. Mix the eggs, sugar and vanilla in a container until fluffy and creamy.
2. Put in the sour cream and mix thoroughly then fold in the dry ingredients.
3. Stir in using a spatula the raspberries and white chocolate.
4. Spoon the batter in a muffin tin covered with muffin papers and preheat your oven and bake at 350F for about twenty minutes or until a golden-brown colour is achieved and it rises significantly.
5. Let the muffins cool to room temperature before you serve.

Nutritional Content of One Serving:

Calories: 164 ‖ Fat: 5.2g ‖ Protein: 3.4g ‖ Carbohydrates: 26.4g

RASPBERRY VANILLA CUPCAKES

Total Time Taken: 1 ½ hours
Yield: 12 Servings
Ingredients:

Cupcakes:

- ½ cup butter, softened
- 2 eggs
- 1 tablespoon vanilla extract
- 1 ½ cups all-purpose flour
- ¼ teaspoon salt
- 1 ½ teaspoons baking powder
- 2/3 cup white sugar
- 2/3 cup buttermilk

Frosting:

- 1 cup fresh raspberries
- 1 teaspoon vanilla extract
- 2 cups heavy cream
- 2 tablespoons powdered sugar

Directions:

1. To make the cupcakes, combine the butter and sugar until pale and light.
2. Put in the eggs, one at a time, then mix in the vanilla and buttermilk.
3. Fold in the flour, salt and baking powder then spoon the batter in a muffin tin covered with muffin papers.
4. Preheat your oven and bake the cupcakes at 350F for about twenty minutes until a toothpick inserted into them comes out dry then allow them to cool down.
5. To make the frosting, whip the cream in a container until airy and puffed up. Put in the sugar and vanilla and mix thoroughly.
6. Drop a dollop of cream over each cupcake and garnish with a few raspberries.

Nutritional Content of One Serving:

Calories: 267 ‖ Fat: 16.1g ‖ Protein: 3.6g ‖ Carbohydrates: 27.3g

RASPBERRY RICOTTA MUFFINS

Total Time Taken: 1 hour
Yield: 12 Servings
Ingredients:

- 2 eggs
- 1/3 cup white sugar
- 1/3 cup butter, softened
- 1 teaspoon vanilla extract
- 1 cup raspberries
- 1 ¾ cups all-purpose flour
- 1 ½ teaspoons baking powder
- ¾ cup ricotta cheese
- ½ cup milk
- ¼ teaspoon salt

Directions:

1. Mix the butter, cheese, sugar, eggs, milk and vanilla in a container.
2. Put in the flour, salt and baking powder then spoon the batter in a muffin tin covered with muffin papers.
3. Top each muffin with fresh raspberries and preheat your oven and bake at 350F for about twenty minutes or until it rises significantly and starts to appear golden-brown.

These muffins taste best chilled.

Nutritional Content of One Serving:

Calories: 176 ‖ Fat: 7.5g ‖ Protein: 5.1g ‖ Carbohydrates: 22.4g

RASPBERRY MUFFINS

Total Time Taken: 1 hour
Yield: 10 Servings
Ingredients:

- ½ cup milk
- ½ cup white sugar
- ½ teaspoon salt
- 1 ½ teaspoons baking powder
- 1 cup fresh raspberries
- 1 teaspoon vanilla extract
- 2 cups all-purpose flour
- 3 eggs

Directions:

1. Mix the flour, sugar, salt and baking powder in a container.
2. Put in the remaining ingredients and mix using a spatula.
3. Spoon the batter in a muffin tin covered with muffin papers.
4. Preheat your oven and bake the muffins at 350F for about twenty minutes or until a toothpick inserted into the center of a muffin comes out clean.

These muffins taste best chilled.

Nutritional Content of One Serving:

Calories: 162 ‖ Fat: 1.9g ‖ Protein: 4.8g ‖ Carbohydrates: 31.7g

RASPBERRY JAM MUFFINS

Total Time Taken: 1 hour

Yield: 12 Servings

Ingredients:

- 2 eggs
- 1 teaspoon vanilla extract
- ½ cup canola oil
- ¾ cup sour cream
- 1 ¾ cups all-purpose flour
- ½ teaspoon salt
- 1 ½ teaspoons baking powder
- 1 cup raspberry jam
- 2/3 cup white sugar

Directions:

1. Mix the eggs and sugar in a container until fluffy and pale, minimum volume increases to twice what it was.
2. Stir in the vanilla, sour cream and oil and mix thoroughly.
3. Fold in the flour, salt and baking powder then spoon the batter in a muffin tin coated with baking muffin papers.
4. Spoon the jam over each muffin and preheat your oven and bake at 350F for about twenty minutes or until a golden-brown colour is achieved and it rises significantly.
5. Let cool down before you serve.

Nutritional Content of One Serving:

Calories: 298 ‖ Fat: 13.0g ‖ Protein: 3.4g ‖ Carbohydrates: 43.4g

RAISIN BRAN MUFFINS

Total Time Taken: 1 hour

Yield: 10 Servings

Ingredients:

- ¼ teaspoon ground ginger
- ½ cup canola oil

- ½ cup golden raisins
- ½ cup white sugar
- ½ cup whole milk
- ½ teaspoon cinnamon powder
- ½ teaspoon salt
- 1 cup all-purpose flour
- 1 cup wheat bran
- 2 eggs
- 2 teaspoons baking powder

Directions:

1. Mix the flour, wheat bran, baking powder, salt, cinnamon, ginger and raisins in a container.
2. Put in the sugar, canola oil and eggs, as well as milk and mix using a spatula.
3. Spoon the batter in a muffin tin covered with muffin papers.
4. Preheat your oven and bake the muffins at 350F for about twenty minutes or until it rises significantly and starts to appear golden-brown.
5. These muffins taste best cold.

Nutritional Content of One Serving:

Calories: 235 ‖ Fat: 12.6g ‖ Protein: 3.9g ‖ Carbohydrates: 30.1g

QUINOA PEACH MUFFINS

Total Time Taken: 1 hour
Yield: 12 Servings
Ingredients:

- 2 cups all-purpose flour
- 1 teaspoon vanilla extract
- 1 teaspoon baking powder
- 1 egg
- 1 cup cooked quinoa
- 1 cup buttermilk
- ¾ cups light brown sugar
- ½ teaspoon baking soda
- ¼ teaspoon salt
- ¼ cup canola oil

Directions:

1. Mix the quinoa, canola oil, egg, buttermilk and vanilla in a container.
2. Stir in the sugar and mix thoroughly then put in the flour, salt, baking powder and baking soda.
3. Spoon the batter in a muffin tin covered with muffin papers.
4. Pre-heat the oven and bake at 350F for about twenty minutes or until well risen.
5. Let cool down before you serve.

Nutritional Content of One Serving:

Calories: 217 ‖ Fat: 6.1g ‖ Protein: 5.3g ‖ Carbohydrates: 35.1g

QUINOA CRANBERRY MUFFINS

Total Time Taken: 1 hour
Yield: 12 Servings
Ingredients:

- ¼ cup all-purpose flour
- ¼ cup butter, melted
- ¼ cup white sugar
- ¼ teaspoon salt
- ½ cup quinoa flour
- 1 cup cranberries
- 1 cup plain yogurt
- 1 cup whole wheat flour
- 2 eggs
- 2 tablespoons sunflower seeds
- 2 teaspoons baking powder

Directions:

1. Mix the flours, salt, baking powder, sunflower seeds in a container.
2. Put in the yogurt, eggs, sugar and butter and stir for a few seconds to mix.
3. Fold in the cranberries then spoon the batter in a muffin tin coated with baking muffin papers.
4. Pre-heat the oven and bake at 350F for about twenty minutes or until it rises significantly and seems golden.
5. Let cool down before you serve.

Nutritional Content of One Serving:

Calories: 149 ‖ Fat: 5.7g ‖ Protein: 5.2g ‖ Carbohydrates: 18.1g

QUICK COFFEE MUFFINS

Total Time Taken: 1 hour

Yield: 12 Servings

Ingredients:

- ¼ cup brewed espresso
- ¼ teaspoon salt
- ½ cup canola oil
- ½ cup hot water
- ½ teaspoon baking soda
- ¾ cup cocoa powder
- 1 ½ cups white sugar
- 1 ¾ cups all-purpose flour
- 1 cup buttermilk
- 1 teaspoon baking powder
- 1 teaspoon vanilla extract
- 2 eggs

Directions:

1. Mix the dry ingredients in a container.
2. Put in the remaining ingredients and stir for a few seconds to mix.
3. Pour the batter in a muffin tin covered with muffin papers and preheat your oven and bake at 350F for about twenty minutes or until a toothpick inserted into them comes out dry.
4. Let cool down before you serve.

Nutritional Content of One Serving:

Calories: 277 ‖ Fat: 10.9g ‖ Protein: 4.6g ‖ Carbohydrates: 44.1g

PURE VANILLA MUFFINS

Total Time Taken: 1 hour
Yield: 10 Servings
Ingredients:

- ¼ cup sour cream
- ½ cup canola oil
- ½ cup white sugar
- ½ teaspoon salt
- 1 ½ cups all-purpose flour
- 1 teaspoon baking powder
- 1 teaspoon vanilla extract
- 2 eggs

Directions:

1. Mix the eggs and sugar in a container until pale and light.
2. Put in the canola oil, vanilla and sour cream and mix thoroughly.
3. Fold in the flour, salt and baking powder then spoon the batter in a muffin tin covered with muffin papers.
4. Pre-heat the oven and bake at 350F for about twenty minutes or until it rises significantly and seems golden.

These muffins taste best chilled.

Nutritional Content of One Serving:

Calories: 229 ‖ Fat: 13.2g ‖ Protein: 3.2g ‖ Carbohydrates: 24.9g

PUMPKIN PECAN CRUNCH MUFFINS

Total Time Taken: 1 ¼ hours
Yield: 12 Servings
Ingredients:

Muffins:

- ¼ cup butter, chilled
- ¼ teaspoon salt
- ½ cup all-purpose flour
- ½ cup coconut milk Pecan crunch:
- ½ cup coconut oil, melted

- ½ cup ground pecans
- ½ cup light brown sugar
- ½ cup pecans, chopped
- 1 ½ cups all-purpose flour
- 1 cup pumpkin puree
- 1 teaspoon baking soda
- 1 teaspoon pumpkin pie spices
- 2 eggs
- 2 tablespoons light brown sugar

Directions:

1. For the muffins, combine the dry ingredients in a container.
2. Put in the remaining ingredients, all at once, and stir for a few seconds to mix just until incorporated.
3. Spoon the batter in a muffin tin coated with baking muffin papers.
4. For the pecan crunch, combine the ingredients in a container until sandy.
5. Spread the crunch over the muffins and preheat your oven and bake at 350F for about twenty minutes or until the top is crunchy and golden brown.
6. Let cool in the pan before you serve.

Nutritional Content of One Serving:

Calories: 274 ‖ Fat: 18.0g ‖ Protein: 3.8g ‖ Carbohydrates: 26.0g

PUMPKIN NUTELLA MUFFINS

Total Time Taken: 1 hour
Yield: 12 Servings
Ingredients:

- ¼ teaspoon salt
- ½ cup coconut oil, melted
- ½ cup Nutella
- ½ teaspoon ground ginger
- ⅓ teaspoon ground nutmeg
- 1 ½ cups pumpkin puree
- 1 cup white sugar
- 1 teaspoon baking powder
- 1 teaspoon baking soda

- 1 teaspoon cinnamon powder
- 1 teaspoon vanilla extract
- 2 cups all-purpose flour
- 2 eggs

Directions:

1. Mix the flour, sugar, baking powder, baking soda, salt, cinnamon, nutmeg and ginger.
2. Put in the eggs, vanilla, pumpkin puree and coconut oil and stir for a few seconds to mix.
3. Spoon the batter in a muffin tin covered with muffin papers.
4. Drop a spoonful of Nutella on top of each muffin then swirl it with a toothpick.
5. Pre-heat the oven and bake at 350F for about twenty minutes or until it rises significantly and starts to appear golden-brown.

These muffins taste best chilled.

Nutritional Content of One Serving:

Calories: 256 ‖ Fat: 11.1g ‖ Protein: 3.6g ‖ Carbohydrates: 37.2g

PUMPKIN CHOCOLATE CHIP MUFFINS

Total Time Taken: 1 hour
Yield: 12 Servings
Ingredients:

- 2 eggs
- 1 teaspoon vanilla extract
- 1 teaspoon baking soda
- 1 cup pumpkin puree
- 1 ½ cups all-purpose flour
- ½ teaspoon ground star anise
- ½ teaspoon ground ginger
- ½ teaspoon cinnamon powder
- ½ cup oat flour
- ½ cup dark chocolate chips
- ¼ teaspoon salt

- ¼ cup canola oil

Directions:

1. Mix the pumpkin puree, oil, eggs and vanilla in a container and mix thoroughly.
2. Fold in the flours, salt, baking soda and spices.
3. Spoon the batter in a muffin tin covered with muffin papers.
4. Preheat your oven and bake the muffins at 350F for about twenty minutes or until it rises significantly and starts to appear golden-brown.

These muffins taste best chilled.

Nutritional Content of One Serving:

Calories: 155 ‖ Fat: 7.1g ‖ Protein: 3.6g ‖ Carbohydrates: 19.8g

PUMPKIN APPLE STREUSEL MUFFINS

Total Time Taken: 1 ¼ hours
Yield: 14 Servings
Ingredients:

Muffins:

- ¼ cup canola oil
- ¼ teaspoon salt
- ½ cup oat flour
- 1 ¼ cups pumpkin puree
- 1 cup white sugar
- 1 teaspoon baking powder
- 1 teaspoon baking soda
- 1 teaspoon pumpkin pie spices
- 2 apples, peeled and diced
- 2 cups all-purpose flour
- 2 eggs

Streusel:

- ¼ cup butter
- ¼ cup rolled oats
- ½ cup all-purpose flour

- 1 pinch salt
- 2 tablespoons dark brown sugar

Directions:

1. For the muffins, combine the flours, sugar, baking soda, baking powder, salt and spices in a container.
2. Put in the pumpkin puree, eggs, canola oil and apples and stir for a few seconds to mix.
3. Spoon the batter in a muffin tin covered with muffin papers.
4. Pre-heat the oven and bake at 350F for about twenty minutes or until it rises completely and is aromatic.
5. Let cool down before you serve.

Nutritional Content of One Serving:

Calories: 252 ‖ Fat: 8.5g ‖ Protein: 4.1g ‖ Carbohydrates: 41.5g

PUMPKIN APPLE MUFFINS

Total Time Taken: 1 ¼ hours

Yield: 12 Servings

Ingredients:

- 2 red apples, cored and diced
- 2 eggs
- 1 teaspoon pumpkin pie spices
- 1 teaspoon baking soda
- 1 cup pumpkin puree
- 1 ½ cups whole wheat flour
- ½ teaspoon salt
- ½ teaspoon baking powder
- ½ cup light brown sugar
- ½ cup canola oil
- ½ cup all-purpose flour
- ¼ cup milk

Directions:

1. Mix the flours, baking soda, baking powder, salt and spices in a container.

2. Put in the eggs, pumpkin puree, milk, oil and sugar and stir for a few seconds to mix.
3. Fold in the apples then spoon the batter in a muffin tin covered with muffin papers.
4. Pre-heat the oven and bake at 350F for about twenty minutes or until it rises significantly and starts to appear golden-brown.

These muffins taste best chilled.

Nutritional Content of One Serving:

Calories: 215 ‖ Fat: 10.2g ‖ Protein: 3.6g ‖ Carbohydrates: 28.2g

PLUM WHOLE WHEAT MUFFINS

Total Time Taken: 1 hour
Yield: 12 Servings
Ingredients:

- ¼ cup all-purpose flour
- ¼ cup canola oil
- ½ cup buttermilk
- ½ teaspoon salt
- 1 ½ cups whole wheat flour
- 1 tablespoon chia seeds
- 1 teaspoon vanilla extract
- 2 eggs
- 2 teaspoons baking powder
- 4 plums, pitted and diced

Directions:

1. Mix the flours, baking powder, salt and chia seeds in a container.
2. Put in the remaining ingredients and stir for a few seconds to mix using a spatula.
3. Spoon the batter in a muffin tin covered with muffin papers.
4. Preheat your oven and bake the muffins at 350F for about twenty minutes or until it rises significantly and seems golden.

These muffins taste best chilled.

Nutritional Content of One Serving:

Calories: 142 ‖ Fat: 6.4g ‖ Protein: 3.8g ‖ Carbohydrates: 17.4g

PINK VELVET CUPCAKES

Total Time Taken: 1 ½ hours
Yield: 12 Servings
Ingredients:

Cupcakes:

- ¼ teaspoon red food coloring
- ½ cup sour cream
- ½ cup white sugar
- ½ teaspoon salt
- 1 ½ teaspoon baking powder
- 1 2/3 cups all-purpose flour
- 1 egg
- 1 teaspoon vanilla extract

Frosting:

- 1 cup butter, softened
- 1 teaspoon vanilla extract
- 2 cups powdered sugar

Directions:

1. To make the cupcakes, combine the egg and sugar until pale. Put in the vanilla and mix thoroughly then mix in the sour cream and food coloring.
2. Stir in the remaining ingredients and stir for a few seconds to mix.
3. Spoon the batter in 12 muffin cups covered with muffin papers.
4. Preheat your oven and bake the cupcakes at 350F for about twenty minutes or until the cupcake pass the toothpick test.
5. Let the cupcakes cool down.
6. To make the frosting, combine the butter until pale. Put in the sugar and stir thoroughly until blended.
7. Stir in the vanilla and mix thoroughly then spoon the buttercream in a pastry bag and pipe on each cupcake.

Nutritional Content of One Serving:

Calories: 336 ‖ Fat: 17.9g ‖ Protein: 2.7g ‖ Carbohydrates: 42.3g

PINK LEMONADE CUPCAKES

Total Time Taken: 1 ½ hours
Yield: 12 Servings
Ingredients:

Cupcakes:

- ¼ teaspoon salt
- ½ cup milk
- ¾ cup butter, softened
- 1 cup white sugar
- 1 drop red food coloring
- 1 egg white
- 1 tablespoon lemon zest
- 1 teaspoon vanilla extract
- 2 ½ cups all-purpose flour
- 2 eggs
- 2 tablespoons lemon juice
- 2 teaspoons baking powder

Frosting:

- 1 cup butter
- 1 drop red food coloring
- 2 cups powdered sugar

Directions:

1. To make the cupcakes, combine the butter and sugar in a container until fluffy and pale.
2. Put in the eggs and egg white and mix thoroughly.
3. Stir in the vanilla, lemon juice, lemon zest, milk and food colouring and mix thoroughly.
4. Put in the dry ingredients and fold them in using a spatula.
5. Spoon the batter in a muffin tin covered with muffin papers.
6. Pre-heat the oven and bake at 350F for about twenty minutes or until a golden-brown colour is achieved and it rises significantly.

7. Let cool in the pan.
8. To make the frosting, combine the butter in a container until fluffy. Put in the sugar and continue mixing for a few minutes on high speed.
9. Put in the food colouring then pipe the frosting over each cupcake.

The cupcakes taste best chilled.

Nutritional Content of One Serving:

Calories: 442 ‖ Fat: 24.1g ‖ Protein: 3.9g ‖ Carbohydrates: 54.6g

PINK COCONUT CUPCAKES

Total Time Taken: 1 ½ hours
Yield: 12 Servings
Ingredients:

Cupcakes:

- ½ cup butter, softened
- ½ cup shredded coconut
- ½ cup white sugar
- ½ teaspoon salt
- 1 ½ cups all-purpose flour
- 1 teaspoon baking powder
- 1 teaspoon vanilla extract
- 2 eggs
- 2/3 cup whole milk

Frosting:

- ½ teaspoon pink food coloring
- 1 cup butter, softened
- 2 cups powdered sugar
- 2 tablespoons heavy cream

Directions:

1. To make the cupcakes, combine the butter, sugar and vanilla in a container until fluffy and pale.
2. Put in the eggs and mix thoroughly then fold in the flour, salt, baking powder and coconut, alternating it with milk.

3. Spoon the batter in a muffin tin covered with muffin papers and preheat your oven and bake at 350F for about twenty minutes or until a golden-brown colour is achieved and it rises significantly.
4. Let the cupcakes cool down.
5. To make the frosting, combine the butter and sugar in a container until fluffy and pale.
6. Put in the cream and food colouring and continue mixing a few additional minutes until airy.
7. Spoon the frosting on top of each cupcake before you serve.

Nutritional Content of One Serving:

Calories: 410 Fat:26.4g ‖ Protein: 3.4g ‖ Carbohydrates: 41.7g

PERSIMMON MUFFINS

Total Time Taken: 1 hour
Yield: 12 Servings
Ingredients:

- ½ cup butter, melted
- ½ cup whole wheat flour
- ½ teaspoon cinnamon powder
- ½ teaspoon ground ginger
- ½ teaspoon salt
- ¾ cup buttermilk
- 1 ½ cups all-purpose flour
- 1 teaspoon vanilla extract
- 2 eggs
- 2 persimmon fruits, diced
- 2 teaspoons baking powder

Directions:

1. Mix the flours, salt, baking powder, ginger and cinnamon in a container.
2. Stir in the eggs, butter, buttermilk and vanilla and stir for a few seconds to mix.
3. Fold in the persimmon then spoon the batter in a muffin tin covered with muffin papers.

4. Pre-heat the oven and bake at 350F for about twenty minutes or until it rises significantly and starts to appear golden-brown.
5. Serve the muffins chilled or store them in an airtight container for maximum four days.

Nutritional Content of One Serving:

Calories: 182 ‖ Fat: 8.7g ‖ Protein: 3.8g ‖ Carbohydrates: 22.4g

PECAN PIE MUFFINS

Total Time Taken: 1 hour
Yield: 10 Servings
Ingredients:

- 2 eggs
- 1 teaspoon vanilla extract
- 1 cup light brown sugar
- 1 cup butter, melted
- 1 ½ cups pecans, chopped
- ½ cup all-purpose flour
- ¼ teaspoon salt

Directions:

1. Mix the eggs and sugar in a container until fluffy and volume increases to twice what it was.
2. Put in the vanilla and melted butter and mix thoroughly.
3. Fold in the flour, pecans and salt then spoon the batter in a muffin tin covered with muffin papers.
4. Pre-heat the oven and bake at 350F for about twenty minutes or until a golden-brown colour is achieved.

These muffins taste best chilled.

Nutritional Content of One Serving:

Calories: 264 ‖ Fat: 20.3g ‖ Protein: 2.1g ‖ Carbohydrates: 19.3g

PEAR AND GINGER MUFFINS

Total Time Taken: 1 hour
Yield: 12 Servings
Ingredients:

- ¼ teaspoon salt
- ½ cup buttermilk
- ½ cup canola oil
- ½ cup dark chocolate chips
- ½ cup light brown sugar
- 1 ½ cups all-purpose flour
- 1 teaspoon baking soda
- 1 teaspoon grated ginger
- 1 teaspoon vanilla extract
- 2 eggs
- 2 pears, cored and diced

Directions:

1. Mix the eggs and sugar in a container until fluffy and pale. Stir in the oil and mix thoroughly then put in the buttermilk and mix thoroughly.
2. Stir in the vanilla and ginger then fold in the flour, salt and baking powder.
3. Put in the pears and dark chocolate and stir lightly using a spatula.
4. Spoon the batter in a muffin tin covered with muffin papers and preheat your oven and bake at 350F for about twenty minutes or until it rises significantly and starts to appear golden-brown.

These muffins taste best chilled.

Nutritional Content of One Serving:

Calories: 220 ‖ Fat: 11.4g ‖ Protein: 3.4g ‖ Carbohydrates: 27.2g

PEANUT BUTTER BANANA CUPCAKES

Total Time Taken: 1 ½ hours
Yield: 12 Servings
Ingredients:

Cupcakes:

- ¼ teaspoon salt
- ½ cup canola oil
- ½ cup milk
- 1 ¾ cups all-purpose flour
- 1 egg
- 1 teaspoon baking soda
- 1 teaspoon vanilla extract
- 2 bananas, mashed

Frosting:

- ½ cup smooth peanut butter
- 1 cup cream cheese
- 1 cup powdered sugar

Directions:

1. To make the cupcakes, combine the bananas, canola oil, milk, egg and vanilla.
2. Stir in the flour, salt and baking soda then spoon the batter in a muffin tin covered with muffin papers.
3. Pre-heat the oven and bake at 350F for about twenty minutes or until it rises significantly and starts to appear golden-brown.
4. To make the frosting, combine all the ingredients in a container until creamy and fluffy.
5. Apply the frosting on top of each cupcake and serve them fresh.

Nutritional Content of One Serving:

Calories: 345 ‖ Fat: 22.1g ‖ Protein: 7.0g ‖ Carbohydrates: 31.5g

PEACHY MUFFINS

Total Time Taken: 1 hour
Yield: 12 Servings
Ingredients:

- ½ cup canola oil
- ½ cup plain yogurt
- ½ cup whole wheat flour

- ½ teaspoon salt
- ¾ cup white sugar
- 1 cup all-purpose flour
- 1 teaspoon baking soda
- 2 eggs
- 2 peaches, pitted and diced
- 2 tablespoons chia seeds

Directions:

1. Mix the flours, salt, chia seeds and baking soda in a container.
2. Mix the oil, sugar and eggs in another container and whip until volume increases to twice what it was.
3. Put in the yogurt then mix in the flour. Fold in the peaches.
4. Spoon the batter in a muffin tin covered with muffin papers.
5. Preheat your oven and bake the muffins at 350F for about twenty minutes or until it rises significantly and starts to appear golden-brown.

These muffins taste best chilled.

Nutritional Content of One Serving:

Calories: 219 ‖ Fat: 10.9g ‖ Protein: 3.8g ‖ Carbohydrates: 26.9g

PEACH AND CREAM MUFFINS

Total Time Taken: 1 hour
Yield: 12 Servings
Ingredients:

- ¼ teaspoon salt
- ½ cup white sugar
- 1 cup butter, melted
- 1 cup sour cream
- 1 teaspoon vanilla extract
- 2 cups all-purpose flour
- 2 peaches, pitted and diced
- 2 teaspoons baking powder

Directions:

1. Mix the butter, sour cream, sugar and vanilla in a container until creamy.
2. Put in the flour, baking powder and salt then fold in the peaches.
3. Spoon the batter in a muffin tin covered with muffin papers and preheat your oven and bake at 350F for about twenty minutes or until a golden-brown colour is achieved and it rises significantly.

These muffins taste best chilled.

Nutritional Content of One Serving:

Calories: 292 ‖ Fat: 19.6g ‖ Protein: 3.1g ‖ Carbohydrates: 27.1g

PASSIONFRUIT CUPCAKES

Total Time Taken: 1 ½ hours
Yield: 12 Servings
Ingredients:

Cupcakes:

- ¼ cup passionfruit juice
- ½ cup butter, softened
- ½ cup milk
- ½ cup white sugar
- ½ teaspoon salt
- 1 ½ teaspoons baking powder
- 1 13/4 cups all-purpose flour
- 1 teaspoon vanilla extract
- 2 eggs

Frosting:

- 1 cup butter, softened
- 2 cups powdered sugar
- 2 tablespoons passionfruit juice

Directions:

1. To make the cupcakes, combine the butter and sugar in a container until pale and light.
2. Put in the eggs and mix thoroughly then mix in the vanilla, passionfruit juice and milk.

3. Fold in the flour, salt and baking powder then spoon the batter in a muffin tin covered with muffin papers.
4. Pre-heat the oven and bake at 350F for about twenty minutes or until a golden-brown colour is achieved.
5. Let the cupcakes cool down.
6. To make the frosting, combine the butter and sugar in a container for five minutes until pale.
7. Stir in the passionfruit juice and mix thoroughly.
8. Top each cupcake with the frosting and serve fresh.

Nutritional Content of One Serving:

Calories: 494 ‖ Fat: 24.4g ‖ Protein: 6.1g ‖ Carbohydrates: 63.8g

OREO CREAM CUPCAKES

Total Time Taken: 1 ½ hours
Yield: 12 Servings
Ingredients:

Cupcakes:

- ¼ teaspoon salt
- 1 cup butter, softened
- 1 cup buttermilk
- 1 cup white sugar
- 1 tablespoon vanilla extract
- 2 cups all-purpose flour
- 2 eggs
- 2 teaspoons baking powder
- 6 Oreo cookies, crushed

Topping:

- 2 cups heavy cream, whipped
- 6 Oreo cookies, chopped

Directions:

1. To make the cupcakes, combine the flour, salt, baking powder and sugar in a container.
2. Put in the butter and stir until grainy.

3. In a small container, mix the eggs, buttermilk and vanilla. Pour this mixture progressively over the flour and mix for a minute on high speed.
4. Spoon the batter in a muffin tin covered with muffin papers.
5. Pre-heat the oven and bake at 350F for about twenty minutes or until it rises significantly and starts to appear golden-brown.
6. Let cool down before you serve.

Nutritional Content of One Serving:

Calories: 412 ‖ Fat: 25.8g ‖ Protein: 4.9g ‖ Carbohydrates: 41.9g

ORANGE YOGURT MUFFINS

Total Time Taken: 1 hour
Yield: 12 Servings
Ingredients:

- ¼ cup candied orange peel, chopped
- ½ cup canola oil
- ½ teaspoon salt
- 1 cup plain yogurt
- 1 egg
- 1 orange, zested and juice
- 2 cups all-purpose flour
- 2 teaspoons baking powder

Directions:

1. Mix the flour, baking powder and salt in a container.
2. Put in the yogurt, orange zest, orange juice, oil and egg and mix thoroughly.
3. Fold in the orange peel then spoon the batter in a muffin tin lined using muffin papers of your choice.
4. Pre-heat the oven and bake at 350F for about twenty minutes or until it rises significantly and starts to appear golden-brown.

These muffins taste best chilled.

Nutritional Content of One Serving:

Calories: 186 ‖ Fat: 9.9g ‖ Protein: 3.9g ‖ Carbohydrates: 20.1g

ORANGE SODA CUPCAKES

Total Time Taken: 1 ½ cups
Yield: 12 Servings
Ingredients:

Cupcakes:

- ¼ cup vegetable oil
- ¼ teaspoon salt
- ½ cup butter, softened
- ½ cup white sugar 3 egg whites
- 1 ¼ cups orange soda
- 1 ½ cups all-purpose flour
- 1 ½ teaspoons baking powder
- 1 cup cream cheese
- 1 teaspoon orange zest **Frosting:**
- 1 teaspoon vanilla extract
- 2 cups powdered sugar
- 2 tablespoons heavy cream

Directions:

1. To make the cupcakes, combine the egg whites, oil, orange soda and orange zest in a container.
2. Put in the remaining ingredients then spoon the batter in a muffin tin covered with muffin papers.
3. Pre-heat the oven and bake at 350F for about twenty minutes or until a toothpick inserted into them comes out dry.
4. Let cool in the pan.
5. To make the frosting, combine the butter and cream cheese in a container until fluffy.
6. Put in the sugar and mix for five minutes on high speed.
7. Stir in the cream and vanilla and mix for 1 additional minute.
8. Pipe the frosting over each cupcake and serve them fresh.

Nutritional Content of One Serving:

Calories: 368 ‖ Fat: 20.1g ‖ Protein: 4.1g ‖ Carbohydrates: 44.4g

ORANGE POPPY SEED MUFFINS

Total Time Taken: 1 ½ hours

Yield: 12 Servings

Ingredients:

- ½ cup coconut oil
- ½ cup whole wheat flour
- ½ teaspoon salt
- 1 ½ teaspoon baking powder
- 1 cup all-purpose flour
- 1 orange, washed
- 1 teaspoon vanilla extract
- 2 tablespoons poppy seed
- 3 eggs

Directions:

1. Put the orange in a saucepan and cover it with water. Cook until softened then drain and place the orange in a blender.
2. Put in the coconut oil, eggs and vanilla and blend until the desired smoothness is achieved.
3. Stir in the flours, salt, baking powder and poppy seed and mix using a spatula.
4. Spoon the batter in a muffin tin covered with muffin papers and preheat your oven and bake at 350F for about twenty minutes or until it rises significantly and seems golden.

These muffins taste best chilled.

Nutritional Content of One Serving:

Calories: 168 ‖ Fat: 11.0g ‖ Protein: 3.4g ‖ Carbohydrates: 14.5g

ORANGE PECAN MUFFINS

Total Time Taken: 1 ¼ hours

Yield: 12 Servings

Ingredients:

- ¼ cup fresh orange juice
- ¼ teaspoon cinnamon
- ¼ teaspoon salt
- ½ cup dried cranberries
- ½ cup milk
- ½ cup white sugar
- 1 ½ teaspoons baking powder
- 1 ¾ cups all-purpose flour
- 1 cup pecans, chopped
- 1 tablespoon orange zest
- 2 eggs
- 6 tablespoons butter, melted

Directions:

1. Mix the flour, salt, baking powder, sugar and cinnamon in a container.
2. Put in the eggs, butter, milk, orange juice and orange zest and stir for a few seconds to mix.
3. Fold in the pecans and cranberries then spoon the batter in a muffin tin coated with baking muffin papers.
4. Preheat your oven and bake the muffins at 350F for about twenty minutes or until it rises significantly and seems golden.
5. Let cool down before you serve.

Nutritional Content of One Serving:

Calories: 178 ‖ Fat: 7.7g ‖ Protein: 3.4g ‖ Carbohydrates: 24.4g

ORANGE OLIVE OIL MUFFINS

Total Time Taken: 1 hour
Yield: 12 Servings
Ingredients:

- ¼ cup olive oil
- ¼ teaspoon salt
- ½ cup fresh orange juice
- ½ cup sliced almonds
- 1 cup all-purpose flour
- 1 cup almond flour

- 1 cup white sugar
- 1 tablespoon orange zest
- 1 teaspoon baking powder
- 1 teaspoon vanilla extract
- 4 eggs

Directions:

1. Mix the eggs and sugar in a container until fluffy and pale.
2. Put in the orange juice, oil, vanilla and orange zest and mix thoroughly.
3. Fold in the flours, salt and baking powder then spoon the batter in a muffin tin coated with baking muffin papers.
4. Top each muffin with sliced almonds and preheat your oven and bake at 350F for about twenty minutes or until it rises significantly and starts to appear golden-brown.

These muffins taste best chilled.

Nutritional Content of One Serving:

Calories: 200 ‖ Fat: 8.9g ‖ Protein: 4.4g ‖ Carbohydrates: 27.5g

ORANGE ICED CUPCAKES

Total Time Taken: 1 ¼ hours
Yield: 12 Servings

Ingredients:

- ¼ cup candied orange peel, diced
- ½ cup butter, softened
- ½ cup buttermilk
- ½ teaspoon salt
- ¾ cup white sugar
- 1 ½ teaspoons baking powder
- 1 ¾ cups all-purpose flour
- 1 teaspoon vanilla extract
- 3 eggs

Frosting:

- 1 ½ cups powdered sugar

- 1 tablespoon butter, melted
- 1 tablespoon orange juice
- 1 teaspoon orange zest

Directions:

1. To make the cupcakes, combine the butter and sugar in a container until fluffy and pale.
2. Put in the eggs and mix thoroughly then mix in the vanilla and buttermilk.
3. Fold in the flour, baking powder, salt and orange peel then spoon the batter in a muffin tin covered with muffin papers.
4. Pre-heat the oven and bake at 350F for about twenty minutes or until a toothpick inserted into them comes out dry. Let them cool in the pan.
5. For the glaze, combine all the ingredients in a container and mix thoroughly.
6. Sprinkle each cupcake with frosting.

Nutritional Content of One Serving:

Calories: 272 ‖ Fat: 10.0g ‖ Protein: 3.7g ‖ Carbohydrates: 42.9g

ORANGE GLAZED CUPCAKES

Total Time Taken: 1 ½ hours
Yield: 12 Servings
Ingredients:

Cupcakes:

- ¼ cup candied ginger, chopped
- ¼ cup molasses
- ¼ teaspoon salt
- ½ cup butter, softened
- ½ teaspoon baking powder
- ½ teaspoon ground cloves
- ½ teaspoon ground ginger
- 1 cup light brown sugar
- 1 cup sour cream
- 1 tablespoon orange zest
- 1 teaspoon baking soda
- 1 teaspoon cinnamon powder

- 1 teaspoon grated ginger
- 2 cups all-purpose flour
- 2 eggs

Glaze:

- 1 cup powdered sugar
- 1 tablespoon orange juice
- 1 teaspoon vanilla extract

Directions:

1. To make the cupcakes, combine the butter, molasses and sugar in a container until creamy and pale.
2. Put in the sour cream, orange zest, ginger and eggs and mix thoroughly.
3. Fold in the flour, salt, baking soda, baking powder, cinnamon, ginger and cloves.
4. Fold in the ginger and mix using a spatula.
5. Spoon the batter in a muffin tin coated with baking muffin papers.
6. Pre-heat the oven and bake at 350F for about twenty minutes or until it rises significantly and becomes aromatic.
7. Let them cool down in the pan.
8. For the glaze, combine all the ingredients in a container.
9. Sprinkle the glaze over the cupcakes and serve them fresh.

Nutritional Content of One Serving:

Calories: 304 ‖ Fat: 12.7g ‖ Protein: 3.8g ‖ Carbohydrates: 44.6g

ORANGE ALMOND MUFFINS

Total Time Taken: 1 ½ hours
Yield: 12 Servings

Ingredients:

- ½ teaspoon salt
- 1 cup white sugar
- 1 teaspoon baking powder
- 1 teaspoon vanilla extract
- 2 cups almond flour
- 2 small oranges

- 6 eggs

Directions:

1. Put the oranges in a saucepan and cover them with water. Boil the oranges for about half an hour until softened. Drain the oranges well and place them in a blender. Pulse until the desired smoothness is achieved.
2. Mix the eggs and sugar in a container until fluffy and pale.
3. Stir in the oranges then fold in the almond flour, baking powder and salt.
4. Spoon the batter in a muffin tin covered with muffin papers.
5. Preheat your oven and bake the muffins at 350F for about twenty minutes or until it rises significantly and starts to appear golden-brown.
6. Let the muffins cool to room temperature before you serve.

Nutritional Content of One Serving:

Calories: 130 ‖ Fat: 4.5g ‖ Protein: 3.9g ‖ Carbohydrates: 20.0g

OATMEAL CRANBERRY MUFFINS

Total Time Taken: 1 hour
Yield: 12 Servings
Ingredients:

- ¼ cup candied orange peel, diced
- ¼ cup light brown sugar
- ¼ cup milk
- ¼ cup olive oil
- ¼ teaspoon salt
- 1 cup all-purpose flour
- 1 cup fresh cranberries
- 1 cup rolled oats
- 1 teaspoon vanilla extract
- 2 bananas, mashed
- 2 eggs
- 2 tablespoons ground flaxseeds
- 2 teaspoons baking powder

Directions:

1. Mix the bananas, eggs, milk, olive oil, sugar and vanilla in a container.

2. Fold in the flour, flaxseeds, oats, baking powder and salt then put in the cranberries and orange peel.
3. Spoon the batter in a muffin tin covered with muffin papers.
4. Pre-heat the oven and bake at 350F for about twenty minutes or until it rises completely and is aromatic.
5. Let cool in the pan before you serve.

Nutritional Content of One Serving:

Calories: 157 ‖ Fat: 6.0g ‖ Protein: 3.5g ‖ Carbohydrates: 22.4g

OATMEAL CARROT MUFFINS

Total Time Taken: 1 hour
Yield: 12 Servings
Ingredients:

- 2 eggs
- 2 cups grated carrots
- 1 teaspoon baking powder
- 1 cup rolled oats
- 1 cup buttermilk
- 1 cup all-purpose flour
- ½ teaspoon ground ginger
- ½ teaspoon cinnamon powder
- ½ teaspoon baking soda
- ½ cup light brown sugar
- ½ cup crushed pineapple
- ½ cup canola oil
- ¼ teaspoon salt

Directions:

1. Mix the oats, flour, baking soda, baking powder, salt, cinnamon, ginger and sugar in a container.
2. Stir in the eggs, oil and buttermilk and stir for a few seconds to mix.
3. Fold in the carrots and pineapple then spoon the batter in a muffin tin covered with muffin papers.
4. Preheat your oven and bake the muffins at 350F for about twenty minutes or until it rises significantly and starts to appear golden-brown.

These muffins taste best chilled.

Nutritional Content of One Serving:

Calories: 197 ‖ Fat: 10.5g ‖ Protein: 3.8g ‖ Carbohydrates: 22.5g

NUTTY DOUBLE CHOCOLATE MUFFINS

Total Time Taken: 1 hour
Yield: 12 Servings
Ingredients:

- ¼ cup canola oil
- ¼ cup cocoa powder
- ½ cup ground hazelnuts
- ½ teaspoon salt
- 1 1/2 cup all-purpose flour
- 1 cup dark chocolate chips
- 1 cup milk
- 1 cup white sugar
- 1 egg
- 1 teaspoon baking powder
- 1 teaspoon vanilla extract

Directions:

1. Mix the flour, cocoa powder, ground hazelnuts, salt, baking powder and sugar in a container.
2. Put in the egg, canola oil, milk and vanilla and stir for a few seconds to mix.
3. Fold in the chocolate chips then spoon the batter in a muffin tin covered with muffin papers.
4. Preheat your oven and bake the muffins at 350F for about twenty minutes or until a toothpick inserted into them comes out dry.

These muffins taste best chilled.

Nutritional Content of One Serving:

Calories: 247 ‖ Fat: 10.3g ‖ Protein: 4.2g ‖ Carbohydrates: 38.0g

NUTTY CHOCOLATE CHIP MUFFINS

Total Time Taken: 1 hour
Yield: 12 Servings
Ingredients:

- 2 eggs
- 1 teaspoon vanilla extract
- 1 teaspoon baking powder
- 1 cup white sugar
- 1 cup walnuts, chopped
- 1 cup buttermilk
- 1 ½ cups all-purpose flour
- ½ teaspoon baking soda
- ½ cup dark chocolate chips
- ½ cup cocoa powder
- ¼ teaspoon salt
- ¼ cup canola oil

Directions:

1. Mix the flour, cocoa powder, sugar, baking soda, baking powder and salt in a container.
2. Put in the eggs, oil, vanilla and buttermilk and stir for a few seconds to mix.
3. Fold in the walnuts and chocolate chips then pour the batter in a muffin tin lined using muffin papers of your choice.
4. Pre-heat the oven and bake at 350F for about twenty minutes or until a toothpick inserted into them comes out dry.

These muffins taste best chilled.

Nutritional Content of One Serving:

Calories: 275 ‖ Fat: 13.6g ‖ Protein: 6.7g ‖ Carbohydrates: 36.2g

NUTELLA STUFFED STRAWBERRY MUFFINS

Total Time Taken: 1 hour
Yield: 12 Servings
Ingredients:

- ¼ teaspoon salt
- ½ cup canola oil
- ½ cup Nutella
- ¾ cup milk
- 1 cup strawberries, sliced
- 1 cup white sugar
- 1 teaspoon vanilla extract
- 2 cups all-purpose flour
- 2 eggs
- 2 teaspoons baking powder

Directions:

1. Mix the eggs and sugar in a container until fluffy and pale.
2. Put in the vanilla and oil and mix thoroughly.
3. Stir in the milk then put in the flour, salt and baking powder and mix using a spatula.
4. Spoon half of the batter evenly in a muffin tin covered with muffin papers.
5. Top with a dollop of Nutella then spoon the rest of the batter over the Nutella.
6. Pre-heat the oven and bake at 350F for about twenty minutes or until fluffy and golden brown.
7. Let cool in the pan before you serve.

Nutritional Content of One Serving:

Calories: 259 ‖ Fat: 11.4g ‖ Protein: 3.8g ‖ Carbohydrates: 36.5g

NUTELLA PEANUT BUTTER CUPCAKES

Total Time Taken: 1 ½ hours
Yield: 12 Servings
Ingredients:

Cupcakes:

- ¼ cup butter, softened

- ¼ teaspoon salt
- ½ cup buttermilk
- ½ cup smooth peanut butter
- ¾ cup light brown sugar
- 1 ½ cups all-purpose flour
- 1 ½ teaspoons baking powder
- 1 teaspoon vanilla extract
- 2 eggs

Frosting:

- 1 cup Nutella

Directions:

1. To make the cupcakes, combine the peanut butter, butter, sugar and vanilla in a container until creamy.
2. Put in the eggs and buttermilk and mix thoroughly.
3. Fold in the remaining ingredients then spoon the batter in a muffin tin covered with muffin papers.
4. Pre-heat the oven and bake at 350F for about twenty minutes or until it rises significantly and starts to appear golden-brown.
5. When chilled, top with Nutella and serve fresh.

Nutritional Content of One Serving:

Calories: 221 ‖ Fat: 11.2g ‖ Protein: 5.8g ‖ Carbohydrates: 25.7g

MULTIGRAIN MUFFINS

Total Time Taken: 1 hour
Yield: 12 Servings
Ingredients:

- ¼ cup canola oil
- ¼ teaspoon salt
- ½ cup all-purpose flour
- ½ cup light brown sugar
- ½ cup walnuts
- ½ cup wheat bran
- 1 ½ cups buttermilk

- 1 cup whole wheat flour
- 2 eggs
- 2 tablespoons pumpkin seeds
- 2 tablespoons sunflower seeds
- 2 teaspoons baking powder

Directions:

1. Mix the flours, bran, baking powder and salt in a container.
2. Put in the eggs, buttermilk, oil, sugar, walnuts and seeds and mix using a spatula.
3. Spoon the batter in a muffin tin covered with muffin papers and preheat your oven and bake at 350F for about twenty minutes or until it rises significantly and starts to appear golden-brown.

These muffins taste best chilled.

Nutritional Content of One Serving:

Calories: 192 ‖ Fat: 9.8g ‖ Protein: 5.6g ‖ Carbohydrates: 22.2g

MUESLI APPLE MUFFINS

Total Time Taken: 1 hour
Yield: 16 Servings
Ingredients:

- ½ cup canola oil
- ½ teaspoon cinnamon powder
- ½ teaspoon salt
- 1 ½ cups milk
- 1 cup muesli
- 2 ½ cups all-purpose flour
- 2 eggs
- 2 red apples, cored and diced
- 2 teaspoons baking powder

Directions:

1. Mix the flour, salt, baking powder, cinnamon and muesli in a container.
2. Put in the eggs, canola oil and milk and mix thoroughly using a spatula.

3. Fold in the apples then spoon the batter in a muffin tin lined using muffin papers of your choice.
4. Pre-heat the oven and bake at 350F for about twenty minutes or until it rises significantly and starts to appear golden-brown.
5. Serve the muffins chilled or store them in an airtight container.

Nutritional Content of One Serving:

Calories: 182 ‖ Fat: 8.4g ‖ Protein: 4.0g ‖ Carbohydrates: 23.5g

MORNING MUFFINS

Total Time Taken: 1 ¼ hours

Yield: 12 Servings

Ingredients:

- ¼ teaspoon salt
- ½ cup dried cranberries
- ½ cup light brown sugar
- ½ cup oat flour
- 1 ½ cups all-purpose flour
- 1 apple, cored and diced
- 1 cup buttermilk
- 1 cup grated carrots
- 1 teaspoon baking soda
- 1 teaspoon vanilla extract
- 2 eggs

Directions:

1. Mix the eggs and sugar in a container until pale and airy.
2. Put in the vanilla and buttermilk and mix thoroughly.
3. Fold in the flours, salt and baking soda then put in the carrots, cranberries and apple.
4. Spoon the batter in a muffin tin lined using muffin papers of your choice.
5. Pre-heat the oven and bake at 350F for about twenty minutes or until a toothpick inserted into them comes out dry.

These muffins taste best chilled.

Nutritional Content of One Serving:

Calories: 129 ‖ Fat: 1.3g ‖ Protein: 3.8g ‖ Carbohydrates: 25.0g

MORNING GLORY MUFFINS

Total Time Taken: 1 hour

Yield: 12 Servings

Ingredients:

- 3 eggs
- 2 tablespoons chia seeds
- 1 teaspoon baking soda
- 1 cup grated carrots
- 1 ¾ cups all-purpose flour
- ½ teaspoon salt
- ½ teaspoon baking powder
- ½ cup walnuts, chopped
- ½ cup shredded coconut
- ½ cup raisins
- ½ cup canola oil
- ½ cup applesauce

Directions:

1. Mix the flour, baking soda, baking powder and salt in a container.
2. Put in the eggs, canola oil and applesauce and stir for a few seconds to mix.
3. Fold in the carrots, raisins, walnuts, coconut and chia seeds then spoon the batter in a muffin tin covered with muffin papers.
4. Pre-heat the oven and bake at 350F for about twenty minutes or until it rises significantly and starts to appear golden-brown.

These muffins taste best chilled.

Nutritional Content of One Serving:

Calories: 259 ‖ Fat: 16.2g ‖ Protein: 6.0g ‖ Carbohydrates: 23.7g

MOIST CHOCOLATE COFFEE CUPCAKES

Total Time Taken: 1 ½ hours
Yield: 12 Servings
Ingredients:

Cupcakes:

- ¼ cup canola oil
- ½ cup buttermilk
- ½ cup cocoa powder
- ½ teaspoon salt
- 1 ½ cups all-purpose flour
- 1 cup brewed coffee
- 1 egg
- 1 teaspoon baking soda
- 1 teaspoon instant coffee
- 1 teaspoon vanilla extract

Frosting:

- 1 cup heavy cream
- 1 teaspoon vanilla extract
- 2 cups dark chocolate chips

Directions:

1. To make the cupcakes, combine the cocoa powder, flour, salt and baking soda in a container.
2. Stir in the egg, coffee, instant coffee, buttermilk, oil and vanilla and mix thoroughly.
3. Pour the batter in a muffin tin covered with muffin papers.
4. Preheat your oven and bake the cupcakes at 350F for about twenty minutes or until well risen. Let them cool in the pan.
5. To make the frosting, bring the cream to a boil. Turn off the heat and
6. put in the chocolate. Stir until melted and smooth then let cool to room temperature.
7. Stir in the vanilla then whip the cream using an electric mixer just until pale and firm.
8. Garnish each cupcake with whipped frosting and serve them fresh.

Nutritional Content of One Serving:

Calories: 244 ‖ Fat: 14.6g ‖ Protein: 4.6g ‖ Carbohydrates: 28.1g

MOIST BANANA MUFFINS

Total Time Taken: 1 hour

Yield: 12 Servings

Ingredients:

- 3 bananas, mashed
- 2 eggs
- 2 cups all-purpose flour
- 1 teaspoon vanilla extract
- 1 teaspoon baking soda
- 1 teaspoon baking powder
- 1 cup white sugar
- ½ cup dark chocolate chips
- ½ cup canola oil

Directions:

1. Mix the flour, baking soda, baking powder and sugar in a container.
2. Put in the remaining ingredients and stir for a few seconds to mix.
3. Fold in the chocolate chips then spoon the batter in a muffin tin covered with muffin papers.
4. Pre-heat the oven and bake at 350F for about twenty minutes or until it rises significantly and becomes aromatic.
5. Serve the muffins chilled or store them in an airtight container.

Nutritional Content of One Serving:

Calories: 280 ‖ Fat: 11.4g ‖ Protein: 3.7g ‖ Carbohydrates: 42.9g

MOIST BANANA MUFFINS

Total Time Taken: 1 hour

Yield: 12 Servings

Ingredients:

- 3 bananas, mashed
- 1 teaspoon vanilla extract
- 2 eggs
- ½ cup sour cream

- ½ cup coconut oil, melted
- 2 cups all-purpose flour
- ¼ teaspoon salt
- 2 teaspoons baking powder
- 2/3 cup white sugar

Directions:

1. Mix the bananas, sugar, vanilla, eggs, sour cream and coconut oil in a container.
2. Put in the flour, salt and baking powder and stir swiftly to combine.
3. Spoon the batter in a muffin tin covered with muffin papers.
4. Pre-heat the oven and bake at 350F for about twenty minutes or until a toothpick inserted into the center of a muffin comes out clean.

These muffins taste best chilled.

Nutritional Content of One Serving:

Calories: 255 ‖ Fat: 12.1g ‖ Protein: 3.7g ‖ Carbohydrates: 34.6g

MOCHA MADNESS CUPCAKES

Total Time Taken: 1 ½ hours
Yield: 12 Servings
Ingredients:

Cupcakes:

- ¼ teaspoon salt
- ½ cup canola oil
- ½ cup cocoa powder
- ½ cup water
- 1 ½ cups all-purpose flour
- 1 cup white sugar
- 1 teaspoon apple cider vinegar
- 1 teaspoon baking soda
- 1 teaspoon instant coffee
- 2 eggs
- 2 teaspoon vanilla extract

Frosting:

- ½ cup white sugar 1 pinch salt
- 1 cup butter, softened
- 1 cup dark chocolate chips, melted and cooled
- 1 teaspoon instant coffee
- 2 egg whites

Directions:

1. To make the cupcakes, combine the eggs and sugar in a container until fluffy and pale.
2. Put in the vanilla, vinegar, water, coffee and oil and mix thoroughly.
3. Stir in the dry ingredients then pour the batter in a muffin tin covered with muffin papers.
4. Preheat your oven and bake the cupcakes at 350F for about twenty minutes or until a toothpick inserted into them comes out dry.
5. Let cool in the pan.
6. To make the frosting, combine the egg whites, sugar and salt in a container and place over a hot water bath. Keep on heat until the sugar has melted then remove and start whipping until firm and shiny and chilled.
7. Put in the butter, all at once, and mix a few minutes until it comes together into a silky cream.
8. Stir in the chocolate and coffee and mix thoroughly.
9. Pipe the frosting over each cupcake and serve them fresh.

Nutritional Content of One Serving:

Calories: 437 ‖ Fat: 28.5g ‖ Protein: 4.6g ‖ Carbohydrates: 45.8g

MOCHA CUPCAKES

Total Time Taken: 1 ½ hours
Yield: 14 Servings
Ingredients:

Cupcakes:

- ½ cup canola oil
- ½ cup espresso
- ½ cup sour cream

- ½ teaspoon salt
- 1 cup light brown sugar
- 1 teaspoon vanilla extract
- 2 cups all-purpose flour
- 2 eggs
- 2 teaspoons baking powder

Frosting:

- ½ cup butter, softened
- ½ cup dark chocolate chips, melted
- 1 cup cream cheese
- 1 teaspoon instant coffee
- 2 cups powdered sugar

Directions:

1. To make the cupcakes, combine the oil and sugar in a container for a couple of minutes then put in the eggs and mix thoroughly.
2. Stir in the vanilla, sour cream and espresso then put in the flour, baking powder and salt.
3. Pour the batter in a muffin tin covered with muffin papers.
4. Preheat your oven and bake the cupcakes at 350F for about twenty minutes.
5. Let cool in the pan.
6. To make the frosting, combine the cream cheese and butter in a container until pale. Put in the sugar and continue whipping until fluffy.
7. Stir in the coffee and melted chocolate.
8. Spoon the frosting in a pastry bag and top the cupcakes with it.

These cupcakes taste best when fresh.

Nutritional Content of One Serving:

Calories: 404 ‖ Fat: 23.8g ‖ Protein: 4.5g ‖ Carbohydrates: 44.9g

MOCHA CHOCOLATE CHIP BANANA MUFFINS

Total Time Taken: 1 hour
Yield: 12 Servings
Ingredients:

- ¼ teaspoon salt
- ½ cup dark chocolate chips
- ½ cup light brown sugar
- ½ cup milk
- ½ teaspoon baking soda
- 1 ½ cups all-purpose flour
- 1 teaspoon baking powder
- 1 teaspoon vanilla extract
- 2 bananas, mashed
- 2 eggs
- 2 teaspoons instant coffee

Directions:

1. Mix the bananas, eggs, instant coffee, vanilla, milk and sugar in a container.
2. Stir in the remaining ingredients and mix thoroughly.
3. Fold in the chocolate chips then spoon the batter in 12 muffin cups covered with muffin papers.
4. Pre-heat the oven and bake at 350F for about twenty minutes or until a golden-brown colour is achieved and it rises significantly.

These muffins taste best chilled.

Nutritional Content of One Serving:

Calories: 138 ‖ Fat: 2.5g ‖ Protein: 3.4g ‖ Carbohydrates: 26.5g

MIXED BERRY BUTTERMILK MUFFINS

Total Time Taken: 1 hour
Yield: 12 Servings
Ingredients:

- ¼ cup olive oil
- ½ cup white sugar
- ½ teaspoon baking soda
- ½ teaspoon salt

- 1 ¼ cups buttermilk
- 1 cup mixed berries
- 1 egg
- 1 teaspoon baking powder
- 1 teaspoon vanilla extract
- 2 cups all-purpose flour

Directions:

1. Mix the flour, salt, baking powder and baking soda in a container.
2. Put in the egg, olive oil, buttermilk and vanilla and mix thoroughly then mix in the sugar.
3. Fold in the berries then spoon the batter in a muffin tin lined using muffin papers of your choice.
4. Preheat your oven and bake the muffins at 350F for about twenty minutes or until a toothpick inserted into them comes out dry.

These muffins taste best chilled.

Nutritional Content of One Serving:

Calories: 167 ‖ Fat: 5.0g ‖ Protein: 3.5g ‖ Carbohydrates: 27.1g

MINTY CHOCOLATE CUPCAKES

Total Time Taken: 1 ½ hours
Yield: 12 Servings
Ingredients:

Cupcakes:

- ¼ cup canola oil
- ½ cup cocoa powder
- ½ teaspoon baking powder
- ½ teaspoon salt
- 1 ½ cups all-purpose flour
- 1 cup buttermilk
- 1 cup white sugar
- 1 teaspoon baking soda

- 1 teaspoon vanilla extract
- 2 eggs

Frosting:

- 1 ½ cups dark chocolate chips
- 1 teaspoon peppermint extract
- 2 tablespoons butter
- 2/3 cup heavy cream

Directions:

1. To make the cupcakes, combine the flour, cocoa powder, sugar, baking soda, baking powder and salt in a container.
2. Put in the buttermilk, eggs, canola oil and vanilla and stir swiftly to combine.
3. Spoon the batter in a muffin cup covered with muffin papers.
4. Preheat your oven and bake the cupcakes at 350F for about twenty minutes or until well risen.
5. Let cool in the pan.
6. To make the frosting, bring the cream to the boiling in a saucepan. Turn off the heat and mix in the chocolate chips. Stir until melted and smooth then put in the peppermint extract and butter and mix thoroughly.
7. Let the frosting cool then put the frosting on top of each cupcake.

Best served chilled.

Nutritional Content of One Serving:

Calories: 298 ‖ Fat: 14.5g ‖ Protein: 5.0g ‖ Carbohydrates: 42.0g

MILLET FLOUR PLUM MUFFINS

Total Time Taken: 1 hour
Yield: 12 Servings
Ingredients:

- ¼ cup coconut oil, melted
- ¼ teaspoon salt
- ½ cup light brown sugar
- 1 cup almond milk
- 1 cup millet flour

- 1 cup whole wheat flour
- 1 teaspoon baking soda
- 2 eggs
- 6 plums, pitted and sliced

Directions:

1. Mix the flours, salt, sugar and baking soda in a container.
2. Put in the remaining ingredients and mix thoroughly.
3. Fold in the plums then spoon the batter in a muffin tin lined with special muffin papers.
4. Preheat your oven and bake the muffins at 350F for about twenty minutes or until a golden-brown colour is achieved and it rises significantly.
5. Let cool down before you serve.

Nutritional Content of One Serving:

Calories: 210 ‖ Fat: 10.7g ‖ Protein: 4.0g ‖ Carbohydrates: 26.2g

MILKY BANANA MUFFINS

Total Time Taken: 1 hour
Yield: 12 Servings
Ingredients:

- ¼ cup canola oil
- ½ cup heavy cream
- ½ teaspoon salt
- 1 ½ cups all-purpose flour
- 1 teaspoon baking soda
- 1 teaspoon vanilla extract
- 2 bananas, mashed
- 2 eggs

Directions:

1. Mix the bananas, eggs, cream, oil and vanilla in a container.
2. Put in the flour, salt and baking soda then spoon the batter in a muffin tin covered with muffin papers.
3. Preheat your oven and bake the muffins at 350F for about twenty minutes or until it rises significantly and becomes aromatic.

These muffins taste best chilled.

Nutritional Content of One Serving:

Calories: 143 ‖ Fat: 7.3g ‖ Protein: 2.8g ‖ Carbohydrates: 16.7g

MILK CHOCOLATE CUPCAKES

Total Time Taken: 1 ½ hours
Yield: 12 Servings
Ingredients:

Cupcakes:

- ½ cup butter, softened
- ½ teaspoon salt
- ¾ cup white sugar
- 1 cup milk
- 1 teaspoon vanilla extract
- 2 cups all-purpose flour
- 2 eggs
- 2 teaspoons baking powder

Frosting:

- ½ cup milk chocolate chips, melted and chilled
- 1 cup butter, softened
- 2 cups powdered sugar

Directions:

1. To make the cupcakes, combine the butter and sugar until fluffy and pale.
2. Put in the eggs, one at a time, then mix in the vanilla and milk.
3. Put in the flour, baking powder and salt and mix using a spatula.
4. Spoon the batter into 12 muffin cups covered with muffin papers.
5. Preheat your oven and bake the cupcakes at 350F for about twenty minutes or until a golden-brown colour is achieved and it rises significantly.
6. Let cool down.
7. To make the frosting, combine the butter in a container until fluffy and pale.
8. Put in the sugar and stir thoroughly for five minutes.
9. Stir in the chocolate and mix thoroughly.
10. Spoon the frosting in a pastry bag and top each cupcake with it.

These cupcakes taste best when fresh.

Nutritional Content of One Serving:

Calories: 438 ‖ Fat: 25.0g ‖ Protein: 4.0g ‖ Carbohydrates: 51.3g

MEXICAN CHOCOLATE MUFFINS

Total Time Taken: 1 hour
Yield: 12 Servings
Ingredients:

- ¼ cup cocoa powder
- ¼ cup milk
- ¼ teaspoon baking soda
- ¼ teaspoon salt
- ½ cup butter, melted
- ½ teaspoon chili powder
- ¾ cup white sugar
- 1 ½ cups all-purpose flour
- 1 cup dark chocolate chips
- 1 egg
- 1 teaspoon baking powder
- 3 bananas, mashed

Directions:

1. Mix the flour, cocoa powder, sugar, salt, baking powder, baking soda and chili powder.
2. Put in the bananas, egg, butter and milk and stir for a few seconds to mix.
3. Fold in the chocolate chips then spoon the batter in a muffin tin covered with muffin papers.
4. Preheat your oven and bake the muffins at 350F for about twenty minutes or until it rises significantly and becomes aromatic.

These muffins taste best chilled.

Nutritional Content of One Serving:

Calories: 257 ‖ Fat: 11.3g ‖ Protein: 3.6g ‖ Carbohydrates: 39.4g

MATCHA STRAWBERRY CUPCAKES

Total Time Taken: 1 ½ hours
Yield: 14 Servings
Ingredients:

Cupcakes:

- ¼ cup cornstarch
- ½ cup butter, softened
- ½ teaspoon salt
- 1 ½ cups all-purpose flour
- 1 cup white sugar
- 1 tablespoon matcha
- 1 teaspoon baking powder
- 1 teaspoon vanilla extract
- 2/3 cup whole milk
- 3 eggs

Frosting:

- 1 cup butter, softened
- 1 cup fresh strawberries, sliced
- 2 cups powdered sugar

Directions:

1. To make the cupcakes, combine the butter and sugar in a container until fluffy and pale.
2. Put in the eggs and vanilla and mix thoroughly.
3. Fold in the dry ingredients, alternating them with milk.
4. Spoon the batter in a muffin tin covered with muffin papers.
5. Preheat your oven and bake the cupcakes at 350F for about twenty minutes or until well risen.
6. Let the cupcakes cool down.
7. To make the frosting, combine the butter and sugar in a container until airy and fluffy.
8. Spoon the frosting into a pastry bag and top the cupcakes with it. Top each cupcake with a strawberry and serve fresh.

Nutritional Content of One Serving:

Calories: 377 ‖ Fat: 21.2g ‖ Protein: 3.2g ‖ Carbohydrates: 45.3g

MAPLE SYRUP PECAN CUPCAKES

Total Time Taken: 1 ½ hours
Yield: 12 Servings
Ingredients:

Cupcakes:

- ¼ cup butter, softened
- ¼ cup heavy cream
- ¼ cup maple syrup
- ½ cup white sugar
- ½ teaspoon salt
- 1 cup all-purpose flour
- 1 cup dates, pitted and chopped
- 1 cup ground pecans
- 1 teaspoon baking powder
- 1 teaspoon vanilla extract
- 2 eggs

Frosting:

- ¼ cup maple syrup
- 1 cup butter, softened

Directions:

1. For the syrup, combine the butter, cream, sugar and maple syrup in a container until pale and creamy.
2. Put in the eggs and vanilla and mix thoroughly.
3. Fold in the pecans, flour, salt and baking powder then put in the dates.
4. Spoon the batter in a muffin tin covered with muffin papers.
5. Pre-heat the oven and bake at 350F for about twenty minutes or until a golden-brown colour is achieved and it rises significantly.
6. Let them cool in the pan.
7. To make the frosting, combine the butter and cream in a container.
8. Sprinkle the frosting over each cupcake and serve fresh.

Nutritional Content of One Serving:

Calories: 343 ‖ Fat: 21.9g ‖ Protein: 2.7g ‖ Carbohydrates: 36.8g

MAPLE SPICE MUFFINS

Total Time Taken: 1 hour
Yield: 12 Servings
Ingredients:

- ¼ teaspoon salt
- ½ cup canola oil
- ½ cup dark chocolate chips
- ½ cup milk
- ½ cup walnuts, chopped
- ½ teaspoon all-spice powder
- ½ teaspoon cinnamon powder
- ½ teaspoon ground ginger
- ¾ cup maple syrup
- 1 egg
- 1 teaspoon vanilla extract
- 2 ¼ cups all-purpose flour
- 2 teaspoons baking powder

Directions:

1. Mix the flour, salt, baking powder and spices in a container.
2. Put in the remaining ingredients and stir thoroughly until blended.
3. Fold in the walnuts and chocolate chips then spoon the batter in a muffin tin covered with muffin papers.
4. Pre-heat the oven and bake at 350F for about twenty minutes or until a toothpick inserted into them comes out dry.

These muffins taste best chilled.

Nutritional Content of One Serving:

Calories: 285 ‖ Fat: 14.3g ‖ Protein: 4.8g ‖ Carbohydrates: 36.0g

MANGO BUTTERMILK MUFFINS

Total Time Taken: 1 hour
Yield: 12 Servings
Ingredients:

- ¼ cup canola oil
- ¼ teaspoon salt
- ½ cup white sugar
- 1 ½ cups buttermilk
- 1 mango, peeled and diced
- 1 teaspoon baking soda
- 1 teaspoon vanilla extract
- 2 cups all-purpose flour
- 2 eggs

Directions:

1. Mix the flour, sugar, salt and baking soda in a container.
2. Put in the eggs, buttermilk, oil and vanilla and stir for a few seconds to mix.
3. Fold in the mango then spoon the batter in a muffin tin covered with muffin papers.
4. Preheat your oven and bake the muffins at 350F for about twenty minutes or until it rises significantly and starts to appear golden-brown.

These muffins taste best chilled.

Nutritional Content of One Serving:

Calories: 171 ‖ Fat: 5.7g ‖ Protein: 4.1g ‖ Carbohydrates: 25.8g

LOADED MUFFINS

Total Time Taken: 1 ¼ hours
Yield: 10 Servings

Ingredients:

- ¼ cup canola oil
- ¼ cup cocoa powder
- ¼ cup dried apricots, chopped
- ¼ cup dried cranberries
- ½ cup milk
- ½ teaspoon salt
- 1 ½ cups all-purpose flour
- 1 ½ teaspoons baking powder
- 2 eggs

- 2 tablespoons candied orange peel, chopped

Directions:

1. Mix the dry ingredients in a container.
2. Put in the remaining ingredients and stir for a few seconds to mix.
3. Spoon the batter in a muffin tin covered with muffin papers.
4. Preheat your oven and bake the muffins at 350F for about twenty minutes or until a golden-brown colour is achieved and it rises significantly.

These muffins taste best chilled.

Nutritional Content of One Serving:

Calories: 145 ‖ Fat: 7.1g ‖ Protein: 3.9g ‖ Carbohydrates: 17.5g

LEMON RICOTTA MUFFINS

Total Time Taken: 1 hour
Yield: 12 Servings
Ingredients:

- ¼ cup milk
- ½ cup butter, melted
- ½ cup ricotta cheese
- ½ teaspoon salt
- 1 ½ teaspoons baking powder
- 1 cup all-purpose flour
- 1 cup almond flour
- 1 tablespoon lemon zest
- 1 teaspoon vanilla extract
- 2 eggs

Directions:

1. Mix the butter, vanilla, eggs, ricotta, milk and lemon zest in a container.
2. Put in the flours, salt and baking powder and mix using a spatula.
3. Spoon the batter in 12 muffin cups coated with baking muffin papers of your desire.
4. Pre-heat the oven and bake at 350F for about twenty minutes or until it rises significantly and starts to appear golden-brown.

These muffins taste best chilled.

Nutritional Content of One Serving:

Calories: 148 ‖ Fat: 10.6g ‖ Protein: 3.9g ‖ Carbohydrates: 9.7g

LEMON POPPY SEED MUFFINS

Total Time Taken: 1 hour
Yield: 12 Servings
Ingredients:

- ½ cup canola oil
- ½ cup milk
- ½ cup white sugar
- ½ teaspoon salt
- 1 ½ teaspoons baking powder
- 1 ¾ cups all-purpose flour
- 1 tablespoon lemon zest
- 2 eggs
- 2 tablespoons lemon juice
- 2 tablespoons poppy seeds

Directions:

1. Mix the flour, salt, baking powder and poppy seeds in a container.
2. In a separate container, combine the eggs and sugar until fluffy and pale. Put in the oil and milk and mix thoroughly then mix in the lemon zest and juice.
3. Fold in the flour mixture then spoon the batter in 12 muffin cups covered with muffin papers.
4. Preheat your oven and bake the muffins at 350F for about twenty minutes or until a golden-brown colour is achieved and it rises significantly.

These muffins taste best chilled.

Nutritional Content of One Serving:

Calories: 203 ‖ Fat: 10.9g ‖ Protein: 3.4g ‖ Carbohydrates: 23.6g

LEMON GLAZED APPLE CIDER MUFFINS

Total Time Taken: 1 hour
Yield: 12 Servings
Ingredients:

- ¼ teaspoon salt
- ½ cup apple cider
- ½ cup coconut oil
- ½ cup light brown sugar
- ½ teaspoon baking soda
- ½ teaspoon cinnamon powder
- 1 cup powdered sugar
- 1 tablespoon lemon juice
- 1 teaspoon baking powder
- 1 teaspoon vanilla extract
- 2 cups all-purpose flour
- 2 eggs
- 2 red apples, cored and diced

Directions:

1. Mix the coconut oil and sugar in a container for a couple of minutes. Put in the eggs and vanilla and mix thoroughly.
2. Stir in the apple cider then fold in the flour, baking powder, baking soda, salt and cinnamon and mix using a spatula.
3. Fold in the apples then spoon the batter in a muffin tin covered with muffin papers.
4. Pre-heat the oven and bake at 350F for about twenty minutes or until set and golden brown.
5. For the glaze, combine the lemon juice and sugar in a container.
6. Sprinkle the mixture over the muffins and serve chilled.

Nutritional Content of One Serving:

Calories: 249 ‖ Fat: 10.1g ‖ Protein: 3.2g ‖ Carbohydrates: 37.5g

LEMON FIG MUFFINS

Total Time Taken: 1 hour
Yield: 12 Servings
Ingredients:

- ½ cup buttermilk
- ½ cup white sugar
- ½ teaspoon salt
- 1 cup all-purpose flour
- 1 cup ground almonds
- 1 lemon, zested and juiced
- 1 teaspoon baking soda
- 1/3 cup butter, melted
- 3 eggs
- 4 fresh figs, chopped

Directions:

1. Mix the butter, sugar, eggs, buttermilk, lemon zest and lemon juice in a container until creamy.
2. Put in the flour, salt and baking soda and mix using a spatula.
3. Fold in the figs then spoon the batter in a muffin tin covered with muffin papers.
4. Pre-heat the oven and bake at 350F for about twenty minutes or until a toothpick inserted into them comes out dry.
5. Best served chilled.

Nutritional Content of One Serving:

Calories: 197 ‖ Fat: 10.4g ‖ Protein: 4.8g ‖ Carbohydrates: 23.0g

LEMON CURD CUPCAKES

Total Time Taken: 1 ½ hours
Yield: 12 Servings

Ingredients:

- ½ cup almond flour
- ½ teaspoon salt
- ¾ cup butter, softened
- ¾ cup white sugar

- 1 ½ cups all-purpose flour
- 1 cup lemon curd
- 1 tablespoon lemon zest
- 1 teaspoon vanilla extract
- 2 tablespoons lemon juice
- 2 teaspoons baking powder
- 3 eggs

Directions:

1. Mix the butter and sugar in a container until pale and fluffy.
2. Put in the eggs, one at a time, and mix thoroughly then mix in the lemon zest and juice, as well as vanilla.
3. Fold in the flours, salt and baking powder then spoon the batter in 12 muffin cups covered with muffin papers.
4. Preheat your oven and bake the cupcakes at 350F for about twenty minutes or until it rises significantly and starts to appear golden-brown.
5. When finished, let cool and top each cupcake with a dollop of lemon curd.

Nutritional Content of One Serving:

Calories: 311 ‖ Fat: 21.4g ‖ Protein: 4.7g ‖ Carbohydrates: 30.7g

LEMON CHIA SEED MUFFINS

Total Time Taken: 1 hour
Yield: 12 Servings
Ingredients:

- ¼ teaspoon salt
- ½ cup coconut oil, melted
- ½ teaspoon baking soda
- 1 ½ teaspoons baking powder
- 1 cup plain yogurt
- 1 cup white sugar
- 1 teaspoon vanilla extract
- 2 cups all-purpose flour
- 2 eggs
- 2 tablespoons chia seeds

Directions:

1. Mix the chia seeds, flour, baking powder, baking soda and salt in a container.
2. Put in the yogurt, coconut oil, vanilla, sugar and eggs and stir for a few seconds to mix.
3. Spoon the batter in a muffin tin covered with muffin papers.
4. Pre-heat the oven and bake at 350F for about twenty minutes or until a toothpick inserted into them comes out dry.

These muffins taste best chilled.

Nutritional Content of One Serving:

Calories: 269 ‖ Fat: 11.9g ‖ Protein: 5.3g ‖ Carbohydrates: 36.2g

LEMON BLUEBERRY MUFFINS

Total Time Taken: 1 hour
Yield: 12 Servings
Ingredients:

- ½ cup white sugar
- ½ teaspoon salt
- 1 cup buttermilk
- 1 cup fresh blueberries
- 1 tablespoon lemon zest
- 1 teaspoon vanilla extract
- 2 cups all-purpose flour
- 2 eggs
- 2 tablespoons chia seeds
- 2 teaspoons baking powder

Directions:

1. Mix the flour, baking powder, salt, chia seeds and sugar in a container.
2. Put in the remaining ingredients and mix using a spatula.
3. Spoon the batter into 12 muffin cups covered with muffin papers.
4. Preheat your oven and bake the muffins at 350F for about twenty minutes or until it rises significantly and starts to appear golden-brown.

These muffins taste best chilled.

Nutritional Content of One Serving:

Calories: 146 ‖ Fat: 1.9g ‖ Protein: 4.4g ‖ Carbohydrates: 27.7g

INTENSE CHOCOLATE CUPCAKES

Total Time Taken: 1 ½ hours
Yield: 12 Servings
Ingredients:

Cupcakes:

- ¼ cup canola oil
- ¼ cup cocoa powder
- ½ cup buttermilk
- ½ teaspoon baking powder
- ½ teaspoon salt
- 1 ½ cups all-purpose flour
- 1 cup brewed coffee
- 1 egg
- 1 teaspoon baking soda
- 1 teaspoon vanilla extract
- 3 oz. dark chocolate

Frosting:

- 1 cup butter, softened
- 2 cups powdered sugar
- 2 tablespoons cocoa powder
- 2 tablespoons heavy cream

Directions:

1. To make the cupcakes, combine the wet ingredients in a container. Put in the dry ingredients and stir swiftly to combine.
2. Pour the cupcakes in 12 muffin cups covered with muffin papers.
3. Preheat your oven and bake the cupcakes at 350F for about twenty minutes.
4. To make the frosting, combine the butter and sugar in a container until fluffy and pale.
5. Put in the remaining ingredients and mix thoroughly.
6. Spoon the frosting in a pastry bag and top each cupcake with it.

Nutritional Content of One Serving:

Calories: 374 ‖ Fat: 23.9g ‖ Protein: 3.7g ‖ Carbohydrates: 38.3g

---

HUMMINGBIRD MUFFINS

Total Time Taken: 1 ½ hours
Yield: 12 Servings

Ingredients:

- ¼ teaspoon cinnamon powder
- ½ cup canola oil
- ½ cup crushed pineapple
- ½ cup grated carrots
- ½ cup shredded coconut
- ½ cup walnuts, chopped
- ½ cup white sugar
- ½ teaspoon salt
- 1 ½ cups all-purpose flour
- 1 ½ teaspoons baking powder
- 1 teaspoon orange zest
- 1 teaspoon vanilla extract
- 2 bananas, mashed
- 2 eggs

Directions:

1. Mix the eggs and sugar in a container until fluffy and pale.
2. Put in the bananas and oil, as well as vanilla and mix thoroughly.
3. Fold in the flour, salt, baking powder and cinnamon then put in the coconut, walnuts, pineapple, carrots and orange zest.
4. Pour the batter in a muffin tin covered with muffin papers.
5. Preheat your oven and bake the muffins at 350F for about twenty minutes or until a golden-brown colour is achieved and it rises significantly.

These muffins taste best chilled.

Nutritional Content of One Serving:

Calories: 247 ‖ Fat: 14.2g ‖ Protein: 4.2g ‖ Carbohydrates: 27.6g

HONEY SPICED MUFFINS

Total Time Taken: 1 hour

Yield: 12 Servings

Ingredients:

- ½ cup butter, melted
- ½ cup honey
- ½ teaspoon cinnamon powder
- ½ teaspoon ground cardamom
- ½ teaspoon ground ginger
- ½ teaspoon ground star anise
- ½ teaspoon salt
- 1 cup all-purpose flour
- 1 cup ground almonds
- 1 teaspoon baking soda
- 1 teaspoon vanilla extract
- 2 eggs
- 2 tablespoons dark brown sugar

Directions:

1. Mix the butter, eggs, honey and sugar in a container.
2. Stir in the remaining ingredients and mix using a spatula just until incorporated.
3. Pour the batter in a muffin tin covered with muffin papers.
4. Pre-heat the oven and bake at 350F for about twenty minutes or until it rises completely and is aromatic.

These muffins taste best chilled.

Nutritional Content of One Serving:

Calories: 213 ‖ Fat: 12.5g ‖ Protein: 3.9g ‖ Carbohydrates: 23.1g

HONEY PUMPKIN MUFFINS

Total Time Taken: 1 hour

Yield: 12 Servings

Ingredients:

- 2 teaspoons baking powder
- 2 tablespoons pumpkin seeds
- 2 eggs
- 1 teaspoon vanilla extract
- 1 cup pumpkin puree
- 1 cup oat flour
- 1 cup all-purpose flour
- ½ cup honey
- ¼ teaspoon salt

Directions:

1. Mix the honey, pumpkin puree, vanilla and eggs in a container.
2. Put in the remaining ingredients then pour the batter in a muffin tin covered with muffin papers of your desire.
3. Pre-heat the oven and bake at 350F for about twenty minutes or until it rises significantly and starts to appear golden-brown.

These muffins taste best chilled.

Nutritional Content of One Serving:

Calories: 138 ‖ Fat: 2.1g ‖ Protein: 3.6g ‖ Carbohydrates: 27.2g

HONEY PEAR MUFFINS

Total Time Taken: 1 hour
Yield: 12 Servings
Ingredients:

- ¼ cup butter, melted
- ¼ teaspoon ground nutmeg
- ½ cup buttermilk
- ½ cup light brown sugar
- ½ teaspoon cinnamon powder
- ½ teaspoon salt
- 1 ½ cups all-purpose flour
- 1 ½ teaspoons baking powder
- 1 teaspoon vanilla extract
- 2 eggs

- 2 pears, cored and diced

Directions:

1. Mix the dry ingredients in a container and the wet ingredients in a separate container.
2. Combine the two mixtures together and mix quickly with a whisk or spatula.
3. Fold in the pears then spoon the batter in a muffin tin covered with muffin papers.
4. Preheat your oven and bake the muffins at 350F for about twenty minutes or until a golden-brown colour is achieved and it rises significantly.

These muffins taste best chilled.

Nutritional Content of One Serving:

Calories: 150 ‖ Fat: 4.9g ‖ Protein: 3.0g ‖ Carbohydrates: 24.1g

HONEY NUTMEG PEACH MUFFINS

Total Time Taken: 1 hour
Yield: 12 Servings
Ingredients:

- ¼ cup honey
- ¼ teaspoon salt
- ½ cup buttermilk
- ½ cup ground walnuts
- ½ cup white sugar
- ½ teaspoon ground nutmeg
- 1 ½ cups all-purpose flour
- 1 banana, mashed
- 1 teaspoon baking soda
- 2 eggs
- 2 peaches, pitted and diced

Directions:

1. Mix the dry ingredients in a container.
2. Stir in the eggs, honey, banana and buttermilk and stir for a few seconds to mix.

3. Fold in the peaches and spoon the batter in a muffin tin covered with muffin papers.
4. Pre-heat the oven and bake at 350F for about twenty minutes or until it rises significantly and starts to appear golden-brown.
5. Let the muffins cool in the pan before you serve.

Nutritional Content of One Serving:

Calories: 172 ‖ Fat: 4.1g ‖ Protein: 4.4g ‖ Carbohydrates: 31.0g

HONEY LEMON MUFFINS

Total Time Taken: 1 hour
Yield: 12 Servings
Ingredients:

- ¼ cup canola oil
- ¼ cup honey
- ¼ teaspoon salt
- ½ cup milk
- ½ cup white chocolate chips
- 1 ½ cups all-purpose flour
- 1 ½ teaspoons baking powder
- 1 tablespoon lemon zest
- 2 eggs
- 2 tablespoons lemon juice

Directions:

1. Mix the flour, salt and baking powder in a container.
2. Put in the remaining ingredients and mix thoroughly.
3. Spoon the batter in a muffin tin coated with baking muffin papers and preheat your oven and bake at 350F for about twenty minutes or until it rises significantly and starts to appear golden-brown.
4. Let cool down before you serve.

Nutritional Content of One Serving:

Calories: 174 ‖ Fat: 7.9g ‖ Protein: 3.3g ‖ Carbohydrates: 23.0g

HONEY CARDAMOM CUPCAKES

Total Time Taken: 1 ½ hours
Yield: 12 Servings
Ingredients:

Cupcakes:

- ½ cup butter, softened
- ½ cup honey
- ½ teaspoon salt
- 1 ½ cups all-purpose flour
- 1 ½ teaspoons baking powder
- 1 teaspoon ground cardamom
- 1 teaspoon vanilla extract
- 1/3 cup milk
- 2 eggs
- 2 tablespoons dark brown sugar

Frosting:

- ¼ cup honey
- 1 cup butter, softened
- 1 teaspoon vanilla extract
- 2 cups powdered sugar

Directions:

1. To make the cupcakes, combine the butter, honey and sugar in a container until fluffy and pale. Put in the vanilla and eggs and mix thoroughly.
2. Fold in the flour, salt, baking powder and cardamom, alternating them with milk.
3. Spoon the batter in a muffin tin covered with muffin papers.
4. Pre-heat the oven and bake at 350F for about twenty minutes or until a golden-brown colour is achieved.
5. Let them cool in the pan.
6. To make the frosting, combine the butter and sugar in a container for about five to seven minutes until fluffy and pale. Stir in the vanilla and mix thoroughly.
7. Spoon the frosting into a pastry and top each cupcake with it.
8. Sprinkle the frosted cupcakes with honey.

Nutritional Content of One Serving:

Calories: 425 ‖ Fat: 24.1g ‖ Protein: 3.1g ‖ Carbohydrates: 51.7g

HEALTHY CHOCOLATE MUFFINS

Total Time Taken: 1 hour
Yield: 12 Servings
Ingredients:

- ¼ teaspoon salt
- ½ cup cocoa powder
- ½ cup low fat milk
- ½ cup maple syrup
- 1 ½ cups whole wheat flour
- 1 ½ teaspoons baking powder
- 1 cup plain yogurt
- 1 egg
- 1 teaspoon vanilla extract

Directions:

1. Mix the flour, baking powder, salt and cocoa powder in a container.
2. Put in the remaining ingredients and stir for a few seconds to mix.
3. Spoon the batter in a muffin tin covered with muffin papers and preheat your oven and bake at 350F for about twenty minutes or until a toothpick inserted into them comes out dry.
4. Let cool in the pan before you serve.

Nutritional Content of One Serving:

Calories: 125 ‖ Fat: 1.4g ‖ Protein: 4.2g ‖ Carbohydrates: 25.0g

HAZELNUT FIG MUFFINS

Total Time Taken: 1 hour
Yield: 12 Servings
Ingredients:

- ¼ cup canola oil

- ½ cup all-purpose flour
- ½ cup light brown sugar
- ½ teaspoon salt
- 1 cup ground hazelnuts
- 1 teaspoon baking powder
- 12 fresh figs
- 4 eggs

Directions:

1. Mix the hazelnuts, flour, salt and baking powder in a container.
2. Mix the eggs and sugar in a container until pale and light. Put in the oil and mix thoroughly.
3. Fold in the flour and hazelnut mixture then pour the batter in a muffin tin covered with muffin papers.
4. Top each muffin with a fig and preheat your oven and bake at 350F for about twenty minutes or until it rises significantly and seems golden.

These muffins taste best chilled.

Nutritional Content of One Serving:

Calories: 190 ‖ Fat: 10.0g ‖ Protein: 4.0g ‖ Carbohydrates: 23.4g

HARVEST MUFFINS

Total Time Taken: 1 hour
Yield: 12 Servings
Ingredients:

- 2 eggs
- 2 cups all-purpose flour
- 1 teaspoon baking powder
- 1 pear, cored and diced
- 1 cup milk
- 1 apple, cored and diced
- ½ teaspoon ground ginger
- ½ teaspoon cinnamon powder
- ½ teaspoon baking soda
- ½ cup light brown sugar

- ½ cup dried cranberries
- ½ cup butter, melted
- ¼ teaspoon salt

Directions:

1. Mix the flour, baking powder, baking soda, salt, cinnamon, ginger and sugar in a container.
2. Put in the eggs, milk and butter and stir for a few seconds to mix.
3. Fold in the apple, pear and cranberries then spoon the batter in a muffin pan coated with muffin papers.
4. Pre-heat the oven and bake at 350F for about twenty minutes or until it rises significantly and becomes aromatic.
5. Let the muffins cool to room temperature before you serve.

Nutritional Content of One Serving:

Calories: 205 ‖ Fat: 9.1g ‖ Protein: 3.9g ‖ Carbohydrates: 27.4g

GRAPEFRUIT CREAM CHEESE CUPCAKES

Total Time Taken: 1 ½ hours
Yield: 12 Servings
Ingredients:

Cupcakes:

- ½ cup butter, softened
- ½ teaspoon salt
- ¾ cup buttermilk
- ¾ cup white sugar
- 1 ½ teaspoons baking powder
- 1 ¾ cups all-purpose flour
- 1 teaspoon grapefruit zest
- 2 eggs

Frosting:

- ½ cup butter
- 1 cup cream cheese

- 1 tablespoon grapefruit zest
- 2 cups powder sugar

Directions:

1. To make the cupcakes, combine the butter and sugar in a container until fluffy and creamy.
2. Put in the zest and eggs and mix thoroughly.
3. Stir in the flour, salt and baking powder then put in the milk and mix thoroughly.
4. Spoon the batter in a muffin tin covered with muffin papers and preheat your oven and bake at 350F for about twenty minutes.
5. Let the cupcakes cool in the pan.
6. To make the frosting, combine the cream cheese and butter in a container until fluffy.
7. Put in the eggs and stir thoroughly for 4-5 minutes then mix in the zest.
8. Garnish each cupcake with frosting and serve them fresh.

Nutritional Content of One Serving:

Calories: 412 ‖ Fat: 23.1g ‖ Protein: 4.9g ‖ Carbohydrates: 48.1g

GRAIN FREE APPLE CINNAMON

Total Time Taken: 1 ¼ hours

Yield: 12 Servings

Ingredients:

- ¼ cup coconut oil, melted
- ¼ cup honey
- ¼ teaspoon salt
- ½ cup coconut milk
- ½ cup tapioca flour
- ½ teaspoon baking powder
- ½ teaspoon baking soda
- 1 ½ cups almond flour
- 1 teaspoon cinnamon powder
- 1 teaspoon lemon juice
- 1 teaspoon vanilla extract

- 2 red apples, cored and diced
- 3 eggs

Directions:

1. Mix the flours, cinnamon, baking soda, baking powder and salt in a container.
2. Put in the eggs and the remaining ingredients and mix thoroughly.
3. Spoon the batter in a muffin tin coated with baking muffin papers then preheat your oven and bake at 350F for about twenty minutes or until a golden-brown colour is achieved and it rises significantly.

These muffins taste best chilled.

Nutritional Content of One Serving:

Calories: 163 ‖ Fat: 9.8g ‖ Protein: 2.5g ‖ Carbohydrates: 18.5g

GLUTEN FREE MAPLE MUFFINS

Total Time Taken: 1 hour
Yield: 12 Servings
Ingredients:

- ¼ cup tapioca flour
- ¼ teaspoon salt
- ½ cup butter, melted
- ½ cup coconut flour
- ½ cup maple syrup
- ½ cup sorghum flour
- ¾ cup milk
- 1 ½ teaspoons baking powder
- 1 teaspoon vanilla extract
- 2 eggs
- 2 tablespoons dark brown sugar

Directions:

1. Mix the eggs, butter, maple syrup, sugar and vanilla in a container until creamy.
2. Put in the remaining ingredients and mix thoroughly.

3. Pour the batter in a muffin tin covered with muffin papers.
4. Pre-heat the oven and bake at 350F for about twenty minutes or until a toothpick inserted into the center of a muffin comes out clean.
5. Let the muffins cool to room temperature before you serve.

Nutritional Content of One Serving:

Calories: 203 ‖ Fat: 9.7g ‖ Protein: 3.1g ‖ Carbohydrates: 27.3g

GLUTEN FREE CHOCOLATE MUFFINS

Total Time Taken: 1 hour

Yield: 10 Servings

Ingredients:

- ¼ cup cocoa powder
- ½ cup canola oil
- ½ cup dark chocolate chips
- ½ cup shredded coconut
- ½ cup tapioca flour
- ½ cup white rice flour
- ½ cup white sugar
- ½ teaspoon salt
- 1 teaspoon baking powder
- 1 teaspoon vanilla extract
- 3 eggs

Directions:

1. Mix the eggs, sugar and vanilla in a container until fluffy and pale.
2. Put in the oil then mix in the remaining ingredients.
3. Spoon the batter in a muffin tin covered with muffin papers and preheat your oven and bake at 350F for about twenty minutes or until it rises significantly and becomes aromatic.

These muffins taste best chilled.

Nutritional Content of One Serving:

Calories: 251 ‖ Fat: 15.4g ‖ Protein: 2.9g ‖ Carbohydrates: 28.7g

GLUTEN FREE CHOCOLATE CUPCAKES WITH PUMPKIN FROSTING

Total Time Taken: 1 ½ hours
Yield: 12 Servings
Ingredients:

Cupcakes:

- ¼ cup coconut oil, melted
- ¼ teaspoon salt
- ½ cup buckwheat flour
- ½ cup cocoa powder
- ½ cup coconut flour
- ½ cup maple syrup
- 1 cup shredded coconut
- 1 cup sparkling water
- 1 teaspoon baking soda
- 1 teaspoon vanilla extract

Frosting:

- ¼ teaspoon cinnamon powder
- ¼ teaspoon ground ginger
- ½ cup pumpkin puree
- ½ cup walnuts
- 1 cup dates, pitted
- 2 tablespoons coconut oil
- 2 tablespoons maple syrup

Directions:

1. To make the cupcakes, combine the flours, shredded coconut, cocoa powder, baking soda and salt in a container.
2. In a separate container, mix the maple syrup, sparkling water, coconut oil and vanilla and mix thoroughly. Put in the dry ingredients and stir for a few seconds to mix.
3. Pour the batter in a muffin tin covered with muffin papers and preheat your oven and bake at 350F for about twenty minutes or until a toothpick inserted into them comes out dry.
4. Let the cupcakes cool down.

5. To make the frosting, place the dates and the rest of the ingredients in a food processor or blender and pulse until well mixed.
6. Top each cupcake with the frosting and serve fresh.

Nutritional Content of One Serving:

Calories: 249 ‖ Fat: 13.5g ‖ Protein: 3.9g ‖ Carbohydrates: 32.8g

GINGERBREAD MUFFINS

Total Time Taken: 1 hour
Yield: 12 Servings
Ingredients:

- ½ cup raisins
- ½ cup wheat bran
- ½ cup white sugar
- ½ teaspoon ground ginger
- ½ teaspoon ground star anise
- ½ teaspoon salt
- 1 ½ cups all-purpose flour
- 1 cup buttermilk
- 1 egg
- 1 teaspoon cinnamon powder
- 1 teaspoon vanilla extract
- 2 tablespoons dark molasses

Directions:

1. Mix the dry ingredients in a container.
2. Put in the wet ingredients and stir for a few seconds to mix.
3. Spoon the batter in a muffin tin covered with muffin papers.
4. Preheat your oven and bake the muffins at 350F for about twenty minutes or until it is aromatic and appears golden.
5. Best served chilled.

Nutritional Content of One Serving:

Calories: 137 ‖ Fat: 0.8g ‖ Protein: 3.4g ‖ Carbohydrates: 30.3g

GINGER PINEAPPLE MUFFINS

Total Time Taken: 1 hour
Yield: 12 Servings
Ingredients:

- ½ cup canola oil
- ½ cup milk
- ½ cup shredded coconut
- ½ teaspoon cinnamon powder
- ½ teaspoon salt
- ¾ cup light brown sugar
- 1 ½ cups all-purpose flour
- 1 ½ teaspoons baking powder
- 1 cup crushed pineapple
- 1 egg
- 1 teaspoon ground ginger

Directions:

1. Mix the oil and sugar until creamy. Put in the egg and mix thoroughly then mix in the milk and mix very well.
2. Fold in the flour, coconut, salt, baking powder, ginger and cinnamon and mix thoroughly.
3. Fold in the pineapple then spoon the batter in a muffin tin covered with muffin papers.
4. Pre-heat the oven and bake at 350F for about twenty minutes or until it rises significantly and starts to appear golden-brown.

These muffins taste best chilled.

Nutritional Content of One Serving:

Calories: 202 ‖ Fat: 10.9g ‖ Protein: 2.6g ‖ Carbohydrates: 24.1g

GERMAN CHOCOLATE CUPCAKES

Total Time Taken: 1 ½ hours
Yield: Servings 18
Ingredients:

Cupcakes:

- 1 cup butter, softened
- ¼ cup light brown sugar
- 2 eggs
- 1 teaspoon vanilla extract
- 1 cup buttermilk
- ½ cup sour cream
- 1 cup cocoa powder
- ¼ teaspoon salt
- 1 ½ teaspoons baking powder
- ½ teaspoon baking soda
- 2/3 cup white sugar
- 1 3/4 cups all-purpose flour

Frosting:

- ½ cup pecans, chopped
- 1 cup butter, softened
- 1 cup evaporated milk
- 1 cup light brown sugar
- 1 cup sliced almonds
- 2 cups shredded coconut

Directions:

1. To make the cupcakes, combine the butter, sugars and vanilla in a container until fluffy and pale.
2. Put in the eggs, one at a time, and mix thoroughly then mix in the buttermilk and sour cream.
3. Fold in the flour, cocoa powder, salt, baking powder and baking soda.
4. Spoon the batter in a muffin tin covered with muffin papers.
5. Pre-heat the oven and bake at 350F for about twenty minutes.
6. To make the frosting, combine the butter, sugar and evaporated milk in a container until creamy and fluffy.
7. Put in the coconut, almonds and pecans and mix thoroughly.
8. Top each cupcake with the frosting and serve them fresh.

Nutritional Content of One Serving:

Calories: 415 ‖ Fat: 30.4g ‖ Protein: 6.1g ‖ Carbohydrates: 34.4g

FUNFETTI CREAM CHEESE CUPCAKES

Total Time Taken: 1 ½ hours
Yield: 12 Servings
Ingredients:

Cupcakes:

- ½ cup colourful sprinkles
- ½ cup butter, softened
- ½ cup milk
- ½ cup sour cream
- ½ teaspoon baking soda
- ½ teaspoon salt
- 1 ¾ cups all-purpose flour
- 1 teaspoon baking powder
- 1 teaspoon vanilla extract
- 2 eggs
- 2/3 cup white sugar

Frosting:

- ½ cup butter, softened
- 1 cup cream cheese
- 2 cups powdered sugar
- Sprinkles to garnish

Directions:

1. To make the cupcakes, combine the butter and sugar in a container until creamy and pale.
2. Put in the eggs and mix thoroughly then mix in the sour cream, milk and vanilla.
3. Fold in the sprinkles then spoon the batter in a muffin tin coated with baking muffin papers.
4. Pre-heat the oven and bake at 350F for about twenty minutes or until it rises significantly and starts to appear golden-brown.
5. Let the cupcakes cool down.
6. To make the frosting, combine the cream cheese and butter in a container until pale.
7. Put in the sugar and mix thoroughly for about five to seven minutes or until fluffy and light.

8. Garnish the cupcakes with cream cheese frosting.
9. Top with colourful sprinkles.

Nutritional Content of One Serving:

Calories: 438 ‖ Fat: 25.7g ‖ Protein: 5.2g ‖ Carbohydrates: 48.6g

FUNFETTI BANANA MUFFINS

Total Time Taken: 1 hour
Yield: 12 Servings
Ingredients:

- ¼ cup colourful sprinkles
- ¼ teaspoon salt
- ½ cup almond flour
- ½ cup canola oil
- ½ cup milk
- ½ cup white sugar
- 1 ½ cups all-purpose flour
- 1 teaspoon baking powder
- 1 teaspoon vanilla extract
- 2 eggs

Directions:

1. Mix the eggs and sugar in a container until fluffy and pale.
2. Put in the oil, vanilla and milk and mix thoroughly.
3. Fold in the flours, salt and baking powder then put in the sprinkles.
4. Spoon the batter in a muffin tin covered with muffin papers and preheat your oven and bake at 350F for about twenty minutes or until a golden-brown colour is achieved and it rises significantly.
5. Let cool down before you serve.

Nutritional Content of One Serving:

Calories: 204 ‖ Fat: 11.2g ‖ Protein: 3.3g ‖ Carbohydrates: 23.3g

FUDGY CHOCOLATE MUFFINS

Total Time Taken: 1 hour

Yield: 12 Servings

Ingredients:

- ½ cup canola oil
- ½ teaspoon salt
- 1 ¾ cups all-purpose flour
- 1 cup dark chocolate chips
- 1 cup milk
- 1 egg
- 1 teaspoon vanilla extract
- 2 tablespoons cocoa powder
- 2 teaspoons baking powder
- 3 oz. dark chocolate

Directions:

1. Mix the dark chocolate and canola oil in a heatproof container and place over a hot water bath. Melt them together until smooth then turn off heat and put in the egg, milk, sugar and vanilla.
2. Fold in the flour, cocoa powder, baking powder and salt then put in the chocolate chips.
3. Spoon the batter in a muffin tin covered with muffin papers.
4. Preheat your oven and bake the muffins at 350F for about twenty minutes or until well risen and a toothpick inserted into the center of a muffin comes out clean.

These muffins taste best chilled.

Nutritional Content of One Serving:

Calories: 250 ‖ Fat: 14.9g ‖ Protein: 4.4g ‖ Carbohydrates: 26.7g

FUDGY CHOCOLATE DATE MUFFINS

Total Time Taken: 1 hour

Yield: 12 Servings

Ingredients:

- ¼ cup cornstarch
- ¼ cup milk
- ½ cup cocoa powder
- ½ cup fresh orange juice
- ½ teaspoon salt
- 1 cup all-purpose flour
- 1 cup dates, pitted
- 1 teaspoon baking soda
- 1 teaspoon orange zest
- 1 teaspoon vanilla extract
- 2 eggs

Directions:

1. Mix the dates, orange juice, orange zest, eggs and vanilla in a blender and pulse until the desired smoothness is achieved. Put in the milk and mix thoroughly.
2. Fold in the remaining ingredients and mix thoroughly.
3. Pour the batter in a muffin tin covered with muffin papers.
4. Preheat your oven and bake the muffins at 350F for about twenty minutes or until a toothpick inserted into the center of a muffin comes out clean.

These muffins taste best chilled.

Nutritional Content of One Serving:

Calories: 117 ‖ Fat: 1.5g ‖ Protein: 3.3g ‖ Carbohydrates: 24.9g

FRESH GINGER MUFFINS

Total Time Taken: 1 hour
Yield: 12 Servings
Ingredients:

- ½ cup butter, softened
- ½ cup light brown sugar
- ½ teaspoon salt
- 1 ½ teaspoons grated ginger
- 1 cup buttermilk
- 1 teaspoon vanilla extract

- 2 cups all-purpose flour
- 2 eggs
- 2 teaspoons baking powder

Directions:

1. Mix the butter, eggs, buttermilk, ginger and vanilla in a container.
2. Stir in the sugar and mix thoroughly.
3. Fold in the flour, salt and baking powder then spoon the batter in a muffin tin covered with muffin papers.
4. Pre-heat the oven and bake at 350F for about twenty minutes or until it rises significantly and starts to appear golden-brown.

These muffins taste best chilled.

Nutritional Content of One Serving:

Calories: 188 ‖ Fat: 8.8g ‖ Protein: 3.9g ‖ Carbohydrates: 23.5g

FRAGRANT DATE BANANA MUFFINS

Total Time Taken: 1 ¼ hours
Yield: 12 Servings

Ingredients:

- ¼ teaspoon salt
- ½ cup butter, melted
- ½ cup light brown sugar
- 1 ½ cups all-purpose flour
- 1 cup dates, pitted and chopped
- 2 eggs
- 2 teaspoons baking powder
- 4 bananas, mashed

Directions:

1. Mix the butter, eggs, bananas and sugar in a container.
2. Put in the flour, baking powder and salt and stir swiftly to combine.
3. Fold in the dates then spoon the batter in a muffin tin covered with muffin papers.

4. Pre-heat the oven and bake at 350F for about twenty minutes or until it rises significantly and starts to appear golden-brown.
5. Let cool down before you serve.

Nutritional Content of One Serving:

Calories: 236 ‖ Fat: 8.7g ‖ Protein: 3.4g ‖ Carbohydrates: 38.4g

FLAXSEED PUMPKIN MUFFINS

Total Time Taken: 1 hour
Yield: 12 Servings
Ingredients:

- ¼ cup canola oil
- ¼ cup ground flaxseeds
- ¼ teaspoon baking soda
- ¼ teaspoon salt
- ½ cup buttermilk
- 1 ¼ cups all-purpose flour
- 1 cup pumpkin puree
- 1 egg
- 1 teaspoon baking powder
- 1 teaspoon pumpkin pie spices
- 1 teaspoon vanilla extract

Directions:

1. Mix the flour, flaxseeds, spices, baking powder, baking soda and salt in a container.
2. Put in the remaining ingredients and mix thoroughly.
3. Spoon the batter in a muffin tin lined with special muffin papers.
4. Preheat your oven and bake the muffins at 350F for about twenty minutes or until a toothpick inserted into them comes out dry.
5. Let cool in the pan before you serve.

Nutritional Content of One Serving:

Calories: 118 ‖ Fat: 5.9g ‖ Protein: 2.8g ‖ Carbohydrates: 13.1g

FIG WALNUT MUFFINS

Total Time Taken: 1 hour

Yield: 12 Servings

Ingredients:

- ¼ teaspoon baking soda
- ¼ teaspoon salt
- ½ cup shredded coconut
- ½ cup white sugar
- 1 ½ cups whole wheat flour
- 1 cup coconut milk
- 1 cup ground walnuts
- 1 egg
- 1 pinch cinnamon powder
- 1 teaspoon baking powder
- 1 teaspoon vanilla extract
- 1/3 cup olive oil
- 6 fresh figs, quartered

Directions:

1. Mix the flour, baking powder, baking soda, salt, cinnamon, sugar, coconut and walnuts in a container.
2. Put in the remaining ingredients and mix thoroughly.
3. Pour the batter in a muffin tin covered with muffin papers and top with figs.
4. Pre-heat the oven and bake at 350F for about twenty minutes or until a toothpick inserted into them comes out dry.
5. Let the muffins cool in the pan before you serve.

Nutritional Content of One Serving:

Calories: 289 ‖ Fat: 18.2g ‖ Protein: 5.5g ‖ Carbohydrates: 29.3g

EXTRA CHOCOLATE MUFFINS

Total Time Taken: 1 hour

Yield: 12 Servings

Ingredients:

- ¼ cup cocoa powder
- ½ cup dark chocolate chips
- ½ cup light brown sugar
- ½ cup white chocolate chips
- ½ teaspoon baking powder
- ½ teaspoon baking soda
- ½ teaspoon salt
- 1 ¾ cups all-purpose flour
- 1 cup milk
- 1/3 cup canola oil
- 2 eggs

Directions:

1. Mix the dry ingredients in a container then put in the wet ingredients.
2. Fold in the chocolate chips then spoon the batter in a muffin cups covered with muffin papers.
3. Preheat your oven and bake the muffins at 350F for about twenty minutes or until well risen.

These muffins taste best chilled.

Nutritional Content of One Serving:

Calories: 229 ‖ Fat: 11.2g ‖ Protein: 4.5g ‖ Carbohydrates: 29.5g

ESPRESSO SOUR CREAM CUPCAKES

Total Time Taken: 1 ½ hours
Yield: 12 Servings
Ingredients:

Cupcakes:

- 1 teaspoon vanilla extract
- 2 eggs
- ½ cup sour cream
- ¼ cup brewed espresso
- 1 ½ cups all-purpose flour
- ½ teaspoon salt
- 1 ½ teaspoons baking powder

- ¼ cup cornstarch
- 2/3 cup butter, softened
- 2/3 cup white sugar

Frosting:

- 1 cup butter, softened
- 1 teaspoon vanilla extract
- 2 cups powdered sugar
- 2 teaspoons instant coffee

Directions:

1. To make the cupcakes, combine the butter and sugar in a container until pale and creamy.
2. Put in the vanilla and eggs and mix thoroughly. Stir in the espresso and sour cream.
3. Put in the remaining ingredients and mix using a spatula.
4. Spoon the batter in a muffin tin covered with muffin papers.
5. Pre-heat the oven and bake at 350F for about twenty minutes or until it rises significantly and starts to appear golden-brown.
6. Let the cupcakes cool in the pan.
7. To make the frosting, combine the butter and sugar in a container for minimum five minutes or until pale and creamy.
8. Put in the coffee and vanilla and mix thoroughly.
9. Spoon the frosting in a pastry bag and top the cupcakes with it.

These are best enjoyed fresh.

Nutritional Content of One Serving:

Calories: 447 ‖ Fat: 28.5g ‖ Protein: 3.1g ‖ Carbohydrates: 46.4g

EGGLESS PUMPKIN MUFFINS

Total Time Taken: 1 hour
Yield: 12 Servings
Ingredients:

- ¼ teaspoon salt
- ½ cup coconut oil, melted
- ½ cup maple syrup

- 1 cup pumpkin puree
- 1 teaspoon lemon juice
- 1 teaspoon pumpkin pie spices
- 1 teaspoon vanilla extract
- 2 cups all-purpose flour
- 2 teaspoons baking powder
- 3/4 cup almond milk

Directions:

1. Mix the wet ingredients in a container.
2. Put in the remaining ingredients and stir for a few seconds to mix.
3. Spoon the batter in a muffin tin covered with muffin papers and preheat your oven and bake at 350F for about twenty minutes or until a toothpick inserted into them comes out dry.

These muffins taste best chilled.

Nutritional Content of One Serving:

Calories: 232 ‖ Fat: 13.0g ‖ Protein: 2.7g ‖ Carbohydrates: 27.7g

DUO CHOCOLATE CHIP MUFFINS

Total Time Taken: 1 hour
Yield: 12 Servings
Ingredients:

- ½ cup canola oil
- ½ cup dark chocolate chips
- ½ cup white chocolate chips
- ½ teaspoon salt
- 1 ½ teaspoons baking powder
- 1 cup milk
- 1 cup white sugar
- 2 cups all-purpose flour
- 2 eggs

Directions:

1. Mix the oil and sugar in a container. Put in the eggs and mix thoroughly then mix in the milk.
2. Fold in the flour, salt and baking powder then put in the chocolate chips.
3. Spoon the batter in a muffin tin covered with muffin papers and preheat your oven and bake at 350F for about twenty minutes or until a golden-brown colour is achieved.

These muffins taste best chilled.

Nutritional Content of One Serving:

Calories: 301 ‖ Fat: 14.0g ‖ Protein: 4.5g ‖ Carbohydrates: 41.4g

DOUBLE CHOCOLATE NUTELLA MUFFINS

Total Time Taken: 1 hour
Yield: 12 Servings
Ingredients:

- ¼ cup cocoa powder
- ¼ cup white sugar
- ¼ teaspoon salt
- ½ cup canola oil
- ½ cup chopped hazelnuts
- ½ cup dark chocolate chips
- ½ cup milk
- ½ cup Nutella
- ½ teaspoon baking soda
- 1 teaspoon baking powder
- 1 teaspoon vanilla extract
- 2 cups all-purpose flour
- 3 eggs

Directions:

1. Mix the Nutella, eggs, vanilla, oil and milk in a container.
2. Put in the flour, cocoa powder, sugar, salt, baking powder and baking soda and stir for a few seconds to mix.

3. Fold in the chocolate chips then spoon the batter in a muffin tin lined using muffin papers of your choice.
4. Top with chopped hazelnuts and preheat your oven and bake at 350F for about twenty minutes or until a toothpick inserted into them comes out dry.
5. Let cool in the pan before you serve or storing away.

Nutritional Content of One Serving:

Calories: 258 ‖ Fat: 15.0g ‖ Protein: 5.1g ‖ Carbohydrates: 27.5g

DOUBLE CHOCOLATE MUFFINS

Total Time Taken: 1 hour
Yield: 12 Servings
Ingredients:

- ½ cup canola oil
- ½ cup cocoa powder
- ½ cup dark chocolate chips
- ½ cup whole milk
- ½ teaspoon salt
- 1 ½ cups all-purpose flour
- 1 teaspoon baking powder
- 1 teaspoon vanilla extract
- 2 eggs

Directions:

1. Mix the flour, cocoa powder, salt and baking powder in a container.
2. Put in the remaining ingredients and stir for a few seconds to mix with a whisk.
3. Spoon the batter into 12 muffin cups covered with muffin papers and preheat your oven and bake at 350F for about twenty minutes.

These muffins taste best chilled.

Nutritional Content of One Serving:

Calories: 186 ‖ Fat: 12.1g ‖ Protein: 3.8g ‖ Carbohydrates: 18.0g

DOUBLE CHOCOLATE CUPCAKES

Total Time Taken: 1 ½ hours
Yield: 12 Servings
Ingredients:

Cupcakes:

- ½ cup canola oil
- ½ cup cocoa powder
- ½ teaspoon salt
- ¾ cup white sugar
- 1 ½ cups all-purpose flour
- 1 cup brewed coffee
- 1 teaspoon baking soda
- 1 teaspoon lemon juice
- 1 teaspoon vanilla extract
- 2 eggs

Frosting:

- 1 cup heavy cream
- 1 teaspoon vanilla extract
- 2 cups dark chocolate chips

Directions:

1. To make the cupcakes, combine all the ingredients in a container and stir for a few seconds to mix.
2. Pour the batter into 12 muffin cups covered with muffin papers.
3. Preheat your oven and bake the cupcakes at 350F for about twenty minutes or until well risen and set.
4. Let cool in the pan.
5. To make the frosting, bring the cream to a boil in a saucepan.
6. Put in the chocolate chips and stir thoroughly until melted. Stir in the vanilla and mix thoroughly.
7. Let the frosting cool down.

Apply the frosting on top of each cupcake.

Nutritional Content of One Serving:

Calories: 333 ‖ Fat: 19.5g ‖ Protein: 4.7g ‖ Carbohydrates: 40.1g

DOUBLE BERRY CUPCAKES

Total Time Taken: 1 ½ hours
Yield: 12 Servings
Ingredients:

Cupcakes:

- ½ cup almond flour
- ½ cup butter, softened
- ½ cup white sugar
- ½ teaspoon salt
- 1 ¼ cups all-purpose flour
- 1 ½ teaspoons baking powder
- 1 cup fresh strawberries, sliced
- 1 teaspoon vanilla extract
- 2 eggs
- 2/3 cup buttermilk

Frosting:

- 1 cup fresh raspberries
- 2 cups heavy cream

Directions:

1. To make the cupcakes, combine the butter and sugar in a container until creamy and pale. Put in the eggs and vanilla and mix thoroughly.
2. Stir in the buttermilk then fold in the flours, salt and baking powder.
3. Put in the strawberries and stir lightly.
4. Spoon the batter in a muffin tin coated with baking muffin papers and preheat your oven and bake at 350F for about twenty minutes or until a golden-brown colour is achieved and it rises significantly.
5. Let them cool in the pan.
6. Apply whipped cream on top of each cupcake and garnish with raspberries.

Nutritional Content of One Serving:

Calories: 249 ‖ Fat: 16.7g ‖ Protein: 3.7g ‖ Carbohydrates: 22.3g

DEEP CHOCOLATE PUMPKIN MUFFINS

Total Time Taken: 1 hour
Yield: 12 Servings
Ingredients:

- ¼ cup cocoa powder
- ¼ teaspoon cinnamon powder
- ½ cup buttermilk
- ½ cup canola oil
- ½ cup dark chocolate chips
- ½ teaspoon baking powder
- 1 ½ cups all-purpose flour
- 1 cup pumpkin puree
- 1 pinch nutmeg
- 1 teaspoon baking soda
- 1 teaspoon vanilla extract
- 2/3 cup light brown sugar
- 3 eggs

Directions:

1. Mix the eggs and sugar in a container until fluffy and pale.
2. Put in the canola oil and vanilla, as well as buttermilk and pumpkin puree.
3. Fold in the dry ingredients then put in the chocolate chips.
4. Spoon the batter in a muffin tin covered with muffin papers.
5. Preheat your oven and bake the muffins at 350F for about twenty minutes or until a toothpick inserted into them comes out dry.
6. Let cool in the pan before you serve.

Nutritional Content of One Serving:

Calories: 223 ‖ Fat: 12.0g ‖ Protein: 4.2g ‖ Carbohydrates: 26.5g

DECADENT BROWNIE MUFFINS

Total Time Taken: 1 hour
Yield: 12 Servings
Ingredients:

- ¼ teaspoon salt
- ½ teaspoon baking soda

- ¾ cup butter
- 1 ½ cups dark chocolate chips
- 1 cup all-purpose flour
- 1 cup light brown sugar
- 1 teaspoon vanilla extract
- 4 eggs

Directions:

1. Melt the butter and chocolate in a heatproof container over a hot water bath. Let cool down slightly.
2. Mix the eggs and sugar in a container until fluffy and pale. Put in the vanilla then mix in the chocolate mixture.
3. Fold in the flour, baking soda and salt then spoon the batter in a muffin tin covered with muffin papers.
4. Pre-heat the oven and bake at 350F for about fifteen minutes or until set.
5. Let cool in the pan then serve.

Nutritional Content of One Serving:

Calories: 278 ‖ Fat: 17.1g ‖ Protein: 4.1g ‖ Carbohydrates: 30.0g

CRANBERRY EGGNOG MUFFINS

Total Time Taken: 1 hour
Yield: 12 Servings
Ingredients:

- ¼ teaspoon salt
- ½ cup butter, softened
- ½ cup eggnog
- ¾ cup light brown sugar
- 1 cup dried cranberries
- 1 cup eggnog
- 1 teaspoon vanilla extract
- 2 cups all-purpose flour
- 2 eggs
- 2 teaspoons baking powder

Directions:

1. Mix the cranberries and eggnog in a container and set aside for later to soak up.
2. Mix the butter, sugar, eggnog, eggs and vanilla in a container until creamy.
3. Fold in the flour and mix thoroughly then put in the cranberries.
4. Spoon the batter in a muffin tin covered with muffin papers.
5. Pre-heat the oven and bake at 350F for about twenty minutes or until it rises significantly and starts to appear golden-brown.

These muffins taste best chilled.

Nutritional Content of One Serving:

Calories: 238 ‖ Fat: 11.0g ‖ Protein: 4.4g ‖ Carbohydrates: 30.4g

COCONUT MUFFINS

Total Time Taken: 1 hour
Yield: 12 Servings
Ingredients:

- ½ cup canola oil
- ½ cup light brown sugar
- ½ cup quinoa flour
- ½ cup raspberry jam
- ½ cup shredded coconut
- ½ teaspoon salt
- 1 ½ cups all-purpose flour
- 1 egg
- 1 teaspoon baking soda
- 1 teaspoon vanilla extract
- 2/3 cup milk

Directions:

1. Mix the flours, baking soda, salt, coconut and sugar.
2. Stir in the egg, milk, oil and vanilla and stir for a few seconds to mix using a spatula.
3. Spoon the batter in a muffin tin covered with muffin papers.

4. Drop a dollop of raspberry jam on top of each muffin and preheat your oven and bake at 350F for about twenty minutes or until it rises significantly and starts to appear golden-brown.

These muffins taste best chilled.

Nutritional Content of One Serving:

Calories: 237 ‖ Fat: 11.5g ‖ Protein: 4.4g ‖ Carbohydrates: 28.9g

COCONUT MANGO MUFFINS

Total Time Taken: 1 hour
Yield: 12 Servings
Ingredients:

- ½ cup canola oil
- ½ cup coconut milk
- ½ cup white sugar
- ½ teaspoon salt
- 1 ½ teaspoons baking powder
- 1 cup all-purpose flour
- 1 cup shredded coconut
- 1 mango, peeled and diced
- 1 teaspoon vanilla extract
- 2 eggs

Directions:

1. Mix the oil, eggs, sugar, vanilla and coconut milk in a container.
2. Put in the coconut, flour, salt and baking powder then fold in the mango.
3. Spoon the batter in a muffin tin covered with muffin papers or greased and preheat your oven and bake at 350F for about twenty minutes or until it rises significantly and starts to appear golden-brown.

These muffins taste best chilled.

Nutritional Content of One Serving:

Calories: 220 ‖ Fat: 14.6g ‖ Protein: 2.5g ‖ Carbohydrates: 21.2g

COCONUT LEMON CHIA SEED MUFFINS

Total Time Taken: 1 hour
Yield: 10 Servings
Ingredients:

- ¼ cup coconut oil, melted
- ¼ teaspoon salt
- ½ cup honey
- ½ cup milk
- 1 ½ cups almond flour
- 1 teaspoon baking powder
- 1 teaspoon lemon juice
- 1 teaspoon lemon zest
- 1 teaspoon vanilla extract
- 2 tablespoons chia seeds
- 4 eggs

Directions:

1. Mix the chia seeds, almond flour, salt and baking powder in a container.
2. Put in the remaining ingredients and stir for a few seconds to mix.
3. Pour the batter in a muffin tin covered with muffin papers.
4. Pre-heat the oven and bake at 350F for about twenty minutes or until it rises significantly and seems golden.
5. Let the muffins cool in the pan before you serve.

Nutritional Content of One Serving:

Calories: 187 ‖ Fat: 11.5g ‖ Protein: 4.8g ‖ Carbohydrates: 18.0g

COCONUT FLAKES CUPCAKES

Total Time Taken: 1 ½ hours
Yield: 12 Servings
Ingredients:

Cupcakes:

- ¼ teaspoon salt
- ½ cup butter, softened

- ½ cup white sugar
- 1 cup all-purpose flour
- 1 cup shredded coconut
- 1 teaspoon baking powder
- 1 teaspoon coconut extract
- 3 eggs

Frosting:

- 1 cup butter, softened
- 1 cup coconut flakes
- 2 cups powdered sugar

Directions:

1. To make the cupcakes, combine the butter and sugar in a container until pale and light.
2. Put in the coconut extract and eggs and mix thoroughly.
3. Fold in the flour, salt, baking powder and shredded coconut.
4. Spoon the batter in a muffin tin covered with muffin papers.
5. Preheat your oven and bake the cupcakes at 350F for about twenty minutes or until it rises significantly and seems golden. Let the cupcakes cool down.
6. To make the frosting, combine the butter until pale. Put in the sugar and stir thoroughly for five minutes.
7. Spoon the frosting in a pastry bag and top each cupcake with it.
8. Garnish the frosted cupcakes with coconut flakes.

These cupcakes taste best when fresh.

Nutritional Content of One Serving:

Calories: 415 ‖ Fat: 28.7g ‖ Protein: 3.2g ‖ Carbohydrates: 38.6g

COCONUT CUPCAKES

Total Time Taken: 1 ½ hours
Yield: 12 Servings
Ingredients:

Cupcakes:

- ½ cup butter, softened
- ½ cup shredded coconut
- ½ teaspoon salt
- ¾ cup coconut milk
- ¾ cup white sugar
- 1 ½ teaspoons baking powder
- 1 ¾ cup all-purpose flour
- 1 teaspoon vanilla extract
- 3 eggs

Frosting:

- ½ cup butter, softened
- ½ cup cream cheese, softened
- 1 teaspoon vanilla extract
- 2 cups powdered sugar

Directions:

1. To make the cupcakes, combine the butter, sugar and vanilla in a container until fluffy and pale.
2. Put in the eggs, one at a time, then fold in the flour, baking powder, salt and coconut, alternating it with milk. Begin with flour and finish with flour.
3. Spoon the batter in 12 muffin cups covered with muffin papers.
4. Pre-heat the oven and bake at 350F for about twenty minutes or until it rises significantly and starts to appear golden-brown.
5. Let the cupcakes cool in the pan.
6. To make the frosting, combine the butter, cream cheese and sugar in a container for five minutes or until fluffy and pale.
7. Stir in the vanilla and mix thoroughly then spoon the frosting in a pastry bag and top the cupcakes with it.

Nutritional Content of One Serving:

Calories: 425 ‖ Fat: 24.7g ‖ Protein: 4.6g ‖ Carbohydrates: 48.4g

COCONUT CARAMEL CUPCAKES

Total Time Taken: 1 ½ hours
Yield: 14 Servings
Ingredients:

Cupcakes:

- ½ cup butter, softened
- ½ cup coconut cream
- ½ cup coconut milk
- ½ teaspoon salt
- 1 ½ cups all-purpose flour
- 1 cup white sugar
- 1 teaspoon vanilla extract
- 2 teaspoons baking powder
- 2/3 cup shredded coconut
- 3 eggs

Frosting:

- ½ cup caramel sauce
- 1 cup butter, softened
- 1 cup coconut flakes
- 1 teaspoon vanilla extract
- 2 cups powdered sugar

Directions:

1. To make the cupcakes, combine the butter and sugar in a container until fluffy and pale.
2. Put in the eggs and mix thoroughly then mix in the coconut cream, milk and vanilla.
3. Fold in the flour, coconut, salt and baking powder.
4. Spoon the batter in a muffin tin covered with muffin papers and preheat your oven and bake at 350F for about twenty minutes or until a golden-brown colour is achieved and it rises significantly.
5. Let the cupcakes cool down.
6. To make the frosting, combine the butter and sugar in a container for about five to seven minutes or until fluffy and pale.
7. Put in the vanilla and mix thoroughly. Top each cupcake with the frosting then garnish with coconut flakes.
8. Just before you serve, sprinkle the cupcakes with caramel sauce.

Nutritional Content of One Serving:

Calories: 462 || Fat: 28.1g || Protein: 3.7g || Carbohydrates: 52.2g

CITRUS ICED COCONUT CUPCAKES

Total Time Taken: 1 ¼ hours
Yield: 12 Servings
Ingredients:

Cupcakes:

- ¼ teaspoon salt
- ½ cup coconut butter
- ½ cup coconut flakes
- ½ cup coconut milk
- ½ cup white sugar
- 1 ½ cups all-purpose flour
- 1 ½ teaspoons baking powder
- 2 eggs

Icing:

- 1 ½ cups powdered sugar
- 1 tablespoon lime juice
- 1 teaspoon lemon zest
- 1 teaspoon lime zest

Directions:

1. To make the cupcakes, combine the coconut butter and sugar until creamy.
2. Put in the eggs, one at a time, then mix in the coconut milk.
3. Fold in the flour, coconut flakes, salt and baking powder then spoon the batter in a muffin tin covered with muffin papers.
4. Preheat your oven and bake the muffins at 350F for about twenty minutes or until a golden-brown colour is achieved and it rises significantly. Let them cool in the pan.
5. For the icing, combine all the ingredients in a container.
6. Sprinkle the icing over each cupcake and serve them fresh.

Nutritional Content of One Serving:

Calories: 212 ‖ Fat: 6.2g ‖ Protein: 3.1g ‖ Carbohydrates: 37.7g

CITRUS COCONUT MUFFINS

Total Time Taken: 1 hour
Yield: 12 Servings
Ingredients:

- ¼ cup milk
- ½ cup butter, melted
- ½ cup white sugar
- ½ teaspoon salt
- 1 cup coconut flakes
- 1 teaspoon lemon zest
- 1 teaspoon lime zest
- 1 teaspoon orange zest
- 2 cups all-purpose flour
- 2 eggs
- 2 teaspoons baking powder

Directions:

1. Mix the eggs and sugar in a container until pale and light. Put in the melted butter and citrus zest and mix thoroughly.
2. Fold in the dry ingredients, as well as the coconut flakes then spoon the batter in 12 muffin cups covered with muffin papers.
3. Preheat your oven and bake the muffins at 350F for about twenty minutes or until a golden-brown colour is achieved and it rises significantly.
4. Let cool in the pan before you serve.

Nutritional Content of One Serving:

Calories: 213 ‖ Fat: 10.9g ‖ Protein: 3.5g ‖ Carbohydrates: 26.1g

CINNAMON PLUM MUFFINS

Total Time Taken: 1 hour
Yield: 12 Servings
Ingredients:

- ¼ cup canola oil
- ½ cup ground walnuts
- ½ cup light brown sugar
- ½ teaspoon ground ginger

- 1 ½ cups all-purpose flour
- 1 cup buttermilk
- 1 egg
- 1 teaspoon baking soda
- 1 teaspoon cinnamon powder
- 1 teaspoon vanilla extract
- 6 plums, pitted and diced

Directions:

1. Mix the flour, sugar, baking soda, cinnamon, ginger and walnuts in a container.
2. Put in the remaining ingredients and mix thoroughly. Put in the plums as well.
3. Spoon the batter in a muffin tin lined using muffin papers of your choice.
4. Pre-heat the oven and bake at 350F for about twenty minutes or until it rises significantly and starts to appear golden-brown.

These muffins taste best chilled.

Nutritional Content of One Serving:

Calories: 177 ‖ Fat: 8.4g ‖ Protein: 4.2g ‖ Carbohydrates: 22.0g

CINNAMON BLUEBERRY MUFFINS

Total Time Taken: 1 hour
Yield: 12 Servings
Ingredients:

- ½ cup butter, melted
- ½ cup light brown sugar
- ½ cup milk
- ½ teaspoon cinnamon powder
- ½ teaspoon salt
- 1 cup blueberries
- 1 teaspoon baking soda
- 2 cups all-purpose flour
- 2 eggs

Directions:

1. Mix the flour, sugar, salt, baking soda and cinnamon in a container.
2. Put in the milk, eggs and melted butter and fold in the blueberries then spoon the batter in a muffin tin covered with muffin papers.
3. Preheat your oven and bake the muffins at 350F for about twenty minutes or until it rises significantly and starts to appear golden-brown.

These muffins taste best chilled.

Nutritional Content of One Serving:

Calories: 189 ‖ Fat: 8.8g ‖ Protein: 3.6g ‖ Carbohydrates: 24.1g

CINNAMON AUTUMN MUFFINS

Total Time Taken: 1 hour
Yield: 12 Servings
Ingredients:

- ½ cup butter, melted
- ½ cup butternut squash cubes
- ½ cup milk
- ½ teaspoon salt
- 1 apple, cored and diced
- 1 pear, cored and diced
- 1 teaspoon cinnamon powder
- 1 teaspoon vanilla extract
- 2 cups all-purpose flour
- 2 eggs
- 2 teaspoons baking powder
- 2/3 cup light brown sugar

Directions:

1. Mix the flour, salt, baking powder, cinnamon and sugar in a container.
2. Put in the butter, eggs, milk and vanilla and mix thoroughly.
3. Fold in the apple, pear and butternut squash cubes.
4. Spoon the batter in a muffin tin coated with baking muffin papers.
5. Pre-heat the oven and bake at 350F for about twenty minutes or until it rises significantly and seems golden.

These muffins taste best chilled.

Nutritional Content of One Serving:

Calories: 208 ‖ Fat: 8.9g ‖ Protein: 3.6g ‖ Carbohydrates: 29.1g

CINNAMON APPLE CUPCAKES

Total Time Taken: 1 ½ hours
Yield: 12 Servings
Ingredients:

Cupcakes:

- ¼ cup milk
- ½ cup butter, softened
- ½ cup light brown sugar
- ½ teaspoon salt
- 1 ½ cups all-purpose flour
- 1 teaspoon baking powder
- 1 teaspoon grated ginger
- 1 teaspoon vanilla extract
- 2 red apples, cored and diced
- 3 eggs

Frosting:

- 1 cup butter, softened
- 1 teaspoon cinnamon powder
- 1 teaspoon vanilla extract
- 2 cups powdered sugar

Directions:

1. To make the cupcakes, combine the butter and sugar in a container until fluffy and creamy.
2. Put in the eggs, one at a time, and mix thoroughly then mix in the vanilla and ginger.
3. Fold in the flour, salt and baking powder, alternating it with milk. Fold in the apples.
4. Spoon the batter in a muffin tin covered with muffin papers.
5. Preheat your oven and bake the cupcakes at 350F for about twenty minutes. Let the cupcakes cool in the pan.

6. To make the frosting, combine the butter in a container until fluffy. Put in the sugar and mix thoroughly then mix in the cinnamon and vanilla. Whip on high speed for five minutes.
7. Top each cupcake with the frosting and serve them fresh.

Nutritional Content of One Serving:

Calories: 398 ‖ Fat: 24.4g ‖ Protein: 3.5g ‖ Carbohydrates: 42.7g

CHUNKY BANANA MUFFINS

Total Time Taken: 1 hour
Yield: 12 Servings
Ingredients:

- ¼ cup butter, melted
- ¼ teaspoon salt
- ½ cup cocoa powder
- ½ cup light brown sugar
- 1 ½ cups all-purpose flour
- 1 cup buttermilk
- 1 teaspoon vanilla extract
- 2 bananas, sliced
- 2 eggs
- 2 tablespoons molasses
- 2 teaspoons baking powder

Directions:

1. Mix the eggs and sugar in a container until pale and light. Put in the molasses and vanilla and mix thoroughly.
2. Stir in the butter and buttermilk then put in the flour, cocoa powder, salt and baking powder.
3. Fold in the banana slices and spoon the batter in a muffin tin lined using muffin papers of your choice.
4. Pre-heat the oven and bake at 350F for about twenty minutes. When finished, allow them to cool in the pan before you serve.

Nutritional Content of One Serving:

Calories: 169 ‖ Fat: 5.4g ‖ Protein: 4.1g ‖ Carbohydrates: 28.3g

CHOCOLATE TAHINI MUFFINS

Total Time Taken: 1 hour
Yield: 12 Servings
Ingredients:

- ¼ cup cocoa powder
- ¼ cup light brown sugar
- ¼ cup maple syrup
- ¼ cup milk
- ¼ cup tahini paste
- ¼ teaspoon salt
- 1 ½ cups all-purpose flour
- 1 teaspoon baking powder
- 1 teaspoon vanilla extract
- 4 eggs

Directions:

1. Mix the eggs, tahini paste, maple syrup, sugar, vanilla and milk in a container.
2. Put in the flour, cocoa powder, salt and baking powder and stir for a few seconds to mix.
3. Spoon the batter in a muffin tin coated with baking muffin papers.
4. Pre-heat the oven and bake at 350F for about twenty minutes or until a toothpick inserted in the center of the muffins comes out clean.
5. Allow the muffins to cool to room temperature in the pan.

Nutritional Content of One Serving:

Calories: 144 ‖ Fat: 4.6g ‖ Protein: 4.8g ‖ Carbohydrates: 21.9g

CHOCOLATE SPICE CUPCAKES

Total Time Taken: 1 ½ hours
Yield: 12 Servings
Ingredients:

Cupcakes:

- ¼ cup cocoa powder

- ½ cup white sugar
- ½ teaspoon cinnamon powder
- ½ teaspoon ground ginger
- ½ teaspoon ground star anise
- ½ teaspoon salt
- ¾ cup milk
- 1 ¼ cups all-purpose flour
- 1 ½ teaspoons baking powder
- 1 teaspoon vanilla extract
- 1/2 cup butter, softened
- 2 eggs

Frosting:

- ½ cup heavy cream
- 1 cup dark chocolate chips

Directions:

1. To make the cupcakes, combine the butter, sugar and vanilla in a container until fluffy and pale.
2. Put in the eggs and mix thoroughly then mix in the milk.
3. Fold in the flour, cocoa powder, salt, baking powder, cinnamon, ginger and star anise.
4. Spoon the batter in a muffin tin covered with muffin papers.
5. Preheat your oven and bake the cupcakes at 350F for about twenty minutes or until it rises completely and is aromatic.
6. Let the cupcakes cool down.
7. To make the frosting, bring the cream to a boil in a saucepan. Turn off the heat and mix in the chocolate chips. Stir until melted then spoon the frosting over each cupcake.
8. Serve immediately or store them in an airtight container.

Nutritional Content of One Serving:

Calories: 235 ‖ Fat: 13.6g ‖ Protein: 4.0g ‖ Carbohydrates: 27.4g

CHOCOLATE RASPBERRY CUPCAKES

Total Time Taken: 1 ½ hours
Yield: 12 Servings
Ingredients:

Cupcakes:

- 2 eggs
- 1 teaspoon vanilla extract
- ¼ cup milk
- 1 ½ cups all-purpose flour
- ½ teaspoon salt
- 1 ½ teaspoons baking powder
- ¼ cup cocoa powder
- 2/3 cup butter, softened
- 2/3 cup white sugar

Frosting:

- ½ cup dark chocolate chips, melted and chilled
- 1 cup butter, softened
- 1 cup cream cheese
- 2 cups powdered sugar

Directions:

1. To make the cupcakes, combine the butter and sugar in a container until fluffy and airy.
2. Put in the eggs and vanilla and mix thoroughly. Stir in the milk.
3. Fold in the flour, salt, baking powder and cocoa and mix using a spatula.
4. Spoon the batter in a muffin tin covered with muffin papers and preheat your oven and bake at 350F for about twenty minutes or until well risen.
5. Let them cool in the pan.
6. For frosting, combine the cream cheese and butter in a container until pale.
7. Put in the sugar, progressively, and mix for five minutes on high speed.
8. Stir in the melted chocolate then spoon a dollop of frosting over each cupcake and serve fresh.

Nutritional Content of One Serving:

Calories: 512 ‖ Fat: 34.9g ‖ Protein: 5.1g ‖ Carbohydrates: 48.5g

CHOCOLATE RASPBERRY CRUMBLE MUFFINS

Total Time Taken: 1 ¼ hours
Yield: 12 Servings
Ingredients:

Muffins:

- ¼ cup cocoa powder
- ½ cup butter, melted
- ½ cup milk
- ½ cup white sugar
- ½ teaspoon salt
- 1 ½ cups all-purpose flour
- 1 cup fresh raspberries
- 1 teaspoon vanilla extract
- 2 teaspoons baking powder
- 3 eggs

Crumble Topping:

- ¼ cup butter, chilled
- ¼ teaspoon salt
- ½ cup all-purpose flour

Directions:

1. For the muffins, combine the eggs, sugar and vanilla in a container until creamy.
2. Stir in the milk and butter and mix thoroughly.
3. Fold in the flour, cocoa powder, salt and baking powder then spoon the batter in a muffin pan coated with muffin papers.
4. For the topping, combine the ingredients in a container until grainy.
5. Top the muffins with the crumble topping and preheat your oven and bake at 350F for about twenty minutes or until well risen.

These muffins taste best chilled.

Nutritional Content of One Serving:

Calories: 241 ‖ Fat: 13.3g ‖ Protein: 4.4g ‖ Carbohydrates: 27.5g

CHOCOLATE PRETZEL MUFFINS

Total Time Taken: 1 ½ hours
Yield: 12 Servings
Ingredients:

Cupcakes:

- ¼ cup canola oil
- ¼ cup cocoa powder
- ¼ teaspoon salt
- ½ cup brewed coffee
- 1 ¼ cups all-purpose flour
- 1 ½ teaspoons baking powder
- 1 cup buttermilk
- 1 teaspoon vanilla extract
- 2 eggs

Frosting:

- ½ cup dark chocolate chips, melted and chilled
- 1 cup butter, softened
- 1 cup pretzels2 cups powdered sugar
- , crushed

Directions:

1. To make the cupcakes, combine the flour, cocoa powder, salt and baking powder in a container.
2. Put in the remaining ingredients and stir for a few seconds to mix.
3. Pour the batter in a muffin tin covered with muffin papers.
4. Pre-heat the oven and bake at 350F for about twenty minutes or until a toothpick inserted into the center of a muffin comes out clean.
5. Let cool down.
6. To make the frosting, combine the butter and sugar in a container until fluffy and pale.
7. Stir in the chocolate and mix thoroughly.
8. Top each cupcake with the frosting and drizzle with pretzels.

These cupcakes taste best when fresh.

Nutritional Content of One Serving:

Calories: 368 ‖ Fat: 22.6g ‖ Protein: 4.3g ‖ Carbohydrates: 39.5g

CHOCOLATE PEAR MUFFINS

Total Time Taken: 1 hour

Yield: 12 Servings

Ingredients:

- ½ cup buttermilk
- ½ cup light brown sugar
- ½ cup milk
- ½ teaspoon salt
- 1 1/3 cups all-purpose flour
- 1 teaspoon baking powder
- 1/3 cup cocoa powder
- 2 eggs
- 2 pears, peeled and diced

Directions:

1. Mix the eggs, milk, sugar and buttermilk in a container.
2. Stir in the dry ingredients and stir for a few seconds to mix.
3. Fold in the pears then spoon the batter in a muffin tin covered with muffin papers.
4. Preheat your oven and bake the muffins at 350F for about twenty minutes or until well risen.

These muffins taste best chilled.

Nutritional Content of One Serving:

Calories: 119 ‖ Fat: 1.5g ‖ Protein: 3.6g ‖ Carbohydrates: 24.4g

CHOCOLATE PEANUT BUTTER CUPCAKES

Total Time Taken: 1 ½ hours

Yield: 12 Servings

Ingredients:

Cupcakes:

- ¼ cup smooth peanut butter
- ¼ teaspoon salt
- ½ cup butter, softened
- ½ cup sour cream
- 1 cup all-purpose flour
- 1 cup almond flour
- 1 teaspoon baking powder
- 1 teaspoon vanilla extract
- 2 eggs

Frosting:

- 1 cup heavy cream
- 1 teaspoon vanilla extract
- 2 cups dark chocolate chips

Directions:

1. To make the cupcakes, combine the butter and peanut butter in a container until creamy.
2. Put in the eggs and sour cream and mix thoroughly. Stir in the vanilla too.
3. Put in the flours, salt and baking powder and mix them using a spatula.
4. Spoon the batter in 12 muffin cups covered with muffin papers.
5. Preheat your oven and bake the cupcakes at 350F for about twenty minutes or until it rises significantly and seems golden.
6. Let them cool in the pan.
7. To make the frosting, bring the cream to a boil in a saucepan.
8. Turn off the heat and put in the chocolate chips. Stir until melted and smooth then allow to cool.
9. Spoon the frosting on top of each cupcake.

Nutritional Content of One Serving:

Calories: 312 ‖ Fat: 23.4g ‖ Protein: 5.8g ‖ Carbohydrates: 23.9g

CHOCOLATE MALT CUPCAKES

Total Time Taken: 1 hour
Yield: Servings 18
Ingredients:

Cupcakes:

- ¼ cup canola oil
- ½ teaspoon baking soda
- ½ teaspoon salt
- ¾ cups cocoa powder
- 1 cup malted milk powder
- 1 cup milk
- 1 cup sour cream
- 1 teaspoon baking powder
- 1 teaspoon vanilla extract
- 2 ¼ cups all-purpose flour
- 4 eggs

Frosting:

- ½ cup malted milk powder
- 1 ½ cups butter, softened
- 1 teaspoon vanilla extract
- 2 cups powdered sugar

Directions:

1. To make the cupcakes, combine the milk, milk powder, eggs, sour cream, vanilla and oil in a container.
2. Put in the flour, cocoa powder, salt, baking soda and baking powder and mix using a spatula.
3. Spoon the batter in a muffin tin covered with muffin papers.
4. Pre-heat the oven and bake at 350F for about twenty minutes or until a toothpick inserted into them comes out dry.
5. Let cool down before you serve.
6. To make the frosting, combine the butter in a container until airy.
7. Put in the milk powder and mix 2 minutes on high speed, then mix in the sugar and vanilla and continue mixing for five minutes on high speed.
8. Pipe the frosting on top of the cupcakes and serve them fresh.

Nutritional Content of One Serving:

Calories: 389 ‖ Fat: 23.6g ‖ Protein: 5.8g ‖ Carbohydrates: 41.3g

CHOCOLATE GRAHAM CUPCAKES

Total Time Taken: 1 ½ hours
Yield: 12 Servings
Ingredients:

Cupcakes:

- ¼ cup whole milk
- ½ cup all-purpose flour
- ½ cup crushed graham crackers
- ½ teaspoon salt
- 1 cup butter, softened
- 1 cup light brown sugar
- 1 cup whole wheat flour
- 1 teaspoon baking soda
- 1 teaspoon vanilla extract
- 1/2 teaspoon cinnamon powder
- 4 eggs

Frosting:

- ½ cup crushed graham crackers
- 1 cup heavy cream
- 2 cups dark chocolate chips

Directions:

1. To make the cupcakes, combine the butter and sugar in a container until pale and creamy.
2. Put in the vanilla and eggs, one at a time and mix thoroughly.
3. Fold in the flours, graham crackers, salt, baking soda and cinnamon powder, alternating it with the milk.
4. Spoon the batter in a muffin tin coated with baking muffin papers.
5. Pre-heat the oven and bake at 350F for about twenty minutes or until the cupcakes pass the toothpick test.
6. Let cool in the pan.
7. To make the frosting, bring the cream to a boil in a saucepan. Turn off the heat and put in the chocolate. Stir until melted and smooth then let cool down.
8. Apply the frosting on top of each cupcake and drizzle with crushed graham crackers.

Nutritional Content of One Serving:

Calories: 421 ‖ Fat: 26.9g ‖ Protein: 5.8g ‖ Carbohydrates: 43.2g

CHOCOLATE DRIZZLE CUPCAKES

Total Time Taken: 1 ½ hours
Yield: 12 Servings
Ingredients:

Cupcakes:

- ¼ cup brewed coffee
- ¼ cup canola oil
- ¼ cup cocoa powder
- ½ teaspoon salt
- 1 ½ cups all-purpose flour
- 1 ½ teaspoons baking powder
- 1 cup buttermilk
- 1 teaspoon vanilla extract
- 2 eggs

Frosting:

- 1 cup butter, softened
- 1 tablespoon cocoa powder
- 1 tablespoon dark rum
- 2 cups powdered sugar

Directions:

1. To make the cupcakes, combine the flour, salt, baking powder and cocoa powder in a container.
2. Put in the eggs, vanilla, buttermilk, coffee and canola oil and stir for a few seconds to mix.
3. Pour the batter in 12 muffin cups covered with muffin papers and preheat your oven and bake at 350F for about twenty minutes or until a toothpick inserted into them comes out dry.
4. Let cool down.
5. To make the frosting, combine the butter until fluffy. Put in the sugar and mix for about five to seven minutes or until pale and light.

6. Stir in the rum and mix thoroughly.
7. Top each cupcake with the frosting and serve them fresh.

Nutritional Content of One Serving:

Calories: 338 ‖ Fat: 21.3g ‖ Protein: 3.8g ‖ Carbohydrates: 34.5g

CHOCOLATE CUPCAKES WITH PEANUT BUTTER FROSTING

Total Time Taken: 1 ½ hours
Yield: 16 Servings
Ingredients:

Cupcakes:

- ¼ teaspoon salt
- ½ cup butter, softened
- ½ cup cocoa powder
- ½ cup sour cream
- 1 ½ cups all-purpose flour
- 1 ½ teaspoons baking powder
- 1 cup buttermilk
- 1 cup white sugar
- 1 teaspoon vanilla extract
- 3 eggs

Frosting:

- ½ cup butter, softened
- 1 cup powdered sugar
- 1 cup smooth peanut butter
- 1 teaspoon vanilla extract
- 2 tablespoons heavy cream

Directions:

1. To make the cupcakes, combine the butter and sugar in a container until creamy and pale.
2. Put in the eggs and mix thoroughly then mix in the vanilla, sour cream and buttermilk.

3. Fold in the flour, cocoa powder, salt and baking powder then spoon the batter in a muffin tin covered with muffin papers.
4. Preheat your oven and bake the muffins at 350F for about twenty minutes.
5. Let the cupcakes cool down.
6. To make the frosting, combine the peanut butter, butter and sugar in a container until fluffy and pale.
7. Put in the vanilla and cream and continue whipping for five minutes until fluffy and airy.
8. Garnish the cupcakes with the peanut butter frosting.

These cupcakes taste best when fresh.

Nutritional Content of One Serving:

Calories: 363 ‖ Fat: 23.3g ‖ Protein: 7.7g ‖ Carbohydrates: 35.0g

CHOCOLATE CHUNK CUPCAKES

Total Time Taken: 1 ½ hours
Yield: 12 Servings
Ingredients:

Cupcakes:

- ½ cup butter, melted
- ½ cup sour cream
- ½ cup white sugar
- ½ teaspoon salt
- 2 cups all-purpose flour
- 2 eggs
- 2 teaspoons baking powder
- 4 oz. dark chocolate, chopped

Frosting:

- 1 ½ cups heavy cream, whipped
- 2 oz. dark chocolate, chopped

Directions:

1. To make the cupcakes, combine the butter, sugar and eggs in a container until pale.

2. Put in the sour cream and mix thoroughly.
3. Fold in the flour, baking powder and salt then fold in the dark chocolate.
4. Spoon the batter in a muffin tin covered with muffin papers.
5. Preheat your oven and bake the cupcakes at 350F for about twenty minutes or until a golden-brown colour is achieved and it rises significantly.
6. Let the cupcakes cool then top each of them with a dollop of whipped cream.
7. Drizzle each cream with chopped chocolate and serve.

Nutritional Content of One Serving:

Calories: 334 ‖ Fat: 20.4g ‖ Protein: 4.8g ‖ Carbohydrates: 33.9g

CHOCOLATE CHIP MUFFINS

Total Time Taken: 1 hour
Yield: 12 Servings
Ingredients:

- ½ cup canola oil
- ½ cup chocolate chips
- ½ cup white sugar
- ½ teaspoon salt
- 1 ½ teaspoons baking powder
- 1 cup all-purpose flour
- 1 cup whole wheat flour
- 1 egg
- 1 teaspoon vanilla extract
- 2/3 cup milk

Directions:

1. Mix the flours, baking powder and salt in a container.
2. Put in the sugar, egg, milk, oil and vanilla and mix using a spatula.
3. Fold in the chocolate chips then spoon the batter in a muffin tin covered with muffin papers.
4. Preheat your oven and bake the muffins at 350F for about twenty minutes or until a golden-brown colour is achieved and it rises significantly.

These muffins taste best chilled.

Nutritional Content of One Serving:

Calories: 238 ‖ Fat: 12.0g ‖ Protein: 3.6g ‖ Carbohydrates: 29.4g

CHOCOLATE CHIP CINNAMON MUFFINS

Total Time Taken: 1 hour
Yield: 12 Servings
Ingredients:

- ¼ cup milk
- ½ cup butter, melted
- ½ cup dark chocolate chips
- ½ cup white sugar
- ½ teaspoon salt
- 1 cup all-purpose flour
- 1 teaspoon baking powder
- 1 teaspoon cinnamon powder
- 1 teaspoon orange zest
- 1 teaspoon vanilla extract
- 2 tablespoons dark brown sugar
- 4 eggs

Directions:

1. Mix the eggs and sugars in a container until fluffy and pale.
2. Put in the vanilla, orange zest and melted butter.
3. Fold in the flour, cinnamon, salt and baking powder then put in the milk and chocolate chips.
4. Spoon the batter in a muffin tin covered with muffin papers.
5. Pre-heat the oven and bake at 350F for about twenty minutes or until a golden-brown colour is achieved and it rises significantly.

These muffins taste best chilled.

Nutritional Content of One Serving:

Calories: 191 ‖ Fat: 10.7g ‖ Protein: 3.5g ‖ Carbohydrates: 21.7g

CHOCOLATE CANDIED ORANGE MUFFINS

Total Time Taken: 1 hour
Yield: 12 Servings
Ingredients:

- ¼ cup candied orange peel, chopped
- ½ cup canola oil
- ½ cup dark chocolate chips
- ½ cup fresh orange juice
- ½ cup plain yogurt
- ½ cup white sugar
- ½ teaspoon salt
- 1 ½ cups all-purpose flour
- 1 ½ teaspoons baking powder
- 1 teaspoon orange zest
- 2 eggs

Directions:

1. Mix the sugar, orange juice, eggs, oil, yogurt and orange zest in a container.
2. Stir in the flour, salt, baking powder, chocolate chips and orange peel and mix using a spatula.
3. Pour the batter in a muffin tin covered with muffin papers and preheat your oven and bake at 350F for about twenty minutes or until a toothpick inserted into them comes out dry.

These muffins taste best chilled.

Nutritional Content of One Serving:

Calories: 217

Fat:11.4g ‖ Protein: 3.5g ‖ Carbohydrates: 26.3g

CHOCOLATE AVOCADO CUPCAKES

Total Time Taken: 1 ½ hours
Yield: 12 Servings
Ingredients:

Cupcakes:

- 1 large avocado, mashed
- 1 cup coconut milk
- 1 teaspoon vanilla extract
- 1 egg
- 2 egg whites
- 1 cup whole wheat flour
- 1 cup all-purpose flour
- ¼ teaspoon salt
- 2 teaspoons baking powder
- ½ cup cocoa powder
- 2/3 cup coconut sugar

Frosting:

- ¼ cup cocoa powder
- ½ teaspoon vanilla extract
- 1 large avocado, mashed
- 2 tablespoons coconut oil
- 2 tablespoons coconut sugar

Directions:

1. To make the cupcakes, combine the avocado, coconut sugar, coconut milk, vanilla, egg and egg whites in a container until creamy.
2. Put in the remaining ingredients and stir swiftly to combine.
3. Spoon the batter in a muffin tin covered with muffin papers.
4. Pre-heat the oven and bake at 350F for about twenty minutes or until a toothpick inserted in the muffins comes out clean.
5. Let cool in the pan.
6. To make the frosting, combine all the ingredients in a blender or food processor and pulse until well mixed.
7. Pipe the frosting over each cupcake and serve fresh.

Nutritional Content of One Serving:

Calories: 280 ‖ Fat: 14.8g ‖ Protein: 5.3g ‖ Carbohydrates: 36.0g

CHERRY MUFFINS

Total Time Taken: 1 hour
Yield: 10 Servings
Ingredients:

- ¼ teaspoon salt
- ½ cup butter, melted
- ½ cup white sugar
- 1 cup all-purpose flour
- 1 cup cherries, pitted
- 1 teaspoon baking powder
- 1 teaspoon vanilla extract
- 4 eggs

Directions:

1. Mix the eggs, sugar and vanilla in a container until its volume increases to almost three times it was.
2. Stir in the butter and mix thoroughly.
3. Fold in the flour, salt and baking powder.
4. Put in the cherries then spoon the batter in a muffin tin covered with muffin papers.
5. Preheat your oven and bake the muffins at 350F for about twenty minutes or until a golden-brown colour is achieved and it rises significantly.

These muffins taste best chilled.

Nutritional Content of One Serving:

Calories: 200 ‖ Fat: 11.1g ‖ Protein: 3.6g ‖ Carbohydrates: 22.0g

CHERRY COCONUT MUFFINS

Total Time Taken: 1 hour
Yield: 12 Servings
Ingredients:

- ¼ cup canola oil
- ½ cup white sugar

- ½ teaspoon salt
- ¾ cup coconut milk
- 1 cup all-purpose flour
- 1 cup cherries, pitted
- 1 cup shredded coconut
- 1 teaspoon baking soda
- 2 eggs

Directions:

1. Mix the eggs and sugar in a container until fluffy and pale. Put in the oil and milk and mix thoroughly.
2. Fold in the coconut, flour, salt, baking soda and cherries.
3. Spoon the batter in a muffin tin covered with muffin papers.
4. Preheat your oven and bake the muffins at 350F for about twenty minutes or until a toothpick inserted into them comes out dry.

These muffins taste best chilled.

Nutritional Content of One Serving:

Calories: 185 ‖ Fat: 11.2g ‖ Protein: 2.6g ‖ Carbohydrates: 19.9g

CHAI VANILLA FROSTED CUPCAKES

Total Time Taken: 1 ½ hours
Yield: 12 Servings
Ingredients:

Cupcakes:

- ½ cup butter, softened
- 2 eggs
- 1 teaspoon vanilla extract
- 1 ½ cups all-purpose flour
- 1 teaspoon baking powder
- ½ teaspoon baking soda
- ¼ teaspoon cinnamon powder
- ¼ teaspoon ground ginger
- ¼ teaspoon ground star anise
- ¼ teaspoon ground cardamom

- 2/3 cup white sugar
- 2/3 cup buttermilk

Frosting:

- 1 cup butter, softened
- 1 teaspoon vanilla extract
- 2 cups powdered sugar

Directions:

1. To make the cupcakes, combine the butter and sugar in a container until creamy and firm.
2. Put in the eggs and vanilla, then mix in the buttermilk.
3. Put in the flour, baking powder, baking soda, cinnamon powder, ginger, star anise and cardamom, as well as a pinch of salt.
4. Pour the batter in a muffin tin covered with muffin papers and preheat your oven and bake at 350F for about twenty minutes or until a golden-brown colour is achieved.
5. Let cool down in the pan.
6. To make the frosting, combine the butter in a container until creamy and light.
7. Put in the sugar, ½ cup at a time, and stir thoroughly for at least five minutes.
8. Put in the vanilla and mix thoroughly.
9. Top each cupcake with the frosting and serve fresh.

Nutritional Content of One Serving:

Calories: 399 ‖ Fat: 24.0g ‖ Protein: 3.2g ‖ Carbohydrates: 44.1g

CARROT WHITE CHOCOLATE MUFFINS

Total Time Taken: 1 hour
Yield: 12 Servings
Ingredients:

- ¼ cup canola oil
- ¼ teaspoon baking soda
- ½ cup plain yogurt
- ½ cup white chocolate chips

- ½ cup white sugar
- ½ cup whole wheat flour
- ½ teaspoon salt
- ½ teaspoon salt
- 1 cup all-purpose flour
- 1 cup crushed pineapple
- 1 cup grated carrots
- 1 egg
- 1 teaspoon baking powder

Directions:

1. Mix the egg and sugar in a container until pale and light.
2. Put in the oil and yogurt and mix thoroughly.
3. Fold in the flours, salt, baking powder, baking soda and salt.
4. Put in the crushed pineapple, carrots and chocolate chips.
5. Spoon the batter in a muffin tin covered with muffin papers and preheat your oven and bake at 350F for about twenty minutes or until a toothpick inserted into the center of a muffin comes out clean.

These muffins taste best chilled.

Nutritional Content of One Serving:

Calories: 190 ‖ Fat: 7.5g ‖ Protein: 3.2g ‖ Carbohydrates: 28.1g

CARROT CAKE PECAN MUFFINS

Total Time Taken: 1 hour
Yield: 12 Servings
Ingredients:

- ¼ teaspoon salt
- ½ cup canola oil
- ½ cup crushed pineapple
- ½ cup light brown sugar
- ½ cup milk
- ½ cup walnuts, chopped
- ½ teaspoon ground ginger
- 1 ½ cups all-purpose flour

- 1 cup grated carrot
- 1 egg
- 1 teaspoon baking soda
- 1 teaspoon cinnamon powder

Directions:

1. Mix the flour, salt, baking soda, cinnamon and ginger.
2. Put in the milk, egg, oil, sugar, carrot, pineapple and walnuts and mix thoroughly.
3. Spoon the batter in a muffin tin covered with muffin papers.
4. Pre-heat the oven and bake at 350F for about twenty minutes or until it rises significantly and becomes aromatic.
5. Serve the muffins chilled or store them in an airtight container for maximum four days.

Nutritional Content of One Serving:

Calories: 210 ‖ Fat: 12.9g ‖ Protein: 3.8g ‖ Carbohydrates: 20.8g

CARIBBEAN MUFFINS

Total Time Taken: 1 hour
Yield: 12 Servings
Ingredients:

- ¼ cup wheat bran
- ¼ teaspoon salt
- ½ cup shredded coconut
- 1 ½ cups all-purpose flour
- 1 ½ teaspoons baking powder
- 1 cup buttermilk
- 1 cup crushed pineapple
- 1 egg
- 1 mango, peeled and diced
- 2 tablespoons chia seeds

Directions:

1. Mix the flour, wheat bran, salt, baking powder, chia seeds and coconut in a container.

2. Put in the egg, buttermilk and pineapple and mix thoroughly.
3. Fold in the mango then spoon the batter in a muffin tin covered with muffin papers.
4. Preheat your oven and bake the muffins at 350F for about twenty minutes or until it rises significantly and starts to appear golden-brown.

These muffins taste best chilled.

Nutritional Content of One Serving:

Calories: 130 ‖ Fat: 3.5g ‖ Protein: 4.3g ‖ Carbohydrates: 21.0g

CARAMEL VANILLA CUPCAKES

Total Time Taken: 1 ½ hours
Yield: 12 Servings
Ingredients:

Cupcakes:

- 2 eggs
- 1/3 cup butter, melted
- 1 teaspoon vanilla extract
- 1 egg
- 1 cup milk
- 1 ¾ cups all-purpose flour
- 1 ½ teaspoons baking powder
- ¼ teaspoon salt

Frosting:

- 2 cups powdered sugar
- 1 teaspoon vanilla extract
- 1 cup butter, softened
- ½ cup caramel sauce

Directions:

1. To make the cupcakes, combine the flour, salt and baking powder in a container.

2. Combine the eggs, butter, milk, egg and vanilla then pour this mixture over the flour. Give it a quick mix then spoon the batter in a muffin tin covered with muffin papers.
3. Pre-heat the oven and bake at 350F for about twenty minutes or until it rises significantly and starts to appear golden-brown. Let them cool down.
4. To make the frosting, combine the butter in a container until fluffy. Put in the sugar and vanilla and keep mixing for five minutes.
5. Pipe the frosting over the cupcakes and sprinkle them with caramel sauce.

These cupcakes taste best when fresh.

Nutritional Content of One Serving:

Calories: 388 ‖ Fat: 22.2g ‖ Protein: 4.3g ‖ Carbohydrates: 44.3g

CAKEY BLUEBERRY MUFFINS

Total Time Taken: 1 hour
Yield: 12 Servings
Ingredients:

- ¼ cup cornstarch
- ¼ teaspoon salt
- ½ cup canola oil
- ¾ cup white sugar
- 1 ½ cups all-purpose flour
- 1 ½ teaspoons baking powder
- 1 cup blueberries
- 1 teaspoon vanilla extract
- 2 eggs
- 2/3 cup sour cream

Directions:

1. Mix the eggs and sugar in a container until volume increases to twice what it was. Stir in the vanilla and oil and mix thoroughly then put in the sour cream and stir thoroughly until blended.
2. Fold in the flour, cornstarch, salt and baking powder then fold in the blueberries.
3. Spoon the batter in a muffin tin covered with muffin papers.

4. Pre-heat the oven and bake at 350F for about twenty minutes or until a toothpick inserted into them comes out dry.

These muffins taste best chilled.

Nutritional Content of One Serving:

Calories: 241 || Fat: 12.7g || Protein: 3.0g || Carbohydrates: 29.6g

BUTTERNUT ALMOND MUFFINS

Total Time Taken: 1 hour
Yield: 12 Servings
Ingredients:

- ¼ cup canola oil
- ¼ cup sliced almonds
- ½ cup golden syrup
- ½ teaspoon salt
- 1 ½ teaspoons baking powder
- 1 cup all-purpose flour
- 1 cup almond flour
- 1 cup butternut squash puree
- 1 teaspoon pumpkin pie spices
- 1 teaspoon vanilla extract
- 2 eggs

Directions:

1. Mix the butternut squash puree, golden syrup, eggs, vanilla and canola oil in a container.
2. Put in the flours, salt, baking powder and spices and stir lightly.
3. Spoon the batter in a muffin tin covered with muffin papers and top with sliced almonds.
4. Pre-heat the oven and bake at 350F for about twenty minutes or until a golden-brown colour is achieved and it rises significantly.

These muffins taste best chilled.

Nutritional Content of One Serving:

Calories: 158 || Fat: 7.6g || Protein: 3.0g || Carbohydrates: 20.9g

BROWN SUGAR BOURBON CUPCAKES

Total Time Taken: 1 hour
Yield: 12 Servings
Ingredients:

Cupcakes:

- ¼ teaspoon salt
- ½ cup butter, softened
- ½ cup heavy cream
- 1 ½ teaspoons baking powder
- 1 ¾ cups all-purpose flour
- 1 cup light brown sugar
- 1 teaspoon vanilla extract
- 2 tablespoons bourbon
- 3 eggs

Frosting:

- ½ cup dark brown sugar
- 1 cup butter, softened
- 1 cup powdered sugar

Directions:

1. To make the cupcakes, combine the sugar and butter in a container until creamy.
2. Put in the cream, vanilla and bourbon and mix thoroughly.
3. Stir in the eggs and stir thoroughly until blended.
4. Fold in the flour, salt and baking powder then spoon the batter in a muffin tin covered with muffin papers.
5. Pre-heat the oven and bake at 350F for about twenty minutes or until a toothpick inserted into them comes out dry.
6. Let cool in the pan.
7. To make the frosting, combine all the ingredients in a container for about five to seven minutes or until fluffy and pale.
8. Top the cupcakes with the frosting and serve them fresh.

Nutritional Content of One Serving:

Calories: 418 ‖ Fat: 26.2g ‖ Protein: 3.6g ‖ Carbohydrates: 42.2g

BROWN BUTTER STREUSEL PUMPKIN MUFFINS

Total Time Taken: 1 hour
Yield: 12 Servings
Ingredients:

Muffins:

- ¼ cup canola oil
- ½ cup buttermilk
- ½ cup light brown sugar
- ½ teaspoon baking powder
- ½ teaspoon baking soda
- 1 ½ cups all-purpose flour
- 1 cup pumpkin puree
- 1 pinch salt
- 1 teaspoon pumpkin pie spices
- 1 teaspoon vanilla extract
- 2 eggs

Streusel:

- ¼ cup brown sugar
- ½ cup all-purpose flour
- 1 pinch salt
- 2 tablespoons light brown sugar
- 2 tablespoons pumpkin seeds

Directions:

1. For the muffins, combine the wet ingredients in a container.
2. Put in the dry ingredients and stir for a few seconds to mix.
3. Spoon the batter in a muffin tin covered with muffin papers.
4. For the streusel, combine all the ingredients in a container and stir until grainy.
5. Spread the streusel over the muffins and preheat your oven and bake at 350F for about twenty minutes or until they're fragrant and it rises significantly.
6. Let cool in the pan before you serve.

Nutritional Content of One Serving:

Calories: 187 || Fat: 6.3g || Protein: 4.0g || Carbohydrates: 29.0g

BROWN BUTTER CHOCOLATE CHIP MUFFINS

Total Time Taken: 1 ¼ hours
Yield: 14 Servings

Ingredients:

- ¼ teaspoon salt
- ½ cup brown butter
- ½ cup dark chocolate chips
- ¾ cup milk
- ¾ cup white sugar
- 1 ½ cups all-purpose flour
- 1 ½ teaspoons baking powder
- 2 eggs

Directions:

1. Mix the brown butter and sugar in a container until creamy. Put in the eggs and milk and mix thoroughly then mix in the flour, baking powder and salt.
2. Spoon the batter in a muffin tin covered with muffin papers.
3. Top with chocolate chips and preheat your oven and bake at 350F for about twenty minutes or until it rises significantly and starts to appear golden-brown.
4. When finished, let cool in the pan before you serve.

Nutritional Content of One Serving:

Calories: 267 || Fat: 10.6g || Protein: 7.4g || Carbohydrates: 36.4g

BROWN BUTTER BANANA MUFFINS

Total Time Taken: 1 hour
Yield: 12 Servings
Ingredients:

- ¼ teaspoon salt
- ½ cup butter
- ½ teaspoon baking powder
- ½ teaspoon baking soda
- ¾ cup light brown sugar
- 1 cup all-purpose flour
- 1 cup ground walnuts
- 1/2 cup milk
- 2 eggs
- 4 bananas, mashed

Directions:

1. Put the butter in a saucepan and place over medium flame. Cook the butter until it starts to turn golden brown, slightly caramelized.
2. Mix the butter, sugar, milk and eggs in a container.
3. Stir in the walnuts, flour, baking soda, salt and baking powder.
4. Spoon the batter in a muffin tin lined with special muffin papers and preheat your oven and bake at 350F for about twenty minutes or until it rises significantly and starts to appear golden-brown.

These muffins taste best chilled.

Nutritional Content of One Serving:

Calories: 255 ‖ Fat: 15.0g ‖ Protein: 5.4g ‖ Carbohydrates: 27.5g

BROWN BUTTER BANANA CUPCAKES

Total Time Taken: 1 ½ hours
Yield: Servings 20
Ingredients:

Cupcakes:

- ¼ cup coconut oil, melted
- ¼ teaspoon salt

- ½ cup brown butter
- ½ cup buttermilk
- ½ teaspoon baking soda
- ¾ cup light brown sugar
- ¾ cup whole wheat flour
- 1 cup all-purpose flour
- 1 teaspoon baking powder
- 2 bananas, mashed
- 2 eggs

Frosting:

- ½ teaspoon cinnamon powder
- 1 cup butter, softened
- 2 cups powdered sugar

Directions:

1. To make the cupcakes, combine the flours, salt, baking soda and baking powder in a container.
2. In a separate container, combine the butter, coconut oil and sugar in a container until fluffy and creamy.
3. Put in the eggs and mix thoroughly then mix in the buttermilk and bananas.
4. Fold in the flour then spoon the batter in a muffin tin covered with muffin papers.
5. Pre-heat the oven and bake at 350F for about twenty minutes or until it is aromatic and appears golden.
6. Let cool in the pan.
7. To make the frosting, combine all the ingredients in a container for about five to seven minutes until pale and fluffy.
8. Top each cupcake with the butter frosting.

Best served chilled.

Nutritional Content of One Serving:

Calories: 331 ‖ Fat: 18.5g ‖ Protein: 5.3g ‖ Carbohydrates: 37.0g

BROOKLYN BLACKOUT CUPCAKES

Total Time Taken: 1 ½ hours
Yield: 12 Servings
Ingredients:

Cupcakes:

- ¼ teaspoon salt
- ½ cup butter, softened
- ½ cup buttermilk
- ½ cup cocoa powder
- ½ teaspoon baking soda
- 1 cup all-purpose flour
- 1 cup white sugar
- 1 teaspoon baking powder
- 1 teaspoon vanilla extract
- 2 eggs
- 2 teaspoons instant coffee

Frosting:

- ¼ cup white sugar
- 1 cup milk
- 1 pinch salt
- 1 teaspoon instant coffee
- 2 tablespoons butter
- 2 tablespoons cocoa powder
- 2 tablespoons cornstarch

Directions:

1. To make the cupcakes, combine the butter and sugar in a container until creamy.
2. Put in the eggs, one at a time, and mix thoroughly then mix in the coffee powder, buttermilk and vanilla.
3. Put in the flour, cocoa powder, baking soda, baking powder and salt and mix using a spatula or whisk.
4. Pour the batter in a muffin tin covered with muffin papers and preheat your oven and bake at 350F for about twenty minutes or until a toothpick inserted into them comes out dry.
5. Let cool down in the pan.
6. To make the frosting, bring the milk to the boiling point in a saucepan.
7. In a container, mix the remaining ingredients.

8. Pour in the milk and mix thoroughly then return on low heat and cook until it becomes thick.
9. Let the frosting cool down then spoon it over each cupcake.

The cupcakes taste best chilled.

Nutritional Content of One Serving:

Calories: 242 ‖ Fat: 11.5g ‖ Protein: 3.9g ‖ Carbohydrates: 34.2g

BREAKFAST MUFFINS

Total Time Taken: 1 hour
Yield: 16 Servings
Ingredients:

- 2 teaspoons baking powder
- 2 eggs
- 1 cup rolled oats
- 1 cup milk
- 1 cup grated carrots
- 1 cup golden raisins
- 1 banana, mashed
- 1 ½ cups all-purpose flour
- ½ teaspoon salt
- ½ teaspoon ground nutmeg
- ½ teaspoon ground ginger
- ½ teaspoon cinnamon powder
- ½ cup shredded coconut
- ½ cup olive oil

Directions:

1. Mix the oats, flour, baking powder, salt and spices in a container. Stir in the raisins and coconut.
2. Put in the olive oil, eggs, milk, carrots and banana and mix using a spatula.
3. Spoon the batter in a muffin tin lined using muffin papers of your choice.
4. Pre-heat the oven and bake at 350F for about twenty minutes or until well risen and a toothpick inserted into the center of a muffin comes out clean.

These muffins taste best chilled.

Nutritional Content of One Serving:

Calories: 178 ‖ Fat: 8.5g ‖ Protein: 3.6g ‖ Carbohydrates: 23.5g

BRAN FLAX BLUEBERRY MUFFINS

Total Time Taken: 1 hour
Yield: 12 Servings
Ingredients:

- 2 teaspoons baking powder
- 2 eggs
- 1 teaspoon vanilla extract
- 1 red apple, peeled and grated
- 1 cup milk
- 1 cup grated carrots
- 1 cup blueberries
- 1 ½ cups all-purpose flour
- ½ teaspoon salt
- ½ cup raisins
- ½ cup oat bran
- ½ cup ground flax seeds
- ½ cup canola oil

Directions:

1. Mix the flour, flax seeds, oat bran, baking powder and salt in a container.
2. Put in the milk, eggs, canola oil and vanilla and stir for a few seconds to mix.
3. Fold in the carrots, apple, raisins and blueberries then spoon the batter in a muffin tin covered with muffin papers.
4. Preheat your oven and bake the muffins at 350F for about twenty minutes or until a toothpick inserted into the center of a muffin comes out clean.

These muffins taste best chilled.

Nutritional Content of One Serving:

Calories: 227 ‖ Fat: 12.1g ‖ Protein: 4.9g ‖ Carbohydrates: 25.9g

BOURBON GLAZED PUMPKIN MUFFINS

Total Time Taken: 1 hour
Yield: 12 Servings
Ingredients:

Muffins:

- ¼ cup coconut oil
- ½ cup buttermilk
- ½ cup white sugar
- ½ teaspoon ground ginger
- ½ teaspoon salt
- 1 ½ cups whole wheat flour
- 1 cup pumpkin puree
- 1 egg
- 1 teaspoon cinnamon powder
- 2 teaspoons baking powder

Glaze:

- 1 ½ cups powdered sugar
- 2 tablespoons bourbon

Directions:

1. For the muffins, combine the dry ingredients in a container.
2. Put in the wet ingredients and stir for a few seconds to mix.
3. Spoon the batter in a muffin tin covered with muffin papers.
4. Pre-heat the oven and bake at 350F for about twenty minutes.
5. When finished, let cool in the pan.
6. For the glaze, combine the ingredients in a container.
7. Sprinkle the glaze over each muffin and serve the muffins chilled.

Nutritional Content of One Serving:

Calories: 208 ‖ Fat: 5.2g ‖ Protein: 2.6g ‖ Carbohydrates: 37.8g

BLUEBERRY WHITE CHOCOLATE MUFFINS

Total Time Taken: 1 hour
Yield: 12 Servings
Ingredients:

- ¼ cup canola oil
- ½ cup shredded coconut
- ½ cup white chocolate chips
- ½ teaspoon salt
- 1 1/2 cups all-purpose flour
- 1 cup milk
- 1 teaspoon vanilla extract
- 2 eggs
- 2 teaspoons baking powder

Directions:

1. Mix the flour, baking powder, salt, coconut and chocolate chips in a container.
2. Put in the remaining ingredients and mix thoroughly.
3. Spoon the batter in a muffin tin lined with special muffin papers.
4. Preheat your oven and bake the muffins at 350F for about twenty minutes or until a golden-brown colour is achieved and it rises significantly.

These muffins taste best chilled.

Nutritional Content of One Serving:

Calories: 169 ‖ Fat: 9.2g ‖ Protein: 3.7g ‖ Carbohydrates: 18.1g

BLUEBERRY POPPY SEED MUFFINS

Total Time Taken: 1 hour
Yield: 12 Servings
Ingredients:

- ½ cup canola oil
- ½ cup white sugar
- ½ teaspoon salt
- 1 1/2 cups all-purpose flour 2 teaspoons baking powder
- 1 cup fresh blueberries
- 1 cup plain yogurt

- 1 tablespoon lemon juice
- 1 tablespoon lemon zest
- 2 eggs
- 2 tablespoons poppy seeds

Directions:

1. Mix the eggs, yogurt, lemon zest, lemon juice and oil in a container.
2. Put in the sugar and mix thoroughly then fold in the remaining ingredients.
3. Spoon the batter in a muffin tin covered with muffin papers and preheat your oven and bake at 350F for about twenty minutes or until a toothpick inserted into them comes out dry.
4. Best served chilled.

Nutritional Content of One Serving:

Calories: 210 ‖ Fat: 10.9g ‖ Protein: 4.1g ‖ Carbohydrates: 24.4g

BLUEBERRY OATMEAL MUFFINS

Total Time Taken: 1 hour
Yield: 12 Servings
Ingredients:

- ¼ teaspoon salt
- ½ cup canola oil
- ½ teaspoon baking soda
- ¾ cup light brown sugar
- 1 cup all-purpose flour
- 1 cup buttermilk
- 1 cup fresh blueberries
- 1 cup oat flour
- 1 teaspoon baking powder
- 2 eggs

Directions:

1. Mix the flours, baking powder, baking soda, salt and sugar in a container.
2. Put in the eggs, buttermilk and canola oil and mix thoroughly.
3. Fold in the blueberries then spoon the batter in a muffin tin covered with muffin papers of your desire.

4. Pre-heat the oven and bake at 350F for about twenty minutes or until it rises significantly and starts to appear golden-brown.
5. Let cool in the pan before you serve.

Nutritional Content of One Serving:

Calories: 209 ‖ Fat: 10.6g ‖ Protein: 3.8g ‖ Carbohydrates: 25.1g

BLUEBERRY LEMON CUPCAKES

Total Time Taken: 1 ½ hours
Yield: 12 Servings
Ingredients:

Cupcakes:

- ½ cup butter, softened
- ½ teaspoon salt
- 1 ½ teaspoons baking powder
- 1 ¾ cups all-purpose flour
- 1 cup fresh blueberries
- 1 cup white sugar
- 1 tablespoon lemon zest
- 1 teaspoon vanilla extract
- 2 tablespoons lemon juice
- 3 eggs

Frosting:

- ½ cup butter
- 1 cup white sugar
- 3 lemons, zested and juiced
- 4 egg yolks

Directions:

1. To make the cupcakes, combine the butter and sugar in a container until fluffy and creamy.
2. Put in the eggs and mix thoroughly then mix in the lemon zest, lemon juice and vanilla.
3. Fold in the flour, salt, baking powder and blueberries.
4. Spoon the batter in a muffin tin covered with muffin papers.

5. Pre-heat the oven and bake at 350F for about twenty minutes or until a toothpick inserted into them comes out dry.
6. Let them cool in the pan.
7. To make the frosting, combine all the ingredients in a heatproof container and place over a hot water bath.
8. Cook the mixture for about twenty minutes, stirring all the time with a whisk until it thickens and it looks smooth and shiny.
9. Let cool and then top each cupcake with the lemon cream.

Nutritional Content of One Serving:

Calories: 374 ‖ Fat: 18.2g ‖ Protein: 4.6g ‖ Carbohydrates: 51.1g

BLUEBERRY FROSTED CUPCAKES

Total Time Taken: 1 ½ hours
Yield: 12 Servings
Ingredients:

Cupcakes:

- ½ cup butter, softened
- 2 tablespoons dark brown sugar
- 3 eggs
- 1 teaspoon vanilla extract
- 1 ¾ cups all-purpose flour
- 1 teaspoon baking powder
- ½ teaspoon salt
- 1 cup buttermilk
- 1 cup fresh blueberries
- 2/3 cup white sugar

Frosting:

- ¼ cup blueberry puree
- 1 cup butter, softened
- 2 ½ cups powdered sugar

Directions:

1. To make the cupcakes, combine the butter and sugars in a container until fluffy and pale.

2. Put in the eggs and vanilla and mix thoroughly then fold in the flour, baking powder and salt.
3. Stir in the buttermilk then fold in the blueberries.
4. Spoon the batter in 12 muffin cups covered with muffin papers.
5. Preheat your oven and bake the cupcakes at 350F for about twenty minutes or until it rises significantly and starts to appear golden-brown.
6. Let the cupcakes cool down in the pan.
7. To make the frosting, combine the butter and sugar in a container until fluffy and pale, at least five minutes.
8. Put in the blueberry puree and mix thoroughly.
9. Spoon the frosting into a pastry bag and top the cupcakes with it.

Nutritional Content of One Serving:

Calories: 463 ‖ Fat: 24.5g ‖ Protein: 4.3g ‖ Carbohydrates: 58.8g

BLUEBERRY CHEESE MUFFINS

Total Time Taken: 1 hour
Yield: 12 Servings
Ingredients:

- ¼ cup white rice flour
- ¼ teaspoon salt
- ½ cup coconut flour
- ½ cup cream cheese
- ½ cup sorghum flour
- ½ cup tapioca flour
- ¾ cup butter, melted
- 1 ½ teaspoons baking powder
- 1 cup fresh blueberries
- 1 cup milk
- 1 cup white sugar
- 2 eggs

Directions:

1. Mix the butter, sugar and eggs in a container until creamy.
2. Put in the milk and mix thoroughly then mix in the flours, salt and baking powder.

3. Put in the blueberries then spoon the batter in a muffin tin coated with baking muffin papers.
4. Top each muffin with a dollop of cream cheese and preheat your oven and bake at 350F for about twenty minutes or until a golden-brown colour is achieved and it rises significantly.
5. Let the muffins cool to room temperature before you serve.

Nutritional Content of One Serving:

Calories: 314 ‖ Fat: 17.1g ‖ Protein: 4.3g ‖ Carbohydrates: 38.6g

BLUEBERRY BANANA MUFFINS

Total Time Taken: 1 hour
Yield: 12 Servings
Ingredients:

- ½ cup canola oil
- ½ teaspoon cinnamon powder
- ½ teaspoon salt
- 1 cup all-purpose flour
- 1 cup fresh blueberries
- 1 cup plain yogurt
- 1 cup wheat flour
- 2 bananas, mashed
- 2 eggs
- 2 teaspoons baking powder

Directions:

1. Mix the flours, cinnamon, salt and baking powder in a container.
2. Put in the remaining ingredients and stir for a few seconds to mix.
3. Fold in the blueberries then spoon the batter in a muffin tin lined.
4. Pre-heat the oven and bake at 350F for about twenty minutes or until it rises significantly and starts to appear golden-brown.

These muffins taste best chilled.

Nutritional Content of One Serving:

Calories: 206 ‖ Fat: 10.4g ‖ Protein: 4.5g ‖ Carbohydrates: 24.0g

BLACKBERRY WHITE CHOCOLATE MUFFINS

Total Time Taken: 1 hour
Yield: 12 Servings
Ingredients:

- 2 teaspoons baking powder
- 2 eggs
- 2 cups all-purpose flour
- 1 teaspoon vanilla extract
- 1 cup milk
- 1 cup blueberries
- ½ teaspoon salt
- ½ cup white sugar
- ½ cup white chocolate chips
- ½ cup canola oil
- ¼ cup shredded coconut

Directions:

1. Mix the flour, baking powder, salt, sugar, coconut and chocolate chips in a container.
2. Stir in the milk, eggs, canola oil and vanilla and mix using a spatula.
3. Fold in the blueberries then spoon the batter in a muffin tin coated with baking muffin papers.
4. Preheat your oven and bake the muffins at 350F for about twenty minutes or until it rises significantly and starts to appear golden-brown.

These muffins taste best chilled.

Nutritional Content of One Serving:

Calories: 261 ‖ Fat: 13.3g ‖ Protein: 4.3g ‖ Carbohydrates: 31.9g

BLACKBERRY OAT BRAN MUFFINS

Total Time Taken: 1 hour
Yield: 12 Servings
Ingredients:

- 2 eggs
- 1 teaspoon vanilla extract
- 1 cup buttermilk
- 1 cup blackberries
- 1 ½ teaspoons baking powder
- 1 ½ cups all-purpose flour
- ½ teaspoon cinnamon powder
- ½ cup white sugar
- ½ cup oat bran
- ½ cup butter, melted
- ¼ teaspoon salt

Directions:

1. Mix the flour, oat bran, baking powder, salt and cinnamon in a container.
2. In a separate container, mix the butter, sugar, eggs, buttermilk and vanilla. Pour this mixture over the dry ingredients and give them a quick whisk.
3. Fold in the blackberries then spoon the batter in a muffin tin lined using muffin papers of your choice.
4. Pre-heat the oven and bake at 350F for about twenty minutes or until it rises significantly and seems golden.

These muffins taste best chilled.

Nutritional Content of One Serving:

Calories: 188 ‖ Fat: 9.0g ‖ Protein: 3.9g ‖ Carbohydrates: 24.5g

BLACKBERRY MUFFINS

Total Time Taken: 1 hour
Yield: 10 Servings
Ingredients:

- ½ cup rolled oats
- ½ teaspoon salt
- 1 ½ cups all-purpose flour

- 1 cup buttermilk
- 1 cup fresh blackberries
- 1 teaspoon baking soda
- 1 teaspoon vanilla extract
- 2 eggs
- 2/3 cup white sugar

Directions:

1. Mix the flour, oats, baking soda, salt and sugar in a container.
2. Put in the eggs, buttermilk and vanilla and stir swiftly to combine.
3. Fold in the blackberries then scoop the batter in a muffin tin covered with muffin papers.
4. Preheat your oven and bake the muffins at 350F for about twenty minutes or until it rises significantly and seems golden.

These muffins taste best chilled.

Nutritional Content of One Serving:

Calories: 164 ‖ Fat: 1.6g ‖ Protein: 4.6g ‖ Carbohydrates: 33.1g

BLACKBERRY BRAN MUFFINS

Total Time Taken: 1 hour
Yield: 12 Servings
Ingredients:

- ¼ cup honey
- ¼ cup light brown sugar
- ¼ cup rice bran oil
- ½ cup wheat bran
- ½ teaspoon salt
- ¾ cup milk
- 1 cup all-purpose flour
- 1 cup fresh blackberries
- 1 teaspoon baking soda
- 2 eggs

Directions:

1. Mix the flour, wheat bran, baking soda and salt in a container.
2. Stir in the eggs, milk, honey, sugar and oil and stir for a few seconds to mix.
3. Fold in the blackberries then spoon the batter in a muffin tin covered with muffin papers.
4. Pre-heat the oven and bake at 350F for about twenty minutes or until it rises significantly and seems golden.

These muffins taste best chilled.

Nutritional Content of One Serving:

Calories: 140 ‖ Fat: 5.8g ‖ Protein: 3.1g ‖ Carbohydrates: 20.2g

BLACK SESAME CUPCAKES WITH CREAM CHEESE FROSTING

Total Time Taken: 1 ½ hours
Yield: 14 Servings
Ingredients:

Cupcakes:

- ¼ cup black sesame powder
- ½ teaspoon salt
- ¾ cup milk
- 1 ½ cups all-purpose flour
- 1 cup white sugar
- 1 teaspoon baking powder
- 1 teaspoon vanilla extract
- 2 eggs
- 2/3 cup butter, softened

Frosting:

- 1 cup cream cheese
- 2/3 cup butter, softened
- 3 cups powdered sugar

Directions:

1. To make the cupcakes, combine the butter and sugar in a container until fluffy and airy. Put in the eggs, one at a time, then mix in the milk and vanilla.
2. Fold in the dry ingredients and mix using a spatula.
3. Spoon the batter into 12 muffin cups covered with muffin papers.
4. Preheat your oven and bake the cupcakes at 350F for about twenty minutes or until the cupcakes pass the toothpick test.
5. Let cool in the pan.
6. To make the frosting, combine the butter and cream cheese in a container until creamy.
7. Put in the sugar and continue stirring thoroughly until fluffy and pale.
8. Spoon the frosting in a pastry bag and top each cupcake with it.

Nutritional Content of One Serving:

Calories: 445 ‖ Fat: 25.0g ‖ Protein: 4.0g ‖ Carbohydrates: 53.3g

BLACK MAGIC CUPCAKES

Total Time Taken: 1 ½ hours
Yield: 14 Servings
Ingredients:

Cupcakes:

- ¼ cup butter, softened
- ¼ teaspoon salt
- ½ cup buttermilk
- ½ cup canola oil
- ¾ cup cocoa powder
- 1 ½ cups all-purpose flour
- 1 ½ teaspoons baking powder
- 1 cup white sugar
- 1 teaspoon instant coffee
- 1 teaspoon vanilla extract
- 2 eggs

Frosting:

- ¼ cup cocoa powder
- 1 cup butter, softened

- 1 teaspoon instant coffee
- 2 cups powdered sugar
- 2 tablespoons milk

Directions:

1. To make the cupcakes, combine the butter, oil and sugar in a container until creamy and pale.
2. Put in the eggs and mix thoroughly. Stir in the vanilla and buttermilk then put in the remaining ingredients and mix using a spatula.
3. Spoon the batter in a muffin tin covered with muffin papers.
4. Preheat your oven and bake the muffins at 350F for about twenty minutes or until a toothpick inserted into them comes out dry.
5. Let cool in the pan.
6. To make the frosting, combine the butter in a container until creamy and pale.
7. Put in the sugar, progressively, then whip until fluffy.
8. Stir in the coffee, cocoa powder and milk and mix for a few additional minutes.
9. Spoon the frosting in a pastry bag and top each cupcake with it.

The cupcakes taste best chilled.

Nutritional Content of One Serving:

Calories: 412 ‖ Fat: 25.9g ‖ Protein: 3.8g ‖ Carbohydrates: 45.8g

BLACK FOREST MUFFINS

Total Time Taken: 1 hour
Yield: 12 Servings
Ingredients:

- ¼ cup canola oil
- ¼ cup cocoa powder
- ¼ teaspoon salt
- ½ cup brewed coffee
- ½ teaspoon baking soda
- 1 ½ cups all-purpose flour
- 1 cup buttermilk

- 1 cup cherries, pitted
- 1 teaspoon baking powder
- 1 teaspoon vanilla extract
- 2 eggs

Directions:

1. Mix the eggs, buttermilk, coffee, oil and vanilla and mix thoroughly.
2. Fold in the flour, cocoa powder, baking soda, baking powder and salt then put in the cherries and mix them in gently.
3. Spoon the batter in a muffin tin coated with baking muffin papers and preheat your oven and bake at 350F for about twenty minutes or until well risen.

These muffins taste best chilled.

Nutritional Content of One Serving:

Calories: 128 ‖ Fat: 5.8g ‖ Protein: 3.6g ‖ Carbohydrates: 15.9g

BLACK FOREST CUPCAKES

Total Time Taken: 1 ½ hours
Yield: 12 Servings
Ingredients:

Cupcakes:

- ¼ cup cocoa powder
- ½ cup canola oil
- ½ teaspoon salt
- 1 ¼ cups all-purpose flour
- 1 cup brewed coffee
- 1 egg
- 1 teaspoon baking soda
- 1 teaspoon vanilla extract

Frosting:

- 1 cup sour cherries, pitted
- 2 cups heavy cream, whipped

Directions:

1. To make the cupcakes, combine the coffee, oil, egg and vanilla in a container.
2. Stir in the flour, cocoa powder, salt and baking soda and stir for a few seconds to mix.
3. Pour the batter in a muffin tin covered with muffin papers.
4. Pre-heat the oven and bake at 350F for about twenty minutes or until it rises significantly and becomes aromatic.
5. Let the muffins cool to room temperature.
6. Spread the whipped cream on top of each muffin and decorate with sour cherries.

Nutritional Content of One Serving:

Calories: 264 ‖ Fat: 17.2g ‖ Protein: 2.7g ‖ Carbohydrates: 25.4g

BLACK BOTTOM MUFFINS

Total Time Taken: 1 hour
Yield: 12 Servings
Ingredients:

- ¼ cup white sugar
- ½ cup butter, melted
- ½ cup light brown sugar
- ½ teaspoon salt
- 1 ½ cups almond flour
- 1 cup cream cheese
- 1 egg
- 1 teaspoon baking powder
- 1/3 cup all-purpose flour
- 2 eggs

Directions:

1. Mix the cream cheese,
2. 1 egg and ¼ cup sugar in a container.
3. Spoon the mixture into 12 muffin cups covered with muffin papers.
4. Combine
5. 2 eggs with butter and sugar until pale.
6. Put in the flour, almond flour, baking powder and salt.

7. Spoon the batter over the cream cheese mixture.
8. Preheat your oven and bake the muffins at 350F for about twenty minutes or until well risen.

These muffins taste best chilled.

Nutritional Content of One Serving:

Calories: 223 ‖ Fat: 17.3g ‖ Protein: 4.0g ‖ Carbohydrates: 14.3g

BEETROOT RASPBERRY MUFFINS

Total Time Taken: 1 ½ hours
Yield: 12 Servings

Ingredients:

- ½ cup buttermilk
- ½ cup canola oil
- ½ cup white sugar
- ½ teaspoon salt
- 1 ½ teaspoons baking powder
- 1 cup beetroot puree
- 1 cup fresh raspberries
- 1 egg
- 1 teaspoon vanilla extract
- 2 cups all-purpose flour

Directions:

1. Mix the beetroot puree, egg, buttermilk and oil in a container.
2. Put in the sugar and vanilla and mix thoroughly then fold in the flour, salt and baking powder.
3. Fold in the raspberries then spoon the batter in a muffin tin coated with baking muffin papers.
4. Pre-heat the oven and bake at 350F for about twenty minutes or until it rises significantly and starts to appear golden-brown.

These muffins taste best chilled.

Nutritional Content of One Serving:

Calories: 206 ‖ Fat: 9.8g ‖ Protein: 3.2g ‖ Carbohydrates: 26.8g

BASIC MUFFINS

Total Time Taken: 1 hour
Yield: 12 Servings
Ingredients:

- ¼ teaspoon salt
- ½ cup canola oil
- ½ teaspoon baking powder
- ½ teaspoon baking soda
- ¾ cup white sugar
- 1 cup whole milk
- 1 egg
- 1 teaspoon vanilla extract
- 2 ¼ cups all-purpose flour

Directions:

1. Mix the flour, sugar, salt, baking powder and baking soda in a container.
2. Stir in the egg, oil, milk and vanilla and stir for a few seconds to mix.
3. Spoon the batter in a muffin tin covered with muffin papers and preheat your oven and bake at 350F for about twenty minutes or until it rises significantly and seems golden.

These muffins taste best chilled.

Nutritional Content of One Serving:
Calories: 231 ‖ Fat: 10.3g ‖ Protein: 3.5g ‖ Carbohydrates: 31.5g

BASIC CHOCOLATE MUFFINS

Total Time Taken: 1 hour
Yield: 12 Servings
Ingredients:

- 2 tablespoons cocoa powder

- 2 eggs
- 2 cups all-purpose flour
- 1 teaspoon vanilla extract
- 1 ½ teaspoons baking powder
- ¾ cup light brown sugar
- ½ cup milk
- ½ cup canola oil
- ¼ teaspoon salt

Directions:

1. Mix the flour, cocoa powder, salt and baking powder.
2. Mix the sugar and oil in a container for a couple of minutes. Put in the eggs, vanilla and milk and mix thoroughly.
3. Fold in the flour then spoon the batter in a muffin tin covered with muffin papers of your desire.
4. Pre-heat the oven and bake at 350F for about twenty minutes or until a toothpick inserted into them comes out dry.

These muffins taste best chilled.

Nutritional Content of One Serving:

Calories: 210 ‖ Fat: 10.3g ‖ Protein: 3.6g ‖ Carbohydrates: 26.2g

BANANA YOGURT MUFFINS

Total Time Taken: 1 hour
Yield: 12 Servings
Ingredients:

- ½ cup canola oil
- ½ cup light brown sugar
- ½ teaspoon baking soda
- ½ teaspoon salt
- 1 bananas, mashed
- 1 cup plain yogurt
- 1 egg
- 1 teaspoon baking powder
- 2 cups all-purpose flour

Directions:

1. Mix the bananas, yogurt, egg, sugar and oil in a container until creamy.
2. Put in the remaining ingredients and stir for a few seconds to mix.
3. Spoon the batter in a muffin tin covered with muffin papers.
4. Preheat your oven and bake the muffins at 350F for about twenty minutes or until a golden-brown colour is achieved and it rises significantly.

These muffins taste best chilled.

Nutritional Content of One Serving:

Calories: 208 ‖ Fat: 9.9g ‖ Protein: 3.9g ‖ Carbohydrates: 25.7g

BANANA PEAR MUFFINS

Total Time Taken: 1 hour
Yield: 12 Servings
Ingredients:

- ¼ cup buttermilk
- ¼ cup canola oil
- ¼ teaspoon salt
- ½ cup white sugar
- ½ cup whole wheat flour
- ½ teaspoon ground ginger
- 1 cup all-purpose flour
- 1 egg
- 1 teaspoon baking soda
- 1 teaspoon cinnamon powder
- 2 bananas, mashed
- 2 pears, cored and diced

Directions:

1. Mix the bananas, egg, oil, buttermilk and sugar in a container.
2. Put in the flours, salt, spices and baking soda and stir for a few seconds to mix just until incorporated.
3. Fold in the pears then spoon the batter in a muffin tin covered with muffin papers.

4. Pre-heat the oven and bake at 350F for about twenty minutes or until a golden-brown colour is achieved and fragrant.

These muffins taste best chilled.

Nutritional Content of One Serving:

Calories: 173 ‖ Fat: 5.2g ‖ Protein: 2.6g ‖ Carbohydrates: 30.4g

BANANA PEANUT BUTTER MUFFINS

Total Time Taken: 1 hour
Yield: 12 Servings
Ingredients:

- ¼ cup canola oil
- ¼ cup smooth peanut butter
- ½ cup buttermilk
- ½ cup light brown sugar
- ½ teaspoon salt
- 1 ½ cups all-purpose flour
- 1 teaspoon baking soda
- 1 teaspoon vanilla extract
- 2 eggs
- 2 ripe bananas, mashed

Directions:

1. Mix the peanut butter, bananas, oil, eggs and buttermilk in a container.
2. Put in the vanilla and mix thoroughly then fold in the remaining ingredients.
3. Spoon the batter in 12 muffin cups covered with muffin papers.
4. Preheat your oven and bake the muffins at 350F for about twenty minutes or until it rises significantly and becomes aromatic.

These muffins taste best chilled.

Nutritional Content of One Serving:

Calories: 185 ‖ Fat: 8.3g ‖ Protein: 4.4g ‖ Carbohydrates: 24.0g

BANANA PEANUT BUTTER CUPS MUFFINS

Total Time Taken: 1 hour
Yield: 12 Servings
Ingredients:

- ½ cup light brown sugar
- ½ peanut butter cups, chopped
- ½ teaspoon salt
- 1 ½ cups all-purpose flour
- 1 cup buttermilk
- 1 teaspoon baking soda
- 1 teaspoon vanilla extract
- 2 bananas, mashed
- 2 eggs

Directions:

1. Mix the bananas, eggs, buttermilk and vanilla in a container.
2. Put in the sugar, flour, salt and baking soda and mix using a spatula.
3. Fold in the peanut butter cups then spoon the batter in a muffin tin covered with muffin papers.
4. Preheat your oven and bake the muffins at 350F for about twenty minutes or until a golden-brown colour is achieved and it rises significantly.

These muffins taste best chilled.

Nutritional Content of One Serving:

Calories: 180 || Fat: 6.5g || Protein: 6.1g || Carbohydrates: 25.5g

BANANA OLIVE OIL MUFFINS

Total Time Taken: 1 hour
Yield: 12 Servings
Ingredients:

- ¼ cup extra virgin olive oil

- ½ cup buttermilk
- ½ cup light brown sugar
- ½ teaspoon salt
- 1 ½ cups all-purpose flour
- 1 ½ teaspoons baking powder
- 1 tablespoon lemon juice
- 1 teaspoon lemon zest
- 2 bananas, mashed
- 2 eggs

Directions:

1. Mix the eggs and sugar in a container until creamy. Put in the olive oil and lemon zest and mix thoroughly. Stir in the lemon juice and bananas, as well as the buttermilk.
2. Fold in the flour, salt and baking powder then spoon the batter in a muffin tin covered with muffin papers.
3. Pre-heat the oven and bake at 350F for about twenty minutes or until it rises significantly and seems golden.

These muffins taste best chilled.

Nutritional Content of One Serving:

Calories: 149 ‖ Fat: 5.2g ‖ Protein: 3.1g ‖ Carbohydrates: 23.3g

BANANA MASCARPONE CUPCAKES

Total Time Taken: 1 ½ hours
Yield: 12 Servings
Ingredients:

Cupcakes:

- ¼ cup canola oil
- ½ cup oat flour
- ½ teaspoon salt
- 1 ½ cups all-purpose flour
- 1 cup buttermilk
- 1 teaspoon vanilla extract
- 2 bananas, mashed

- 2 eggs
- 2 teaspoons baking powder

Frosting:

- 1 ½ cups mascarpone cheese
- 1 cup powdered sugar
- 1 teaspoon vanilla extract

Directions:

1. To make the cupcakes, combine the bananas, eggs, vanilla, oil and buttermilk in a container.
2. Put in the remaining ingredients and mix thoroughly.
3. Spoon the batter in a muffin tin covered with muffin papers.
4. Pre-heat the oven and bake at 350F for about twenty minutes or until a golden-brown colour is achieved and it rises significantly.
5. Let them cool in the pan.
6. To make the frosting, combine the mascarpone cheese and sugar in a container until pale and fluffy.
7. Put in the vanilla and mix thoroughly.
8. Apply the frosting on top of the cupcakes and serve them fresh.

Nutritional Content of One Serving:

Calories: 244 ‖ Fat: 9.9g ‖ Protein: 7.4g ‖ Carbohydrates: 31.5g

BANANA HONEY MUFFINS

Total Time Taken: 1 hour
Yield: 12 Servings
Ingredients:

- ½ cup buttermilk
- ½ cup honey
- ½ cup rolled oats
- ½ teaspoon salt
- 1 ½ cups all-purpose flour
- 1 egg
- 1 teaspoon baking soda
- 1 teaspoon vanilla extract

- 2 ripe bananas, mashed

Directions:

1. Mix the bananas, honey, buttermilk, egg and vanilla in a container.
2. Put in the remaining ingredients and mix using a spatula.
3. Spoon the batter in a muffin tin covered with muffin papers and preheat your oven and bake at 350F for about twenty minutes or until it rises significantly and starts to appear golden-brown.

These muffins taste best chilled.

Nutritional Content of One Serving:

Calories: 141 ‖ Fat: 0.9g ‖ Protein: 3.1g ‖ Carbohydrates: 30.9g

BANANA CRUNCH MUFFINS

Total Time Taken: 1 hour
Yield: 12 Servings
Ingredients:

- ¼ teaspoon salt
- ½ cup canola oil
- ½ cup light brown sugar
- ½ cup milk
- ½ cup shredded coconut
- 1 ½ teaspoons baking powder
- 1 cup rolled oats
- 1 teaspoon vanilla extract
- 2 bananas, mashed
- 2 cups all-purpose flour
- 2 eggs

Directions:

1. Mix the bananas, sugar, eggs, milk, vanilla and oil in a container.
2. Stir in the flour, salt, baking powder and coconut and mix using a spatula.
3. Spoon the batter in a muffin tin covered with muffin papers and top each muffin with rolled oats.

4. Pre-heat the oven and bake at 350F for about twenty minutes or until it rises significantly and starts to appear golden-brown.

These muffins taste best chilled.

Nutritional Content of One Serving:

Calories: 251 ‖ Fat: 11.8g ‖ Protein: 4.6g ‖ Carbohydrates: 32.3g

BANANA CHOCOLATE CHIP MUFFINS

Total Time Taken: 1 hour
Yield: 12 Servings
Ingredients:

- ¼ cup milk
- ½ cup dark chocolate chips
- ½ cup white sugar
- ½ teaspoon salt
- 1 ½ cups all-purpose flour
- 1 egg
- 1 teaspoon baking soda
- 1/3 cup butter, melted
- 3 bananas, mashed

Directions:

1. Mix the bananas, sugar, egg, butter and milk in a container until creamy.
2. Put in the remaining ingredients and fold them in using a spatula.
3. Spoon the batter into 12 muffin cups covered with muffin papers.
4. Pre-heat the oven and bake at 350F for about twenty minutes.

These muffins taste best chilled.

Nutritional Content of One Serving:

Calories: 191 ‖ Fat: 7.2g ‖ Protein: 2.9g ‖ Carbohydrates: 30.6g

BANANA CHIA MUFFINS

Total Time Taken: 1 hour
Yield: 12 Servings
Ingredients:

- ¼ cup whole milk
- ½ cup canola oil
- ½ cup white sugar
- ½ teaspoon salt
- 1 cup buttermilk
- 2 bananas, mashed
- 2 cups all-purpose flour
- 2 eggs
- 2 teaspoons baking powder
- 3 tablespoons chia seeds

Directions:

1. Mix the flour, chia seeds, sugar, salt and baking powder in a container.
2. Put in the remaining ingredients and stir for a few seconds to mix.
3. Spoon the batter in a muffin tin covered with muffin papers and preheat your oven and bake at 350F for about twenty minutes or until a toothpick inserted into the center of a muffin comes out clean.
4. Let them cool in the pan before you serve.

Nutritional Content of One Serving:

Calories: 266 ‖ Fat: 12.8g ‖ Protein: 5.7g ‖ Carbohydrates: 33.0g

BANANA BUTTERMILK MUFFINS

Total Time Taken: 1 hour
Yield: 12 Servings
Ingredients:

- ¼ cup butter, melted
- ½ cup rolled oats
- ½ cup white sugar
- ½ teaspoon salt
- 1 ¾ cups all-purpose flour
- 1 cup buttermilk

- 1 egg
- 1 teaspoon baking powder
- 1 teaspoon baking soda
- 2 ripe bananas, mashed

Directions:

1. Mix the dry ingredients in a container and the wet ingredients in a separate container.
2. Pour the wet ingredients over the dry ones and stir swiftly to combine.
3. Spoon the batter in a muffin pan coated with muffin papers.
4. Preheat your oven and bake the muffins at 350F for about twenty minutes or until a golden-brown colour is achieved or until mildly golden-brown and it rises significantly.

These muffins taste best chilled.

Nutritional Content of One Serving:

Calories: 176 ‖ Fat: 4.8g ‖ Protein: 3.7g ‖ Carbohydrates: 30.2g

APRICOT ROSEMARY MUFFINS

Total Time Taken: 1 hour
Yield: 12 Servings
Ingredients:

- ¼ cup milk
- ¼ teaspoon salt
- ½ cup dried apricots, chopped
- ½ cup ground almonds
- ½ cup honey
- ½ cup plain yogurt
- ½ cup rolled oats
- 1 ½ cups all-purpose flour
- 1 egg
- 1 teaspoon baking powder
- 1 teaspoon dried rosemary

Directions:

1. Mix the flour, salt, baking powder, oats, almonds and rosemary in a container.
2. Stir in the honey, yogurt, milk and egg and mix thoroughly then fold in the apricots.
3. Spoon the batter in a muffin pan coated with your favorite muffin papers and preheat your oven and bake at 350F for about twenty minutes or until it rises significantly and starts to appear golden-brown.

These muffins taste best chilled.

Nutritional Content of One Serving:

Calories: 155 ‖ Fat: 3.0g ‖ Protein: 4.2g ‖ Carbohydrates: 28.7g

APRICOT ORANGE MUFFINS

Total Time Taken: 1 hour
Yield: 12 Servings
Ingredients:

- ¼ cup wheat bran
- ¼ teaspoon orange juice
- ½ cup buttermilk
- ½ cup canola oil
- ½ cup light brown sugar
- ½ teaspoon salt
- 1 ½ cups all-purpose flour
- 1 ½ teaspoons baking powder
- 1 tablespoon orange zest
- 2 eggs
- 6 apricots, halved

Directions:

1. Mix the flour, wheat bran, salt and baking powder in a container.
2. Put in the eggs, sugar, buttermilk, orange zest and orange juice and stir for a few seconds to mix.
3. Spoon the batter in a muffin tin covered with muffin papers.

4. Top each muffin with one apricot half and preheat your oven and bake at 350F for about twenty minutes or until a golden-brown colour is achieved and it rises significantly.

These muffins taste best chilled.

Nutritional Content of One Serving:

Calories: 187 ‖ Fat: 10.2g ‖ Protein: 3.3g ‖ Carbohydrates: 21.5g

APPLE PUREE MUFFINS

Total Time Taken: 1 hour
Yield: 12 Servings
Ingredients:

- 1 ½ cups all-purpose flour
- 1 teaspoon cinnamon powder
- ½ teaspoon ground ginger
- 1 teaspoon baking soda
- 2 eggs
- ½ cup apple puree
- ¼ cup peanut oil
- 1 teaspoon vanilla extract
- 2 apples, cored and diced
- ½ cup golden raisins
- 2/3 cup light brown sugar

Directions:

1. Mix the flour, sugar, cinnamon, ginger and baking soda in a container.
2. Put in the remaining ingredients and stir for a few seconds to mix.
3. Pour the batter in a muffin tin coated with baking muffin papers.
4. Preheat your oven and bake the muffins at 350F for about twenty minutes or until it is aromatic and appears golden brown.

These muffins taste best chilled.

Nutritional Content of One Serving:

Calories: 179 ‖ Fat: 5.5g ‖ Protein: 2.8g ‖ Carbohydrates: 30.4g

APPLE PIE CARAMEL CUPCAKES

Total Time Taken: 1 ½ hours

Yield: 14 Servings

Ingredients:

- ½ teaspoon baking soda
- ½ teaspoon ground ginger
- 1 ½ cups all-purpose flour
- 1 pinch salt
- 1 teaspoon baking powder
- 1 teaspoon vanilla extract
- 2 eggs
- 2/3 cup butter, softened
- 2/3 cup buttermilk
- 2/3 cup light brown sugar

Frosting:

- ½ teaspoon cinnamon powder
- 1 cup butter, softened
- 2 cups powdered sugar

Topping:

- ¼ cup light brown sugar
- 1 tablespoon lemon juice
- 2 apples, peeled, cored and diced

Directions:

1. To make the cupcakes, combine the butter and sugar in a container until creamy and fluffy.
2. Put in the eggs and vanilla and mix thoroughly then mix in the buttermilk.
3. Put in the flour, spices, baking powder, baking soda and salt then pour the batter in a muffin tin covered with muffin papers.
4. Pre-heat the oven and bake at 350F for about twenty minutes or until a toothpick inserted into them comes out dry.
5. To make the frosting, combine the butter and sugar in a container for five minutes until pale and airy. Put in the cinnamon and mix thoroughly.
6. Top each cupcake with the frosting.

7. For the topping, mix the ingredients in a saucepan and cook over low heat just until the apples are tender. Let cool down then top each cupcake with a spoonfuls of apple mixture.

These cupcakes taste best when fresh.

Nutritional Content of One Serving:

Calories: 374 ‖ Fat: 22.9g ‖ Protein: 2.9g ‖ Carbohydrates: 41.1g

APPLE MUFFINS

Total Time Taken: 1 hour
Yield: 12 Servings
Ingredients:

- ¼ cup canola oil
- ½ cup ground walnuts
- ½ cup plain yogurt
- ½ cup white sugar
- ½ cup whole wheat flour
- ½ teaspoon cinnamon powder
- ½ teaspoon salt
- 1 cup all-purpose flour
- 1 teaspoon baking soda
- 1 teaspoon vanilla extract
- 2 apples, peeled, cored and diced
- 2 eggs

Directions:

1. Mix the eggs and sugar until fluffy and pale.
2. Put in the vanilla, oil and yogurt and stir thoroughly until blended.
3. Fold in the flour mixture then put in the apples.
4. Spoon the batter in a muffin tin covered with muffin papers and preheat your oven and bake at 350F for about twenty minutes or until a golden-brown colour is achieved and it rises significantly.

These muffins taste best chilled.

Nutritional Content of One Serving:

Calories: 195 || Fat: 8.7g || Protein: 4.5g || Carbohydrates: 25.8g

APPLE CRANBERRY MUFFINS

Total Time Taken: 1 hour
Yield: 12 Servings
Ingredients:

- ¼ teaspoon salt
- ½ cup butter, melted
- ½ cup dried cranberries
- ½ cup light brown sugar
- ½ cup milk
- ½ teaspoon cinnamon powder
- 1 ¾ cups all-purpose flour
- 1 egg
- 1 red apple, cored and diced
- 1 teaspoon baking soda
- 1 teaspoon vanilla extract

Directions:

1. Mix the flour, sugar, baking soda, salt and cinnamon in a container.
2. Stir in the butter, milk, egg and vanilla and stir for a few seconds to mix.
3. Fold in the apple and cranberries and spoon the batter in a muffin tin lined using muffin papers of your choice.
4. Preheat your oven and bake the muffins at 350F for about twenty minutes or until it rises significantly and seems golden.

These muffins taste best chilled.

Nutritional Content of One Serving:

Calories: 179 || Fat: 8.4g || Protein: 2.8g || Carbohydrates: 22.9g

ALMOND WHITE CHOCOLATE CUPCAKES

Total Time Taken: 1 ½ hours
Yield: 12 Servings
Ingredients:

Cupcakes:

- ½ cup all-purpose flour
- ½ cup butter, softened
- ½ cup plain yogurt
- ½ teaspoon almond extract
- ½ teaspoon salt
- ¾ cup white sugar
- 1 ½ teaspoons baking powder
- 1 cup almond flour
- 1 teaspoon vanilla extract
- 3 eggs

Frosting:

- 1 cup heavy cream
- 2 cups white chocolate chips

Directions:

1. To make the cupcakes, combine the butter and sugar in a container until fluffy and pale.
2. Put in the vanilla, almond extract and eggs and mix thoroughly.
3. Stir in the yogurt and stir thoroughly until blended.
4. Fold in the flours, salt, baking powder and mix using a spatula.
5. Spoon the batter in a muffin tin covered with muffin papers and preheat your oven and bake at 350F for about twenty minutes or until it rises significantly and seems golden.
6. Let them cool in the pan.
7. To make the frosting, bring the cream to a boil then remove from the
8. heat and put in the chocolate. Stir until melted and smooth then let cool in your refrigerator for a few hours.
9. When chilled, whip the frosting until airy and fluffy. Spoon the frosting in a pastry bag and top the cupcakes with it.

10. Serve immediately.

Nutritional Content of One Serving:

Calories: 359 ‖ Fat: 22.9g ‖ Protein: 5.0g ‖ Carbohydrates: 35.2g

ALMOND VANILLA CUPCAKES

Total Time Taken: 1 ½ hours
Yield: 12 Servings
Ingredients:

Cupcakes:

- ¼ cup milk
- ½ cup butter, softened
- ½ cup white sugar
- ½ teaspoon salt
- 1 cup all-purpose flour
- 1 cup ground almonds
- 1 teaspoon baking powder
- 1 teaspoon lemon zest
- 1 teaspoon vanilla extract
- 2 eggs

Glaze:

- 1 cup powdered sugar
- 1 tablespoon butter, melted
- 1 teaspoon lemon zest

Directions:

1. To make the cupcakes, combine the butter, sugar and vanilla in a container until fluffy and pale.
2. Put in the eggs, one at a time, then mix in the lemon zest and put in the flour, almonds, salt and baking powder.
3. Stir in the milk and mix for a minute on high speed.
4. Spoon the batter in a muffin tin covered with muffin papers and preheat your oven and bake at 350F for about twenty minutes or until a golden-brown colour is achieved and it rises significantly.
5. Let the cupcakes cool in the pan.

6. For the glaze, combine all the ingredients in a container. Sprinkle the glaze over each cupcake and serve fresh.

Nutritional Content of One Serving:

Calories: 245 ‖ Fat: 13.5g ‖ Protein: 3.9g ‖ Carbohydrates: 28.6g

ALMOND VANILLA CUPCAKES

Total Time Taken: 1 ½ hours
Yield: 12 Servings
Ingredients:

Cupcakes:

- ½ cup all-purpose flour
- ½ cup butter, softened
- ½ cup buttermilk
- ½ cup white sugar
- ½ teaspoon almond extract
- ½ teaspoon salt
- 1 ½ cups almond flour
- 1 teaspoon baking soda
- 1 teaspoon vanilla extract
- 2 eggs

Frosting:

- 1 cup butter, softened
- 1 tablespoon vanilla extract
- 2 cups powdered sugar

Directions:

1. To make the cupcakes, combine the flours, salt and baking soda in a container.
2. In a separate container, combine the butter, sugar and vanilla until fluffy and creamy.
3. Put in the eggs, one at a time, then mix in the buttermilk and almond extract.
4. Fold in the flour mixture then spoon the batter in a muffin tin covered with muffin papers.

5. Pre-heat the oven and bake at 350F for about twenty minutes or until a golden-brown colour is achieved.
6. Let them cool in the pan.
7. To make the frosting, combine the butter and sugar for five minutes until pale and fluffy.
8. Put in the vanilla and mix thoroughly.
9. Spoon the frosting in a pastry bag and top the cupcakes with it.

Nutritional Content of One Serving:

Calories: 371 ‖ Fat: 25.7g ‖ Protein: 2.8g ‖ Carbohydrates: 33.8g

ALMOND ROSE CUPCAKES

Total Time Taken: 1 ½ hours
Yield: 12 Servings
Ingredients:

Cupcakes:

- ¼ cup all-purpose flour
- ¼ teaspoon salt
- ½ cup butter, softened
- ½ cup white sugar
- 1/2 teaspoon almond extract
- 1 ¼ cups almond flour
- 1 ½ teaspoons baking powder
- 1 teaspoon rose water
- 2 eggs

Frosting:

- 1 cup butter, softened
- 1 teaspoon rose water Rose petals to garnish
- 2 cups powdered sugar

Directions:

1. To make the cupcakes, combine the butter and sugar in a container until creamy and fluffy. Put in the rose water and almond extract, as well as the eggs and mix thoroughly.
2. Fold in the flours, salt and baking powder and mix using a spatula.

3. Spoon the batter in a muffin tin covered with muffin papers and preheat your oven and bake at 350F for about twenty minutes or until it rises significantly and starts to appear golden-brown.
4. Let cool in the pan.
5. To make the frosting, combine the butter and sugar in a container until creamy and fluffy and
6. pale.
7. Put in the rose water and mix thoroughly.
8. Pipe the frosting on top of each cupcake and garnish with rose petals.

Nutritional Content of One Serving:

Calories: 350 ‖ Fat: 25.3g ‖ Protein: 2.1g ‖ Carbohydrates: 31.3g

ALMOND POPPY SEED MUFFINS

Total Time Taken: 1 hour
Yield: 12 Servings
Ingredients:

- ¼ teaspoon salt
- ½ cup butter, melted
- ½ cup sour cream
- ½ cup white sugar
- 1 ½ cups almond flour
- 1 pinch salt
- 1 teaspoon baking powder
- 1 teaspoon lemon zest
- 1 teaspoon vanilla extract
- 2 eggs
- 2 tablespoons poppy seeds

Directions:

1. Mix the almond flour, baking powder, salt and poppy seeds in a container.
2. In another container, combine the sugar, butter, eggs, sour cream, lemon zest and salt. Pour this mixture over the dry ingredients and mix thoroughly.
3. Spoon the batter in a muffin tin covered with muffin papers.
4. Pre-heat the oven and bake at 350F for about twenty minutes or until a golden-brown colour is achieved and it rises significantly.

5. Let the muffins cool in the pan before you serve.

Nutritional Content of One Serving:

Calories: 159 ‖ Fat: 12.8g ‖ Protein: 2.3g ‖ Carbohydrates: 10.2g

BONUS: FRENCH DESSERTS

No one makes desserts like the French!

CHOCOLATE TART

Total Time Taken: 1 ½ hour
Yield: 10 Servings
Ingredients:

Crust:

- ¼ cup cocoa powder
- ¼ teaspoon salt
- ½ cup butter, softened
- ½ cup powdered sugar
- 1 ¾ cups all-purpose flour
- 1 egg
- 1 teaspoon vanilla extract

Filling:

- 1 ½ cups heavy cream
- 1 pinch salt
- 1 tablespoon vanilla extract
- 2 cups dark chocolate chips

Directions:

1. For the crust, combine the butter, sugar and vanilla and mix thoroughly.
2. Stir in the egg and fold in the flour, cocoa powder and salt and stir until the dough comes together.
3. Put the dough on a floured working surface and roll it into a slim sheet.
4. Move the sheet of dough to a tart pan and press it well on the bottom and sides of the pan.
5. Preheat your oven and bake the crust at 350F for about twenty minutes or until set.
6. For the filling, bring the cream to a boil in a saucepan.
7. Turn off the heat and put in the chocolate chips and stir until melted and

8. smooth.
9. Put in the vanilla and salt and mix thoroughly.
10. Pour the filling in the chilled crust and let cool in the pan.
11. Serve the chocolate tart chilled.

Nutritional Content of One Serving:

Calories: 374 ‖ Fat: 23.2g ‖ Protein: 5.3g ‖ Carbohydrates: 40.6g

CHOCOLATE ÉCLAIRS

Total Time Taken: 1 ½ hours
Yield: 20 Servings
Ingredients: Éclairs:

- ½ cup milk
- ½ cup water
- ½ teaspoon salt
- ¾ cup butter
- 1 cup all-purpose flour
- 1 teaspoon sugar
- 5 eggs, beaten

Chocolate Filling:

- 1 ½ cups dark chocolate chips
- 1 ½ cups heavy cream
- 1 teaspoon vanilla extract

Glaze:

- 1 ½ cups dark chocolate chips
- 1 tablespoon canola oil

Directions:

1. For the éclairs, combine the water, milk, butter, sugar and salt in a saucepan.
2. Put over moderate heat and bring to its boiling point.
3. Put in the flour, all at once, and mix thoroughly using a spatula until it becomes thick and the dough comes together into a ball.
4. Let the dough cool down for about ten minutes then mix in the eggs and mix thoroughly.

5. Spoon the batter in a pastry bag and pipe it on a baking tray lined with
6. parchment paper.
7. Pre-heat the oven and bake at 350F for about twenty minutes or until well risen, golden and crunchy.
8. Let cool in the pan.
9. For the filling, bring the cream to a boil. Turn off the heat and put in the chocolate. Stir until melted and smooth then let cool down and mix in the vanilla.
10. Fill the éclairs with the chocolate cream.
11. To make the glaze, melt the chocolate with the oil in a heatproof container over a hot water bath.
12. Immerse the éclairs in the glaze and place on a wire rack.
13. Best served chilled and set.

Nutritional Content of One Serving:

Calories: 225 ‖ Fat: 17.0g ‖ Protein: 3.7g ‖ Carbohydrates: 17.6g

CHEWY ALMOND MACAROONS

Total Time Taken: 1 hour
Yield: 20 Servings
Ingredients:

- ¼ cup Amaretto liqueur
- ¼ teaspoon salt
- ½ cup white sugar
- 1 cup powdered sugar
- 16 oz. almond paste

Directions:

1. Mix the almond paste, sugar and salt in a container until creamy.
2. Put in the liqueur and mix thoroughly.
3. Put the sugar on a platter.
4. Make small balls of mixture and roll them through the powdered sugar. Position the macaroons on a baking tray covered with parchment paper. Allow to rest for about twenty minutes then preheat your oven and bake at 350F for fifteen minutes or until golden.
5. Best served chilled.

Nutritional Content of One Serving:

Calories: 155 ‖ Fat: 6.3g ‖ Protein: 2.0g ‖ Carbohydrates: 21.8g

CHERRY CLAFOUTIS

Total Time Taken: 1 hour

Yield: 8 Servings

Ingredients:

- ¼ teaspoon salt
- ½ cup white sugar
- ¾ cup all-purpose flour
- 1 ½ cups milk
- 1 teaspoon vanilla extract
- 2 tablespoons brandy
- 3 cups cherries, pitted or unpitted
- 6 eggs

Directions:

1. Mix the milk, vanilla, sugar, brandy and eggs in a container.
2. Stir in the flour and salt and mix thoroughly.
3. Put the cherries in a deep dish baking tray lined using butter.
4. Pour the batter over the cherries and preheat your oven and bake at 350F for about twenty-five minutes or until set.

Best served chilled.

Nutritional Content of One Serving:

Calories: 203 ‖ Fat: 4.4g ‖ Protein: 7.3g ‖ Carbohydrates: 31.0g

BUTTERY MADELEINES

Total Time Taken: 1 hour

Yield: 12 Servings

Ingredients:

- ½ cup butter, melted and cooled
- ½ cup white sugar
- ½ teaspoon baking powder
- ¾ cup all-purpose flour
- 1 pinch salt
- 1 teaspoon vanilla extract
- 2 eggs

Directions:

1. Sift the flour, salt and baking powder in a container.
2. Mix the eggs and sugar in a container until fluffy and light. Put in the vanilla and mix thoroughly.
3. Fold in the flour then put in the butter, mixing it gently using a spatula.
4. Spoon the batter in a madeleine pan and preheat your oven and bake at 350F for about ten minutes or until a golden-brown colour is achieved and it rises significantly.

Tastes best chilled.

Nutritional Content of One Serving:

Calories: 139 ‖ Fat: 8.5g ‖ Protein: 1.8g ‖ Carbohydrates: 14.5g

BUTTER COOKIES

Total Time Taken: 1 ½ hours
Yield: 20 Servings

Ingredients:

- ¼ teaspoon salt
- ½ cup butter, softened
- ½ cup ground almonds
- ½ cup powdered sugar
- 1 egg
- 1 teaspoon vanilla extract
- 2 cups all-purpose flour

Directions:

1. Mix the butter and sugar in a container until fluffy and pale.

2. Put in the vanilla and egg and mix thoroughly then mix in the almonds, flour and salt.
3. Shape the dough into a ball and wrap it in foil. Place in your refrigerator for about half an hour.
4. Transfer the dough to a floured working surface and roll it into a slim sheet.
5. Cut into small cookies using a cookie cutter of your choices and arrange them on a baking sheet coated with baking papers.
6. Pre-heat the oven and bake at 350F for about ten minutes or until the edges turn mildly golden brown.
7. Let the cookies cool down before you serve.

Nutritional Content of One Serving:

Calories: 115 ‖ Fat: 6.1g ‖ Protein: 2.1g ‖ Carbohydrates: 13.1g

BOOZY CHOCOLATE TRUFFLES

Total Time Taken: 2 hours

Yield: Servings 30

Ingredients:

- ¼ cup Amaretto liqueur
- ¼ teaspoon salt
- ½ cup butter
- ½ cup heavy cream
- 1 pound dark chocolate chips

Directions:

1. Combine the chocolate, salt, butter and heavy cream in a container over a hot water bath.
2. When melted and smooth, turn off heat and mix in the Amaretto liqueur.
3. Cover the mixture using plastic wrap and store in the refrigerator for minimum an hour.
4. Make small balls of mixture and roll them through cocoa powder.
5. Serve the truffles chilled or store them in an airtight container.

Nutritional Content of One Serving:

Calories: 111 ‖ Fat: 7.8g ‖ Protein: 1.1g ‖ Carbohydrates: 10.1g

FIADONE – *FRENCH CHEESECAKE*

Total Time Taken: 1 ¼ hours

Yield: 10 Servings

Ingredients:

- 1 cup white sugar
- 1 lemon, zested
- 1 tablespoon vanilla extract
- 2 pounds ricotta cheese
- 8 eggs
- Butter to grease the pan

Directions:

1. Combine all the ingredients in a container.
2. Grease a 9-inch round cake pan with butter then pour the mixture in the pan.
3. Pre-heat the oven and bake at 350F for about forty minutes or until a golden-brown colour is achieved on the edges.
4. Let the cheesecake cool down before you serve.

Nutritional Content of One Serving:

Calories: 256 ‖ Fat: 10.7g ‖ Protein: 14.8g ‖ Carbohydrates: 25.6g

ALMOND SABLES

Total Time Taken: 2 hours

Yield: 20 Servings

Ingredients:

- ¼ cup light brown sugar
- ¼ teaspoon salt
- ½ cup butter, softened
- ½ cup ground almonds
- ½ cup powdered sugar
- 1 cup almonds, chopped
- 1 egg
- 1 egg white, beaten

- 1 teaspoon vanilla extract
- 2 cups all-purpose flour

Directions:

1. Mix the butter and sugar in a container until fluffy and pale.
2. Put in the egg and vanilla and mix thoroughly then fold in the almonds, flour and salt and knead just until the dough comes together.
3. Shape the dough into an even log.
4. Mix the almonds and sugar on a platter.
5. Brush the log with egg white then roll it through the almond mixture. Cover using plastic wrap and store in your freezer for an hour.
6. After an hour, cut the log into ¼-inch thin slices and place them with the cut facing up on a baking tray covered with parchment paper.
7. Pre-heat the oven and bake at 350F for about fifteen minutes or until golden on the edges.
8. Serve the sables chilled.

Nutritional Content of One Serving:

Calories: 151 ‖ Fat: 8.5g ‖ Protein: 3.3g ‖ Carbohydrates: 15.9g

FRENCH BEIGNETS

Total Time Taken: 1 hour
Yield: 20 Servings
Ingredients:

- ¼ cup butter, melted
- ¼ cup sugar
- ¼ teaspoon salt
- 1 teaspoon orange blossom water
- 1 teaspoon vanilla extract
- 2 cups all-purpose flour
- 2 eggs
- Oil for frying

Directions:

1. Mix the sugar, eggs, butter, orange water and vanilla in a container until pale and creamy.
2. Put in the flour and salt and knead the dough for a few minutes until elastic.
3. Let the dough rest for about ten minutes then place it on a floured working surface and roll it into a slim sheet.
4. Cut strips of dough using a sharp knife.
5. Heat sufficient oil in a deep frying pan.
6. Drop the strips of dough in the hot pan and fry them on each side until a golden-brown colour is achieved.
7. Transfer the brignets to paper towels and serve them with powdered sugar on the side.

Nutritional Content of One Serving:

Calories: 82 ‖ Fat: 2.9g ‖ Protein: 1.9g ‖ Carbohydrates: 12.1g

FRENCH APPLE TART

Total Time Taken: 1 ½ hours
Yield: 10 Servings
Ingredients: Crust:

- ¼ teaspoon salt
- 1 ¼ cups all-purpose flour
- 2 tablespoons powdered sugar
- 3/4 cup butter, chilled and cubed
- 4-6 tablespoons cold water

Filling:

- 4 egg yolks
- ¼ cup cornstarch
- 2 cups milk
- 1 teaspoon vanilla extract
- 1 pinch salt
- 4 apples, peeled and finely sliced
- 2/3 cup white sugar

Directions:

1. For the crust, combine the flour, salt and sugar in a container. Put in the butter and stir until grainy.
2. Stir in the water, spoon by spoon, and stir until the dough comes together.
3. Cover the dough with plastic wrap and store in the refrigerator for about half an hour.
4. Meanwhile, bring the milk to a boil in a saucepan.
5. Mix the eggs, sugar and cornstarch in a container until fluffy and pale.
6. Put in the hot milk and place back on heat. Cook until it becomes thick then turn off heat and allow to cool. Stir in the vanilla extract.
7. Put the dough on a floured working surface and roll it into a slim sheet. Move the dough to a 9-inch tart pan and press it well on the bottom and sides of the pan. Trim the edges if required.
8. Preheat your oven and bake the crust at 350F for about ten minutes.
9. Take out of the oven and fill the crust with the vanilla pastry cream.
10. Top with apple slices and continue baking for another fifteen minutes or so.
11. Best served chilled.

Nutritional Content of One Serving:

Calories: 332 ‖ Fat: 16.9g ‖ Protein: 4.6g ‖ Carbohydrates: 42.5g

FIG GALETTE

Total Time Taken: 1 hour
Yield: 10 Servings
Ingredients:

- ¼ cup sour cream
- ¼ teaspoon salt
- ½ cup butter, chilled and cubed
- ½ cup butter, softened
- ½ cup light brown sugar
- 1 ½ cups all-purpose flour
- 1 cup ground almonds
- 1 egg
- 1 pound fresh figs, quartered
- 2 tablespoons powdered sugar

Directions:

1. For the dough, combine the chilled butter, flour, sugar and salt in a container until grainy.
2. Put in the sour cream and stir until the dough comes together.
3. Put the dough on a floured working surface and roll it into a slim sheet.
4. Mix the softened butter, light brown sugar and egg in a container until creamy and pale.
5. Put in the almonds and stir lightly. Spoon the mixture over the center of the dough.
6. Put fresh figs on top then pull the edges of the dough over the filling, leaving the center exposed.
7. Pre-heat the oven and bake at 350F for about half an hour or until crisp and golden on the edges.

Tastes best chilled.

Nutritional Content of One Serving:

Calories: 451 ‖ Fat: 25.4g ‖ Protein: 6.4g ‖ Carbohydrates: 54.3g

FAR BRETON

Total Time Taken: 1 hour
Yield: 10 Servings
Ingredients:

- ¼ teaspoon salt
- ½ cup heavy cream
- 1 ½ cups all-purpose flour
- 1 ½ cups dried prunes, pitted
- 1 teaspoon vanilla extract
- 3 cups milk
- 4 eggs

Directions:

1. Mix the eggs, milk, cream and vanilla in a container.
2. Put in the flour and salt and mix thoroughly.
3. Fold in the prunes then pour the mixture in a greased deep dish baking pan.
4. Pre-heat the oven and bake at 350F for about twenty-five minutes or until set.

This dessert tastes best chilled

Nutritional Content of One Serving:

Calories: 213 ‖ Fat: 5.8g ‖ Protein: 7.2g ‖ Carbohydrates: 34.6g

DRIED CRANBERRY PEAR CLAFOUTIS

Total Time Taken: 1 hour
Yield: 8 Servings
Ingredients:

- ¼ cup milk
- ¼ teaspoon salt
- ½ cup dried cranberries
- 1 cup heavy cream
- 1 teaspoon vanilla extract
- 1/3 cup white sugar
- 2/3 cup all-purpose flour
- 4 eggs
- 4 pears, ripe but firm
- Butter to grease the pan

Directions:

1. Grease a 9-inch deep dish baking pan with butter.
2. Put the pears and cranberries on the bottom of the pan.
3. Mix the cream, milk, sugar, flour, salt and vanilla in container.
4. Pour this mixture over the pears and preheat your oven and bake at 350F for a little more than half an hour or until a golden-brown colour is achieved on the edges.

Best served chilled.

Nutritional Content of One Serving:

Calories: 222 ‖ Fat: 8.2g ‖ Protein: 4.8g ‖ Carbohydrates: 33.9g

DEEP CHOCOLATE SOUFFLÉ

Total Time Taken: 1 hour

Yield: 4 Servings

Ingredients:

- ¼ cup cocoa powder
- ¼ cup white sugar
- ¼ teaspoon salt
- 1 cup milk
- 2 tablespoons all-purpose flour
- 4 egg yolks
- 4 oz. dark chocolate, chopped
- 6 egg whites

Directions:

1. Mix the milk and sugar in a saucepan and place over low heat. Bring to its boiling point then put in the flour and cocoa and cook until it becomes thick.
2. Turn off the heat and mix in the chocolate. Stir until melted and smooth.
3. Let cool down then put in the egg yolks.
4. Whip the whites with the salt until fluffy and firm.
5. Fold the meringue into the chocolate mixture then pour the mixture into 4 ramekins.
6. Pre-heat the oven and bake at 350F for about twenty-five minutes.
7. Serve the soufflés freshly made.

Nutritional Content of One Serving:

Calories: 335 ‖ Fat: 15.0g ‖ Protein: 13.6g ‖ Carbohydrates: 39.2g

CREPES SUZZETTE

Total Time Taken: 1 hour

Yield: 4 Servings

Ingredients:

- ¼ cup brandy
- ¾ cup all-purpose flour
- 1 ½ cups milk

- 1 pinch salt
- 1 teaspoon vanilla extract
- 2 eggs
- 2 tablespoons canola oil
- 3 tablespoons butter
- 4 oranges, cut into segments

Directions:

1. Mix the milk, eggs, vanilla, oil, flour and salt in a container until creamy.
2. Heat a non-stick pan over moderate-high heat then pour a few tablespoons of batter in the hot pan and swirl it around to uniformly cover the bottom of the pan.
3. Cook on each side until golden and pile the crepes on a platter.
4. Melt the butter in a saucepan.
5. Put in the oranges and brandy and cook for a couple of minutes.
6. Put the wrapped crepes in the mixture and cook for another minute.
7. Best served warm, topped with powdered sugar to taste.

Nutritional Content of One Serving:

Calories: 404 ‖ Fat: 20.1g ‖ Protein: 10.0g ‖ Carbohydrates: 44.3g

CRÈME CARAMEL

Total Time Taken: 1 hour
Yield: 6 Servings
Ingredients:

- ¼ cup light brown sugar
- 1 ¼ cups white sugar
- 1 pinch salt
- 1 tablespoon vanilla extract
- 3 cups milk
- 6 eggs

Directions:

1. Melt the sugar in a heavy saucepan until it sppears amber in colour.
2. Pour the hot sugar in a 8-inch deep dish baking pan and swirl it around to cover the bottom and sides. Be cautious as it's hot.

3. Mix the eggs, milk, vanilla, brown sugar and salt in a container.
4. Pour this mixture in the pan , preheat your oven and bake at 300F for around forty minutes.
5. Let cool down for an hour then turn the crème upside down on a platter.

Best served chilled.

Nutritional Content of One Serving:

Calories: 309 ‖ Fat: 6.9g ‖ Protein: 9.5g ‖ Carbohydrates: 54.2g

CRÈME BRULEE

Total Time Taken: 1 hour
Yield: 6 Servings
Ingredients:

- 1 cup heavy cream
- 1 cup white sugar
- 1 teaspoon vanilla extract
- 2 cups milk
- 6 egg yolks

Directions:

1. Mix the milk, cream, egg yolks and vanilla in a container.
2. Pour the mixture in 4 ramekins and place them in a deep dish baking pan.
3. Pour hot water in the pan, around the ramekins , preheat your oven and bake at 300F for forty minutes.
4. When finished, top the ramekins with sugar and place under the broiler for a couple of minutes until caramelized and golden.

Best served chilled.

Nutritional Content of One Serving:

Calories: 291 ‖ Fat: 13.6g ‖ Protein: 5.8g ‖ Carbohydrates: 38.6g

CLASSIC FRENCH TOAST WITH HONEY

Total Time Taken: 20 minutes

Yield: 4 Servings

Ingredients:

- ¼ cup honey for serving
- 1 cup milk
- 1 teaspoon vanilla extract
- 2 eggs, beaten
- 2 tablespoons butter
- 4 slices brioche bread

Directions:

1. Mix the eggs, milk and vanilla in a container.
2. Heat the butter in a frying pan.
3. Immerse the bread slices in the egg and milk mixture then drop them in the hot butter.
4. Fry on each side until a golden-brown colour is achieved and crusty.
5. Serve the French toast warm, sprinkled with honey.

Nutritional Content of One Serving:

Calories: 302 ‖ Fat: 12.3g ‖ Protein: 7.7g ‖ Carbohydrates: 41.1g

PURE CHOCOLATE BUCHE DE NOEL

Total Time Taken: 1 ½ hours

Yield: 10 Servings

Ingredients:

Cake:

- ¼ cup cocoa powder
- ¼ teaspoon salt
- ½ teaspoon baking powder
- ¾ cup white sugar
- 1 cup all-purpose flour
- 1 teaspoon vanilla extract
- 2 tablespoons butter, melted
- 6 eggs

Filling:

- 1 cup heavy cream
- 1 tablespoon vanilla extract
- 2 cups dark chocolate chips

Glaze:

- ¾ cup heavy cream
- 1 ½ cups dark chocolate chips

Directions:

1. For the cake, combine the eggs, sugar and vanilla in a container until fluffy and pale and volume increases to twice what it was.
2. Fold in the flour, salt, baking powder and cocoa powder then put in the butter and mix using a spatula.
3. Spread the batter in a large baking pan coated with baking paper and preheat your oven and bake at 350F for fifteen minutes or until set.
4. Let the cake cool in the pan.
5. For the filling, melt the cream and chocolate together in a heatproof container. Put in the vanilla then allow the filling to cool completely in your refrigerator for a few hours.
6. Whip the filling until airy and pale.
7. Spread the filling over the cake and roll it firmly. Place it on a platter.
8. To make the glaze, bring the cream to a boil. Put in the chocolate and stir until it melts completely. Let cool completely and set then spread it over the cake.
9. Use a fork to score the top of the cake roulade to resemble a tree.
10. Serve fresh and chilled.

Nutritional Content of One Serving:

Calories: 438 ‖ Fat: 24.3g ‖ Protein: 8.2g ‖ Carbohydrates: 54.8g

PORT WINE POACHED PEARS

Total Time Taken: 1 hour
Yield: 4 Servings
Ingredients:

- ½ lemon, sliced
- 1 cinnamon stick

- 1 cup fresh orange juice
- 1 star anise
- 2 cardamom pods, crushed
- 2 cups Port wine
- 2 whole cloves
- 4 pears, ripe but firm

Directions:

1. Mix the wine, Port wine, orange juice, lemon slices, star anise, cloves, cinnamon and cardamom in a saucepan.
2. Bring to its boiling point.
3. Meanwhile, peel the pears and cautiously remove their core.
4. Drop them in the hot liquid then turn the heat on low and cover with a lid.
5. Cook for about half an hour or until tender.
6. Let the pears cool in the liquid before you serve.

Nutritional Content of One Serving:

Calories: 256 ‖ Fat: 0.8g ‖ Protein: 1.5g ‖ Carbohydrates: 43.4g

PISTACHIO FINANCIERS

Total Time Taken: 1 hour
Yield: 16 Servings
Ingredients:

- ¼ cup all-purpose flour
- ½ cup butter, melted
- ½ cup pistachio, chopped
- ½ cup white sugar
- 1 cup ground almonds
- 2 eggs

Directions:

1. Mix the almonds and sugar in a container. Stir in the eggs and mix thoroughly then put in the butter and stir thoroughly until blended.
2. Fold in the flour and pistachio, as well as a pinch of salt.

3. Spoon the batter in small financier pans and preheat your oven and bake at 350F for about fifteen minutes or until it rises significantly and seems golden on the edges.
4. Serve the financiers chilled.

Nutritional Content of One Serving:

Calories: 134 ‖ Fat: 10.2g ‖ Protein: 2.6g ‖ Carbohydrates: 9.5g

PEPIN'S APPLE TART

Total Time Taken: 1 ¼ hours
Yield: 10 Servings

Ingredients:

- ¼ cup milk
- ¼ teaspoon salt
- ½ cup butter, softened
- ½ cup powdered sugar
- ½ teaspoon cinnamon powder
- 1 ¼ cups all-purpose flour
- 1 teaspoon baking powder
- 1 teaspoon vanilla extract
- 2 eggs
- 4 apples, cored and sliced

Directions:

1. Mix the butter and sugar in a container until creamy and pale.
2. Put in the eggs, milk and vanilla and mix thoroughly.
3. Fold in the flour, salt and baking powder then spoon the batter in a 9-inch tart pan.
4. Top with apple slices and drizzle with cinnamon.
5. Bake the tart in the preheated oven at 350F for around forty minutes until it rises significantly and starts to appear golden-brown.
6. Best served chilled.

Nutritional Content of One Serving:

Calories: 217 ‖ Fat: 10.5g ‖ Protein: 3.2g ‖ Carbohydrates: 28.6g

ORANGE MARMALADE SOUFFLÉS

Total Time Taken: 1 hour

Yield: 6 Servings

Ingredients:

- ¼ cup heavy cream
- ¼ teaspoon salt
- 1 cup orange marmalade
- 1 tablespoon Cointreau
- 2 tablespoons lemon juice
- 4 egg whites
- Butter to grease the ramekins

Directions:

1. Grease 6 ramekins with butter.
2. Mix the marmalade with the cream, lemon juice and Cointreau in a container.
3. Whip the egg whites and salt in a container until fluffy and firm.
4. Put in the egg whites into the marmalade, folding it slowly using a spatula.
5. Spoon the batter in the greased ramekins and preheat your oven and bake at 350F for about twenty minutes.
6. Serve the soufflés immediately.

Nutritional Content of One Serving:

Calories: 174 || Fat: 1.9g || Protein: 2.7g || Carbohydrates: 35.8g

ORANGE APPLE TERRINE

Total Time Taken: 2 hours

Yield: 8 Servings

Ingredients:

- ½ cup light brown sugar
- 2 oranges
- 2 pounds Granny Smith apples

Directions:

1. Peel the apples and cautiously core them. Cut them into small slices.

2. Cut the oranges into segments as well.
3. Start layering the apple slices and orange segments in a loaf cake pan coated with baking paper. Drizzle with brown sugar between layers.
4. Pre-heat the oven and bake at 300F for about ninety minutes.
5. When finished, take it out of the oven and place a weight on top of your terrine. Let it cool to room temperature then flip it over on a platter.
6. Serve the terrine chilled.

Nutritional Content of One Serving:

Calories: 115 || Fat: 0.3g || Protein: 0.8g || Carbohydrates: 30.0g

MOUSSE AU CHOCOLAT

Total Time Taken: 1 hour
Yield: 4 Servings
Ingredients:

- ¼ cup white sugar
- ¼ teaspoon salt
- 1 cup heavy cream
- 1 cup heavy cream, whipped
- 4 egg yolks
- 6 oz. dark chocolate chips

Directions:

1. Bring 1 cup of cream to a boil.
2. Mix the egg yolks and sugar in a container until creamy. Put in the cream and mix thoroughly then place back on heat and cook until it becomes thick.
3. Turn off the heat and mix in the salt and chocolate. Combine until the desired smoothness is achieved.
4. Let cool down then fold in the whipped cream.
5. Spoon the mousse into small glasses and serve it chilled.

Nutritional Content of One Serving:

Calories: 506 || Fat: 38.0g || Protein: 6.8g || Carbohydrates: 43.1g

MOCHA POTS DE CRÈME

Total Time Taken: 1 ½ hours
Yield: 6 Servings

Ingredients:

- 1 ½ cups dark chocolate chips
- 1 cup milk
- 1 pinch salt
- 1 teaspoon vanilla extract
- 2 cups heavy cream
- 2 teaspoons instant coffee
- 6 egg yolks

Directions:

1. Bring the milk to a boil in a saucepan. Turn off the heat and mix in the chocolate. Stir until melted then let cool down slightly.
2. Stir in the remaining ingredients and mix thoroughly.
3. Pour the mixture in 4 ramekins and place them in a deep baking pan. Pour hot water in the deep pan, around the ramekins. Pre-heat the oven and bake at 300F for about half an hour until set.
4. Let cool in the pan before you serve.

Nutritional Content of One Serving:

Calories: 354 ‖ Fat: 28.1g ‖ Protein: 6.9g ‖ Carbohydrates: 23.8g

RED WINE CHOCOLATE CAKE:

Total Time Taken: 1 ¼ hours
Yield: 10 Servings

Ingredients:

- ½ cup canola oil
- ½ teaspoon salt
- ¾ cup cocoa powder
- 1 cup buttermilk
- 1 cup dark chocolate chips
- 1 cup red wine
- 1 teaspoon baking powder
- 1 teaspoon baking soda

- 1 teaspoon vanilla extract
- 2 cups all-purpose flour
- 2 eggs

Directions:

1. Mix the dry ingredients in a container.
2. Stir in the red wine, buttermilk, oil, vanilla and eggs and stir for a few seconds to mix.
3. Fold in the chocolate chips then pour the batter in a 9-inch round cake pan coated with baking paper.
4. Pre-heat the oven and bake at 350F for forty minutes or until a toothpick inserted into the center of the cake comes out clean.
5. The cake tastes best chilled.

Nutritional Content of One Serving:

Calories: 301 ‖ Fat: 16.3g ‖ Protein: 6.5g ‖ Carbohydrates: 32.8g

MERINGUES

Total Time Taken: 2 hours
Yield: 20 Servings
Ingredients:

- ¼ teaspoon salt
- 1 cup white sugar
- 1 tablespoon vanilla extract
- 4 egg whites

Directions:

1. Mix the egg whites, sugar and salt in a heatproof container. Put the container over a hot water bath and stir until the sugar is melted.
2. Turn off the heat and whip the egg whites for 7-9 minutes or until fluffy, stiff and shiny.
3. Put in the vanilla extract then spoon the meringue in a pastry bag and pipe small dollops of mixture on a baking tray coated with baking paper.
4. Pre-heat the oven and bake at 250F for about ninety minutes.

Tastes best chilled.

Nutritional Content of One Serving:

Calories: 43 ‖ Fat: 0.0g ‖ Protein: 0.7g ‖ Carbohydrates: 10.1g

LEMON CHEESE SOUFFLÉ

Total Time Taken: 1 hour
Yield: 4 Servings
Ingredients:

- 6 tablespoons butter, softened
- ¾ cup water
- ¼ teaspoon salt
- ¾ cup all-purpose flour
- 5 egg yolks
- 1 lemon, zested and juiced
- 1 cup ricotta cheese
- 5 egg whites
- 1/2 cup white sugar

Directions:

1. Mix the butter, sugar, water and salt in a saucepan. Put over moderate heat and bring to its boiling point.
2. Put in the flour, all at once, and stir thoroughly until a dough forms.
3. Turn off the heat and let cool down then mix in the egg yolks, lemon zest and lemon juice.
4. Stir in the cheese.
5. Whip the egg whites in a container until fluffy and firm.
6. Fold the meringue into the batter then spoon the mixture into 4 ramekins lined using butter.
7. Pre-heat the oven and bake at 350F for about twenty minutes until it rises significantly and starts to appear golden-brown.
8. Serve the soufflés warm and fresh out of the oven.

Nutritional Content of One Serving:

Calories: 510 ‖ Fat: 28.2g ‖ Protein: 17.7g ‖ Carbohydrates: 48.5g

ILES FLOTTANTES

Total Time Taken: 1 ½ hours
Yield: 4 Servings
Ingredients:

Crème anglaise:

- ½ cup white sugar
- 1 pinch nutmeg
- 1 teaspoon vanilla extract
- 2 cups milk
- 4 egg yolks

Iles flottantes:

- ½ cup white sugar
- ½ teaspoon lemon zest
- 1 pinch salt
- 2 cups milk
- 2 egg whites

Directions:

1. To make the crème anglaise, bring the milk to a boil. Mix the egg yolks and sugar in a container until creamy. Put in the hot milk and mix thoroughly then place the mixture back on heat and cook until it becomes thick. Turn off the heat and put in the vanilla and nutmeg. Let cool down.
2. For the iles flottante, combine the egg whites, lemon zest and salt in a container until fluffy.
3. Put in the sugar and continue whipping until shiny and firm.
4. Bring the milk to its boiling point in a saucepan. Drop spoonfuls of whipped egg whites in the hot milk and cook for a couple of minutes. Cautiously transfer to serving platters.
5. Put the crème anglaise on top before you serve.

Nutritional Content of One Serving:

Calories: 376 ‖ Fat: 9.6g ‖ Protein: 12.5g ‖ Carbohydrates: 62.9g

HONEY FIG AND GOAT CHEESE TART

Total Time Taken: 1 hour

Yield: 10 Servings

Ingredients:

- ¼ cup honey
- ½ cup goat cheese
- ½ cup walnuts, chopped
- 1 cup cream cheese
- 1 pound fresh figs, quartered
- 1 sheet puff pastry
- 2 eggs
- Extra honey for serving

Directions:

1. Mix the cream cheese, goat cheese, eggs and honey in a container.
2. Position the puff pastry dough in a baking tray coated with baking paper.
3. Spread the goat cheese mixture over the dough and top with fresh figs.
4. Drizzle with walnuts and preheat your oven and bake at 350F for about half an hour.
5. Best served chilled, sprinkled with extra honey.

Nutritional Content of One Serving:

Calories: 304 ‖ Fat: 15.5g ‖ Protein: 6.9g ‖ Carbohydrates: 39.3g

GATEAU BASQUE

Total Time Taken: 1 hour

Yield: 8 Servings

Ingredients:

- ½ cup cornstarch
- ½ cup white sugar
- 1 cup glace cherries
- 1 egg for brushing the dough
- 1 tablespoon vanilla extract
- 2 ½ cups milk
- 2 sheets puff pastry dough
- 2 tablespoons brandy

- 4 egg yolks

Directions:

1. Bring the milk to its boiling point in a saucepan.
2. Mix the egg yolks, cornstarch and sugar in a container. Pour in the hot milk then place back on heat and cook until it becomes thick.
3. Turn off the heat and mix in the vanilla and brandy. Let cool completely.
4. Place on sheet of puff pastry dough on a floured working surface.
5. Spoon the vanilla cream in the center of the dough. Top with cherries and cover with the rest of the sheet of dough.
6. Trim the edges around the filling and brush the top with egg.
7. Pre-heat the oven and bake at 350F for a little more than half an hour or until it rises significantly and starts to appear golden-brown.
8. Serve the gateau chilled.

Nutritional Content of One Serving:

Calories: 243 ‖ Fat: 8.9g ‖ Protein: 5.6g ‖ Carbohydrates: 31.9g

GASCON FLAN

Total Time Taken: 1 ¼ hours
Yield: 10 Servings

Ingredients:

- ¼ teaspoon salt
- ½ cup white sugar
- 1 ½ cups all-purpose flour
- 1 teaspoon vanilla extract
- 4 cups milk
- 4 eggs

Directions:

1. Combine all the ingredients in a blender and pulse until the desired smoothness is achieved.
2. Pour the batter in a deep dish baking pan lined using butter and preheat your oven and bake at 350F for around forty minutes or until a golden-brown colour is achieved.
3. Serve the flan chilled.

Nutritional Content of One Serving:

Calories: 181 ‖ Fat: 3.9g ‖ Protein: 7.4g ‖ Carbohydrates: 29.3g

FRENCH LEMON TART

Total Time Taken: 1 ½ hour
Yield: 10 Servings
Ingredients:

Tart:

- ¼ teaspoon salt
- ½ cup butter, softened
- ½ cup powdered sugar
- ½ teaspoon baking powder
- 1 egg
- 2 cups all-purpose flour

Filling:

- ½ cup butter
- ½ cup lemon juice
- 1 cup white sugar
- 1 pinch salt
- 2 tablespoons lemon zest

Directions:

1. For the tart crust, combine the butter with sugar until creamy and fluffy.
2. Put in the egg and mix thoroughly then mix in the flour, baking powder and salt.
3. Put the dough on a floured working surface and roll it into a slim sheet.
4. Put the dough on a tart pan and press it on the bottom and sides. Trim off the edges.
5. Preheat your oven and bake the crust at 350F for about twenty minutes or until a golden-brown colour is achieved on the edges.
6. Allow the crust to cool down.
7. For the filling, combine all the ingredients in a heatproof container. Place over a hot
8. water bath and cook until it becomes thick.

9. Pour the filling into the crust and let cool down and set before you serve.

Nutritional Content of One Serving:

Calories: 362 ‖ Fat: 19.2g ‖ Protein: 3.5g ‖ Carbohydrates: 45.7g

FRENCH CANNELES

Total Time Taken: 1 ½ hours
Yield: 20 Servings

Ingredients:

- ½ cup white sugar
- 1 pinch salt
- 1 teaspoon vanilla extract
- 2 cups milk
- 2 tablespoons butter
- 2 tablespoons dark rum
- 3 eggs

Directions:

1. Combine all the ingredients in a container until creamy.
2. Pour the canneles in a caneles pan. Put the pan in another pan, slightly deeper and pour hot water into the pan.
3. Pre-heat the oven and bake at 350F until they turn golden brown.
4. Let them cool down slightly then take them out of the pan and serve them chilled.

Nutritional Content of One Serving:

Calories: 54 ‖ Fat: 2.3g ‖ Protein: 1.6g ‖ Carbohydrates: 6.3g

TARTE TROPEZIENNE

Total Time Taken: 2 hours
Yield: 10 Servings
Ingredients:

Brioche dough:

- ¼ cup white sugar
- ¼ teaspoon instant yeast
- ¼ teaspoon salt
- 1 teaspoon vanilla extract
- 1/4 cup butter, melted
- 2 cups all-purpose flour
- 2 tablespoons milk
- 3 eggs

Filling:

- ¼ cup cornstarch
- ¼ teaspoon salt
- ½ cup white sugar
- 1 cup butter, softened
- 1 tablespoon vanilla extract
- 2 cups milk
- 4 egg yolks

Directions:

1. To make the brioche dough, combine the warm milk with the yeast in a container until melted.
2. Put in the eggs, sugar, vanilla and butter then mix in the flour and salt.
3. Knead the dough for a few minutes until elastic.
4. Let the dough rest and rise for an hour.
5. Put the dough on a floured working surface and roll it into a disc.
6. Preheat your oven and bake the brioche at 350F for about half an hour or until it rises significantly and starts to appear golden-brown.
7. Let cool down.
8. For the filling, combine the egg yolks, sugar and cornstarch in a container.
9. Heat the milk and pour it over the egg yolks. Put back on heat and cook until it becomes thick.
10. Let the cream cool down then mix in the vanilla.
11. Whip the butter in a container until fluffy. Put in the pastry cream, spoon by spoon, and mix thoroughly.
12. Cut the brioche disc in half along the length and fill it with the pastry cream.
13. Best served fresh.

Nutritional Content of One Serving:

Calories: 435 ‖ Fat: 27.4g ‖ Protein: 7.3g ‖ Carbohydrates: 40.1g

TART TATIN

Total Time Taken: 1 hour

Yield: 8 Servings

Ingredients:

- ¼ teaspoon salt
- ½ cup butter, chilled and cubed
- 1 ¼ cups all-purpose flour
- 1 cup white sugar
- 1 teaspoon cinnamon powder
- 4 apples, peeled, cored and quartered
- 4-6 tablespoons cold water

Directions:

1. Melt the sugar in a heavy saucepan until it sppears amber in colour.
2. Sprinkle the sugar on the bottom of a round cake pan.
3. Position the apple slices over the dark color.
4. For the dough, combine the butter, flour and salt in a container until grainy.
5. Put in the water, spoon after spoon, until the dough comes together.
6. Put the dough on a floured working surface and roll it into a slim sheet, as large as your pan.
7. Put the dough over the apples.
8. Pre-heat the oven and bake at 350F for about twenty-five minutes or until a golden-brown colour is achieved.
9. When the tart is done, flip it over on a platter and serve it chilled.

Nutritional Content of One Serving:

Calories: 314 ‖ Fat: 11.9g ‖ Protein: 2.4g ‖ Carbohydrates: 52.5g

RUSTIC PEAR GALETTE

Total Time Taken: 1 hour

Yield: 8 Servings

Ingredients:

- ¼ cup milk
- ¼ cup whole wheat flour

- ¼ teaspoon salt
- ½ cup butter, chilled
- ½ teaspoon baking powder
- 1 cup all-purpose flour
- 2 tablespoons dark brown sugar
- 3 tablespoons powdered sugar
- 4 pears, cored and sliced

Directions:

1. Mix the flours, sugar, salt and baking powder in a container. Put in the butter and stir until grainy.
2. Stir in the milk and stir until the dough comes together.
3. Put the dough on a floured working surface and roll it into a slim sheet.
4. Put the pear slices in the center of the dough and wrap the edges over the pears, leaving the center exposed.
5. Drizzle the pears with brown sugar and bake the galette in the preheated oven at 350F for about half an hour or until a golden-brown colour is achieved and crunchy.

Tastes best chilled.

Nutritional Content of One Serving:

Calories: 258 ‖ Fat: 12.0g ‖ Protein: 2.8g ‖ Carbohydrates: 36.6g

RHUBARB TART

Total Time Taken: 1 hour
Yield: 10 Servings
Ingredients:

Crust:

- 1 ½ cups all-purpose flour
- 1 egg
- 1 pinch salt
- 2 tablespoons cold water
- 2 tablespoons powdered sugar
- 4 oz. butter, chilled and cubed

Filling:

- 1 cup heavy cream
- 1 cup white sugar
- 1 pinch salt
- 1 teaspoon vanilla extract
- 2 egg yolks
- 2 eggs
- 2 pounds rhubarb stalks, sliced

Directions:

1. For the crust, combine the flour, sugar, salt and butter in a container until grainy.
2. Put in the egg and water and stir thoroughly until the dough comes together.
3. Put the dough on a floured working surface and roll it into a slim sheet.
4. Put the dough in a tart baking pan and press it well on the bottom and sides of the pan. Trim the edges.
5. Position the rhubarb slices in the crust.
6. Mix the sugar, cream, egg yolks, eggs, salt and vanilla in a container. Pour this mixture over the rhubarb. Pre-heat the oven and bake at 350F for a little more than half an hour.
7. Let cool down before you serve.

Nutritional Content of One Serving:

Calories: 322 ‖ Fat: 16.2g ‖ Protein: 5.3g ‖ Carbohydrates: 40.6g

ABOUT THE AUTHOR

Anna Goldman is an American professional baker. Born and raised in Kentucky, Anna loved her mother's baking and gradually developed an affinity to it. She started baking with her mother's recipes, and eventually came up with recipes of her own. She had always wanted to write a book about baking, but never got the time to do so until she had to shut down her bakery temporarily due to the coronavirus. Every cloud has a silver lining!

Printed in Poland
by Amazon Fulfillment
Poland Sp. z o.o., Wrocław